## Whitestein Series in Software Agent Technologies

Series Editors:
Marius Walliser
Monique Calisti
Thomas Hempfling
Stefan Brantschen

This series reports new developments in agent-based software technologies and agent-oriented software engineering methodologies, with particular emphasis on applications in various scientific and industrial areas. It includes research level monographs, polished notes arising from research and industrial projects, outstanding PhD theses, and proceedings of focused meetings and conferences. The series aims at promoting advanced research as well as at facilitating know-how transfer to industrial use.

## About Whitestein Technologies

Whitestein Technologies AG was founded in 1999 with the mission to become a leading provider of advanced software agent technologies, products, solutions, and services for various applications and industries. Whitestein Technologies strongly believes that software agent technologies, in combination with other leading-edge technologies like web services and mobile wireless computing, will enable attractive opportunities for the design and the implementation of a new generation of distributed information systems and network infrastructures.

www.whitestein.com

# Agent-based Supply Network Event Management

**Roland Zimmermann**

Birkhäuser Verlag
Basel · Boston · Berlin

Author

Roland Zimmermann
Witschaftsinformatik II
Universität Erlangen-Nürnberg
Lange Gasse 20
D-90403 Nürnberg

2000 Mathematical Subject Classification 68T20, 68T35, 68T37, 94A99, 94C99

A CIP catalogue record for this book is available from the Library of Congress,
Washington D.C., USA

Bibliographic information published by Die Deutsche Bibliothek
Die Deutsche Bibliothek lists this publication in the Deutsche Nationalbibliografie;
detailed bibliographic data is available in the Internet at <http://dnb.ddb.de>.

ISBN 3-7643-7486-1 Birkhäuser Verlag, Basel – Boston – Berlin

© 2006 Birkhäuser Verlag, P.O. Box 133, CH-4010 Basel, Switzerland
Part of Springer Science+Business Media
Cover design: Micha Lotrovsky, CH-4106 Therwil, Switzerland
Printed on acid-free paper produced from chlorine-free pulp. TCF ∞

ISBN   3-7643-7486-1
ISBN   978-3-7643-7486-0      ISBN 978-3-7643-7487-7  (eBook)
DOI 10.1007/978-3-7643-7487-7

9 8 7 6 5 4 3 2 1                                         www.birkhauser.ch

# Contents

# Preface

After all that I was able to observe in the last years, IT-based supply chain management on the one hand still focuses on planning and scheduling issues while on the other hand an increasing awareness for negative effects of disruptive events is observable. Such events often render schedules in production, transportation and even in warehousing processes obsolete and ripple effects in following processes are encountered. This second focus in application-oriented supply chain management is often referred to as *Supply Chain Event Management (SCEM)* and an increasing number of IT-systems promise to cure the underlying fulfillment problems. However, in my opinion many such solutions lack conceptual precision and currently available client-server SCEM systems are ill-suited for complex supply networks in today's business environment: True integration of event management solutions among different enterprises is currently only achievable with centralized server architectures which contradict the autonomy of partners in a supply network. This is the main motivation why in this book I present a concept for distributed, decentralized event management. The concept permits network partners to implement individual strategies for event management and to hide information from network partners, if they wish to (e.g. for strategic reasons). Besides, this concept builds upon existing data sources and provides mechanisms to integrate information from different levels of a supply network while it prevents information overflow due to unconstrained monitoring activities.

Agent technology is selected since it provides the flexibility and individualized control required in a distributed event management environment. Agent interaction based on communicative acts is a means to facilitate the inter-organizational integration of event management activities. In essence, a complex system of agent societies at different enterprises in a supply network evolves. These societies interact and an inter-organizational event management based on order monitoring activities emerges. This concept promises benefits not realized by today's SCEM solutions due to its loosely coupled integration of event management agent societies.

It was my objective in this book to provide a thorough analysis of the event management problem domain from which to develop a generic agent-based approach to *Supply Network Event Management*. The main focus lies on practical issues of event management (e.g. semantic interoperability) and economic benefits to be achieved with agent technology in this state-of-the-art problem domain.

This book is the result of my PhD studies undertaken in recent years at the Department of Information Systems in Nuremberg. I would especially like to thank Prof. Dr. Freimut

Bodendorf who provided me with the opportunity to work and research as part of his staff on this interesting research project. The project was largely funded by the Deutsche Forschungsgemeinschaft (DFG) as part of the priority research program 1083 which focuses on applications of agent technology in realistic scenarios. The research project is conducted in cooperation with the chair of Artificial Intelligence in Erlangen, hence many thanks to Prof. Dr. Günter Görz and his crew, especially Bernhard Schiemann who contributed so much to the overall DFG research project.

I owe specific gratitude to Prof. Peter Klaus who accepted to be the second reviewer for my PhD thesis and to Whitestein Technologies, specifically Dr. Monique Calisti, Dr. Dominic Greenwood and Marius Walliser, for publication of this book.

On the long journey to finalization of such a project many people have contributed in long discussions with helpful advice. Among them are many students, namely Adrian Paschke, Simone Käs, Thomas Schnocklake, Martin Baumann, Clemens Meyreiss, Ulf Schreiber, Kristina Makedonska, Moritz Goeb, Dirk Stepan and certainly others I have missed but who have contributed in varying aspects to the overall DFG research project and thus also brightened the path to this book. A large handful of thanks go to all team members at Wi II (= the Department of Information Systems). I would especially like to thank Dr. Oliver Hofmann who had the initial idea for this research project, Dr. Stefan Reinheimer for many valuable subprojects conducted with industrial partners and Julian Keck as well as Dr. Bernd Weiser for reading part of the early manuscript. All others, namely Christian Bauer, Robert Butscher, Michael Durst, Kai Götzelt, Florian Lang, Marc Langendorf, Dr. Susanne Robra-Bissantz, Dr. Manfred Schertler, Günter Schicker, Mustafa Soy, Dr. Sascha Uelpenich, Stefan Winkler and Angela Zabel, also know the struggles one undergoes in preparing such a book and they are the major source of motivation and support in this process.

Besides, the research work would not have been possible without industry partners who provided knowledge and resources for an industry showcase. Among them are Jörg Buff and Cornelia Bakir who always had remarkable interest in new IT-trends and Prof. Dr. Jörg Müller, Prof. Dr. Bernhard Bauer and Dr. Michael Berger from Siemens Corporate Technology who opened up the opportunity to fruitful research cooperation.

Last - but not the very bit least - my family has always encouraged me on this path and I owe the deepest thanks to my parents Amrei and Horst and my beloved wife Ina for without them this book would never have been written.

*Nuremberg, November 2005*                                     *Roland Zimmermann*

# Chapter 1

# Introduction

Operational problems in fulfillment processes occur in every industry. These problems have severe negative effects within a given enterprise and multiply in multi-enterprise supply networks. However, *Supply Chain Management* has for a long time focused on the optimization of procurement, production and distribution planning (e.g. *Stadtler et al. 2002*), while neglecting fulfillment problems: The execution of fulfillment plans regularly deviates from original plans due to unexpected events. Interdependent processes are affected negatively by these events, and ripple effects in inter-organizational networks are common. The awareness for these operational problems increased in the last years, although in management science concepts such as *Management-by-Exception* already existed. Terms such as *Supply Chain Monitoring* or *Supply Chain Event Management* (e.g. *Bittner 2000*) illustrate the interest in operational problems of fulfillment processes in supply networks. However, current solutions primarily focus on intra-organizational processes within single enterprises, while implementations with a true inter-organizational supply network perspective are rare (*Masing 2003*, pp. 88). One reason is that current offerings of SCEM systems build upon centralized architectures which prevent the integration of multiple systems among different enterprises. This is illustrated by an initiative of the automotive industry to interconnect existing supply chain monitoring systems. In its official recommendation it points out that decentralized infrastructures are needed which aim at the cooperation between enterprises. But such solutions are not available (*Odette 2003, pp. 26*).

As a consequence, the work presented here has the objective to analyze those problems which result from disruptive events in supply networks with emphasis on relationships between independently acting enterprises. To achieve this, the constraints and requirements for inter-organizational event management are identified, and a concept based on a decentralized IT-solution is proposed which employs innovative agent technology. This concept provides proactive event management in the distributed environment of supply networks. Proofs-of-concept and an evaluation of economic benefits to be achieved with this concept complete the work. A short overview is given in fig. 1-1. Chapter 2 provides a detailed analysis of the information deficits which disruptive events cause in supply networks. These deficits have to be reduced by an event management solution. The analysis is concluded with a formal definition of the problem. From this definition the requirements of an event management solution are derived. With respect to these requirements the potential benefits of event management solutions are analyzed and the existing approaches to event management are assessed.

Chapters 3 and 4 define the information base and the functions needed for event management. The information base consists of a data model and an ontology which facilitates interoperability among different enterprises in supply networks. In addition, the main data sources relevant for event management are identified (chapter 3). In chapter 4 mechanisms are proposed which are needed to fulfill the functional requirements, as defined in chapter 2. Since the inter-organizational supply network perspective guides the development of the concept, mechanisms for proactive information gathering in inter-organizational settings are proposed. Further functions concern the interpretation and distribution of the gathered event-related data. An integrated event management process is defined, based on all functions. This process is applicable to every enterprise in a supply network, and it provides a focus on interdependencies between enterprises.

In chapter 5 the data model and the event management functions are integrated in an agent-based concept. The use of software agents in the domain of event management in supply networks is discussed, and a structured method for designing an agent-based application is introduced. This method is then used to develop an agent-based event management system. Two prototypes are presented in chapter 6: One is situated in a laboratory environment needed to conduct experiments, and the second provides an industry showcase to apply the agent-based event management concept to a realistic environment.

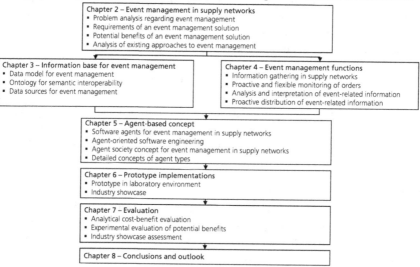

Fig. 1-1. Overview of chapters

An evaluation is conducted in chapter 7 to find out whether an agent-based event management concept can truly realize monetary benefits. Three perspectives for the evaluation are selected: First, a theoretical cost-benefit-model is developed to compare the agent-based concept with existing approaches to event management. Second, experimental results from the laboratory prototype are used to substantiate hypotheses of the cost-benefit-model. Third, the industrial showcase is assessed, and cost measurements for the showcase are analyzed. In all three perspectives, constraints of the agent-based concept are identified and discussed with respect to their effect on a possible implementation of an agent-based event management. Concluding, chapter 8 summarizes the results and provides an outlook on future developments and further research opportunities.

# Chapter 2

# Event Management in Supply Networks

A detailed analysis of the supply network domain is conducted with special attention to issues of nondeterministic problems in operational processes of enterprise networks (see section 2.1). Results of this analysis are used to determine basic requirements for a solution to these *event management* issues (see section 2.2). Potential benefits of event management are identified for the supply network domain and existing IT-systems are evaluated (see sections 2.3 and 2.4) to illustrate the potential for improvement.

## 2.1 Problem

The problem of event management is analyzed regarding two major aspects: First, characteristics of nondeterministic events and their effects on information logistics are assessed (see section 2.1.1). Second, specific characteristics of operational fulfillment processes in multi-enterprise networks are reviewed (see section 2.1.2). Both results are integrated in a model which formally describes the problem and tasks of event management in complex supply networks (see section 2.1.3).

### 2.1.1 Event-related Information Logistics

#### 2.1.1.1 Information Deficits in Supply Networks

In every industry problems occur during the execution of processes. These problems have an impact on the performance of enterprises and their supply networks[1]. Performance is

---

[1.] An enterprise takes, for instance, the role of a supplier which provides basic parts to manufacturers which in turn sell their goods to other network partners.

affected negatively with respect to timeliness, quality, cost and revenues of supply network partners. Some examples illustrate these impacts which are at the heart of the problem to be solved by event management in supply networks.

In the automotive industry just-in-time partnerships between first-tier suppliers and car
producers are very common. They rely on very tight schedules for delivery of parts often
directly to the production line. Thus, inventory costs are reduced to a minimum (*Shingo
1993, pp.171*). One of the side effects is the requirement for high reliability of the delivery
processes. Otherwise complete production lines have to be stopped in a matter of hours,
if only one supplier fails to meet the pre-planned schedule of delivery. A very extreme example occurred at General Motors in 1996 when an 18-day labor strike at a supplier of
brakes halted production in 26 production plants (*Radjou et al. 2002, p.3*). However, even
small problems in suppliers' processes result in deviations from globally planned and optimized schedules with serious impacts on supply network performance. Only warnings
of such events, if provided in a timely fashion, enable affected network partners to react
to arising problems. For instance, a supplier can only deliver a fraction of the ordered
quantity: If this information is conveyed directly to his customer (e.g. a production facility) and other parts planned for later delivery can already be shipped, the customer might
be able to change his own schedule for production provided that enough time for rescheduling is given.

Customers in the consumer goods industry are very sensitive to temporarily unavail-
able goods during shopping hours. One of the largest problems for producers of consumer
goods is the lost-sale problem due to unavailability of their products in the shelves of su-
permarkets. Studies reveal that about three percent of the potential sales volume in the re-
tail sector are lost due to out-of-stock situations (*Seifert 2001, p.87*). In consequence, any
kind of delay or shortage of deliveries from production to warehouses and from warehouses to market facilities pose the threat of lost sales and consumers turning their attention to
competitors' products (*Wagner et al. 2002a, pp.353*). Early warnings on delays permit,
for instance, to use express deliveries from other warehouses of the producers or wholesalers which still have inventories on stock.

Additional examples of problems associated with supply networks underline the relevance of unanticipated events for supply network performance as illustrated in table 2-1.
Although such extreme situations may occur rarely, they emphasize the need to react as
soon as possible. In some cases these actions may even be vital for the survival of supply
network partners, and the impact of failures in supply networks can have major negative
effects on shareholder value[2].

| Company | Supply network exception | Cost of lost transactions |
|---------|--------------------------|---------------------------|
| Boeing | Two key suppliers fail to deliver criti-cal parts on time (1997) | Deals lost worth $2.6 billion |
| Sony | Shortage of PlayStation 2 graphics chip (2000) | Console shipment in US was 50% less than planned |

Table 2-1. Consequences of supply network events (*Radjou et al. 2002*)

| Company | Supply network exception | Cost of lost transactions |
|---------|--------------------------|---------------------------|
| Ericsson | Fire in a plant (Philips Electronics) disrupts chip supplies for new handset | Loss of 3% market share against Nokia in 2000 and exit from handset market |

Table 2-1. Consequences of supply network events (*Radjou et al. 2002*)

All examples share the following features:
- Initial triggers for the problems are unexpected events that cannot be prevented by one of the actors involved. These events can be characterized as disturbances, disruptions or malfunctions of processes.
- Most of the events occur during processes of actual order fulfillment - i.e. production, warehousing and transportation or closely related administrative processes.
- Consequences of the events affect not only the single enterprise where the event occurs, but also related companies. Many of those are direct customers, but also customers of customers on different levels of the supply network.
- Consequences may be avoided or at least reduced to an acceptable level, if decision-supporting information on serious events is available as soon as possible.
- In reality time-lags between the occurrence of events, their identification and the communication of related information to affected actors in a supply network reduce the ability of reacting to a problem. In many cases such information is neither identified nor communicated at all, and the consequences affect the network with their full impact (*Bretzke et al. 2002, pp.1*).

In summary, negative consequences for supply network processes are due to unavoidable events. But consequences can be reduced, if high-quality information is provided to supply network partners at an early stage shortly after such events have occurred. However, a lack of reliable and accurate information on events and insufficient communication of event-related data between network partners is observed. The resulting information deficit regarding event-related information will be referred to as the *Supply Network Event Management (SNEM) problem*.

### 2.1.1.2 Role of Information Logistics

Information management in supply networks needs to be improved to solve the SNEM problem outlined in section 2.1.1.1. It is a task in the field of *information logistics*, which is a major area of research in logistics sciences.

Management of information that accompanies physical processes in supply networks is an important task for information logistics. The associated information processes can either be directly value-adding (e.g. product design) or supporting in the sense of controlling and managing the associated physical processes (*Augustin 1998*).

---

[2.] On average an 11% decrease of stock prices is attributed to each severe supply network problem made public by a company (adjusted to market and industry movements) (for details see (*Singhal 2003*)).

A more general definition of information logistics is based on the assumption that information consists of data which is relevant for somebody. Information represents input for decisions that are the basis of economic behavior resulting in transactions and their fulfillment. Consequently, the aim of information logistics is to provide relevant information to actors (*Kloth 1999, pp. 57*). Three basic dimensions have been proposed, that characterize this aim in greater detail (*Föcker et al. 2000, p.20*):

- *Content*

  Only selected information is relevant for a decision-maker (actor) in a given context. Therefore, content has to be matched with the current situation of the actor.

- *Time*

  Information is only useful, if it is available at the point in time when the actor needs it. A second aspect is the timeliness of information. It restricts its use for decisions, if it is outdated.

- *Location*

  Information needed by an actor has to be communicated to the location where the actor is situated when he is meant to act upon the information.

In the context of the SNEM problem, information logistics has to provide a solution for overcoming the information deficit and thereby improving the management of the supply network processes. It has to consider the three basic dimensions of *content* (e.g. characterization of an event), *time* (e.g. real-time quality of information) and *location* (e.g. where is an affected supply network partner located and who is the relevant contact). Regarding the SNEM problem, deficits in information logistics exist because the required content is often not available or at least not at the right time and not for the relevant actors (the supply network partners) that could react upon the information.

### 2.1.1.3    Disruptive Events

Non-deterministic events as the triggers of the SNEM problem are characterized on an abstract level as triggers for state transitions of some kind of object. In fig. 2-1 an example is depicted as an UML state chart. The object that changes its state might either be some kind of actor, physical resource, process or, in general, some kind of system endowed with a behavior. The event that triggers the transition of the object into a new state (e.g. from "idle" to "occupied") is characterized as "a significant occurrence" (*Larman 1997, p.379*).

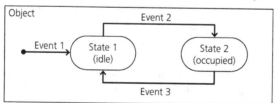

Fig. 2-1. UML state chart of an abstract object

The term "occurrence" can be illustrated by a few examples which highlight different types of events:

- "A disturbance occurred at machine X at time Y"

- "The milestone 'Delivery to customer' was achieved on date Z"
- "Measurement of production tolerances indicates a deviation of X % from the required
  tolerances"
- "Company XY has issued an order for Z pieces of product P"

These types of events change the states of different objects. A machine failure results in the state *blocked*, whereas the achievement of the final milestone of an order changes the order's state to *finished*. Not every type of event is important from the SNEM problem's point of view. If the occurrence of an event is certain, it is irrelevant whether it has a negative impact on processes in a supply network or not. It can be assumed that in such a case the event is integrated into any kind of plan and schedule, and processes are already optimized under the restriction of this event occurring at some point in time. However, if an event in a supply network is uncertain but has no impact or at least no negative impact on the performance of the network's processes there is no need to communicate such events to other network partners or to take any managerial actions. The only case where an information logistics solution is required, is characterized by an uncertain event that has a negative impact on processes of a supply network.

Disturbances, disruptions, malfunctions and other concepts for describing uncertain events with a negative impact will be referred to as *disruptive events*. They can propagate across many levels of a system (see section 2.1.1.1). Consequences of a specific disruptive event will affect only certain orders. Any order is characterized by different attributes (e.g. order quantity, destination, planned milestones, price) which are affected by disruptive events. Two scenarios illustrate the relationships:

- A traffic jam during transportation results in a delay with the consequence of an exceeded time-limit of the milestone for delivery of an order.
- Quality defects due to a lack of maintenance are identified during quality control, and only part of the ordered quantity is released for actual delivery.

Diagnosis of such consequences (e.g. a delay of an order) can point to disruptive events that are not identified explicitly (e.g. a slowdown of a machine). Indirect identification of disruptive events based on measurements is considered to be a disruptive event itself that has to be taken into account by an information logistics solution for the SNEM problem.

## 2.1.2  Supply Networks

### 2.1.2.1    Fulfillment Processes

To further analyze the SNEM problem, a characterization of the supply network domain is necessary. A supply network consists of all processes necessary to supply goods and services to customers and markets (*Klaus 1998, p. 434*). On a short- to medium-term basis these networks are mostly stable regarding their main participants, but changes of participants occur in the long run (*Marbacher 2001, p.19*). Supply networks in industrial environments are characterized by three main operational process types: demand communication, fulfillment and payment (*Klaus et al. 2000, pp.17*) (see fig. 2-2). Triggered by customers, the demand - articulated via orders that are placed with wholesalers, manufacturers or service providers - is propagated throughout the network and triggers suborders where necessary. Fulfillment of the orders is characterized by the physical processes of production, warehousing and transportation that "head" towards the final customers who articulated the initial demand. Payment processes finalize the transactions with the transfer of funds to the vendors of the goods and services.

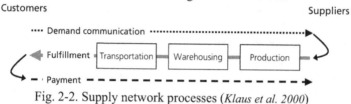

Fig. 2-2. Supply network processes (*Klaus et al. 2000*)

The examples of disruptive events (see section 2.1.1.1) which propagate in supply networks mainly occur during fulfillment processes. Although demand fluctuations are serious phenomena that amplify across supply networks (e.g. the bullwhip-effect as the most famous phenomenon (*Lee et al. 1997*)), a focus on fulfillment processes is chosen. Research on effects of demand fluctuations and on optimized methodologies for demand communication management has been conducted intensively (e.g. research related to the ECR- and CPFR-Initiatives[3]), whereas the execution of these plans and related controlling activities are often neglected (*Bretzke et al. 2002, pp.29*).

In the following the SNEM problem is analyzed with a focus on the information logistics tasks which arise in the fulfillment processes of supply networks - namely production, warehousing and transportation.

## 2.1.2.2    Relationships between Orders

Supply networks can be characterized as a special form of an institutionalized division of labor (many different enterprises cooperating under market conditions to produce goods and services). Here, division of labor is established by means of placing orders with suppliers or other types of enterprises that fulfill certain activities needed to produce a good or service. These activities encompass e.g. procurement of parts by a producer that are manufactured by a supplier and transported by a logistics service provider to the producer. Such (sub-)orders are characterized as pre-conditions which have to be fulfilled before certain other (value-adding) activities (e.g. the assembly of parts at the producer's site) can be initiated.

A supply network consists of a number of enterprises that may have different relationships at different times with each other. This results in a general supply network structure as depicted in fig. 2-3 (left side).

---

[3.] ECR = Efficient Consumer Response (http://www.ecrnet.org/) and CPFR = Collaborative Planning Forecasting and Replenishment (http://www.cpfr.org/)

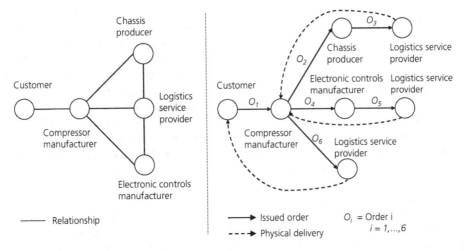

Fig. 2-3. Graphical representations of supply networks

However, the examples mentioned in section 2.1.1.1 refer to specific instances of orders and their related suborders, because disruptive events directly threaten certain orders while other orders between the same enterprises may not be affected at all. For instance, a different product for the same customer produced at a different site will not be affected by a specific machine breakdown.

To analyze the effects of events on certain orders, actual instances of orders $O_i$ and their relationships have to be identified. As suborders represent pre-conditions for their superorders, the relationships between orders can be depicted as a directed graph (see fig. 2-3 right side): Suborder $O_2$ issued to the chassis producer has to be fulfilled before the compressor manufacturer can complete order $O_1$. However, the chassis producer itself can only fulfill his order $O_2$ completely, when suborder $O_3$ to the logistics service provider (LSP) has been fulfilled. This order relationship implies that the chassis has to be delivered by the LSP to the compressor manufacturer to complete order $O_2$.

Although in the example of fig. 2-3 all three manufacturers have relationships with the same logistics service provider (left side), the three different orders placed with this LSP by the manufacturers to deliver parts and products to their customers ($O_3$, $O_5$, $O_6$) have to be reflected separately in the directed graph of order relationships. The LSP appears three times in the directed graph and as a result the complex network structure is reduced to a sequenced "order-tree" which is the basis for further analysis.

### 2.1.2.3    Effects of Disruptive Events in Supply Networks

Effects of disruptive events are analyzed with regard to the complex structures in supply networks (see section 2.1.2.2). Since the SNEM problem is the result of an information deficit concerning these events, a need for information management is established (see section 2.1.1.2). Consequently, the effects of disruptive events in supply networks are analyzed in scenarios with and without an information logistics solution. In the following, three scenarios are developed in a thought experiment and analyzed as depicted in table 2-2. A "certain world" is assumed in the first scenario and all events that might occur in the future are known. In consequence, ideal plans can be devised for a supply network by taking into account every possible situation (compare section 2.1.1.3) and information logistics is not required. Efficient value creation in the supply network is possible. No measures have to be taken when an event occurs, because it has already been incorporated into every schedule (e.g. work plans and transportation plans) in the supply network.

However, in reality the assumption of complete certainty is, of course, not tenable and therefore abandoned in scenario 2. It is assumed that no communication on disruptive events within a company and between the partners of a supply network is possible (no information logistics). In this situation, order relationships have to be taken into account (see section 2.1.2.2).

| Scenario | Assumptions | Effects on supply network | Possible counter measures |
|---|---|---|---|
| 1 | Certain world; No information logistics provided | Ideal Plans<br>- No deviations<br>- Efficient value creation | Not necessary |
| 2 | Uncertain world; No information logistics provided | Worst Case<br>- No advance information on events<br>- Propagation of events in supply network<br>- No event-specific management actions possible to forestall negative consequences | Buffers<br>- Physical stock (parts, goods)<br>- Assets (machines, personnel)<br>- Time (buffers in processes)<br>- Money (liquidity) |
| 3 | Uncertain world; Ideal information logistics on disruptive events in real-time | Improved Situation<br>- Advance information on events result in more reaction time<br>- Propagation of events can be decreased/stopped<br>- Event-specific management in advance of effects | Replace buffers with information<br>- Alternative processes<br>- Dynamic rescheduling<br>- Controlling activities |

Table 2-2. Scenarios for uncertainty of events

A disruptive event such as a machine failure might propagate in the network along the path defined by the relationships and amplify over time (see fig. 2-4). As no communication concerning disruptive events that occur is possible during fulfillment, no advance information on the consequences to be anticipated by supply network partners is available. Managerial actions can only be taken when negative effects have ultimately reached the partners (i.e. a delay is recognized). Even then decisions on corrective actions can hardly be attained because information on the type and consequences of the unknown event (e.g.

when the delayed delivery will ultimately arrive) is lacking. The only appropriate measures to forestall such consequences consist in increasing buffers of inventories, resources, time and liquidity in the fulfillment processes of a supply network. In consequence, negative effects of propagating disruptive events can be reduced only at the huge expense of costly buffers.

The third scenario assumes perfect information logistics regarding any disruptive event that occurs in a supply network. Timely identification and communication of event-related information is facilitated across the whole supply network. Gain in reaction time for affected supply network partners due to advance notice of events enables them to forecast consequences on their own processes and opens up alternatives to handle arising problems. Besides alternative processes, a dynamic rescheduling of orders is enabled. The increase in available event-related information will be accompanied by a decrease in the necessary buffers. To sum up, the uncertainty of disruptive events induces expensive buffers of different kinds in fulfillment processes of supply networks. Buffers can be reduced if information logistics can effectively provide information on disruptive events to supply network partners.

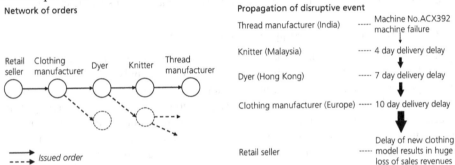

Fig. 2-4. Amplification of a disruptive event in a supply network (*Radjou et al. 2002*)

### 2.1.2.4    Autonomy of Supply Network Partners

The current situation in supply networks presumably lacks effective event-related information logistics (see section 2.1.1.1). A structural factor adds complexity to the development of an information logistics solution: the autonomy of the supply network participants (see fig. 2-5).

Every supply network partner is (in most cases) an independent enterprise with individual goals (e.g. "maximize individual gain"). Depending on its organization an enterprise can follow different behavior patterns that are developed to accomplish its individual goals. Cooperation of enterprises in supply networks due to the division of labor cannot prevent that conflicts between goals of different partners arise (e.g. a supplier minimizes quality control efforts to reduce its costs while the customer wants reliable products without rising prices for the service). Consequently, the behavior patterns of individual companies influence each other because every partner is trying to accomplish its own goals while interacting with other partners. That situation can result in a desire to hide information from partners, to act strategically or even opportunistic.

Fig. 2-5. Autonomy of supply network partners

An information logistics solution for the SNEM problem has to accept individual goals and behavior of the supply network partners and must not interfere with individual strategies. Therefore, each company has to be able to adapt its information logistics services to its own goals and strategies (e.g. define an information policy) as well as govern the behavior of these services (e.g. host its own information logistics solution, implement individual strategies, restrict data availability for external partners in specific cases).

### 2.1.2.5    Heterogeneity of Supply Network Partners

A second structural factor which adds even more complexity to the information logistics task is the heterogeneity of different partners involved in a supply network. Dimensions such as products, processes, size of companies and differences in management culture influence each other already within a company (e.g. a certain product type requires specific processes that are designed according to the management culture in the company). The more so they vary between supply network partners. Partners like logistics service providers cooperate in supply networks with producers of various goods, which can range from raw material (e.g. oil) to industrial products (e.g. electronic parts). In addition, small and medium enterprises with a simple organizational structure often supply to larger corporations that use sophisticated tools and methods in their complex organizations. And every industry has specialized processes and different management cultures that affect the way information is exchanged internally and externally with partners. As a result very different informational needs evolve in a supply network with respect to the information which is to be provided by an information logistics solution (e.g. a producer requires quality measures on product specifications of an order whereas a logistics service provider focuses on transportation milestones). Such needs have to be considered in a generic yet open and flexible solution for the SNEM problem.

## 2.1.3    Formal Specification of the Problem

The findings in section 2.1.1 and section 2.1.2 are summarized in a formalized model of the SNEM domain and the SNEM problem. It serves both as the starting point for further analysis and for the development of an information logistics solution for the SNEM problem[4].

### 2.1.3.1    Definitions

- *Legal Entity* - a *Legal Entity* $LE_k$ with $k \in N$ is an entity which can enter into a legal contract. It is either a person or a corporation.
- *Disruptive Event* - a *Disruptive Event* $DE_h$ with $h \in N$ is the term for any kind of disruption, malfunction or anomaly of behavior with a probability of occurrence between zero and one and a negative effect on the fulfillment processes of a supply network. A $DE_h$ originates at a certain legal entity $LE_k$ and occurs at a point in time $T_t$ and is written as $DE_h(LE_k;T_t)$.
- *Order* - an *Order* $O_i$ with $i \in N$ is a legally binding contract concerning a transaction between two or more legal entities $LE_k$. It is issued by one $LE_k$ and received by another which is written as $O_i(LE_k;LE_{k-x})$ for $x \in N$ where $LE_k$ issues and $LE_{k-x}$ receives the order $O_i$.
- *Order Relationship* - division of labor results in suborders that have to be fulfilled before a superorder can be fulfilled. An *Order Relationship* $OR_{ji}$ between a superorder $O_j$ and a suborder $O_i$ is defined as $OR_{ji} = (O_j;O_i)$.
- *Order Attribute* - an *Order* $O_i$ has one or more characteristic *Order Attributes* $OA_n$ with $n \in N$. Some of the $OA_n$ have a constant value while others may change during the fulfillment of $O_i$. Therefore, $OA_n(T_t)$ is the value of an order attribute $OA_n$ at a certain point in time $T_t$. An $OA_n(T_t)$ can also represent an aggregated value calculated from different $OA_{n-x}(T_t)$ for $x \in N$. A value of an order attribute $OA_n$ is characterized by the parameters order $O_i$ and time $T_t$: $OA_n(O_i;T_t)$.
- *Order Status* - the situation depicted by the values of all order attributes $OA_n(O_i;T_t)$ of an order $O_i$ at a certain point in time $T_t$ is defined as the *Order Status* $OS_i(T_t) = \{OA_n(O_i;T_t)\}$ for $n \in N$.
- *Location* - any legal entity $LE_k$ has a *Location* $L_r$ which defines where and how it can be contacted with the help of communication technology.
- *Activity* - an *Activity* $A_v$ is something that is executed over a certain interval of time, with "something" referring to physical and/or mental tasks that are conducted by some entity.

The following basic definitions are detailed in statements defined in section 2.1.3.2:

- *Demand* - a *Demand* $D_q$ is the need of an actor (e.g. a *Legal Entity*) for goods or information.
- *Message* - a written or spoken piece of information that is sent from one actor to another is defined as a *Message $M_s$*.
- *Content* - the *Content* $C_p$ is defined as the subject contained in a piece of information (e.g. in a *Message*).
- *Reaction* - an *Activity* that is a direct result of some event (e.g. a *Disruptive Event*) is a *Reaction* $R_u$.
- *Consequence* - a *Consequence* $CSQ_w$ is a result of a particular *Reaction* that is executed.

---

[4.] An information logistics solution for the SNEM problem is referred to as a *SNEM solution* or *SNEM system*.

### 2.1.3.2    Statements

The following statements are based upon the concepts defined above and characterize the SNEM problem:

A disruptive event $DE_h(LE_{k-x};T_1)$ that occurs at time $T_1$ and originates at legal entity $LE_{k-x}$ will affect one or more orders $O_i$ which results in a change of values of order attributes $OA_n$ (depicted as $\Delta OA_n(O_i;T_1)$) and a change of order status $OS_i(T_t)$ represented by $\Delta OS_i(T_1)$.

(1) $DE_h(LE_{k-x};T_1) \Rightarrow \{\Delta OA_n(O_i;T_1)\} \Rightarrow \Delta OS_i(T_1)$ for $n \in N$ (read as
   $\quad$ $IF \Rightarrow THEN$)

The information concerning the relationship between the disruptive event $DE_h$ and the changed order status $\Delta OS_i(T_1)$ is defined as the potential *Content* $C_p$ of a message.

(2) $C_p(DE_h;\Delta OS_i(T_1))$

As for the interdependencies that exist between orders and their suborders, the change of order attributes $\Delta OA_n(O_i;T_1)$ and the respective change of the order status $\Delta OS_i(T_1)$ will affect a related superorder $O_j$ of legal entity $LE_k$ at some future point in time $T_y$.

(3) $((OR_{ji} = (O_j;O_i)) \wedge (\Delta OS_i(T_1) \neq 0)) \Rightarrow \{\Delta OA_n(O_j;T_y)\} \Rightarrow \Delta OS_j(T_y)$ for $n \in N$
   $\quad$ with $T_y > T_1$

With the deviation $\Delta OS_i(T_1)$ in (1) an implicit *Demand* $D_q$ for information arises at time $T_1$ at the supply network partner that will eventually be affected by the disruptive event $DE_h$ in the future as described in (3). This demand $D_q$ cannot actually be articulated, because it is unknown to the partners at the time of occurrence of the disruptive event $DE_h$. This implicit demand $D_q$ is located at the legal entity $LE_k$ that issued the suborder $O_i$ and that has to fulfill its superorder $O_j$. The content $C_p$ defined in (2) is required at time $T_1$ (as soon as the $DE_h$ has occurred), and it is needed at the *Location* $L_r$ of the recipient $LE_k$.

(4) $((OR_{ji} = (O_j;O_i)) \wedge (\Delta OS_i(T_1) \neq 0)) \Rightarrow D_q(LE_k;C_p;T_1;L_r)$ with $O_i(LE_k;LE_{k-x})$

Ideally, the demand $D_q$ is satisfied by a *Message* $M_s$ that is communicated from the legal entity $LE_{k-x}$, where the event occurred, to the potentially affected legal entity $LE_k$. It contains the content $C_p$ and is transmitted at time $T_2$ to location $L_r$ from sender $LE_{k-x}$ to recipient $LE_k$.

(5) $D_q(LE_k;C_p;T_1;L_r) \Rightarrow M_s(C_p;T_2;L_r;LE_{k-x};LE_k)$ with $T_2 > T_1$

Based on the content $C_p$ communicated in message $M_s$ the recipient $LE_k$ is able to react upon it in order to reduce the potential negative effects that will propagate from the suborder $O_i$ and affect its own order $O_j$ negatively. The *Reaction* $R_u$ is characterized by the parameters $LE_k$ depicting the actor, an *Activity* $A_v$, the order $O_j$ that is the target of the activity, and a time-stamp $T_3$.

(6) $M_s(C_p;T_2;L_r;LE_{k-x};LE_k) \Rightarrow R_u(LE_k;A_v;O_j;T_3)$ with $T_3 > T_2 > T_1$

Any reaction $R_u$ as defined in (6) will have a *Consequence* $CSQ_w$ regarding the order status $OS_j(T_t)$ of the order $O_j$. The consequence is described by the remaining negative effect $\Delta OS_j(T_y)$ at time $T_y$ of the disruptive event $DE_h$ on the superorder $O_j$. This effect is eliminated or at least reduced to a minimum with respect to the chosen reaction $R_u$.

$$(7) \quad R_u(LE_k;A_v;O_j;T_3) \Rightarrow CSQ_w = \Delta OS_j(T_y) \to min! \quad \text{with} \quad T_y > T_3 > T_2 > T_1$$

### 2.1.3.3 Implications

The goal of minimizing the negative effects of disruptive events on supply networks, by using communication of event information to enable precautionary actions, is defined in formula (7) in section 2.1.3.2 with the term $\Delta OS_j(T_y) \to min!$. An analysis of the preceding formulae regarding potential problems in the sequence of statements puts forth one obvious critical fact: the "implicity" of the demand $D_q(LE_k;C_p;T_1;L_r)$ experienced by an affected partner $LE_k$ in the supply network (see formula (4)). This actor cannot specify its actual demand for information on a disruptive event at time $T_1$ when a new disruptive event $DE_h$ occurs. Although this information is already available as content $C_p(DE_h;\Delta OS_i(T_1))$ at $LE_{k-x}$, the potential sender of the information $LE_{k-x}$ is not queried by $LE_k$ for information concerning the disruptive event $DE_h$. An information deficit at $LE_k$ is the consequence - the SNEM problem. Therefore, a proactive management of the information flow is needed that satisfies the implicit demand $D_q$ defined in formula (4) in a timely manner. This is the information logistics task to solve the SNEM problem.

The relatively vague need for proactive information logistics management in a supply network, which became visible in statement (4), is refined in formula (5) by defining the necessary message $M_s(C_p;T_2;L_r;LE_{k-x};LE_k)$ to satisfy the implicit demand $D_q$. $M_s$ includes the content $C_p$ and several parameters which are the starting point for identifying requirements of a SNEM solution to solve the SNEM problem (see section 2.2).

The formalized model presented above considers the autonomy of supply network partners (see section 2.1.2.4): This autonomy is reflected in the notion of different legal entities $LE_k$ who willfully enter into contracts by means of orders. Implicitly, the model also considers the heterogeneity of the participants and their different information needs (see section 2.1.2.5), since the demand $D_q$ is defined without any data restrictions. It is to be satisfied with content $C_p$ that contains changes in an order status $OS_i$. An order status itself is based on a flexible number of order attributes $OA_n$. Since both restrictions of heterogeneity and autonomy are reflected in the formal model of the SNEM problem, the model is used as the basis for further analysis of the SNEM domain.

## 2.2 Requirements of an Event Management Solution

Both, formulae (4) and (5) in section 2.1.3.2, which define the implicit demand $D_q$ and the necessary message $M_s$ to satisfy this demand, are used to identify relevant aspects of the information logistics task as depicted in fig. 2-6.

Three main fields of requirements are distinguished:

1. Since demand $D_q$ is not apparent to a potential recipient of event information ("implicity"), a behavioral framework is needed to which supply network partners commit themselves. Basic behavioral agreements are addressed as general requirements of a SNEM solution in section 2.2.1.

2. Information that can satisfy the implicit demand $D_q$ is defined in the content $C_p$ of a message $M_s$. This content consists of various types of data relevant to the SNEM problem. Therefore, a data model is needed for a SNEM solution. Certain requirements for this model are identified in section 2.2.3.

3. To generate and transmit a message $M_s$, different information logistics activities have to be performed. Three basic types of functions are common to information logistics solutions: content, time and communication management (*Lienemann 2001, pp.4*). Within these limits, specific functional requirements of a SNEM solution are determined in section 2.2.2.

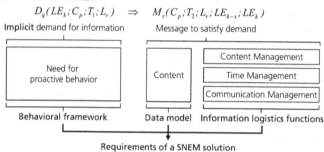

$$D_q(LE_k;C_p;T_1;L_r) \quad \Rightarrow \quad M_s(C_p;T_2;L_r;LE_{k-x};LE_k)$$

Fig. 2-6. Areas of requirements

An overview of all requirements for the three main fields is depicted in fig. 2-7. The requirements are subsequently defined in detail.

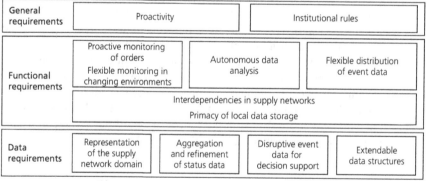

Fig. 2-7. Requirements of a SNEM solution

## 2.2.1    General Requirements

### 2.2.1.1    Proactivity

The main objective of event management in supply networks is to overcome the "implicity" of demand $D_q$ since $D_q$ cannot be made explicit (see section 2.1.3.3). Thus, supply network partners ought to act proactive: First, partners in the network have to "sense" what kind of information might be needed by themselves in the future and act proactive by pulling information from all available data sources including related network partners. Second, information on disruptive events identified by a network partner should be communicated to potentially interested network partners proactively (information push). In consequence, a supply network partner has to act proactively in at least two roles it is adopting at different times: as a sender it has to distribute information concerning disruptive events and as a receiver it will gather information on orders proactively given the assumption that otherwise important information might be identified too late. A SNEM solution has to enable and support both types of proactivity.

### 2.2.1.2    Institutional Rules

Autonomy of supply network partners as outlined in section 2.1.2.4 determines the behavior of actors in a supply network. As they pursue individual goals, conflicts are inevitable. The information logistics task of a SNEM solution has to consider these individual behaviors that are dependent on individual goals and strategies of the participants. To ensure effective SNEM processes and facilitate proactive behavior, some basic behavioral rules have to be established for a SNEM solution. Such a system of rules is called an "institution" and is used as a framework for the behavior of different actors (*Esteva et al. 2002*). This concept borrows from the idea of human institutions like a society or business organizations. An institution defines rights and obligations of actors that want to participate in such an institution (e.g. in a state or a company) and are regarded as the macro-framework in which each actor is allowed to act as long as it complies with the institutional rules. The idea of an institution can be transferred to electronically supported institutions that also need rules of behavior, if different participants with individual behaviors have to cooperate (*Esteva et al. 2001*). This is the case for a SNEM solution which is based upon information technology. Some important aspects that have to be defined as institutional rules of a SNEM solution are:
-   Roles in the institution and hierarchies between roles
-   Communication types and interactions between actors
-   Allowed statements and vocabulary
-   Costs of service provision
-   Behavioral assumptions (benevolence vs. opportunism)

## 2.2.2    Functional Requirements

The process of managing the information logistics task to satisfy the implicit demand $D_q$ is similar to a typical fulfillment process where a product or a service is supplied to a customer (in this case to supply network partner $LE_k$ with its demand $D_q$).

The widely accepted supply chain reference model SCOR (*SCC 2005*) differentiates three main process types: *Source* (procurement), *Make* (transformation/production) and *Deliver* (distribution of goods/services) to define a fulfillment process. With regard to the information logistics domain *Source* refers to the process of gathering information and *Make* refers to an aggregation, interpretation and rearrangement of information. Both process types are part of the content management function (see fig. 2-8) identified as one major area for functional requirements (see also fig. 2-6). The output of the *Make* process is an information product. Distribution of this product, which contains SNEM data, is related to time and communication management functions of information logistics solutions. These functions are mapped to the *Deliver* process (see fig. 2-8).

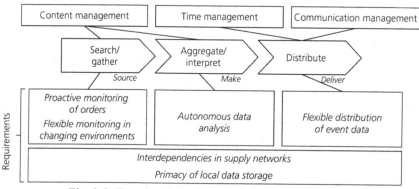

Fig. 2-8. Functional requirements of a SNEM solution

Similar models from other domains concerned with management of information underpin the general applicability of this process model (e.g. *Eisenbiegler et al. 2003*). For instance, the content lifecycle model relevant to the domain of web content management (*Buechner et al. 2000, pp.83*) is based on similar processes: During the *Source* process content is created and information gathered. In the next step it is edited until it is released for publication.

The basic SNEM process model which consists of searching/gathering, aggregation/interpretation and distribution activities is used to derive detailed requirements for the functions of a SNEM solution. Two basic requirements that have consequences in every process step are caused by order relationships and the structural factors of autonomy and heterogeneity in supply networks: *Interdependencies in supply networks* and *Primacy of local data storage* (see fig. 2-8).

### 2.2.2.1    Interdependencies in Supply Networks

During the search process order relationships $OR_{ji}$ between orders and suborders have to be taken into account. Information on suborders has to be gathered in addition to the reception of event information communicated from network partners regarding suborders. In the aggregation and interpretation process data from different network partners has to be aggregated and interpreted to evaluate effects of disruptive events that occurred in the network. In the distribution process order relationships determine potentially affected network partners that have to be informed proactively.

### 2.2.2.2    Primacy of Local Data Storage

The second basic requirement is established as a consequence of taking inter-organizational dependencies (see above) into account. Considering autonomy of supply network partners (see section 2.1.2.4), a replication of all SNEM data in a centralized data storage system for a supply network is neither acceptable to autonomous enterprises in general nor is it feasible. Otherwise, a huge amount of redundant data would have to be communicated, filtered, matched and stored for every supply network partner in one central data base. In addition, heterogeneity of partners regarding data and technological infrastructures makes centralized data storage extremely difficult and complex. In consequence, data sources that are available at each supply network partner should not be replicated unnecessarily elsewhere. Data between network partners shall only be exchanged upon request or when critical situations call for an alert of affected partners.

### 2.2.2.3    Proactive Monitoring of Orders

The first requirement regarding the "search/gathering" process concerns activities of gathering information. They have to be fulfilled proactively (see also section 2.2.1.1) and in a timely manner to provide a data basis for the next process steps. However, gathering information on monitored orders always incurs costs (e.g. communication costs, infrastructure costs, activity costs associated with personnel) that cannot be neglected. Therefore, identification of orders with a high probability of encountering disruptive events is needed. With this knowledge a more focused proactive monitoring has to be realized with the result of an improvement of a SNEM solution's efficiency regarding operational costs.

### 2.2.2.4    Flexible Monitoring in Changing Environments

Intensity of monitoring efforts has to be adapted to the likelihood of disruptive events (see section 2.2.2.3). In dynamic supply networks error-prone order types may evolve over time into reliable ones that need not be monitored as closely as newly evolving critical types. A proactive SNEM solution autonomously adapts to such new conditions in its environment and gathers SNEM data accordingly.

### 2.2.2.5    Autonomous Data Analysis

The set of data gathered from internal and external sources regarding the status of an order and its suborders has to be interpreted automatically by a SNEM solution. In a first step, dependencies between orders and suborders have to be considered while aggregating available SNEM data and calculating effects of deviations on a superorder's fulfillment that are encountered during suborders' fulfillment. In a second step, an evaluation of the situation is necessary to provide a basis for decisions triggered by the following distribution process. A SNEM solution has to be able to autonomously aggregate and interpret gathered data. Otherwise a timely management of information cannot be achieved and benefits of the SNEM solution (see also section 2.3) cannot be realized. In addition, necessary rules have to be editable to provide easy integration of new knowledge (e.g. new rules for interpretation) as it becomes available.

### 2.2.2.6    Flexible Distribution of Event Data

During the distribution process possible recipients of the content defined in previous process steps have to be identified. These can either be specialized actors or a dedicated planning system. An intelligent distribution mechanism is able to decide when the information has to be communicated and to whom. It considers available and appropriate communication channels along with available communication technology and message formats. A SNEM solution has to be able to communicate with intra- and inter-organizational systems as well as users. It can change its communication strategy in accordance with escalation rules based on interpretation of currently available SNEM data.

## 2.2.3    Data Requirements

### 2.2.3.1    Representation of the Supply Network Domain

Data used by a SNEM solution has to reflect static structure of supply networks as well as dynamic behaviors that networks show over time. Therefore, different order relationships $OR_{ji}$ have to be represented in a data model as well as order attributes $OA_n$ that characterize an order (e.g. quantities, delivery dates, quality measures, prices, cost). To assess an order's status, data on the planned fulfillment of processes (e.g. a planned delivery date) is also needed. Some order attributes change their values during fulfillment processes both due to advancement of fulfillment and disruptive events $DE^5$. Data on disruptive events themselves is an essential aspect of message content $C_p$ and has to be represented, too. However, detailed requirements on representation of disruptive events within a SNEM data model are identified separately in section 2.2.3.3. All data types relevant to the SNEM problem are summarized with the term *SNEM data*.

### 2.2.3.2    Aggregation and Refinement of Status Data

Although data types which characterize a supply network's situation should be available according to the requirement defined in section 2.2.3.1, it is not automatically assured that specific questions of actors regarding the fulfillment of their orders can be answered in a structured way. A network partner who tries to evaluate whether he is affected by disruptive events in the network will ask questions such as "*Is delivery of suborder x on-time?*" or "*Will I receive my order completely and in perfect quality?*" which can be answered

---

5. In the following, the index $h$ is not used when a disruptive event is abbreviated with $DE$.

with a Boolean value "true" or "false". To enable an aggregated estimation of the current situation of an order and its corresponding suborders, information has to be available on a detailed level and aggregation has to be feasible. On the other hand, details will be requested by actors in case problems are identified in the fulfillment process.

Top-level questions consider dimensions of order performance such as timeliness, quality, and cost measurements. They need to be enriched with more detailed information. The formal model (see section 2.1.3) conforms to this need as the definition of an order attribute $OA_n$ encompasses the possibility to aggregate different $OA_n$ into an aggregated $OA_{n+1}$:

With $OA_1$ = Planned delivery date and $OA_2$ = Actually achieved delivery date, a composed order attribute $OA_3$ = Delivery delay = $OA_2 - OA_1$ can be calculated. $OA_3$ can be used to define a simple rule which answers a top-level question such as "*Is order x on-time?*":

        If $OA_3$ > 0 Then False Else True

Consequently, the data model of a SNEM solution has to consider aggregation and respectively refinement of information. This enables preparation of statements and assessments of the current situation of an order and its related suborders in a supply network with various degrees of detail.

### 2.2.3.3    Disruptive Event Data for Decision Support

A SNEM solution has to enable reactions on disruptive events $DE$ by satisfying the implicit demand for information. This is depicted by $M_s$ resulting in a reaction $R_u$ (see (6) in section 2.1.3.2). Therefore, the data model has to support effective decision making of actors which react to event management data. Typical examples of information types related to disruptive events and required for making rational decisions are characterizations of events (e.g. type, severity, date of occurrence). They are used for deciding on activities in reactions. For instance, information that a delay of a delivery which has not yet arrived is caused by a traffic accident in which the transportation vehicle has been destroyed - in contrast to the reason *traffic jam* - will result in different reactions of an informed actor. In the first case, the delivery is supposedly completely lost whereas in the latter case, it will still arrive sometime. The SNEM data model has to characterize disruptive events $DE$ explicitly with data types that allow understanding and assessing type and quality of a $DE$.

### 2.2.3.4    Extendable Data Structures

Due to the heterogeneity of network partners and their varying information needs (see section 2.1.2.5) any data model of a SNEM solution has to be open to extensions for individual needs. Individual data types might reflect specialized processes in an industry (e.g. certain milestones of a production process) or specific quality measurements typical for certain products (e.g. temperature-logging in frozen-food-industry).

## 2.2.4  Implications

This set of requirements is used to guide the development process for an innovative SNEM solution: Following an assessment of potential benefits that can be achieved with a SNEM solution, an analysis of existing approaches related to the SNEM problem is conducted. It employs the set of requirements to identify strengths and weaknesses of these solutions (see section 2.4). As a result, main focus points for research are defined that have to be covered by an innovative concept for a SNEM solution.

In chapter 3 the required data structure is analyzed in greater detail, a data model for a SNEM solution is defined and potential SNEM data sources are identified. Functions of a SNEM system are developed in chapter 4. Use of software agent technology for realization of innovative SNEM systems is justified in chapter 5 with the help of the general requirements and technological requirements that arise due to SNEM functions developed in chapter 4. Consequently, an agent-based SNEM concept is proposed in the remainder of chapter 5. Prototypical implementations of agent-based SNEM systems that serve as a proof-of-concept are presented in chapter 6. An evaluation of the SNEM concept and the prototypes with respect to the initial definition of the SNEM problem is conducted in chapter 7.

## 2.3  Potential Benefits

Benefits from event management in supply networks are realized on different levels of a network: Multiple enterprises are affected by propagating disruptive events. Hence, reductions of negative consequences associated with these disruptive events are also realized by all affected partners. To quantify reductions of negative consequences an assessment of benefits for an individual enterprise is conducted. It precedes a cumulative evaluation of these benefits on the network level. All quantifications of benefits are based on a cost-model which is introduced in subsequent sections. Additional empiricial evidence on potential benefits concludes section 2.3.

### 2.3.1  Benefits for Single Enterprises

#### 2.3.1.1    Graphical Model

In fig. 2-9 an aggregated view on potential benefits of a SNEM system for a single enterprise is depicted. The solid curve indicates the ability of an enterprise to react to a problem caused by a disruptive event which occurs during a fulfillment process. The ability degrades as time advances and certain options of reaction become impractical. In contrast, costs related to a specific disruptive event[6] increase over time in relation to a planned ful-

---

[6.] Costs related to a disruptive event are all types of cost that are induced by a certain event. They encompass direct failure costs as well as indirect or follow-up costs that e.g. arise from future lost sales of unsatisfied customers. For details see section 2.3.1.2.

fillment date, because less alternatives for reaction are available and situations cannot be changed anymore (dashed curve in fig. 2-9)[7]. An example within a transportation process is a relatively cheap change of a transportation plan due to a later dispatch by a sender which will no longer be available when the transportation order is due for pick up and other orders for the same destination have already been loaded onto the truck. A loss of capacity has to be accepted with a partly loaded truck traveling to its destination. An early discovery of the situation would have allowed to replan and use a smaller truck or accept other orders for transportation.

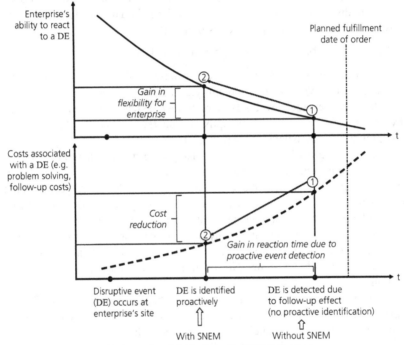

Fig. 2-9. Isolated benefits of a SNEM solution

In a simple scenario (see fig. 2-9) a disruptive event *DE* (e.g. machine breakdown) occurs which has a serious impact on a production order. The *DE* is not detected and results in a delay of production and a delay in shipment. Only few alternatives are left for reaction, e.g. sending the product with express air freight. The enterprise incurs high costs associated with this disruptive event for solving the problem (1). In case the disruptive event is identified earlier with the help of a SNEM solution (2), a larger set of alternatives for re-

---

[7.] A similar line of argument is used by Pfeiffer to define a general relationship between the ability to influence efficiency (time, quality and costs) of a product, process or project and the point in time during their life-cycle where influence is enacted (*Pfeiffer et al. 1994, pp. 162 and pp. 180*). The earlier an attempt to influence is made (e.g. on product characteristics during product development instead of during production) the higher is the leverage effect on efficiency.

action is available and lower costs associated with the *DE* are incurred. A gain in flexibility is realized which is indicated by the longer time for reaction.

### 2.3.1.2     Reduction of Event-related Costs

Detailed analysis of the benefits described above is based on a cost function similar to that depicted in fig. 2-9. Let $CO$ be a cost function of the type $CO(S, \Delta T)$ with $S$ being the metrically measurable severity of a disruptive event $DE$ and $\Delta T$ the positive difference between the point in time of identification respectively communication of a disruptive event $DE$[8] and the point in time of occurrence of the $DE$. The cost function is based on an additive model with two cost parameters $\alpha$ and $\beta$[9]:

(1) $CO(S, \Delta T) = \alpha S + \beta \Delta T$ with $\Delta T_n; S_n > 0$ and $\alpha, \beta > 0$

Any costs associated with a disruptive event can be divided into two parts: costs associated with direct resolving of the problem (e.g. managerial costs) and follow-up costs (e.g. lost sales or higher stock levels). Buffers in stock, assets, money or time that are provided by an enterprise to cope with disruptive events (see section 2.1.2.3) are also taken into account with their associated costs (e.g. costs of capital).

Costs will tend to grow both with an increasing severity of a disruptive event (e.g. a longer break-down of a machine will affect more orders and result in larger delays) and with an increasing $\Delta T$ as argued above (see fig. 2-9). In addition, $\Delta T$ can become very small but never zero, as in reality at least a very short time-period is always needed before any event is identified and communicated. Both cost parameters $\alpha$ and $\beta$ are positive as neither any kind of disruptive event nor any time for reaction $\Delta T$ can reduce costs compared to a situation without a disruptive event. Cases with $S_n = 0$ are not relevant, because in that case no problem occurs. No specific additional costs can be associated with this situation.

The cost parameter $\alpha$ reflects the impact of severity of a disruptive event. This impact is determined by organizational structures and processes in an enterprise which are affected by a disruptive event. Consequently, $\alpha$ cannot be influenced during operational fulfillment, but $\alpha$ can be reduced as a result of strategic process redesign and organizational optimization efforts. Since a SNEM solution focuses on operational fulfillment only $\Delta T$ can be reduced with the help of a SNEM solution. Therefore, the potential benefit in terms of reduced costs due to higher flexibility of reaction is solely determined by the reduction of $\Delta T$ and results in a linear cost reduction according to parameter $\beta$:

---

[8.] Assumption: no time lag exists between identification and communication of this information to actors who are able to react according to the information. For automatic data gathering, analysis and distribution as assumed for a SNEM system, processing time can be neglected. Without SNEM systems the relevant point in time is determined at the time of communication of event information.

[9.] The use of an additive model is applicable as such a model tends to underestimate the increase of costs for larger $\Delta T$ compared for instance to a multiplicative model. Thus, estimates on achievable benefits through reduction of follow-up costs are rather conservative.

(2) $\Delta CO_{isolated} = \beta(\Delta T_1 - \Delta T_2)$ with $\Delta T_1 > \Delta T_2$ and $\Delta T_1$ without SNEM and $\Delta T_2$ with SNEM

## 2.3.2    Analysis of Supply Network Effects

### 2.3.2.1    Propagation of Disruptive Events

As a prerequisite for calculation of supply network benefits the direct effects of a disruptive event on other levels of a supply network (see section 2.1.2.3) have to be calculated. These effects determine the severity of "follow-up disruptive events" on related supply network levels. Although the general structure of a supply network is not necessarily hierarchical, it was shown in section 2.1.2.2 that instances of order relationships result in tree-like structures (see fig. 2-3). Consequences of a disruptive event on a certain order will propagate towards the final customer/consumer along the path defined by order relationships. This results in a step-wise propagation of effects over various supply network levels (see fig. 2-10). Propagation starts at level $n$ towards level $n+1$ and further on to $n+2$ and $n+3$. Possible side-effects on other orders that are not directly related to the specific order are not considered at this stage of analysis, although they will occur in reality and add to the potential benefits of a SNEM solution.

An effect $E$ of a disruptive event $DE$ which occurs at supply network level $n$ and which affects the following level $n+1$, which is the customer on level $n$ (see fig. 2-10), is calculated as a function $E_n(S_n, \Delta T_n)$. $E_n$ is the measurement of severity $S_{n+1}$ of the "follow-up $DE$" on level $n+1$ with

(3) $S_{n+1} = E_n = \gamma S_n + \delta \Delta T_n$ with $\Delta T_n; S_n > 0$, $\gamma \geq 0$ and $\delta \geq 0$

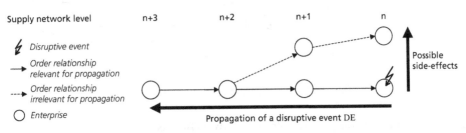

Fig. 2-10. Propagation of a disruptive event

A disruptive event's severity influences effect $E$ for other supply network partners. The intensity of propagation due to a $DE$'s severity is defined by $\gamma$ which is e.g. determined by the structural process design of an enterprise: Some process types are affected severely by small disruptive events $DE$ whereas others (e.g. processes with large stock buffers) are affected less by similar $DEs$. Parameter $\delta$ is a measurement of an enterprise's ability to react to a disruptive event. A large $\delta$ indicates a low ability to react to any disruptive event whereas small $\delta$ characterize enterprises with sophisticated event management capabilities. These capabilities allow to significantly reduce negative effects of $DEs$. The parameter $\gamma$ for calculating effect $E$ is always positive or zero because an occurrence of a disruptive event cannot result in a negative severity of a follow-up disruptive event at the next supply network level. The same holds for the influence of $\Delta T_n$ determined by $\delta$ where a later discovery of a disruptive event cannot result in a reduced severity as long as the problem triggered by the disruptive event is not resolved automatically without managerial interference - in this case no reason for SNEM action exists anyway. Both parameters are specific for each supply network partner but not necessarily specific for a certain type of $DE$.

In fig. 2-11 the influence of different $\Delta T_n$ on $S_{n+1}$ is depicted which results in a linear progression of $S_{n+1}$ since it is assumed that $\Delta T_n$ has no direct influence on the factor $\gamma S_n$ [10]. An increase in $\Delta T_n$ indicates that a disruptive event $DE$ on supply network level $n$ is identified later and its negative effects are propagated to a higher degree to the following supply network partner on level $n+1$.

| $\Delta T_n$ \ $S_n$ | 0,05 | 0,2 | 0,5 | 1 | 2 | 3 | 4 |
|---|---|---|---|---|---|---|---|
| 0,05 | 0,085 | 0,16 | 0,31 | 0,56 | 1,06 | 1,56 | 2,06 |
| 0,2 | 0,265 | 0,34 | 0,49 | 0,74 | 1,24 | 1,74 | 2,24 |
| 0,5 | 0,625 | 0,7 | 0,85 | 1,1 | 1,6 | 2,1 | 2,6 |
| 1 | 1,225 | 1,3 | 1,45 | 1,7 | 2,2 | 2,7 | 3,2 |
| 2 | 2,425 | 2,5 | 2,65 | 2,9 | 3,4 | 3,9 | 4,4 |

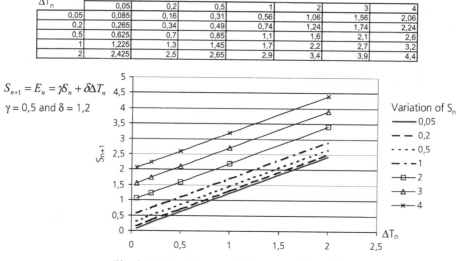

$$S_{n+1} = E_n = \gamma S_n + \delta \Delta T_n$$
$$\gamma = 0,5 \text{ and } \delta = 1,2$$

Variation of $S_n$
—— 0,05
— — 0,2
· · · · 0,5
— · — 1
—□— 2
—△— 3
—×— 4

Fig. 2-11. Variations of follow-up effects $E$

### 2.3.2.2    Propagation in Multi-level Supply Networks

To assess the propagation of a disruptive event in a multi-level supply network, effects $E$ for more than one level have to be calculated. Assuming that $\gamma$ and $\delta$ are identical on all

---

[10.]Although this case seems possible and would result in a non-linear above average curve, the simple case of independent factors is chosen. It underestimates the consequences of disruptive effects. Consequently, in reality any potential benefits may even be higher than those calculated here.

levels[11] the effect $E_{n+1} = S_{n+2}$ at the third level of a supply network which is triggered by an initial disruptive event $DE$ on level $n$ is:

(4) $S_{n+2} = E_{n+1} = \gamma S_{n+1} + \delta \Delta T_{n+1} \Rightarrow \gamma(\gamma S_n + \delta T_n) + \delta \Delta T_{n+1} \Leftrightarrow$
$\gamma^2 S_n + \gamma \delta \Delta T_n + \delta \Delta T_{n+1}$

Under the assumption of identical $\gamma$ on all levels the new restriction $0 \leq \gamma \leq 1$ has to be formulated. In case $\gamma > 1$ would hold, every disruptive event on any level of a supply network would propagate with increasing severity due to the term $\gamma^2 S_n$. Even an almost perfect SNEM solution which would minimize any $\Delta T_x$ could not stop propagation. In reality, any supply network exhibiting such behavior would vanish very soon from the markets. Also, if the assumption of identical $\gamma$ is relaxed, enterprises which exhibit a permanent behavior of propagating every internal disruptive event to their customers were not competitive and would leave the market. Therefore, a realistic interval for $\gamma$ is $0 \leq \gamma \leq 1$. Although a direct measurement of the parameter $\gamma$ is not realistic some further characteristics of $\gamma$ are identified:

- The tightness of relationships between supply network partners is one factor that influences the propagation of disruptive events. The more integrated processes between network partners are, the higher are any effects due to $DEs$. Today, a tendency to higher $\gamma$ is prevailing, because minimization of stock and buffer-times are frequent goals for optimizing logistics processes.
- In different industries, levels of integration differ. For instance, the automotive industry with its just-in-time-relationships presumably has higher $\gamma$ than an industry that traditionally holds large stock. The latter is justified for stock held for speculative reasons. A typical example are producers of consumer goods that are dependent on raw material inputs with highly fluctuating or seasonal prices.
- Taking formula (4) into account, any effect $E$ on a supply network is influenced by $\Delta T_x$. Therefore, minimization of $\Delta T_x$ as provided by a SNEM solution on all supply network levels enables even tighter integration of processes. That allows $\gamma$ to rise while keeping follow-up effects of disruptive events at an acceptable level.

In conclusion, formula (4) clearly indicates that with $0 \leq \gamma \leq 1$ only large $\Delta T_x$ result in a serious propagation of a disruptive event across a supply network. Consequently, calculation of follow-up effects $E$ in supply networks emphasizes the goal to minimize $\Delta T_x$ with the help of a SNEM solution as defined in section 2.1.3. In addition, a tighter process integration made possible by SNEM solutions potentially enables new logistical process designs.

---

[11.]With this assumption calculation of effects on multiple supply network levels is simplified although in reality varying parameters prevail.

## 2.3.3   Benefits for Supply Networks

### 2.3.3.1   Reduction of Costs in Multi-level Supply Networks

Based on the calculation of supply network effects $E$ (see section 2.3.2.2) a calculation of associated costs (see section 2.3.1.2) and an assessment of cumulative effects on possible supply network benefits through cost reduction is possible (see table 2-3)[12].

| Supply network level | Costs per supply network level |
|---|---|
| $n$ | $CO_n(S_n,\Delta T_n) = \alpha S_n + \beta \Delta T_n$ |
| $n+1$ (customer of $n$) | $CO_{n+1} = \alpha S_{n+1} + \beta \Delta T_{n+1} = \alpha(\gamma S_n + \delta \Delta T_n) + \beta \Delta T_{n+1} =$ $\alpha \gamma S_n + \alpha \delta \Delta T_n + \beta \Delta T_{n+1}$ |
| $n+2$ (customer of $n+1$) | $_{+2} = \alpha S_{n+2} + \beta \Delta T_{n+2} = \alpha(\gamma^2 S_n + \gamma \delta \Delta T_n + \delta \Delta T_{n+1}) + \beta \Delta T_{n+2}$ $_n + \alpha \gamma \delta \Delta T_n + \alpha \delta \Delta T_{n+1} + \beta \Delta T_{n+2}$ |

Table 2-3. Costs on multiple supply network levels

The accumulated costs for levels $n$ to $n+2$ are calculated as follows[13]:

(5) $CO_{cum} = \alpha S_n + \beta \Delta T_n + \alpha \gamma S_n + \alpha \delta \Delta T_n + \beta \Delta T_{n+1} +$
    $\alpha \gamma^2 S_n + \alpha \gamma \delta \Delta T_n + \alpha \delta \Delta T_{n+1} + \beta \Delta T_{n+2}$

### 2.3.3.2   Interpretation

By using formula (5) different scenarios with different parameters can be calculated. In fig. 2-12 an example is depicted which reflects general characteristics of possible scenarios. The first column illustrates a situation where no enterprise is using a SNEM solution. The resulting costs of a disruptive event add up to about 300 monetary units with $\Delta T_{1;2;3} = 16$. Most of the costs occur at supply network levels $n+1$ and $n+2$. This behavior corresponds with empirical observations on disruptive events which are detected too late (see section 2.1.1.1). The same effect is visible in the distribution of costs among supply network partners relative to the cumulated supply network costs (see fig. 2-13).

---

[12.]Note again, that costs are defined in a broad sense incorporating indirect costs associated to disruptive events (see section 2.3.1.2).

[13.]For all supply network levels identical cost and event propagation parameters are assumed.

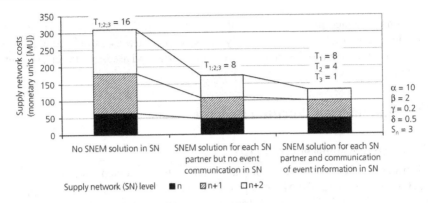

Fig. 2-12. Reduction of supply network costs

In the second column each enterprise in the supply network has implemented a SNEM solution and is able to reduce the time between occurrence of a disruptive event $DE$ at supply network level $n$ respectively its follow-up events at other levels and detection of these events by half (indicated by $\Delta T_{1;2;3} = 8$). However, this information is never actively communicated among supply network partners and no proactive warnings are sent to customers. Therefore, propagation of the initial $DE$ is reduced but the succeeding supply network partners still incur the largest part of resulting costs. If information on the event is communicated proactively by enterprises using a SNEM solution to affected supply network partners an additional reduction of each $\Delta T_x$ on subsequent levels is realizable ($\Delta T_2 = 4$; $\Delta T_3 = 1$) with the result of further reduced costs as depicted in the third column of fig. 2-12. In this case, an efficient mechanism is in place to manage relevant SNEM data and meet the implicit demand $D_q$ of the network partners with information on the disruptive event $DE$ as requested in section 2.2.

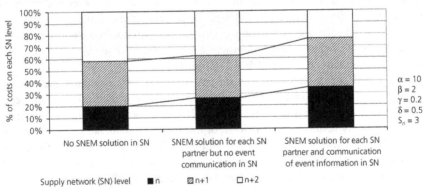

Fig. 2-13. Distribution of supply network costs

Most benefits of a SNEM solution are realized by customers and customers of customers in a supply network (see fig. 2-12 and fig. 2-13). This is considered a fair constellation, since in the situation without a SNEM solution most costs are incurred by those partners not responsible for the initial disruptive event. This insight corresponds to the empirical observations presented in the examples of section 2.1.1.1. A SNEM solution that effectively reduces $\Delta T_x$ is able to reduce supply network costs directly associated with disruptive events (in the scenario described above nearly 60%) and assures a fairer distribution of remaining costs among supply network partners.

## 2.3.4    Summary on Potential Benefits

### 2.3.4.1    Implications of the Model

Fair distribution of benefits is an important incentive for implementation of SNEM solutions: Besides providing SNEM capabilities themselves, every member of a supply network will demand SNEM solutions from its suppliers to achieve the supply network benefits identified above. Since customers will achieve the greatest benefits from event management, if multiple levels of supply networks are covered, they are able to share part of their suppliers' costs for realization of SNEM solutions through adjusted higher prices. Besides the intrinsic motivation every supplier has, due to its own reduced costs of disruptive events (see section 2.3.1), the ability to demand higher prices from customers (see above) and to gain competitive advantage compared to suppliers without SNEM capabilities is an incentive for realization of SNEM solutions.

Due to the theoretical nature of the model presented above some constraints remain to be discussed. The cost-model presented here does not consider the following effects that further increase the potential benefits of a SNEM solution:

-   A disruptive event $DE$ that affects the next level $n+x$ of a supply network will in many cases result in increased costs at level $n+x$ because the superorder affected by a $DE$ represents a larger share of value compared to the order on the supplier level $n$ (e.g. missing material from a suborder halts production of a complex product at the customer). Related costs are in general increasing which can be represented by higher cost parameters for each level $n+x$. Hence, the potential reduction of associated costs will increase on each level of a supply network compared to the example presented above. Fairness of costs' distribution will increase accordingly in a supply network and facilitate dissemination of SNEM solutions.

-   The simplified cost model with a linear cost function for calculating the impact of $\Delta T_x$ tends to underestimate realistic cost functions. A non-linear development of costs along the timeline is more realistic: early warnings that enable a replanning of processes mainly result in informational or transactional costs but no physical goods with associated costs of capital and consumption of fulfillment resources for manipulation of goods are incurred. On the other hand, as reaction time is reduced, costs for unemployed resources, stock, and lost sales increase rapidly. Hence, a non-linear accelerating cost function is realistic. Consequently, benefits due to reduction of $\Delta T_x$ are underestimated using a linear model.

-   Side effects with other orders which result in additional costs associated with a disruptive event $DE$ are not taken into account. For instance, a delayed delivery of a suborder indirectly affects related suborders of a customer: e.g. stock levels of goods procured by other suborders will increase because material scheduled for production cannot be used, if another suborder necessary for the production process is late. This results in increased costs of capital as a side-effect of a *DE*. A SNEM solution will also help to decrease these costs.

Analysis of potential benefits conducted above indicates a large potential to reduce costs associated directly and indirectly with disruptive events in supply networks if a significant reduction of $\Delta T_x$ on all supply network levels can be achieved. The theoretical model consequently underestimates potential benefits and thereby provides strong motivation to implement SNEM solutions on all levels of supply networks. Only if these systems are interconnected and provide SNEM data proactively to customers, the benefits as identified in section 2.3.3.2 can be realized.

### 2.3.4.2    Empirical Evidence of Potential Benefits

Empirical evidence could help to substantiate the results from above. However, no evidence of SNEM systems is found that are implemented and integrated on multiple levels of a supply network, but systems with similar aims as SNEM solutions are identified (see section 2.4). Benefits reported on these approaches point to potential benefits relevant to SNEM solutions.

Current implementations of so called *Supply Chain Event Management (SCEM)* software (see section 2.4.2) are mostly limited to small parts of a supply network: besides single-enterprise applications an inter-organizational setting is primarily realized in the distribution area (*Masing 2003, p.88*). These settings are composed of a large sender and one or more carriers that fulfill transportation orders for this sender (e.g. *Colgate* (*Wieser et al. 2001*), *Texas Instruments* (*Reiter 2002*) and *Philips Consumer Communications* (*Montgomery et al. 2001*)). Only few benefits are reported which are solely realized by a single company (the sender) in these limited settings, e.g. Roth (*Roth 2003*): reduction of transportation costs by 1.7%, process costs by 0.5%, inventory costs by 4.7% and a revenue increase of 0.25% due to reduced cycle times and enhanced order fill rates. In addition, amortization durations are reported of one to three years with implementation costs of 100,000 to 500,000 Euros for SCEM systems and operating costs of around 100,000 Euros per year and system (*Masing 2003, pp. 85*). This indicates benefits of approximately 135,000 to 265,000 Euros per year for one enterprise.

However, no calculations or forecasts concerning benefits in a multi-level supply network exist. Only qualitative assessments of potentially achievable benefits are provided (*Montgomery et al. 2001*), but neither empirical evidence nor analytical models as proposed above concerning network-wide benefits of a SCEM solution are available. Montgomery simply states that a gradual development of SCEM implementations from departmental over enterprise-wide to external integration is needed.

Empirical evidence is primarily available regarding single-enterprise benefits. Since the largest benefits, although not quantified at all, are expected in inter-organizational settings where SCEM systems of different enterprises are interconnected (*Montgomery et al. 2001*), this corresponds to the analytical results presented above in section 2.3.3.

## 2.4   Existing Approaches

An evaluation of existing approaches complements the analysis of the SNEM problem domain. Since the potential benefits of SNEM systems which adhere to the requirements defined in section 2.2 are significant (see section 2.3) any existing approaches are assessed compared to these requirements. Two primary types of software systems exist which address the SNEM problem: *Tracking systems* and *Supply Chain Event Management (SCEM) systems*.

### 2.4.1   Tracking Systems

#### 2.4.1.1   Overview

Tracking-and-tracing (T&T) systems originated from internal systems of parcel services such as FedEx and UPS which introduced such systems in the late 1980s and early 1990s (*Stein et al. 1998, p. 17*). They used these systems as a feature for differentiation in the transportation market. Such systems allow users to access the current status of their transportation orders (e.g. *FedEx 2002, p.11; DHL 2004*). Status information consists of the location of the last milestone achieved, a time stamp and additional information on the type of activity performed (e.g. "in transit", see fig. 2-14).

| Tracking number | 610366672277 | Reference number | SPF3390421 |
| Ship date | Dec 4, 2003 | Delivery location | BANGALORE 560029 |
| Estimated delivery date | Dec 9, 2003 by 12:00 am | | IN |
| | | Service type | International Priority Service |

| Date/Time | | Status | Location | Comments |
|-----------|---|--------|----------|----------|
| Dec 7, 2003 | 10:02 pm | Package status | MUMBAI IN | Package available for clearance |
| | 8:44 pm | Left FedEx Ramp | MUMBAI IN | |
| | 2:05 pm | Arrived at FedEx Ramp | MUMBAI IN | |
| | 2:25 am | Package status | PARIS FR | In transit |
| Dec 5, 2003 | 10:35 pm | Left FedEx Sort Facility | PARIS FR | |
| | 9:12 pm | Package status | PARIS FR | In transit in destination country |
| | 9:15 am | Package status | ROISSY FR | Package in FedEx location |

Fig. 2-14. Excerpt of FedEx T&T website

In most cases, T&T data can be accessed via HTML-Websites. Typically, these systems are limited to a single logistics service provider or to a consortium of service providers that cooperate to transport goods in a national and/or international context. A typical architecture of a T&T system that integrates different small carriers, which are subcontracted by a larger corporation (such as a parcel service) for local distribution, is depicted in fig. 2-15. Its main feature is a central database that aggregates order status data from participating logistics service providers during the transportation process. Every request for information from internal users of one of the corporations and queries from customers are satisfied based upon this central database. Customers can access the system via Internet, internal users via Intranet. Mobile communication technologies such as GSM and mobile web access are sometimes used to gather timely status data from trucks during transportation (e.g. *Kind et al. 2003, Siek et al. 2003, Reichwein 2004*).

The difficulty for small and medium enterprises (SME) to develop T&T capabilities (*Krieger et al. 2001*) has led to the development of light-weight solutions specifically designed to the needs of SMEs in the transportation sector. Such small carriers often cooperate with other carriers to form a transportation network that is able to offer a wide range of transportation services. Vendors of T&T systems offer concepts based on Application Service Providing (ASP) such as Euro-Log (*Dordowsky et al. 1997*) [14] or ZEBRAXX (*Zebraxx 2004*). They offer systems based on large-scale central databases for their customers. These systems provide T&T services to SMEs.

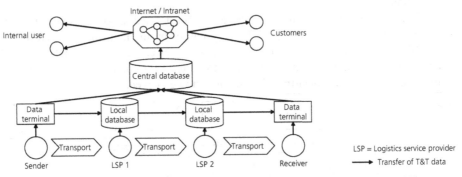

Fig. 2-15. Typical architecture of a T&T system (*Bretzke et al. 2002, p. 25*)

Besides the use of large-scale centralized databases managed by a third party, a concept for a distributed architecture in cooperative transportation networks is developed in the *CargoMan* project (*Stein et al. 1998, pp. 96*). The concept aims at the distribution of status data to transportation partners by sending all status data that is related to a transportation order to the carrier which originally received the order from a customer. As most carriers inherit this role for some of their transportation orders, every carrier has its own local database from which it can answer queries of its customers. A prototype implementation revealed that in general this mechanism is suitable to achieve distributed T&T in cooperative transportation networks but that queries from customers are also often directed to other carriers during the transportation process. This implies replication of status data in the network (*Stein et al. 1998 pp.109*) with the consequence of redundant T&T databases.

### 2.4.1.2    Assessment

In this section, the characteristic features of T&T systems are compared to the requirements for a SNEM solution as defined in section 2.2. Results of this assessment for general, functional and data requirements are depicted in fig. 2-16. They are based on the information presented above and substantiated by a business case.

The *general requirements* (see section 2.2.1) are satisfied to a limited extent by current T&T systems:

---

[14]·http://www.eurolog.com

- *Proactivity*

   Neither a proactive gathering of information nor a proactive dissemination of relevant event information is available in traditional T&T systems. Data that is generated at different milestones during the transportation process is communicated via electronic transmission (EDI, Web-EDI) in batch-files to a central T&T database. This database does not collect information actively to identify critical events. Neither is the active communication of alerts a standard feature of current T&T-systems (*Bretzke et al. 2002, Karrer 2003*).

- *Institutional rules*

   In T&T systems basic institutional rules are either defined in contracts between different carriers who participate in a T&T system or by implicit rules defined by the organization that implements the T&T system. Rules encompass e.g. definitions of data attributes and data formats that have to be used for communication, or certain time-intervals between data-transfers that have to be obeyed.

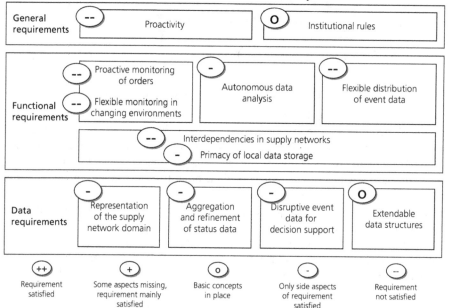

Fig. 2-16. Assessment of T&T-systems against SNEM requirements

The *functional requirements* of a SNEM solution have been defined in section 2.2.2. Current T&T systems cannot fulfill these requirements.

- *Interdependencies in supply networks*

   Since T&T systems only cover transportation processes, they are not built to cover whole supply networks that incorporate such diverse processes as production, warehousing and transportation. This is underlined by the central architecture of these systems which contradicts the autonomy and heterogeneity of supply network partners (see sections 2.1.2.4 and 2.1.2.5).

- *Primacy of local data storage*
  Only few attempts to decentralize data storage of T&T data have been made (e.g. *CargoMan* project), and even those face problems of redundancy of tracking data as a consequence of their concept.
- *Proactive monitoring of orders*
  No proactive data gathering mechanisms are realized and features which identify potentially critical orders at the time of order reception do not exist. Instead, efficiency in communication is achieved by a batch-wise transmission scheme which constrains or even prevents identification of disruptive events on time.
- *Flexible monitoring in changing environments*
  Functions that provide autonomous adaptation in changing environments with regard to the intensity of monitoring orders cannot be identified within traditional T&T systems.
- *Autonomous data analysis*
  T&T systems aggregate data from different sources, but information is limited to a single transportation order. The "analysis task" simply consists of sorting the information into the correct sequence of process steps (e.g. *DHL 2004*). No further interpretation of disruptive events and related situations is achieved. T&T systems do not consider suborders that are related to superorders and thus cannot deal with one-to-many relationships as are common in order-to-suborder-relationships within supply networks (see section 2.1.2.2).
- *Flexible distribution of event data*
  Since most T&T systems are accessed manually by users (e.g. internal staff and customers), no alerts on disruptive events are generated. Mechanisms to proactively push selected information to decision makers are not implemented (*Bretzke et al. 2002, Karrer 2003*).

Data requirements defined in section 2.2.3 are partly satisfied by traditional T&T systems.

- *Representation of the supply network domain*
  Data available from T&T systems represent the current status of transportation orders. The data types are considered to be order attributes of the type $OA_n$. However, important data types for SNEM functions are missing. T&T systems are restricted to the transportation domain and do not cover all processes relevant to a SNEM solution (see section 2.1.2.1). No information is available on data for comparing plans with the current status (e.g. planned dates of achievement) (*Karrer 2003, p. 8*).
- *Aggregation and refinement of status data*
  Typical T&T systems offer two views: a short status with the last status data set retrieved (e.g. "Left Sort Station, 2004-09-22, 12.00") and a detailed view that offers every data set retrieved for an order (see excerpt in fig. 2-14). A further refinement which for instance allows aggregating different order attributes $OA_n$ in one indicator (e.g. delay of an order) is missing.
- *Disruptive event data for decision support*
  In some cases information on different disruption types is available which corresponds to the disruptive events $DE$ in a SNEM solution (e.g. based on the FORTRAS

definitions (*Fortras 2002*)). However, no assessment of disruptive events (e.g. sever-
ity) is provided.
- *Extendable data structures*
  T&T-systems are generally open to different data types as long as those can be inte-
  grated into the underlying data model and database. However, no data standards for
  T&T-systems exist and legacy data formats prevail.

### 2.4.1.3    Business Case

A business case conducted with a 4th-party logistics service provider (LSP) underlines the
deficits of current T&T systems (see fig. 2-17). The LSP manages its own warehouses and
places transportation orders with different carriers. It integrates T&T information from
different carriers in a dedicated database which is filled with about 440,000 EDI-messages
per year induced by a single subsidiary that was analyzed for the business case. On average 2.2 messages are communicated per order. The available tracking information mostly
does not cover detailed process steps and related milestones. During fulfillment processes
only 2% to 5% of the orders experience disruptive events which results in costly overhead
activities and resource consumption for data management (e.g. filtering incoming EDI-
messages, large servers for storing and manipulating data).

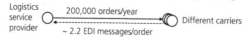

Characteristics of existing tracking system at LSP's subsidiary

- 200,000 orders/year monitored                           → 440,000 EDI messages/year processed
- 95%-98% of orders not critical                          → Only 8,800 - 22,000 messages which may contain data on critical orders
                                                          → Operational costs of tracking system wasted for non-critical orders
- Tracking data received in fixed time-intervals          → Order status outdated
                                                          → Loss of reaction time in case of problems
- No indication of criticality                            → Few carriers indicate problems in fulfillment and never provide
                                                             details on problems
                                                          → No appropriate reactions to disruptive events possible
- Missing automated data analysis                         → Deviations to plans not identified automatically
                                                          → Reactions cannot be triggered automatically
- Missing automated alerts                                → Tracking data only accessed manually by personnel

Fig. 2-17. Business case of a tracking system

Available data is mostly outdated because EDI-transfers are batch-oriented and arrive in
time-intervals at the LSP. Actual dates and times of milestones are provided with a time-
lag of at least four hours and in many cases a day or more after a milestone's achievement.
A huge loss of reaction time is the consequence. In addition, neither any detailed information on the type and occurrence of events nor an indication of criticality of an event are
available. As no mechanisms are in place to filter important information automatically
and in a timely manner from the large data pool, the LSP uses its T&T systems mainly for
controlling purposes and for resolving customer complaints. The potential for actively
managing disruptive events with all the possible benefits identified in section 2.3 cannot
be exploited by the LSP with its current T&T system.

## 2.4.2   SCEM Software

### 2.4.2.1    Overview

T&T-systems are the conceptual basis for a new type of IT-systems that are able to compare the current status of an order to data that is derived from planning processes such as transportation planning: *"Supply Chain Event Management (SCEM)"* systems[15] (*Bretzke et al. 2002, pp.29*). Deviations from planned events (e.g. delayed milestones) trigger alert generators that report these deviations to users and affected participants in an enterprise and/or a supply chain. A general definition for SCEM is given by Lockamy (*Lockamy et al. 2002, p.38)* as "the process of simulating, responding to, and controlling exceptions to planned and unplanned events in the supply chain." This definition is further refined as follows (*Lockamy et al. 2002, p.38)*: "SCEM moves from a single enterprise controlling multiple processes to multiple enterprises that control a single process distributed across trading partners." Consequently, the aim of SCEM systems is very similar to the aim of SNEM systems: to supply relevant information in a timely fashion to decision makers and to automate the management of disruptive events in supply chains where possible. This corresponds to the more precise aim of SNEM systems that try to satisfy the implicit demand $D_q$ of supply network partners with messages $M_s$ (see section 2.1.3).

AMR Research has defined five desirable functions that serve as agreed upon requirements of SCEM solutions (*Bittner 2000*):

- *Monitor* - Information on the current status of supply chain processes and workflows is gathered and disruptive events affecting orders are identified and logged.
- *Notify* - Real-time exception management is provided through alert messaging. Decision-makers are proactively warned of disruptive events or serious deviations in processes that require management reaction.
- *Simulate* - Decision-making is supported through assessment of consequences of disruptive events and simulation of specific management actions to be taken based on optimization methods and trend analysis.
- *Control* - Implementing management decisions is supported. Either users recalibrate process parameters manually or in defined situations an automated intervention is realized to improve the supply chain execution process.
- *Measure* - Measurements for assessing supply chain performance are gathered in data warehouses and made available as *Key Performance Indicators (KPIs)*.

Compared to the SNEM requirements defined in section 2.2 these five SCEM requirements are relatively vague and do not add new specific requirements, because *Control* and *Measurement* are not considered SNEM features: *Control* aims at realizing reactions $R_u$ that are not part of the information logistics task considered relevant to the SNEM problem (see section 2.1.3.3). *Measure* simply logs data for ex-post analysis which can be provided by a SNEM like system as a by-product but is not at the core of the SNEM problem. *Monitor*, *Notify* and *Simulate* are features that are addressed by SNEM requirements in

---

[15.]The term "Supply Chain Event Management (SCEM)" was created by *AMR Research* in 2000 (www.amrresearch.com).

greater detail regarding data gathering, analysis and distribution (see section 2.2.2). Consequently, the SNEM requirements of section 2.2 are used for assessing current SCEM systems.

To distinguish SCEM systems from other supply chain management tools the following characterization applies (*Bodendorf et al. 2005*): SCEM systems are considered to be a part of a technological environment that supports supply chain management. They interact with supply chain planning systems such as *Advanced Planning Systems (APS)* which support inter-organizational planning concepts, e.g. *Collaborative Planning Forecasting and Replenishment (CPFR)*[16] (*Busch et al. 2002, pp. 42*). An APS covers different planning aspects such as long-, mid- and short-term planning and various functional domains, e.g. production and distribution planning (*Fleischmann et al. 2002, Meyr et al. 2002*). SCEM systems, e.g. *SAP's Event Manager (EM)* (see section 2.4.2.2), are not designed to substitute planning applications such as the APS solution *Advanced Planning and Optimization (APO)* offered by *SAP* (*SAP 2004a*). The SCEM approach complements planning functions by providing feedback capabilities from execution processes of a supply chain to the planning domain. As an output they can trigger replanning activities in supply chains thereby enabling a closed-loop supply chain management (*Montgomery et al. 2001, p.4*).

Markets for SCEM systems are yet very immature since specific systems addressing management of disruptive events in supply chains began to evolve since around 2000. A rapid future growth of the SCEM market is predicted by research institutes which underlines the growing importance of SCEM solutions and their idea of event management for supply chain management. For instance *Frost & Sullivan* predict revenues to grow from under 20 Mio. Euros in 2002 to 140 Mio. Euros in 2007 (*Gerhardt 2003*). *Forrester Research* closely monitors the evolving market for SCEM systems. In two studies conducted in 2002 (*Kilgore et al. 2002*) and 2003 (*Tohamy et al. 2003*) active vendors of SCEM solutions were rated regarding their current offerings with respect to SCEM functions and their strategy to penetrate the evolving SCEM market (see fig. 2-18).

A strong offering of a vendor is identified, if solutions "enable end-to-end fulfillment processes" and if analytical capabilities (e.g. trend analysis) are provided (*Tohamy et al. 2003, p.6*). The measurement of strategic strength considers long-term commitment of vendors to their solutions as well as consideration of emerging technologies in their product strategy (*Tohamy et al. 2003, p.6*). Significant shifts in ratings of some companies are due to entry of new players into the SCEM market. For instance, *SAP* has only begun in 2002 to penetrate the SCEM market which it does successfully as is reflected in the 2003 survey. Smaller specialized vendors like *Viewlocity* or *Yantra* that offer innovative functions fall behind large vendors such as *SAP* and *Oracle* regarding their strategy for market penetration. Concluding, a rapidly changing market for SCEM systems currently characterizes the SCEM domain.

---

[16] http://www.cpfr.org

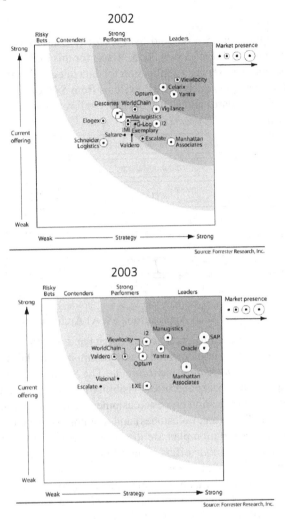

Fig. 2-18. SCEM market studies (*Kilgore et al. 2002, Tohamy et al. 2003*)[17]

### 2.4.2.2    Examples of SCEM Architectures

Two leading representatives of SCEM systems are examined in greater detail: a solution of a specialized vendor (*Viewlocity*) and an integrated system of a large ERP vendor (*SAP*).

---

[17.]A similar study was not conducted in 2004.

*Supply Web Application (Viewlocity)*

The "Supply Web Application (SWA)"sold by *Viewlocity* consists of several modules (see fig. 2-19, *Viewlocity 2003, Viewlocity 2005*). Basis for this SCEM application is the *Integration Center* which represents an application for data integration. It enables integration of data from diverse sources such as ERP-systems from *SAP* or *Oracle*, XML-based documents (Rosetta Net standard) and EDI-messages conforming to EDIFACT or ANSI X.12 standards (*Busch et al. 2002, pp. 82*).

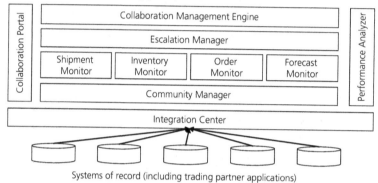

Fig. 2-19. Viewlocity's Supply Web Application (SWA) Architecture (*Viewlocity 2005*)

The *Community Manager is* used to grant access to data and allows to define users and roles. Main SCEM functions are implemented in four monitoring modules, the *Escalation Manager* and the *Collaboration Management Engine*. The *Shipment Monitor* aggregates information on transportation orders and offers visibility into the current order status for all users involved in the transportation process (customers, carriers, senders). In addition, expected events can be defined (e.g. milestones) and monitored during transportation. In case deviations from a transportation plan are identified, alerts are communicated to affected actors. The *Inventory Monitor* offers similar functions for warehousing processes with a focus on different types of inventory such as static inventory, projected inventory and inventory in motion. Alerts are communicated according to predefined roles and can be customized at the user level. The *Order Monitor* is used to track inbound and outbound orders with a focus on production orders and an ability to notify users upon identified deviations. These three monitoring components allow consideration of dependencies between warehousing, transportation and production orders within one SCEM system (e.g. if an enterprise hosts production facilities and warehouses).

The *Forecast Monitor* is an additional module that enables to monitor forecasts regarding inventories and to generate alerts, if forecasts and actual inventory consumption deviate. The *Escalation Manager* is used to manage interaction with users that receive alerts and notifications. It is able to escalate alerts in a defined hierarchy of users and can send messages based on different communication channels including cell phones and PDAs. The *Collaboration Management Engine* is designed to generate alternatives for solutions to disruptive events or other problems identified during supply chain execution, if these are defined up-front by an administrator. Possible alternatives are presented to the user. The *Collaboration Portal* allows users to define views on information they receive and to subscribe to different alert types generated by monitoring components. These views can be integrated into existing enterprise portals. Data gathered from event management is input for the *Performance Analyzer* module which allows to analyze past events, to identify and quantify exception trends and to evaluate the performance of trading partners in the supply chain on an ex-post basis.

*Event Manager (SAP)*

The *Event Manager (EM)* is a SCEM system developed by *SAP* for a broad range of business processes such as transportation, warehousing and production. The core data structure is the *Event Handler* (EH) object that is initialized for any order which is monitored by the *Event Manager* (see fig. 2-20). Every event related to an order, information on expected events (derived from planning systems) and additional data such as rule sets for acting upon events are stored within an *Event Handler* object. *Event Handlers* are initialized and managed by the *Event Controller* which serves as the central module for managing interaction between specialized SCEM modules.

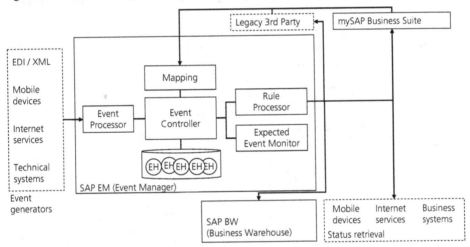

Fig. 2-20. *SAP's Event Manager* architecture (*Roth 2003*)

The *Event Processor* receives incoming event messages in a variety of formats such as EDI/XML, from mobile devices or other technical systems that connect to the *Event Manager* using *SAP's Business Application Programming Interfaces (BAPI)*. It decodes data, validates events and passes messages on to the *Event Controller* which links messages to active *Event Handler* objects. The *Event Controller* passes current event information to the *Expected Event Monitor* which is able to identify deviations from planned events such as a promised date for delivery, a planned due date for a milestone or an ordered quantity. Alerts, responses and performance data is communicated through the *Rule Processor*. It uses predefined business rules to react to certain conditions triggered by identified events. Based on these rules information is communicated to other SAP components such as the APS solution *Advanced Planning and Optimization (APO)* for rescheduling or the business warehouse *SAP BW* to store event data for ex-post business intelligence purposes. In addition, information is made available to actors in an enterprise using communication channels such as the Internet, mobile devices or other business systems and it can be communicated to other partners in a supply chain (e.g. customers) who need event information. The *Mapping* module integrates data from other SAP-modules or external systems of supply chain partners into the *Event Manager*.

### 2.4.2.3    Assessment

Both, rapidly evolving yet immature SCEM markets (see section 2.4.2.1) and heterogeneous designs of SCEM systems (see section 2.4.2.2) induce complexity to the task of assessing existing SCEM approaches. However, main features of current SCEM solutions are identified and compared to the SNEM requirements of section 2.2 (see fig. 2-21). Although current SCEM systems mainly focus on monitoring and notifying features (*Alvarenga et al. 2003, p. 34; Masing 2003, pp. 88*) which are at the heart of the information logistics task of a SNEM system, deficits remain with respect to the SNEM requirements.

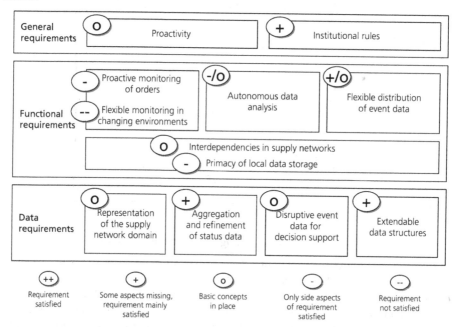

Fig. 2-21. Assessment of SCEM systems

General requirements associated with the behavioral framework (see section 2.2.1) are better satisfied by SCEM systems than by traditional T&T-systems:
- *Proactive behavior*
   One of the key features of SCEM systems is their ability to generate alerts in case deviations from plans or other critical events are identified. This is part of the

required proactive behavior of a SNEM solution. However, current SCEM systems mainly do not conform to the second aspect of proactive behavior: active gathering of data from different data sources to identify problems proactively in fulfillment processes. In contrast, SCEM systems rely on automatic delivery of data from various data sources as input to their event management activities (*Atkinson 2001*).

- *Institutional Rules*
  Compared to T&T-systems SCEM systems implement additional institutional rules regarding generation of alerts (e.g. who is to be alerted and in which case). A problem of current SCEM implementations is the obvious reluctance of supply network partners to communicate their internal data to SCEM systems of partners, while these wait for data inputs (see above) (*Gerhardt 2003*). This is an indicator that further institutional rules are needed that allow participants in a supply network to integrate their enterprises into an inter-organizational SNEM approach.

The requirements for SNEM functions (see section 2.2.2) are realized to a varying degree:

- *Interdependencies in supply networks*
  Only implementations with a very limited number of supply chain levels (mostly two in the distribution domain) are yet reported (e.g. *Reiter 2002, Wieser et al. 2001*). In addition, SCEM systems are presented by vendors with a focus on single companies. Integration of information from different sources is possible but integration of various data formats is addressed primarily and not supply network integration. Alerts to customers are available but no concepts are presented on how interaction between various SCEM systems at different supply network partners is to be realized in a complex supply network. This lack of conceptual support is never addressed clearly yet by SCEM vendors which results in the conclusion that current SCEM systems are mainly single-enterprise focused. This is supported by empirical findings on current SCEM implementations that focus on internal processes and lack integration in "global supply chains" (*Masing 2003, pp. 88*).

- *Primacy of local data storage*
  SCEM solutions wait for data input sent from data sources to a SCEM system. In some cases batch transmission of data is conducted which results in a loss of valuable reaction time. This results in unnecessary redundancy of data storage since all available data is both, stored locally where it originates and communicated to a SCEM system. Even the "promise" to integrate various data sources has a negative side effect, because it also tends to replicate data. This problem becomes even more serious, if more than one level of a supply chain is to be integrated into a SCEM system or if SCEM systems of different supply network partners are to be connected. These designs contradict a policy that prioritizes local data storage as required for a SNEM solution (see section 2.2.2.2).

- *Proactive monitoring of orders*
  Current SCEM systems do not offer specific functions to achieve a focused and cost-efficient monitoring of orders. Resources are wasted on orders with a low probability of disruptive events. However, *SAP* allows to focus on specific orders by defining *Event Handler* objects for order types to be monitored while those without a defined *Event Handler* are not monitored by the *Event Manager* (see section 2.4.2.2). Never-

theless, no specific methods are proposed that allow to decide which orders will encounter disruptive events with a high likelihood and therefore need to be monitored as requested in section 2.2.2.3.

- *Flexible monitoring in changing environments*

Current SCEM systems do not have the ability to identify new types of problems in fulfillment processes autonomously. For instance, over time new critical types of orders can evolve (e.g. longtime roadwork on a certain route or a failed reengineering effort at a partner's site). Affected orders have to be monitored more closely while other order types improve over time and need not be monitored anymore. A SCEM system offering such a feature cannot be identified.

- *Autonomous data analysis*

Rule-based modules of SCEM systems that are used to react on events are implemented with the help of business rules components (e.g. *ILOG 2003*). Such a rule defines a condition and a resulting action to be taken, if the condition is true (see fig. 2-22).

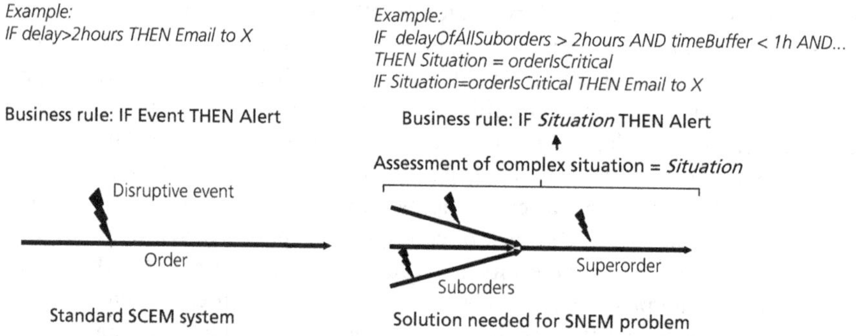

*Example:*
IF delay>2hours THEN Email to X

*Example:*
IF delayOfAllSuborders > 2hours AND timeBuffer < 1h AND...
THEN Situation = orderIsCritical
IF Situation=orderIsCritical THEN Email to X

**Business rule: IF Event THEN Alert**

**Business rule: IF *Situation* THEN Alert**

Assessment of complex situation = *Situation*

Disruptive event

Order

Suborders

Superorder

**Standard SCEM system**

**Solution needed for SNEM problem**

Fig. 2-22. Assessment of complex situations in SNEM domain

A common disadvantage of these systems is a relatively large customizing effort to implement and maintain rule-bases (*Wilson 2001*). For a SNEM solution, consideration of several events that occur in different suborders in parallel is necessary, if these suborders affect the same superorder. Since defining business rules for all realistic combinations of events in different suborders results in extensive rule bases simple business rules cannot be applied. Instead, an analysis of the resulting overall situation of the superorder has to precede an inference mechanism for identifying necessary actions (e.g. an alert) (see fig. 2-22). In most cases, current SCEM systems do not meet this requirement, although business rule components of specialized vendors like *ILOG* (*ILOG 2003*) should be able to fulfill this requirement, if adjusted to the SNEM problem.

- *Flexible distribution of event data*

An alert generated as the resulting action of a business rule must be distributed to actors or systems that have the ability to act upon event information. SCEM systems allow to distribute event information by using various media channels and to escalate alerts to higher hierarchical levels if necessary (e.g. *Viewlocity's SWA*, see section 2.4.2.2). In some cases mechanisms are provided that allow to resolve minor problems automatically (*Montgomery 2003*) or to propose appropriate reactions that have been defined during implementation phase (e.g. *Saltare 2001, Viewlocity 2002*). Regarding this SNEM requirement, SCEM systems offer a broad variety of mechanisms that should be integrated into a SNEM concept.

Data requirements for a SNEM system are basically fulfilled by existing SCEM systems:

- *Representation of the supply network domain*
  Data used by SCEM systems consist of main order attributes $OA_n$ relevant to fulfillment processes which include data derived from fulfillment plans. SCEM systems are not restricted to the transportation domain as are T&T-systems (see section 2.4.1.2) but also cover warehousing and production processes (see section 2.4.2.2). However, SCEM systems do not consider order relationships $OR_{ji}$ as a standard feature although these are vital for the realization of a SNEM solution.

- *Aggregation and refinement of status data*
  One of the main features of SCEM systems is, that they are able to compare current status data to the planned situation of an order (*Bretzke et al. 2002, pp. 29*). This is one of the basic features required to enable aggregation of various data types, to assess the current situation of an order as requested in section 2.2.3 and provide drill-down capabilities for detailed information, if needed by an actor.

- *Disruptive event data for decision support*
  The extent to which SCEM solutions provide background information on disruptive events (e.g. severity measures) that supports the decision-making process of an actor varies. In some cases only type and date of an event will be communicated while other systems may even offer proposals for actions according to predefined business rules (see e.g. *Montgomery 2003* or *Saltare 2001*). However, such features are not common and the requirement is in most cases only fulfilled in part.

- *Extendable data structures*
  SCEM systems are generally open to addition of new data types. Especially the architectural concept of *SAP's Event Manager* is designed to support a wide variety of processes and data types. Other SCEM systems which focus on specific domains or process types are inherently more restricted (e.g. *Viewlocities SWA*, see section 2.4.2.2). However, a common problem is interoperability of data definitions (e.g. *Songini 2001*) to which no solution is explicitly provided by SCEM vendors except *Enterprise Application Integration (EAI)* systems as additional middleware infrastructure (e.g. *Viewlocity 2002*). Data standards for SCEM systems do not exist yet (*Wilson 2001*) and system-specific representations prevail.

## 2.4.3   Conclusion on Existing Approaches

Tracking systems cannot satisfy the requirements for a SNEM solution and have major deficits regarding SNEM functions and SNEM data. They lack proactivity with respect to event detection and communication. However, T&T systems represent the status-quo in most enterprises of the transportation domain in contrast to SCEM systems that only begin to be implemented in supply networks as illustrated by the yet small market volumes, rapidly changing market participants and heterogeneous solutions. All SCEM solutions provide proactive elements regarding notification capabilities but proactive data gathering is not provided. Functional requirements of a SNEM solution are only satisfied to a limited extent although the general aim of SCEM systems is very similar to that of SNEM systems. A standardized SCEM concept is not readily available and especially inter-organizational aspects of multi-level supply networks are at most only vaguely addressed.

Concluding, a major demand for SNEM-like solutions is identified which is illustrated by the rapidly growing SCEM market. However, existing approaches cannot satisfy the SNEM requirements defined in section 2.2. In subsequent chapters a SNEM concept is proposed that aims to overcome these deficits and tackle the significant potential benefits of SNEM solutions that are expected in multi-level supply networks (see section 2.3).

# Chapter 3

# Information Base for Event Management

An information logistics solution to the SNEM problem is supposed to proactively provide messages $M_s$ which satisfy the implicit demand $D_q$ (see section 2.1.3.3). The content $C_p$ of these messages has to be defined and made available in a format suitable for automated data processing: A data model and issues of semantic interoperability among different SNEM systems are presented in sections 3.1 and 3.2. Besides defining SNEM data, information sources which provide event-related data are identified and described in section 3.3.

## 3.1 Data Model

An abstract data model for the SNEM domain is presented in subsequent sections. It satisfies the four data requirements defined in section 2.2.3 and defines a basic set of data types required for event management in supply networks.

### 3.1.1 Representation of the Supply Network Domain

#### 3.1.1.1 Classification Scheme

Due to the requirement *Representation of the Supply Network Domain* (see section 2.2.3.1) a definition of SNEM data structures is needed. They have to represent order relationships $OR_{ji}$ in a supply network and order attributes $OA_n$ that reflect effects of disruptive events $DE$ on an order's status $OS_i$ (see section 2.1.3.1). A classification scheme for SNEM data (*Zimmermann et al. 2002*) is used to classify all data types required for a SNEM solution (see fig. 3-1)[1].

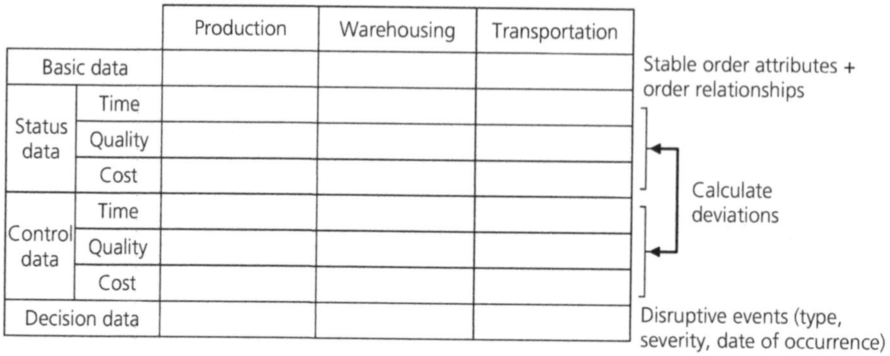

| | | Production | Warehousing | Transportation | |
|---|---|---|---|---|---|
| Basic data | | | | | Stable order attributes + order relationships |
| Status data | Time | | | | |
| | Quality | | | | Calculate deviations |
| | Cost | | | | |
| Control data | Time | | | | |
| | Quality | | | | |
| | Cost | | | | |
| Decision data | | | | | Disruptive events (type, severity, date of occurrence) |

Fig. 3-1. Classification scheme for SNEM data

Four basic categories of data types are defined: basic, status, control and decision data:

1. *Basic data* encompasses all data types that do not change values during fulfillment and that characterize structural features of an order respectively the underlying supply network. Examples are product type, quantity or destination of an order. To identify specific orders as well as to depict relationships between orders, identifiers are needed, e.g. an *Order-ID*.

2. To characterize fulfillment of a single order various performance criteria are used such as cycle time or quality and cost measures. These measures are derived from order attributes $OA_n$. For instance, beginning and end of production for a specific order are attributes that are aggregated within a performance measure "cycle time". Order attributes used for calculation of performance measures are classified as *status data*. The *Supply-Chain-Council* proposes three types of performance measures relevant to the SNEM domain within its SCOR-model (*SCC 2005*): time, quality and cost measures.

3. As identified in section 2.1.3 and addressed by existing approaches of SCEM systems (see section 2.4.2) data on planned events is needed to assess the current status of orders in supply networks. Status data and subsequently derived performance measures are compared to planning data. Scheduled delivery dates, defined tolerances for product quality and target costs are examples of such "benchmark" information which is summarized in the category *control data*.

4. Background information on disruptive events (e.g. a severity measure) is essential to take decisions on managerial reactions but it neither is part of the static attributes of an order (basic data) nor does it reflect the performance of an order as does status data in combination with control data. Consequently, a separate category *decision data* is introduced which will be analyzed separately in section 3.1.3.

---

[1.] The complete data model structured according to this classification scheme is provided in appendix A.

### 3.1.1.2   Basic Data

Typical static data types that characterize an order are order type, material-/product iden-tifiers (often separately for several order items), weight or volume of a delivery and infor-mation about the customer such as a customer identifier, address and priority. These data types do not change during order fulfillment (see fig. 3-2). Some process specific at-tributes are common to the transportation domain such as destination, route and dispatch type (e.g. express vs. regular). Further data types are common for warehousing and pro-duction processes (e.g. a bill-of-material associated to a production order) but these are mostly enterprise-specific and thus are not integrated in the generic data model. However, individual extensions to the data model are possible (see also section 3.1.4).

| | Production | Warehousing | Transportation |
|---|---|---|---|
| Basic data | Order relationships<br>• Superorder-ID<br>• Customer-ID<br>• Suborder-ID<br>• Recipient-ID<br>• Material-/Product-ID<br>• OrderFinished (Y/N)<br>• Order type | Additional basic data<br>*Order*<br>• Order item(s)<br>• Delivery note<br>• Order value<br>*Customer*<br>• Priority<br>• Adress | *Product*<br>• Product/service type<br>*Physical*<br>• Volume<br>• Weight |
| | | | • Destination<br>• Route<br>• Dispatch type |
| | • *Customized data types* | • *Customized data types* | • *Customized data types* |

Fig. 3-2. Basic data of a SNEM solution

A major requirement defined in section 2.2.3.1 refers to order relationships $OR_{ji}$ that ex-ist between a superorder placed by a customer to a company and its related orders that are issued to suppliers or logistics service providers. Two major types of order relationships are identified that are considered for a SNEM solution: direct and decoupled relationships (see fig. 3-3).

- *Direct order relationship*
  A direct order relationship exists if a suborder is issued directly to a supply network partner as part of the fulfillment of a single specific superorder. Goods or services provided by the suborder are needed to fulfill the superorder that triggered the subor-der. Other superorders are not dependent on this external suborder. For instance, spe-cific parts for a product are procured to fulfill a customer order as is common in the automotive industry where, e.g. car seats or other components are manufactured-to-order by suppliers for each individual car.

- *Decoupled order relationship*
  In case a suborder is not directly placed with a supplier, this order represents an inter-nal suborder: Similar internal suborders are gathered and a single order for the accu-mulated amount of goods or services is placed with an external supply network partner. The internal suborders represent a subset of this external suborder's amount ($Amount(O_{sub_{int}}) \subseteq Amount(O_{sub_{ext}})$). No direct link to the supplier exists and the rest of the supply network ($O_4$) is *decoupled* from superorder $O_1$ in fig. 3-3 (right side). This occurs when parts or material are held in stock for production or when suborders for parts are aggregated to achieve economies-of-scale in procurement pro-cesses.

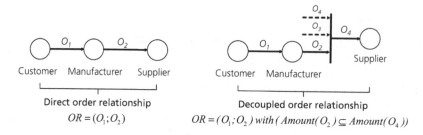

Fig. 3-3. Direct and decoupled order relationships

Direct and decoupled order relationships exist in supply networks at the same time. They are part of complex order networks as depicted in fig. 3-4. A possible scenario in the example is that $O_2$ refers to material sourced from stock for production of the manufacturer, $O_3$ is issued to procure an order-specific part from a supplier and $O_5$ is a transportation order required to deliver the final product to the customer thereby completing $O_1$. At some point in time, stock of material may fall below a certain limit and a replenishment order $O_x$ is issued to a supplier with a suborder $O_y$ to a logistics service provider. Index $x$ and $y$ indicate that orders $O_x$ and $O_y$ are decoupled from the rest of the supply network ($O_1$ to $O_5$).

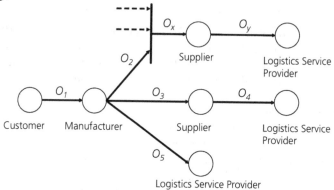

Fig. 3-4. Supply network with direct and decoupled order relationships

For a SNEM solution, links between superorders and suborders are represented for both types of relationships. In a supply network direct order relationships result in one-to-many relationships between external superorders from customers and external suborders to suppliers (see fig. 3-5). In contrast, decoupled order relationships result in a many-to-many relationship between external superorders and external suborders, because more than one customer order is related to a specific external suborder to a supplier (see fig. 3-5 and also fig. 3-3). This situation occurs when e.g. stock is replenished based on forecasts. The concept of *internal suborders* allows for the use of an integrated data model that enables representing both types of order relationships. Assuming internal suborders are directed to the recipient "self", it is determined which external suborder is indirectly linked by a decoupled relationship to a specific superorder (see fig. 3-5): an order attribute $OA_n$ such as a product or material identification number (see also fig. 3-2) is used to identify decoupled external suborders. In addition, an attribute that indicates whether an order is already finished is required. It determines which external suborders are currently active and potentially relevant as suborders to assess the situation of a decoupled order relationship.

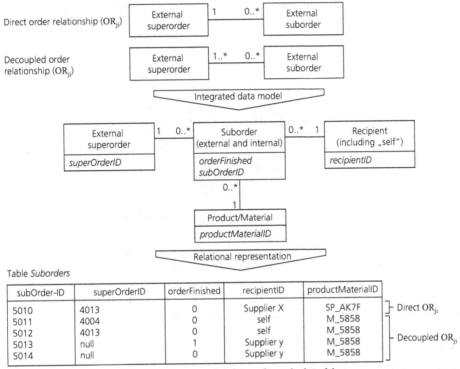

Fig. 3-5. Data model for order relationships

In the example of fig. 3-5 the table *Suborders* contains three external suborders and two internal suborders with *recipientID* = "*self*". Regarding the customer order *4013* two external suborders are relevant to a SNEM system: *5010* and *5014*. The suborder with ID *5010* represents a direct order relationship and suborder *5014* is linked via internal suborder *5012* to external suborders *5013* and *5014* due to an identical *productMaterialID* (*M_5858*). Since suborder *5013* is already finished (*orderFinished=1[true]*) only fulfillment of suborder *5014* is still potentially relevant to fulfillment of superorder *4013*. Concluding, only one data model is needed to represent order relationships for a SNEM solution[2] and an abstraction from the distinction between order relationship types is possible for most parts of the SNEM concept's development process.

Besides order relationships, monitoring of suborders with the help of a SNEM solution has to consider the sequence of fulfillment of suborders. In general, sourcing activities will precede internal processes of a company (e.g. production or warehousing activities) whereas distribution follows these activities.

This is important for a SNEM solution that has to pull information from supply net-work partners to assess the status of suborders: Knowledge on the planned sequence of activities enables a SNEM system to access currently relevant data sources. This means, it will communicate only with those external partners currently actively participating in the fulfillment of a monitored superorder (e.g. during procurement: sourcing orders, for details see section 4.1.2.2).

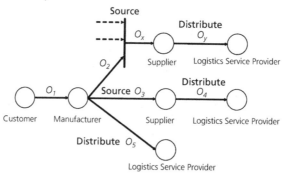

Fig. 3-6. Sequence of suborders: source and distribute

The SNEM data model provides the ability to determine the sequence of suborders with the help of order types associated with the basic types of fulfillment processes in supply networks (see fig. 3-6). The order types are already introduced as basic data types above (see fig. 3-2). They allow a differentiation between sourcing and distribution suborders: Suborders of the order type *Production* or *Warehousing* refer to sourcing processes whereas the type *Transportation* indicates a suborder for distribution.

### 3.1.1.3    Status and Control Data

According to the three basic performance dimensions of time, quality and cost (see sec-tion 3.1.1.1) data types are identified that are applicable to the domain of supply networks in general and required to calculate performance measures. Relevant data types for the three basic fulfillment processes and the performance dimensions are derived from liter-ature. Main sources considered are *Bauer* for production processes (*Bauer 2002*), *Goll-witzer* (*Gollwitzer et al. 1998*) as well as *Ihde* (*Ihde 2001*) for transportation and warehousing processes and the *SCOR* model of the *Supply-Chain-Council* (*SCC 1997*) which defines basic performance measures for all fulfillment process types. Based on

---

[2.] In addition to internal suborders, existing stock levels have to be taken into account for an assessment of a decoupled order relationship. As long as fulfillment of an internal suborder for stocked goods is not yet ongoing, forecasts on stock consumption are needed. Such information is regularly available from warehouse management systems and is therefore not further addressed in detail in the SNEM concept. However, assessment of decoupled replenishment sub-orders is a SNEM specific feature. Consequently, it is integrated in the SNEM data model (see above) and further considered within the proactive data gathering function presented in section 4.1.

these inputs order attributes are identified that are needed for calculation of the performance measurements, because these attributes are mostly not explicitly defined in literature. Order attributes for the main supply network processes of production, warehousing and transportation which are generally applicable to supply networks are summarized in fig. 3-7.

| | | Production | Warehousing | Transportation |
|---|---|---|---|---|
| Status data | Time | • Achieved/estimated date of production start<br>• Achieved/estimated date of production end<br>• Achieved/estimated dates of production milestones | • Achieved/estimated date of dispatch<br>• Achieved/estimated dates of warehousing milestones | • Achieved/estimated date of delivery<br>• Achieved/estimated dates of transportation milestones<br>• Location of order at time x |
| | Quality | • Production quantity<br>• Tolerance in product quality<br>• Number (#) or % of defect parts per order | • Picked / packed quantity<br>• Part quantities<br>• # of picking failures<br>• # of defect goods/pallets/… | • Delivered quantity<br>• Missing quantity<br>• # of defect goods/pallets/… |
| | Costs | • Costs of material / parts<br>• Direct labor costs of order<br>• Activity-based costs | • Costs of packaging material<br>• Activity-based costs | • Transportation costs<br>• Costs of customs procedures<br>• Activity-based costs |

Fig. 3-7. Status data

The dimension *Time* considers start and end dates of processes or activities which are characterized by milestones. For this purpose, three generic process models (see fig. 3-8) are identified based on available process models (*SCC 1997, SCC 2005*) and a business case with a logistics service provider (see section 2.4.1.3). Associated with each process step is a milestone type that defines a measurement point which is used to assess the progress in fulfillment. Hence, achieved or estimated dates of milestones are an integral part of status data (see fig. 3-7).

Quality of a fulfillment process is measured with respect to its output (see fig. 3-7). Output is a physical product itself in case of production processes or a service that is provided in relation to a physical product. Typical quality measures for production are related to produced quantity, tolerances in product quality or number of defect parts per reference unit such as production lots (*Bauer 2002*). For warehousing and transportation processes quantities with respect to actually picked/packed or delivered quantities as well as numbers of failures or defects are quality measurement inputs (*Gollwitzer et al. 1998, SCC 1997*).

Cost performance measurements tend to be highly sensitive: In realistic scenarios network partners very rarely agree to exchange information on costs due to security concerns. However, some potential data types are defined that may be integrated into SNEM solutions, if supply network partners should overcome these concerns. Examples are cost of material, packaging or transportation as well as resource consumption directly related to an order. The latter encompasses accounting figures such as activity-based costs which are directly attributed to process fulfillment.

*Control data* (see section 3.1.1.1) provides data on existing fulfillment plans. It is compared to current status data of an order thus enabling to identify deviations from plans. Control data complements status data. Thus, main order attributes $OA_n$ for this category are derived from status data types defined above (summarized in fig. 3-9). Typical data types are planned dates of achievement of milestones, planned/ordered quantities or planned costs.

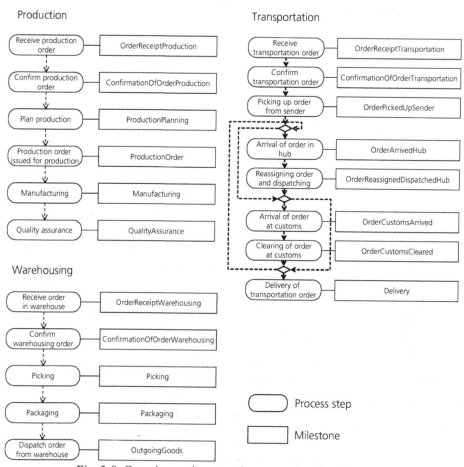

Fig. 3-8. Generic supply network processes and milestones

|  |  | Production | Warehousing | Transportation |
|---|---|---|---|---|
| Control data | Time | • Planned date of production start<br>• Planned date of production end<br>• Planned dates of production milestones | • Planned date of dispatch<br>• Planned dates of warehousing milestones | • Planned/promised date of delivery<br>• Planned dates of transportation milestones<br>• Planned location of order at time x |
|  | Quality | • Planned production quantity<br>• Tolerance limits | • Ordered quantity | • Ordered quantity |
|  | Costs | • Planned costs of material / parts<br>• Planned direct labor costs<br>• Planned activity-based costs | • Planned costs of packaging material<br>• Planned activity-based costs | • Planned transportation costs<br>• Planned customs costs<br>• Planned activity-based costs |

Fig. 3-9. Control data

Data types have been selected with respect to their general applicability to all types of enterprises that conduct at least one of the three basic fulfillment processes production, warehousing or transportation. As mentioned in section 2.1.2.5 heterogeneity of supply network partners results in enterprise-specific data requirements that would represent individual additions to this basic SNEM data set. Further steps of development of the SNEM concept are based upon this data set but options to integrate individual data types in the SNEM concept are addressed wherever relevant.

## 3.1.2    Aggregation and Refinement of Status Data

As defined in section 2.2.3.2, the data model of a SNEM solution has to consider aspects of aggregation respectively refinement of information to derive generalized statements as well as detailed assessments of the current situation of an order and its related suborders to satisfy the implicit demand $D_q$ for event information. While definition of status and control data in section 3.1.1.3 is based on a bottom-up approach, an additional top-down assessment defines main types of top-level questions fundamental to the supply network context. It is shown that these questions can be answered based upon the previously defined status and control data types with the effect of structuring these data types into a coherent hierarchy based upon defined refinement levels.

### 3.1.2.1    Key Performance Indicators

Realizing a top-down approach requires to identify agreed-upon measurements that are associated with important aspects of order fulfillment. For this purpose the SCOR model of the *Supply-Chain-Council* is employed that provides a widely accepted set of key performance indicators for basic supply network processes. Although some of these indicators only refer to processes and not to particular orders, some are directly linked to the fulfillment of individual orders and allow to derive top-level questions for SNEM solutions (*SCC 1997, SCC 2005*) as indicated in fig. 3-10.

All performance indicators highlighted in fig. 3-10 refer to fulfillment of individual orders. Since they address performance issues that affect customers, they inherently focus on inter-organizational interdependencies as required for a SNEM solution. Flexibility issues on how a supply chain adapts to changing demand (*supply chain response time*) and how production processes can be adjusted to different products (*production flexibility*) do not refer to individual orders but to structural process design and are therefore not considered[3].

---

[3.] The second type of performance indicators is in general very sensitive, because cost and asset situations are assessed. As mentioned before, such information will generally not be communicated freely between supply network partners. However, for the purpose of completeness, selected aspects regarding cost situations of orders are considered in the top-level questions for a SNEM solution.

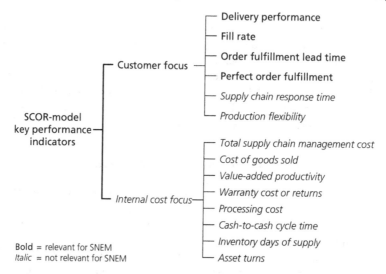

Fig. 3-10. Key performance indicators SCOR model (*SCC 2005*)

Four relevant key performance indicators are defined by the *Supply-Chain-Council* as follows:

- *Delivery performance*
  Delivery performance is measured regarding timeliness of delivery, condition of goods delivered (e.g. defects), completeness of the delivery and its correct delivery location.
- *Fill rate*
  The SCC measures fill rate regarding two aspects: First, the percentage of orders delivered within the delivery target defined by the customer (requested date and receipt date) and second, the percentage of orders that were shipped from stock within 24 hours. The second indicator is of no use for SNEM purposes since it solely focuses on internal warehousing processes.
- *Order fulfillment lead time*
  Time between acceptance of a customer order and delivery of an order to a customer is called order fulfillment lead time. It focuses on fulfillment of single orders, but accumulation of lead times over several levels of a supply network for related orders and suborders is possible.
- *Perfect order fulfillment*
  Perfect order fulfillment is an indicator that is mainly based on other key performance indicators especially delivery performance, fill rate, order fulfillment lead time as well as aspects of product quality. Although it underlines the importance of the above mentioned indicators, it does not offer specific new perspectives on the fulfillment processes.

Key performance indicators proposed by the *Supply-Chain-Council* for performance measurement of inter-organizational processes in supply networks primarily focus on aspects of timeliness of orders and order quality with respect to completeness and damages of products. Cost indicators are not used for assessing inter-organizational relationships. These results point to questions relevant to rate the status of an order's fulfillment processes and thus represent top-level aspects for event management.

### 3.1.2.2    Questions for Event Management

To reflect the top-level aspects for event management identified above several top-level questions are defined for timeliness, completeness and product quality that have to be answered by a SNEM solution (see table 3-1). As requested in section 2.2.3.2, top-level questions are answered with Boolean values true (yes) or false (no). Consequently, $Q1$ to $Q3$ ask whether timeliness, completeness or product quality are achieved as planned.

| No | "Upper-level" SNEM question |
|----|----------------------------|
| $Q1$ | Is an order fulfilled on time ? |
| $Q2$ | Is the ordered quantity delivered completely? |
| $Q3$ | Is product quality according to specifications ? |
| $Q4$ | Are all suborders fulfilled as planned ? |
| $Q5$ | *Do actual costs exceed planned costs?* |

Table 3-1. Top-level SNEM questions

In addition to these three basic aspects, the top-level question $Q4$ explicitly refers to order relationships in supply networks that have to be considered by a SNEM solution. It is answered with $Q1$, $Q2$ and $Q3$ for every individual suborder placed with a supply network partner. Finally $Q5$ is added for completeness: it considers cost aspects. However, since these are considered very sensitive for every enterprise they are included in the SNEM data model but not further used for development of the SNEM concept.

### 3.1.2.3    Refinement Levels

To answer the top-level SNEM questions with *yes* or *no*, detailed data on the actual situation and the planned situation of an order is needed as depicted in fig. 3-11 for $Q1$. On the first level of refinement the current estimation or actually achieved delivery date and time are compared to the planned date of delivery in order to determine whether the delivery is or will be achieved on time. Both input data types are available from SNEM data presented in section 3.1.1.3.

A more detailed analysis of timeliness of delivery is achieved when milestones (for available data types see also section 3.1.1.3) in the order fulfillment process (in the example a transportation process) are analyzed regarding possible deviations between planned and actually achieved dates of fulfillment. This analysis might be further detailed, if data on single activities in fulfillment processes is available.

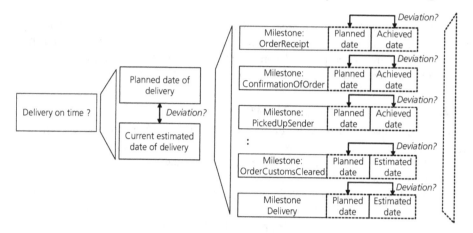

Fig. 3-11. Refinement of a top-level SNEM question

For the SNEM concept two levels of refinement are considered which are based on the available SNEM data defined in section 3.1.1.3 (see table 3-2). Refinement remains generic enough to develop a SNEM concept for a wide range of industries which is detailed to customers' needs, if necessary.

| No | Top-level SNEM question | Refinement level 1 | Refinement level 2 |
|----|------------------------|--------------------|--------------------|
| Q1 | Is an order delivered on time ? | Delivery dates<br>- planned<br>- promised<br>- estimated<br>- achieved | Milestones of main fulfillment processes (planned and estimated / achieved dates)<br>- production<br>- warehousing<br>- transportation |
| Q2 | Is the ordered quantity delivered completely? | Delivery quantity<br>- ordered<br>- delivered | Part quantities<br>- ordered<br>- delivered<br>- delivery dates (see Q1 level 1) |
| Q3 | Is product quality according to specifications ? | Tolerances<br>- predefined limits<br>- statistical measurements of tolerances<br># of Defects<br>- product<br>- packing material | *no further refinement* |

Table 3-2. Levels of refinement

| No | Top-level SNEM question | Refinement level 1 | Refinement level 2 |
|----|------------------------|-------------------|-------------------|
| Q4 | Are all suborders fulfilled as planned ? | *Q1, Q2 and Q3 and their respective refinement levels are considered for suborders placed with supply network partners* | |
| Q5 | *Do actual costs exceed planned costs?* | *Total direct costs of order*<br>*- planned costs*<br>*- actual costs* | *Activity-based cost indicators for processes*<br>*- planned costs*<br>*- actual costs* |

Table 3-2. Levels of refinement

A second refinement level for *Q3* cannot generally be identified since product quality is very specific to a product type and its associated fulfillment processes. However, tolerances and number of defects on level one are considered to be major aspects of product quality derived from the key performance indicators of the SCOR model and from other sources (see section 3.1.1).

## 3.1.3 Disruptive Event Data for Decision Support

### 3.1.3.1 Classification Scheme for Disruptive Events

Besides assessment of the current situation of an order and its suborders, data on disruptive events that affect fulfillment is needed (see section 3.1.1.1). Based on such information, actors in a supply network can react to and manage disruptive events. Disruptive events are characterized by several features, as depicted in fig. 3-12. This classification scheme for disruptive events is developed in a research project which includes explicit models of disruptive events for business process modeling (*ERIKA 2003 pp. 5*). The classification scheme defines five main characteristics of a disruptive event:

1. Origin of a disruptive event is defined by the location of its occurrence, the item that encounters a disruptive event and the process during which a disruptive event takes place.
2. Disruptive events may arise step by step (e.g. decreasing product quality due to an old machine) although many disruptions develop abruptly (e.g. a machine breakdown or traffic jam).
3. Occurrence of a disruptive event is in most cases random although systematic events due to e.g. bad process design are possible, too. A statistical distribution is attributed to each type of disruptive events.
4. Any disruptive event has an effect on an object and the effect is measured using indicators. For a SNEM solution, effects on the input and output of processes (that are the objects of suborders and superorders manipulated by a fulfillment process) are especially important, because these objects are needed to satisfy customers' demand. The relevant indicators (time etc.) are covered by status and control data defined in section 3.1.1.3 which reflect effects of disruptive events on order attributes $OA_n$ as ana-

lyzed in section 2.1.3.

5. Whether a disruptive event propagates to other levels of a supply network or not depends e.g. on its severity. Major events such as a power-outage in a whole region might even affect more than one supply network partner at once, but such events tend to be very rare.

| Disruptive event attribute | | Value | | | | | | |
|---|---|---|---|---|---|---|---|---|
| Origin | Location | Own company | Customer | Supplier | Other | | | |
| | Item | Human | Machine | Input | Output | Software | Other | |
| | Process | Production | Warehousing | Transport | Administration | Other | | |
| Initiation | | Sneaking | | | Abrupt | | | |
| Occurrence | Type | Systematic | | | Random | | | |
| | Distribution | Exponential | Normal | Logarithmic normal | Weibull | Other | | |
| Effect | Item | Human | Machine | Input | Output | Process | Software | Other |
| | Indicator | Time | | Quality | | Cost | | |
| Propagation | | Locally stagnant | | Escalating | | Simultaneously distributed | | |

Fig. 3-12. Classification scheme for disruptive events

An example of two different types of disruptive events and their classification is given in fig. 3-13. It is assumed that, in the example, the breakdown of the fork-lift (machine failure) occurs internally within the boundaries of one enterprise in its warehousing process.

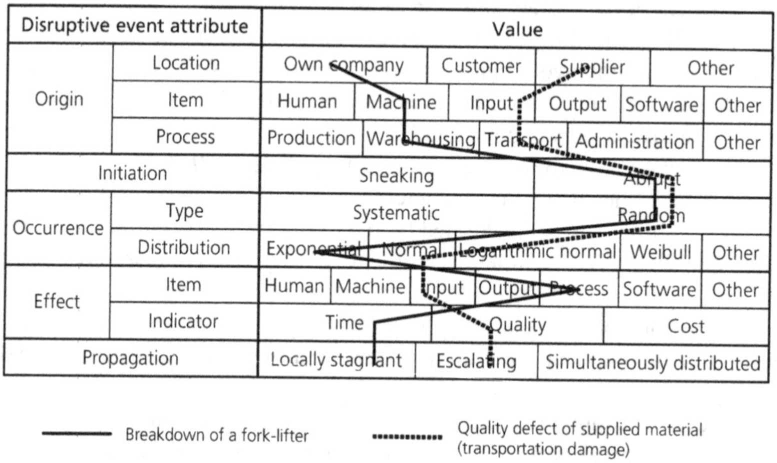

| Disruptive event attribute | | Value | | | | | | |
|---|---|---|---|---|---|---|---|---|
| Origin | Location | Own company | Customer | Supplier | Other | | | |
| | Item | Human | Machine | Input | Output | Software | Other | |
| | Process | Production | Warehousing | Transport | Administration | Other | | |
| Initiation | | Sneaking | | | Abrupt | | | |
| Occurrence | Type | Systematic | | | Random | | | |
| | Distribution | Exponential | Normal | Logarithmic normal | Weibull | Other | | |
| Effect | Item | Human | Machine | Input | Output | Process | Software | Other |
| | Indicator | Time | | Quality | | Cost | | |
| Propagation | | Locally stagnant | | Escalating | | Simultaneously distributed | | |

———— Breakdown of a fork-lifter        ············ Quality defect of supplied material (transportation damage)

Fig. 3-13. Characteristics of disruptive events (examples)

An exponential distribution of the likelihood of such an event is assumed and the warehousing process is affected which results in longer cycle-times for some orders. However, the disruptive event is not severe enough to propagate to other supply network levels (e.g. a second fork-lift with slack resources might be available). On the other hand, quality defects of supplied material due to transportation damages have an escalating effect since they affect following processes of the recipient (e.g. production processes where material is missing or material needs rework before it can be used).

The classification scheme is useful to describe types of disruptive events *DE* but for an operational management of specific *DE* information on *Initiation* and *Occurrence* of *DE* (see fig. 3-13) are of minor importance. Other information is already provided within SNEM data attributes of orders that are affected by a *DE* such as *Location*, i.e. is a *DE* associated to an external suborder or identified internally and the originating process which is covered by the order type defined as basic data in section 3.1.1.2.

As mentioned above, the *Effect* of a *DE* is already covered by status and control data (see section 3.1.1.3). Any additional information on potential effects or characterizations of a *DE* tend to be too enterprise- and situation-specific for a generic data model. They are integrated in a *Description* text field (see fig. 3-14).

| | Production | Warehousing | Transportation |
|---|---|---|---|
| Decision data | • Disruptive event description<br>• Disruptive event severity | • Date of occurrence<br>• Disruptive event identifier | |

Fig. 3-14. Decision data

For an automatic assessment of a disruptive event *DE* by a SNEM system a standard measurement of severity for *DE* types is required which is not proposed in the classification scheme. However, the classification scheme helps to cluster disruptive events in supply networks and subsequently define severity assessments for *DE* types. Consequently, a data type *Disruptive Event Severity* is required. Additionally, each disruptive event is characterized by a *Date of occurrence* and is given a unique identifier (see fig. 3-14).

### 3.1.3.2 Important Disruptive Event Types

Since an enumeration of potential disruptive events is not possible, common disruptive events are identified. An empirical analysis on typical disturbances in industrial environments is summarized in table 3-3 (*Mascada 1998*).

| Disturbance type | Percentage | Disturbance type | Percentage |
|---|---|---|---|
| Equipment failure | 68 % | Late delivery | 37 % |
| Quality miss | 53 % | Unpredictable demand | 21 % |
| Fluctuating demand | 53 % | Missing coordination | 21 % |
| Bad delivery | 42 % | Work force unavailability | 11 % |

Table 3-3. Frequency of disturbances (*Mascada 1998*)

Most of the disturbances reflect events relevant to event management in supply networks. Only fluctuating and unpredictable demand are of minor importance to a SNEM concept because they do not occur during fulfillment of orders but in advance. Missing coordination as a type of disturbance characterizes a relatively vague situation but not an "event" in the exact sense defined in section 2.1.1.3 and is therefore of minor practical relevance to event management. Consequently, main disruptive events linked to fulfillment processes are equipment failures, quality misses and bad or late deliveries.

Further empirical evidence suggests that especially shortages of material, production problems and quality problems in processes have a large impact on supply networks (*Singhal 2003, p.11*) which corresponds to the findings above. Typical problems in the transportation domain are addressed in data definitions of data types for logistic service providers such as the Fortras data set (*Fortras 2002*). A set of potentially important disruptive events based on these empirical findings for all three basic fulfillment processes is depicted in fig. 3-15.

| | Production | Warehousing | Transportation |
|---|---|---|---|
| Examples of common disruptive events | • Machine failure<br>• Material/parts/products defect<br>• Material/parts not available<br>• Capacity shortage<br>• Change of production plan | • Machine failure<br>• Goods damaged<br>• Out-of-stock<br>• Picking failure<br>• Packaging failure<br>• Dispatch deadline missed | Means of transportation<br>• Traffic jam<br>• Truck/Train/Ship/Plane defect<br>• Route blocked<br>• Change of transportation plan<br>Delivery<br>• Address incomplete/wrong<br>• Goods destroyed<br>• Goods lost / not found<br>• Goods damaged<br>• Customs delayed |

Fig. 3-15. Examples of disruptive events

## 3.1.4    Extendable Data Structures

The set of data types defined in the SNEM data model in previous sections focuses on three basic fulfillment processes identified in section 2.1.2.1. Further process types can be integrated in the data model if needed. Possible add-ons are financial processes where payment processes are monitored or product development processes in engineer-to-order industries as part of project management. Potential disruptive events in such processes are delayed payments or overrun project milestones. Besides adding complete process types including all related data categories defined in section 3.1.1, specific data types are added, if required by an enterprise or a community of supply network partners. These add-ons may result in further refinement levels or new aspects of e.g. product quality such as temperature-logging for consumer goods. This openness satisfies the requirement for extendable data structures and allows to reflect heterogeneity of supply network partners (see section 2.1.2.5) adequately.

Furthermore, the extent to which data structures are considered *extendable* also relies on the format chosen for data representation. Aspects of representation, both on a content-related and a technical level as well as problems due to non-standardized representation of SNEM data, are discussed below.

## 3.2  Semantic Interoperability

Automated exchange of messages among supply network partners during event management requires a data format which ensures that every sender as well as recipient of any message has the same understanding of a message's content. Requirements for such a data format are analyzed in the following and the need for an ontology is identified in section 3.2.1. In subsequent sections existing approaches to data standards and ontologies in SNEM-related domains are evaluated and reused where possible to design a SNEM ontology.

### 3.2.1  Requirements for Semantic Interoperability

#### 3.2.1.1  Semantic Needs and Ontologies

The SNEM data types defined in section 3.1 represent the information upon which SNEM solutions at supply network partner sites communicate with each other: They are used to define content $C_p$ that is sent in messages $M_s$ to satisfy the implicit demand $D_q$ of supply network partners for information on disruptive events $DE$ (see section 2.1.3). The *syntax* of terms for this content $C_p$ such as "production quantity" can be derived from section 3.1. However, only if each supply network partner has the same understanding of data types and their relationships, communication is possible (*Mädche et al. 2001*). Therefore, *semantics* of the event management information has to be defined as is illustrated by the following example[4]:

> *A supplier identifies a disruptive event DE in an order's fulfillment. The supplier does not recalculate an estimated delivery date of the order based on the information about the new DE. He only communicates the old estimated delivery date of this order (an $OA_n$) as well as information about the disruptive event to his customer.*
>
> *However, the customer believes that this DE, which is identified by the supplier, is already reflected in the estimated delivery date of the suborder. Hence, the customer revises its process plans without considering the explicit additional information on the DE provided by the supplier. In consequence, the process plan of the customer will be based on a wrong delivery date, because actual delivery of the suborder will be delayed due to the supplier's DE.*
>
> *Although customer and supplier use the same syntax to describe the data type (estimated delivery date) they have different definitions about what information is reflected in an "estimated delivery date" - they use different semantic definitions. Meaningful communication is only possible, if both agree on the same semantic meanings for a given term.*

---

[4.] A simpler example of identical syntax but different semantics in a different domain is given by the term "jaguar". It may either refer to an animal or to the car company. A precise definition is needed to determine what meaning is intended in a specific situation.

The formal definition of a collection of terms (e.g. SNEM data types) and relationships between these terms that conceptualize a domain are represented in a so called "ontology" (*Gruber 1993*). In a SNEM solution, an ontology is used to define semantics of the message content $C_p$ that is communicated between SNEM systems in messages $M_s$. In a more general sense, it defines concepts and relationships between these concepts that represent the "knowledge" which is utilized to realize SNEM functions. In an ontology knowledge is represented in a standardized form which enables to exchange knowledge between actors (humans or machines) (*Guarino 1998*).

Since manipulation of SNEM data and communication between SNEM systems must be automated (see section 2.2), an ontology defines semantics in a machine-readable format. In fig. 3-16 an excerpt of an ontology is depicted. A concept *Order* is defined that has two relationships to other concepts, namely *DisruptiveEvent* (relation: *has_disruptiveEvent*) and an *OrderType* (relation: *has_type*). These concepts and their relations are e.g. defined in a XML-syntax[5] that is machine-readable.

Fig. 3-16. Machine-readable ontology representation

In addition, ontologies defined in a formal representation based on description logics (*Baader et al. 2003*) allow IT-systems to automatically reason about coded knowledge. In the example depicted in fig. 3-17, an ontology defines two subtypes of a concept *Milestone* - a *TransportationMilestone* and a *ProductionMilestone*.

Specific milestones for transportation and production processes are instances of these milestone types (see status data in section 3.1.1.3). A SNEM system which uses this ontology receives information about a milestone (1) (see fig. 3-17), but the specific milestone instance *ProductionSetUp* is new to the SNEM system. Using additional information concerning the order type of this new milestone (*Production*) the SNEM system classifies the milestone as a *ProductionMilestone* (2) and e.g. triggers a production

---

5. Extensible Markup Language

manager to interpret the information. Without reasoning capability, the SNEM system may have to reject this information because it does not fit any of its known milestone types. To ensure maximum openness of SNEM data for SNEM functions (see requirement in section 2.2.3.4) a SNEM ontology is proposed subsequently.

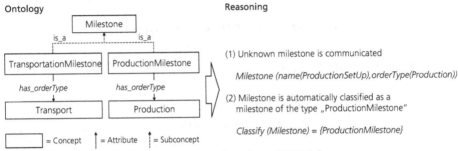

Fig. 3-17. Reasoning about SNEM data

### 3.2.1.2 Ontology Design Process

To design an ontology, functions and users of the ontology are defined (*Uschold et al. 1995*): The primary role of a SNEM ontology is to act as the medium to define content of communication between supply network partners. This implies that the SNEM ontology represents all processes, organizational units, objects and data types that are relevant within the SNEM environment and represented in the SNEM data model defined in section 3.1.

An ontology is generally designed iteratively and refined step by step. Different methods to derive initial and refined ontology designs exist. Holsapple et al. identify five basic approaches to ontology design: inspiration, induction, deduction, synthesis, and collaboration (*Holsapple et al. 2002*). Combinations of these approaches are possible. For the design of the SNEM ontology, a combination of the inductive, deductive and synthetic approach is used.

Definition of the SNEM data types (see section 3.1) is achieved by using a combination of the inductive and deductive approach. Induction is applied in the analysis of a specific business case of a logistics service provider. It provides insight into warehousing and transportation processes which is complemented by process documentations provided in the literature (see section 3.1.1.3). A deductive method is used to define the SNEM problem itself that e.g. allows to analyze the nature and importance of order relationships. Definition and representation of order relationships are primarily based on a deductive approach (see section 3.1.1.2).

For the synthetic approach, concepts from existing ontologies are adopted and integrated into the SNEM ontology. The set of SNEM data types defined in section 3.1 overlaps with a set of existing concepts identified by the synthetic approach (see fig. 3-18) presented in section 3.2.2. The resulting SNEM ontology builds upon existing concepts and newly defined concepts of the SNEM data analysis.

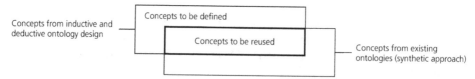

Fig. 3-18. Overlapping sets of concepts

## 3.2.2    Existing Approaches

### 3.2.2.1    Business Data Standards

For development of a generic SNEM concept it would be ideal if an existing data standard could be reused. However, an analysis of existing data standards that cover aspects of business transactions, product specifications and process management reveals that the necessary data types defined in section 3.1 cannot be reflected in one existing standard. In addition, many standards are not defined in a formal representation that is required for a SNEM ontology. In the following, a short overview on related business data standards is given.

The most important standards for business purposes are the *ANSI X.12* standard for America and the *UN/EDIFACT*-standard (United Nations/ Electronic Data Interchange for Administration, Commerce and Transport) used outside America. The *UN/EDIFACT* standard is an international EDI standard currently available in Version D.02B (*Unece 2003*). A common subset of this standard is the *EANCOM* standard, issued by the *EAN.UCC* (*EAN 2003*). It consists of a detailed implementation guideline of selected *EDIFACT* standard messages especially tailored to the needs of distributors and carriers. Besides these standards, further subsets for different industries exist (e.g. *IDS/FORTRAS, ODETTE, SES Siemens EDIFACT*). However, these standards focus on non-structured business messages that do not make use of meta concepts needed to define a coherent ontology (*Haugen et al. 2000*) and they cannot reflect all necessary data types of a SNEM solution.

Currently, the *ebXML* standard for facilitation of electronic business over the internet is developing into a standard that can incorporate ontological definitions of transactions and business processes (*ebXML 2003*). The *Business Process Specification Schema (BPSS)* is a vital part of the *ebXML* standard (*ebXML 2001*). It integrates ontological concepts from the *REA* (Resource-Event-Agent) Ontology (*Geerts et al. 2000*) that was developed to describe transactions between agents[6] in accounting business. *BPSS* focuses on description of process activities and related documents such as contracts or orders. Other data types needed for the SNEM domain are not available.

An extended overview on existing content standards is given by Dörr (*Dörr et al. 2001*). Concluding, no standard currently exists that covers all required data types for a

---

[6] In this context the term "agent" denotes any type of actor such as a human being, a company or a machine/software as long as it is involved in a transaction.

SNEM solution. Therefore, the SNEM ontology presented in section 3.2.3 serves as a generic reference model that is used to assess future developments in the domain of business standards regarding standardization of SNEM systems.

### 3.2.2.2    Formal Ontologies

Besides the mentioned business data standards, a variety of formally defined ontologies exist that cover different areas of the supply network domain. An overview on relevant work which is based on Fox (*Fox et al. 1997*) with extensions on newer ontologies[7] is presented in fig. 3-19.

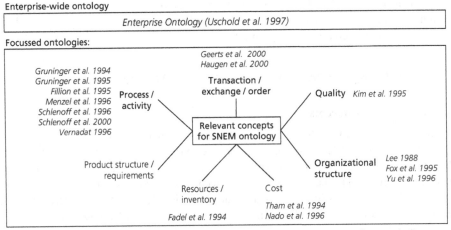

Fig. 3-19. Existing ontologies (adapted from *Fox et al. 1997* and extended)

A broad business context is addressed in the TOVE-project and a large variety of modular ontologies for specific aspects of businesses is developed (*Fox et al. 1997*). Besides general aspects on organizational structures and processes, specific ontologies for quality and cost aspects have been designed (e.g. *Borgo et al. 1996, Grüninger et al. 1995, Kim et al. 1995, Nado et al. 1996*). However, the aspect of *transaction* and *order* has not been addressed directly. The REA ontology addresses these concepts from the point-of-view of the accounting domain. It is based on the REA accounting model proposed by McCarthy (*McCarthy 1982*) and later integrated in the REA ontology (*Geerts et al. 2000*). It also enables to characterize inter-organizational relationships between supply network partners (*Haugen et al. 2000*).Other ontologies focus on detailed definition of processes, e.g. the process specification language (PSL) which was developed in cooperation with the NIST[8]

---

[7.] Development of semantic descriptions currently focuses on design of XML-schemata (not depicted in fig. 3-19) for use in internet-based business applications (see e.g. ebXML initiative (*ebXML 2003*)). However, designing an ontology with formalization in an ontology definition language (see section 3.2.3.3) always permits to automatically derive XML-based schemata but not vice versa. Consequently, the focus is on formally defined ontologies.

[8.] National Institute of Standards and Technology (USA), http://www.nist.gov

(*Schlenoff et al. 1996, Schlenoff et al. 2000*). Another relevant aspect is the specification of physical goods' characteristics addressed in the Physical Markup Language (PML) (*Brock et al. 2001*) defined by the AutoID-Initiative (now EPCglobal[9]).

For development of the SNEM ontology, an enterprise-wide ontology is chosen, which covers a broad set of concepts needed for SNEM solutions with an adequate depth of conceptual detail - the *Enterprise Ontology* (*Uschold et al. 1998a*). Since integration of different ontologies in itself is a complex task (e.g. *Uschold et al. 1998b*), it is preferable to minimize the number of different ontologies reused for ontology design. In addition, ontologies are defined in different ontology description languages which complicates the integration task. Therefore, basic concept and relation definitions are reused and reimplemented in the SNEM ontology while additions from the SNEM data model (see section 3.1) are made where necessary. For these additions, existing concepts from other ontologies are considered where appropriate.

### 3.2.3    Ontology for Supply Network Event Management

#### 3.2.3.1    Main Concepts

The main concepts of the SNEM ontology are depicted in a semantic network in fig. 3-20. The concepts of *Actor, Time* and *Activity* are reused from the *Enterprise Ontology (EO)* and the concept *Milestone* is derived from EO-concepts associated with the *Activity* concept (see fig. 3-21). The central SNEM concept *Order* triggers *Activities*, encounters *DisruptiveEvents* and has further attributes such as basic data or status data derived from section 3.1.1. Further details of the ontology are also described by *Zimmermann et al. 2005.*

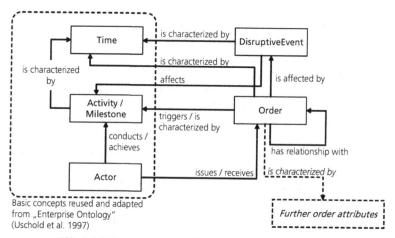

Fig. 3-20. Semantic network of main SNEM concepts

---

[9] http://www.epcglobalinc.org

#### 3.2.3.2     Concepts and Relationships

The SNEM ontology has to adequately represent order relationships in a supply network, which is represented in fig. 3-20 as the recursive relation of the concept *Order*. To model these relationships the data design presented in fig. 3-5 in section 3.1.1.2 is adapted as depicted in fig. 3-21.

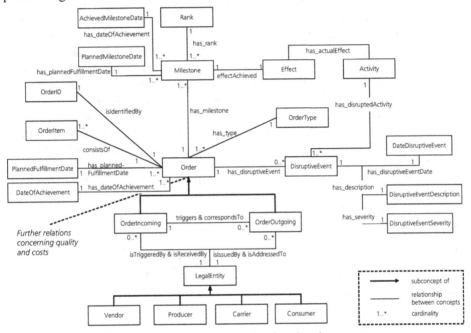

Fig. 3-21. Order concept and main related concepts

An *OrderIncoming* is an *Order* received by a *LegalEntity* (which is actually a subtype of an *Actor*). To fulfill this *Order* it might be necessary to place suborders (*OrderOutgoing*) with suppliers (e.g. a *Producer*) or a *Carrier* for distribution which is denoted by the relation *triggers* (attribute of *OrderIncoming*) and the corresponding attribute *correspondsTo* of an *OrderOutgoing*. Decoupled order relationships as defined in section 3.1.1 are represented with the help of the SNEM ontology by defining an *OrderOutgoing* that *isAddressedTo* the instance of *LegalEntity* which represents the own company (same as "self" in section 3.1.1.2).

The concept of a *Milestone* is closely associated with *Activities*, since the *Effect* (that is the post condition or output) of an *Activity* in combination with the date of achievement of the *Effect* (*MilestoneDate*) denotes a *Milestone*. Since *Milestones* respectively *Activities* are achieved/conducted to fulfill an *Order*, the concept *Rank* is introduced which helps to define the sequence of *Milestones*. For every *Milestone* a planned date of fulfillment and actual date of achievement is defined to allow calculation of deviations (see section 3.1.1.3). Using the *Rank* concept the planned sequence of *Milestones* can be compared to successively achieved *Milestones*.

The third important concept related to *Orders* are *DisruptiveEvents* that cause the SNEM problem. They are characterized by their date of occurrence (*DateDisruptiveEvent*) and by a severity measure that is defined in *DisruptiveEventSeverity* (see section 3.1.3.1). For a qualitative assessment of a *DisruptiveEvent,* a description of an event is needed which supports the decision making process by offering insight into details of the event. Different disruptive event types as identified in section 3.1.3.2 are represented as subconcepts of *DisruptiveEvent* (not depicted in fig. 3-21). Thereby, a SNEM system automatically distinguishes event types and acts upon this information.

To reflect data types other than *Milestones* and *DisruptiveEvents* for measuring the current status of an *Order* various subconcepts of *Measurement* are defined that are grouped into physical, ordinal and monetary types of measurement (see fig. 3-22). These are further detailed, e.g. *Quantity* has subconcepts regarding an *OrderedQuantity, ActualQuantity* and possibly also *PartQuantities* that can occur, if a delivery is only fulfilled partly at a given time. All measurement concepts are related to other concepts of the SNEM ontology. For illustration, subconcepts of *Quantity* and *Dimension* are depicted with their relationships to the concept *OrderItem* that itself is related to *Order* as is shown in fig. 3-21. Monetary concepts are related to *Order* or *OrderType* (e.g. *TransportationCost* has a relationship with the *OrderType TransportationOrder* - not depicted in fig. 3-22). Ordinal measures are related to different concepts, e.g. *Rank* is used in relation with the *Milestone* concept whereas *DisruptiveEventSeverity* has a relation with *DisruptiveEvent* (fig. 3-21).

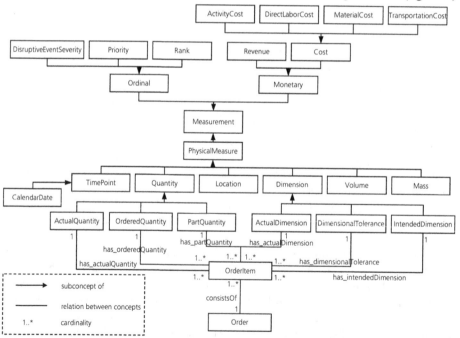

Fig. 3-22. Basic measurements of the SNEM ontology

### 3.2.3.3    Implementation

Different ontology description languages exist for formalization of an ontology. The language *OIL (Ontology Inference Layer)* (*Horrocks et al. 2002*) is used to formally define the SNEM ontology. It is integrated in the new *Ontology Web Language (OWL)* standard format for ontologies (*W3C 2005*) *OIL* combines three important aspects provided by different communities: it inherits the formal semantics and reasoning support from Decision Logics, incorporates essential modeling primitives of frame-based systems, and uses existing Web standards by providing XML and RDF based syntax (*Fensel 2001*). An ontology formalized with *OIL* conforms to the requirement for extendable data structures and opens up a wide variety of technical possibilities for automated manipulation of SNEM data.

For the design of the SNEM ontology, the ontology editor *OilEd* has been used[10]. It provides an easy-to-use connection to the *FaCT* reasoner. The *FaCT* reasoner is a tool that allows to check consistency of all class definitions in an ontology and discovers sub-class/ super-class relationships that are implied by definitions in the ontology but not explicitly stated (*Horrocks et al. 2002*). In addition, other reasoners can be connected to *OilEd* using a special interface (DIG) or by exporting an ontology into a format usable for reasoner software. *OilEd* supports various formats for exporting ontologies such as Simple RDFS, DAML+OIL (Version 2001-03), SHIQ, HTML and OWL. This flexibility allows using the same ontology in different applications with relatively small customizing efforts. The standard format of *OilEd* is an XML-file in the DAML+OIL format.

In fig. 3-23 the concept *TransportationOrder* is defined. For human readers, a documentation allows to describe the concept which is important when e.g. a new supply network partner wants to use the SNEM ontology and has to understand the definitions in order to map the concepts to its own data types. In the next field *TransportationOrder* is defined as a subconcept of *OrderType*[11]. Relations are defined in the field "Restrictions". The *TransportationOrder* has only *Milestones* of the subtype *TransportationMilestones* and a *Route* is related to this order. In addition, specific *TransportationCosts* are associated with such an order (both, actually achieved and planned costs).

Since the SNEM ontology comprises more than 150 concepts and numerous relationships between these concepts, only selected concepts can be depicted (see class hierarchy in fig. 3-24). Other concepts such as the *PlanningConstraints* cover concepts of *Effects* that result from *Activities* which in turn are needed to define the *Milestones* (see also section 3.2.3.2). *MiscSpecDetails* gathers concepts such as *City* or *Street* that cannot be directly subsumed under other concepts but that are needed in the ontology (also e.g. description fields as attributes of concepts).

---

[10.]http://oiled.man.ac.uk/

[11.]In the ontology editor concepts are referred to as classes and thus subconcepts as subclasses.

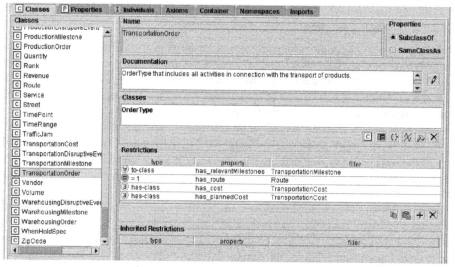

Fig. 3-23. Definition of a concept in OilEd

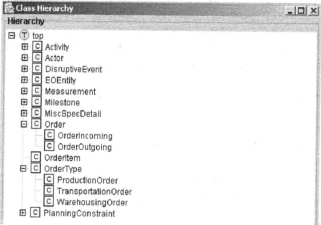

Fig. 3-24. Main concepts of the SNEM ontology

## 3.3  Data Sources

The data model developed in section 3.1 is formalized in the SNEM ontology in section 3.2 and made available for automated usage in IT systems. However, no description of potential data sources has yet been given. To provide SNEM data in the format of the ontology, various data sources are available in supply networks which are analyzed in the following.

## 3.3.1    Data Bases

### 3.3.1.1    Data Types

A SNEM system has to gather data from data bases that are used by supply network partners. The main data source in companies today are enterprise resource planning (ERP)
systems and their data bases. An ERP system is the source of information which manages
data of main business processes such as order fulfillment and accounting. Many applications use this integrated data pool for planning and execution tasks, e.g. production planning or warehouse management. In addition, specific data bases exist in every company
that are linked e.g. to specialized production execution systems which control automated
resources (e.g. CNC production machines) (e.g. *Alvarenga et al. 2003, p. 32*). In many
cases, these systems report important data to centralized ERP-systems or related applications. Consequently, any SNEM system has to be able to access data bases of ERP systems.

A major vendor of ERP systems is *SAP* with its *SAP R/3* ERP system[12] for many aspects of business administration. It is used as an example to illustrate data types typically
available from ERP systems. Data types defined in the SNEM ontology can be related to
data concepts of SAP systems, although in many cases ERP data structures are customized to a specific company and require customized interfaces to a SNEM system. Besides
tables in its data bases SAP provides an object-oriented data interface for external applications that need to access an SAP system. Main data types are encapsulated in so called
*Business Objects (BO)* (*SAP 2001*). Thus, a SNEM system does not need to directly access highly sensitive data bases nor does it need knowledge on how to access and retrieve
information from these data bases. In fig. 3-25 an example of a *BO* is shown - the *Transportation BO* and its parameters that are defined within the method *HeaderData*. A selection of concepts defined in the ontology is depicted with their mapping to the parameters
of the *BO Transportation*. For instance, it is derived from this *BO* whether the milestone
*OrderPickedUpSender* has been achieved or not, but more detailed information on the
date of achievement has to be gathered from other data sources (e.g. other *BOs*), if requested by a SNEM system.

SNEM data types are distributed over many different *Business Objects* and an interface
to a *SAP* ERP system has to be able to automatically select data from different *Business
Objects* or in the case of direct access to the data base from its tables. In table 3-4, a selection of *Business Objects* is presented that offer information for various SNEM data
types. *SalesOrder* and *PurchaseOrder* represent the central ontology concepts of *OrderIncoming* (order received from a customer = *SalesOrder*) and *OrderOutgoing*. The latter
represents suborders (direct or decoupled types) placed with suppliers. The *Shipment BO*
refers to transportation processes and offers information on orders of the *OrderType
TransportationOrder* (see SNEM ontology in section 3.2.3). Milestone information regarding production processes is derived from a *BO* called *ProdOrdConfirmation* which
stores data on various achieved milestones relevant to production. Quality measurements

---

[12.]http://www.sap.com

that are an essential data input for a SNEM solution are accessed using the *QualityNotification BO* that stores information about quality defects and associated orders.

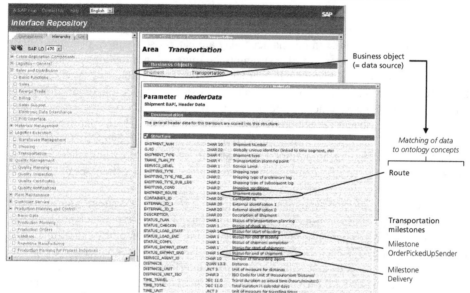

Fig. 3-25. SAP Business Object "Transportation" (*SAP 2005a*)

| Business object | Description |
|---|---|
| SalesOrder | The business object SalesOrder is a contractual arrangement between a sales organization and a sold-to party concerning goods to be delivered or services to be rendered. A SalesOrder contains information about prices, quantities and dates.<br>A SalesOrder consists of several items that contain the quantity of the material or service specified for the order. This total quantity can be divided into different partial quantities with the corresponding delivery dates in the schedule lines. |
| PurchaseOrder | The business object PurchaseOrder is a request or instruction from a purchasing organization to a vendor (external supplier) or a plant to deliver a certain quantity of material or to perform certain services at a certain point in time. |
| Shipment | The business object Shipment is a combination of goods created at a transportation planning point that are transported together from the points of departure to the corresponding destinations. It is the basis for planning, carrying out and monitoring actual physical transportation of goods. |

Table 3-4. Selection of Business Objects (SAP) for SNEM data (*SAP 2005a*)

| Business object | Description |
|---|---|
| ProdOrdConfir-mation *(Production Order Confirma-tion)* | The architecture area ProdOrdConfirmation contains the confirmed activities for the operations, the operation elements and the production tools of a manufacturing order. Furthermore, information on the degree of completion and the expected completion date can be confirmed. |
| QualityNotifica-tion | The business object QualityNotification describes a business object's nonconformance with a quality requirement and contains a request to take appropriate action.<br>A QualityNotification can contain several items. An item describes a single problem. The items in a quality notification can specify the causes for the nonconformance with the quality requirement. |

Table 3-4. Selection of Business Objects (SAP) for SNEM data (*SAP 2005a*)

*BOs* are related to different *Business Components* that represent different modules or solutions of the ERP system. A SNEM system requires data from different *Business Components* e.g. from the *Advanced Planner and Optimizer (APO)* and the *Logistics (LO)* component. Every company has an individual configuration, uses different components and implements various selections of functions (e.g. a transportation company will not implement the production planning module PP). In consequence, each company has to define a custom interface for a SNEM solution to its own ERP system or data bases. The interface enables to access the data source, receive data in a format derived from the SNEM ontology and hide custom features of the data source from the SNEM solution.

### 3.3.1.2    Data Access

A general mechanism to retrieve data from a data base is using queries that are defined in a query language common to a specific data base. Most data bases are accessed with the *Structured Query Language (SQL)*. Each such query consists of a *Select...From...Where...* statement[13].

However, access to large data bases is often more complex than just a few SQL statements and more comfortable methods are provided by vendors to access their systems. Again, SAP's technology is used as an example. Technical access to *Business Objects* (see section 3.3.1.1) is realized by using so called *Business Application Programming Interfaces* (BAPI) that is invoked by external IT systems through *Remote Function Calls* (RFC). A RFC is SAP's equivalent to the concept of a *Remote Procedure Call* (RPC) (*Schissler et al. 2001, pp.8*). Since SAP provides a variety of methods to access its *Business Objects* other mechanisms based on Internet protocols (*HTTP*), CORBA or COM/DCOM are also available (*SAP 2001, p.11*).

---

[13.]SELECT is followed by the data types to be retrieved, FROM determines the table where the data is stored and WHERE provides a condition, e.g. the order identifier for which data is to be selected.

For IT systems that are used in heterogeneous environments a *JAVA*-based implementation is one well suited option (see also section 6.1.1.2). SAP provides the *Java Connector Architecture* (JCO) to enable direct integration of *JAVA* applications with its ERP system (see fig. 3-26). A *JAVA* application is able to access *Business Objects* by using a transparent interface to the SAP system. The interface implements *Remote Function Calls* (RFCs) and alternatively standardized internet protocols to retrieve data needed by the SNEM system via the BAPIs of the *Business Objects (Fewster 2001)*[14].

SAP is developing its interface architecture into a web-enabled environment that allows to use standardized web technologies for accessing its ERP system. The developments are integrated in the *Enterprise Services Architecture* (ESA) strategy with the SAP *NetWeaver* platform that is supported by the *Exchange Infrastructure* (SAP XI) and a *Web Application Server* (SAP Web AS) (*SAP 2005b*). In the future, access of a SNEM system to ERP systems may thus be realized via standardized web interfaces (see below).

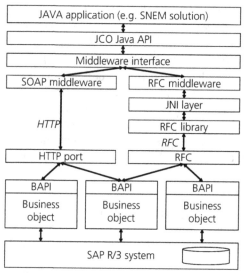

Fig. 3-26. SAP Java Connector Architecture (JCO) (*Fewster 2001*)

## 3.3.2   Internet Sources and Web Services

SNEM information is also gathered from sources that are accessed on the basis of Internet technologies. Three main sources are considered: web pages, web services and to support processes with low-level technologies - email-based data queries.

---

[14.]The Java Connector Application Programming Interface (JCO API) uses a middleware interface that provides two alternative mechanisms: On the one hand, a direct method invocation via a SOAP (Simple Object Access Protocol) message is available which uses HTTP transfer to the BAPI. On the other hand, a layered RFC interface is provided that is composed of a RFC middleware, a JAVA Native Interface (JNI) layer and a RFC library which finally invokes a RFC.

### 3.3.2.1    Web Pages

Information on fulfillment of orders is often made available via web pages for internal and in some cases for external users. If available data is up-to-date and e.g. aggregates various data sources a web page is a viable source of information for a SNEM system. Common examples are tracking websites of carriers, especially those of parcel services such as FedEx, UPS, DHL and others (see section 2.4.1). They offer information on the status of single transportation orders within their own transportation network by using a web front-end. The web front-end can be accessed by customers but it is also used by internal personnel. Other business applications also provide web front-ends (e.g. warehouse management tools) and present data to users which is sometimes integrated in enterprise or process portals.

Technically, a web page is in most cases generated automatically by a web server which selects appropriate data from a data base and then displays the results using the Hypertext Markup Language (HTML). Automatic query of a web page returns a document in HTML code that comprises the SNEM data content and additional information on the layout of the document for display in a browser (see fig. 3-27).

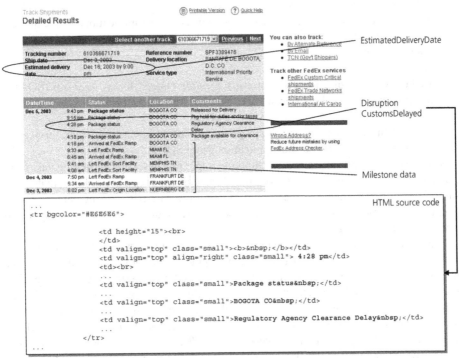

Fig. 3-27. SNEM data source - tracking web page (FedEx example)

Since HTML does not use tags which structure the content of a document a SNEM system has to have advance knowledge about the exact structure of the document to be received. With the help of this knowledge, data is retrieved from a document. This results in a large customizing effort for each web page used as a data source which is reduced significantly, if XML-based[15] syntax with a corresponding Document-Type-Definition (DTD) is used to structure a document. However, in both cases an automatic matching of retrieved information to the SNEM ontology is achieved (see fig. 3-27) and SNEM data is automatically made available to a SNEM solution.

### 3.3.2.2    Web Services

In contrast to web pages that are predominantly developed for interaction with human actors web services are applications that are especially designed to interact directly with other applications. A web service is a software application that delivers a specified service by means of the Internet. Four main features characterize a web service (e.g. *Oracle 2001*):

- *Exposure and self description*
  Functions and attributes of a web service are defined and described in a standard format which enables access to the service for other applications. The *Web Service Definition Language* (WSDL) is used for service description.
- *Publication and location on the web*
  A web service is published in an electronic registry. Other applications locate the service automatically using the *Universal Description Discovery and Integration* (UDDI) standard.
- *Invocation*
  Based on a standardized Internet protocol (*Simple Object Access Protocol* (SOAP)) other applications invoke a web service with their required attributes.
- *Response*
  Results of the web service which are generated due to invocation of the service are communicated to the requesting application using SOAP.

Most web services currently available support simple processes e.g. retrieving data from a data base (e.g. stock quotes, prices) or limited calculations such as currency conversions. Similar web services enable to access SNEM data from carrier's tracking data bases. An example of a response generated by a web service available from FedEx for registered customers is given in fig. 3-28.

Third-party service vendors offer simple access to tracking services of various logistics service providers such as UPS or USPS. They require registration and charge money for their web services (e.g *ServiceObjects 2005*). Compared to accessing traditional websites (see section 3.3.2.1) all data retrieved is XML-structured (see fig. 3-27).

Increasing interest in web services is backed by fast development of web service capabilities provided by data base vendors such as IBM (*WebSphere* platform (*IBM 2005*)) and ORACLE (*Oracle10g Application Server* (*Oracle 2005*)) and ERP vendors such as SAP (*NetWeaver* Suite (*SAP 2005b*)). Concluding, web services will gain importance in the near future as data sources for SNEM solutions.

---

[15.]Extensible Markup Language

```
<?xml version="1.0" encoding="UTF-8" ?>
<TrackShipmentResponse xmlns:xsi="http://www.w3.org/2001/XMLSchemainstance"
xsi:noNamespaceSchemaLocation="TrackShipment.xsd">
        <MoreDataFlag>false</MoreDataFlag>
        <CustomerTransactionIdentifier>20a_#38131</CustomerTransactionIdentifier>
        <TrackProfile>
                        <TrackingNumber>
                        <Number>123456789012</Number>
        </TrackingNumber>
        <Carrier>Express</Carrier>
        ...
        <ShipDate>2003-05-12</ShipDate>
        <DestinationCountryCode>US</DestinationCountryCode>
        <DestinationCity>PANAMA CITY BEACH</DestinationCity>         — Location
        <DestinationState>FL</DestinationState>
        <DestinationPostalCode>32413</DestinationPostalCode>
        <DeliveredDate>2003-05-13</DeliveredDate>
        <DeliveredTime>09:47</DeliveredTime>                         — ActualFulfillmentDate
        ...
        <Weight>
                Amount>1.0</Amount>
                <Units>LBS</Units>                                   — Weight
        </Weight>
        ...
    </TrackProfile>
</TrackShipmentResponse>
```

Fig. 3-28. XML response to query of tracking system (*FedEx 2005*)

### 3.3.2.3    Email-based Data Queries

SNEM data on the current status of an order can also be made available to a SNEM solution by using standardized email forms. The email form is completed by an actor currently responsible for handling an order, e.g. a worker in a warehouse who sends an email form specifying completed activities and time of their fulfillment regarding a specific order. Although this is not a very efficient method of gathering new status data, it is a flexible and robust approach that can be used in many circumstances. For instance, a small carrier might want to provide up-to-date SNEM information to its customers' SNEM solutions. In such a scenario an email-based data provision is a low-cost alternative and a fall-back solution in case other types of data access are not realizable within reasonable cost limits or due to technical problems. An email-based data gathering mechanism may also be used by a SNEM solution to actively gather data from supply network partners that do not regularly participate in a given supply network.

| Request for SNEM data: OrderID = 4292 | Milestone | Date of Achievement | Comments |
|---|---|---|---|
| Request for SNEM data: OrderID = 4292 | ProductionOrder; Manufacturing; ...; | 2004-12-08 15:00; 2003-12-10 13:15; ...; | ; ; ; |

Fig. 3-29. Email form

Email forms are automatically readable as long as their structure is defined and adhered to by all partners. In fig. 3-29 each field of the form is separated by a semicolon which allows to automatically parse fields and their content. In a next processing step, a SNEM system is able to retrieve data from the email form, match it to data types of the SNEM ontology and use it in subsequent SNEM functions[16].

### 3.3.3 Radio Frequency Identification Technologies

#### 3.3.3.1 Alignment of Physical and Virtual Environment

Data bases, web services and other digital sources of information provide a digital representation of the physical situation of an order during fulfillment processes. However, compliance of representation with the actual physical situation cannot be verified in itself by querying a data base since this verification is considered to be a meta-verification of data. The problem is highlighted by deviations that are regularly identified during physical inventory checks: in many cases actual amount of goods in a warehouse deviates from inventory data stored in warehouse management systems. Regarding the SNEM domain, further problems occur, if e.g. the location of a transportation order is "on a truck" according to a transportation planning program but in reality it has not been loaded onto any truck. A SNEM system that relies on such a data base will assume that the transport is being conducted according to plan although in reality a major disruptive event has occurred.

To ensure correct representation of the physical situation in any kind of digital representation an alignment between the physical and informational environment is needed. The alignment has to be achieved on a periodical basis or, if needed, on a real-time basis that might even be triggered on-demand.

Various identification methods and technologies are available that allow to compare actual physical status (e.g. the location) of a physical entity with its digital representation:

- *Manual verification*
  A person locates a physical entity (e.g. a pallet), determines its status (e.g. production is finished) and enters corresponding data into an IT-system (e.g. an ERP system) that allows to store or communicate gathered data. Manual verification is very cost-intensive because human actors are directly involved. It is only appropriate for rare verifications.
- *Barcode Technology*
  A machine readable code that is imprinted on a label and attached to a physical entity is read with the help of a scanner-device. A direct line-of-sight is needed between scanner and label. The code uniquely identifies a physical entity and in combination with additional information (e.g. defined location of the scanner) an automatic update of a data base is realized with reliable data that is verified with the current physical situation. Barcode technology is a low-cost technology and currently state-of-the-art in automated identification.
- *Radio Frequency Identification (RFID) Technology*
  An electronic tag or label attached to a physical entity allows to identify a specific entity by using radio frequency transmission. No direct line-of-sight is needed

---

[16.]A similar function is provided if a web form is used and a link to the form is sent via email.

between the tag and the reader system and the identification cover longer distances than traditional barcode technology. RFID technology is a technology that currently develops into a widely used technology and offers huge development potential regarding the scope of data storage and autonomous data processing (e.g. *Finkenzeller 2002*).

For development of a SNEM solution manual verification and barcode technology are essential techniques but only RFID technology has additional features that will allow to realize innovative SNEM functions in the future.

### 3.3.3.2    Technical Aspects of Electronic Tags

Radio frequency identification (RFID) systems consist of three main elements: an aerial, a transceiver, and a transponder (the electronic tag). As depicted in fig. 3-30 the aerial and the transceiver are often integrated into a reader which can be a handheld or a fixed-mounted device. The reader will generally be linked to some kind of IT-system, e.g. a warehouse-management tool that is linked to an ERP system.

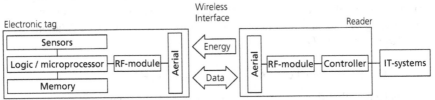

Fig. 3-30. Technical basis of a RFID system (*Pflaum 2001, p.40*)

The transponder is a tag that is mounted onto the object to be identified (e.g. a pallet or a container). A tag consists of memory, processing logic, radio frequency module for transmission and aerial. Sensors are optionally integrated into a tag. The major advantage of radio frequency identification systems is their ability to identify tags without contact between reader and tag and without necessity of a direct line-of-sight between reader and tag as opposed to traditional barcode technology. A detailed overview concerning the relevant technologies currently available is presented by Pflaum (*Pflaum 2001*) and Finkenzeller (*Finkenzeller 2002*). An overview on main attributes of electronic tags and possible values of these is given in fig. 3-31.

| Attribute | Values | | | |
|---|---|---|---|---|
| Memory technology | ROM | EEPROM | SRAM | FRAM |
| Memory capacity | 32-80 Bit | 80-256 Bit | 32-256 Byte | 2-128 kByte |
| Internal logic | State-chart | | Microprocessor | |
| Aerial (integration) | External aerial | | Aerial "on chip" | |
| Anti-collision system | Spatial isolation | Allocation of time slots | Allocation of transmission frequencies | |
| Tag design | Coin, plate | Glass cylinder | Card | Flexible foil |
| Transmission direction | Read only | | Read / write | |
| Power supply | External (passive) | | Internal (active) | |
| Transmission frequency | 120-135 KHz | 13,56 MHz | | 2,45 GHz |

Fig. 3-31. Attributes of electronic tags
(*Pflaum 2001, p.105*, updated with *Finkenzeller 2002*)

Memory sizes range from 32 bit up to 128 Kbytes (and growing) which enables many different applications from identification to storage of detailed information concerning a tagged object. Electronic tags are either passive or active: A passive tag has no internal power supply and power needed to read or write from/to memory is induced by a reader. In contrast, active tags have an internal power supply which allows more power consuming processing activities and greater transmission distances between reader and tag. Power supply and power consumption of an electronic tag are of major importance for applications in supply networks, because goods (with tags attached) are constantly relocated during fulfillment processes. External power supply cannot always be guaranteed (e.g. during transportation).

The design of a tag differs according to its intended functions. For instance, the ability to produce flexible tags from foil opens up possibilities to attach tags to many different objects, just as barcodes are fixed to a large variety of physical entities.

Transmission frequency used in combination with the form of power supply determines the range of a reader and how thick layers of material between reader and tag can be. Active tags have a greater potential range regardless of the frequency used. In general, penetration of material is larger with lower frequencies whereas higher frequencies allow faster processing of data and thus implementation of more complex calculations within the tag (*Pflaum 2001, pp. 112*).

### 3.3.3.3    Electronic Tag Types for Event Management

The various technical options result in different types of electronic tags that are used in different scenarios. Simple RFID tags that only store an identification number have passive power supply and no processing logic (see fig. 3-32).

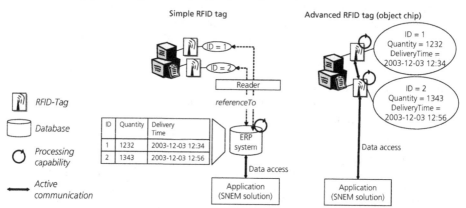

Fig. 3-32. Simple RFID tags and object chips

They represent one end of a continuum of possible technical solutions. These simple tags are cheap and at the brink of mass deployment since their prices of about 50 US-cent and decreasing towards around 15 cent (e.g. *Ward 2004*) currently reach dimensions needed for mass usage. On the other end of the continuum technical innovations from research labs point towards miniaturized chips that actively sense their environment, store large amounts of data, actively process data and proactively initiate communication with other electronic tags or IT systems. Such tags are called *sensor chips,* if they have sensory features and *object chips,* if they act independently and even goal-oriented (*Wacker 2001*). Similar to object chips, so called *Smart-Active-Labels* (*Furness 2004*) are promoted and developed by a consortium of international enterprises (*SAL-C 2005*). However, such chips only exist as prototypes on a laboratory scale yet. In between those extremes some currently available RFID tags allow to store additional information that can be encrypted, if needed. These electronic tags might store additional types of SNEM data.

For a SNEM system simple RFID tags do not change the data access because all relevant data is stored in data bases (see fig. 3-32). Only the alignment of stored data with the physical world is assured and as a result the information in the data bases is especially trustworthy. In contrast, future use of object chips will allow SNEM solutions to directly access objects (e.g. a product) and gather data from their object chips (see fig. 3-32). In addition, object chips will be able to exhibit proactive behavior and inform SNEM solutions of disruptive events they are currently encountering. A generic SNEM concept has to be open to adapt to these new possibilities as soon as they become relevant for industrial use (an outlook on some scenarios is given in section 8.2).

### 3.3.3.4    Constraints of Electronic Tags

Two main aspects currently restrict fast dissemination of simple RFID chips and a technical restriction constrains development of small long-living object chips:

-   *Cost per electronic tag*
    Costs of RFID tags in comparison to simple paper-based barcodes are still immense especially when features like high memory capacity are needed. Although, technological developments enable production of smaller RFID chips and faster production processes, prices for simple electronic tags still range at about 50 US-Cent but falling (e.g. *Ward 2004*) and more complex tags begin at 10 US-Dollar upward (*RFID Journal 2005*). This development is accelerated as large wholesalers (e.g. Wal Mart) demand RFID-tags on every product container from their main suppliers beginning in 2005 (e.g. *Shim et al. 2003*) but technological hurdles and low return-on-investment currently slow these projects down (e.g. *Roberti 2005*). This is due to significant costs of the whole system of readers, adaptation and integration of IT systems and organizational changes necessary to implement such systems

-   *Standards for electronic tags*
    Given technical access to an electronic tag the question of access to data on a tag arises. This raises questions on what kind of data in what format is to be stored and how data is managed within the electronic tag. Different standards are proposed by the *International Organization for Standardization (ISO)* in cooperation with the *International Electrotechnical Comittee (IEC)* for various kinds of electronic tags. An overview on standards is provided by Pflaum (*Pflaum 2001*) and Finkenzeller (*Finkenzeller 2002*). These standards primarily define technical details of how to access data on an electronic tag, but provide no data model. That might be derived from existing data standards such as the UCC/EAN 128 Code (*Pflaum 2001, pp.133*).

However, in section 3.2.2.1 it is shown that existing business data standards do not provide enough SNEM data types. Consequently, direct usage of the SNEM ontology is favorable, if electronic tags can store SNEM data. This is achieved, if data in the memory of the electronic chip is defined in a flexible format, e.g. in a XML-based syntax.

However, current industry focus is on very cheap and simple electronic tags that simply store a unique identification number called *Electronic Product Code (EPC)* proposed by the *EPCglobal* initiative (*EPCglobal 2004a*). The EPC uniquely identifies an object (e.g. a product) which allows to identify and locate this object by using an *Object Name Service (ONS)* that is similar to the *Domain Name Service* of the Internet (*EPCglobal 2004b*). This technology enables the simple scenario in fig. 3-32.

- *Power supply for object chips*

One of the main features of future object chips is their ability to autonomously communicate in an active way. This requires wireless broadcast over a certain distance. Energy required to transmit data theoretically grows with $r^2$ being $r$ the distance between a sender and a receiver. In reality, obstructions from material and reflections result in a growth of up to $r^4$ (*Timmermann 2002*). The available amount of energy, e.g. from miniaturized batteries, is often not enough for the required time horizon of a process' duration (e.g. a multi-step production process). Although improvements of battery capacity are realized, they only add up to an increase of about 30% to 50% increase in five years which is significantly slower than growth of capacities in processors and memory as reflected by Moore's Law (*Timmermann 2002*). This fundamental problem constrains fast development of miniaturized high power object chips as are needed for mass usage in future scenarios in supply network domains.

# Chapter 4

# Event Management Functions

In chapter 4 basic mechanisms to satisfy the functional requirements for a SNEM system (see section 2.2.2) are presented. The presentation is structured according to the basic SNEM process defined in section 2.2.2 and depicted below in fig. 4-1. The SNEM process starts with search activities which proactively gather SNEM information in supply networks, with a focus on consideration of suborders (see section 4.1). To improve efficiency of the proactive data gathering approach, a mechanism based on critical profiles is introduced in section 4.2.

| Search/ gather | Aggregate/ interpret | Distribute |

Fig. 4-1. Basic SNEM process

The process step *aggregate/interpret* focuses on the analysis of the gathered SNEM data (see section 4.3) while proactive distribution of monitoring results and thus satisfaction of the implicit demand $D_q$, as requested by the information logistics task (see section 2.1.3.3), is realized by an alert mechanism proposed in section 4.4.

## 4.1 Information Gathering in Supply Networks

The first requirement of SNEM functions defined in section 2.2.2 calls for consideration of supply network interdependencies (see section 2.2.2.1). In the focus of this requirement are suborders placed with suppliers or carriers. Taking into account the second functional requirement for primacy of local data storage (see section 2.2.2.2), it is concluded that a SNEM system has to proactively seek SNEM data on orders from its supply network partners. This is underlined by the general requirement for proactivity of SNEM systems declared in section 2.2.1.1. To fulfill these requirements, a concept for proactive monitoring of orders in multi-level supply networks is proposed in subsequent sections.

## 4.1.1   Trigger Events

### 4.1.1.1   Definitions

Monitoring of an order and thereby proactive data gathering in supply networks is initiated in a variety of situations. Four categories of situations relevant for a SNEM solution are proposed:

1. An explicit request for information about an order's status is articulated. This request can either be generated by an external actor (mostly customers) or an internal requestor inside the enterprise.
2. An alert, which informs of a disruptive event $DE$ at a suborder recipient, is received by a SNEM system. This alert information is generated and sent by an external partner (e.g. a supplier) where a $DE$ is identified.
3. Knowledge of a certain order becomes available which predicts a high probability of this order to be affected by disruptive events. This knowledge is used to trigger monitoring of the order.
4. A random selection of orders is made. These are then monitored, e.g. to facilitate statistical quality control of order fulfillment processes.

All of these situations are characterized by events that trigger monitoring of an order. Thus, a *Trigger Event TE* is defined as an event which initiates monitoring of an order by a SNEM solution of a specific company. For each of the above categories a certain type of trigger event is defined[1].

1. *Status Request*
   A *Status Request* $TE_{SR}$ describes that a customer or an internal actor requests status information on a specific order. A $TE_{SR}$ has to be answered by a SNEM solution.
2. *Alert Trigger*
   Information concerning a disruptive event $DE$, which is proactively communicated as an alert by an external supplier (system), results in an *Alert Trigger* $TE_{AT}$.
3. *Probabilistic Trigger*
   Selection of an order based on knowledge about its high probability of encountering serious disruptive events is reflected in the notion of a *Probabilistic Trigger* $TE_{PT}$.
4. *Randomized Trigger*
   A *Randomized Trigger* $TE_{RT}$ is the result of random selection of an order for being monitored by a SNEM solution.

### 4.1.1.2   Consequences of Trigger Events

Any trigger event $TE$ signals the beginning of a monitoring process, during which problems of order fulfillment (especially disruptive events and their consequences) are to be identified and communicated to affected actors. A proactive search for data is initiated, during which a company tries to proactively satisfy its own future "implicit" demand $D_q$ for SNEM information (see section 2.1.3.3). In addition, information gathered and analyzed in this process enables this company to actively inform its customers of newly iden-

---

[1] These definitions are used subsequently in chapter 4.

tified disruptive events and their consequences. Thereby, it also aims at satisfying the implicit demand $D_q$ of its customers.

The first step for a SNEM solution, after having received a trigger event $TE$, is to identify the order that is to be monitored[2] and to gather basic and control data related to this order (see sections 3.1.1.2 and 3.1.1.3) from its internal data sources (see section 3.3). Order attributes $OA_n$ that are selected at this point reflect order relationships $OR_{ji}$, order type and control data on the planned date of fulfillment of the order. Depending on the type of trigger event additional activities have to be conducted by a SNEM solution. In case a status request $TE_{SR}$ is received, the SNEM solution memorizes the need to send an answer to the requesting party as soon as (updated) monitoring data is available. An alert trigger $TE_{AT}$ sent by a supplier refers to a suborder that is affected by a disruptive event. Hence, the receiving SNEM system at the customer's site identifies its related superorder first, to determine which order is to be monitored by its SNEM system. In some cases, a specific order is already being monitored by a SNEM solution. This situation arises, e.g., if a probabilistic trigger $TE_{PT}$ has initiated surveillance and at a later point of time a customer sends a status request ($TE_{SR}$). Both triggers occur independently of each other, but the SNEM system avoids duplicated monitoring efforts for the same order.

## 4.1.2  Inter-organizational Information Gathering

### 4.1.2.1  Identification of Suborders

Interdependencies in supply networks are defined by order relationships $OR_{ji}$ (see section 2.1.3.1). A SNEM system, which has initiated the monitoring of an order upon receiving a trigger event $TE$, identifies all its suborders defined by its order relationships $OR_{ji}$ that are available from the already gathered internal data on the order (see section 4.1.1.2). Only direct order relationships are considered for inter-organizational data gathering. Relevant direct suborders are identified by selecting all $OR_{ji} = (O_j;O_i)$ with a superorder $O_j$ (the monitored order) and a suborder $O_i$ for which $O_i(LE_k;LE_{k-x})$ with ($LE_k$ = self $\wedge LE_{k-x}$ = ¬self) holds. Thus, legal entity $LE_k$ places a suborder $O_i$ directly with a supply network partner (e.g. supplier or carrier) represented as $LE_{k-x}$.

In case a suborder is directed to the legal entity "self" - that is the own company - an internal suborder is assumed which belongs to a decoupled order relationship as defined in section 3.1.1.2. These suborders are not directly considered for data gathering from external supply network partners. However, decoupled order relationships are considered based on a mechanism defined in section 4.1.2.7.

---

[2.] An order to be monitored by a SNEM system is always an *OrderIncoming* as defined in the SNEM ontology in section 3.2.3.2. Suborders (*OrderOutgoing*) are only monitored as part of monitoring an *OrderIncoming*.

#### 4.1.2.2     Strategy for Gathering Event Data

Some data on suborders of a monitored order is gathered from an internal data source of an enterprise (e.g. an ERP system (see section 3.3.1)). It indicates whether any of these suborders have already been finished and thus need not be considered any longer. All remaining suborders not yet finished are characterized by their order type and their promised or planned fulfillment date that was negotiated with the supplier or carrier.

Based on this data a SNEM system derives its data gathering strategy. It decides which suborders are currently to be monitored and whether internal processes are to be assessed (see fig. 4-2). At time $t_1$ only *suborder 3* is already finished, assuming that no delay has occurred, while sourcing *suborders 1* and *2* are yet to be finished. This information is based on the data types defined in section 3.1.1.2 to determine the sequence of suborders (*OrderType*). Consequently, at time $t_1$ a SNEM system solely queries the legal entities who fulfill *suborders 1* and *2*. In contrast, in a later update cycle conducted for the order by the SNEM system at time $t_2$, internal data sources are queried exclusively and at $t_3$ only the carrier responsible for distribution of the customer order and thus responsible for *suborder 4* is queried for SNEM data. This strategy guarantees efficient proactive inter-organizational data gathering because no supply network participant is queried as long as it is not actively participating at a given time in the fulfillment of a monitored order.

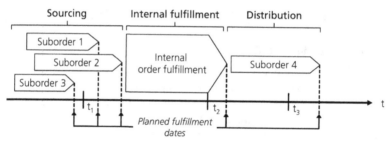

Fig. 4-2. Data gathering strategy

#### 4.1.2.3     Generating Queries

Each query, which is generated to gather information from a suborder recipient, represents a status request. Thus, for the recipient (e.g. a supplier) it is a trigger event $TE_{SR}$ as defined in section 4.1.1. With this request for information data on disruptive events and their negative consequences is sought to satisfy the "implicit" demand $D_q$. As defined in section 2.1.3.2 this demand is satisfied by a message $M_s(C_p;T_2;L_r;LE_{k-x};LE_k)$ that consists of a defined content $C_p$ and a location of the receiver $L_r$. It is communicated between two legal entities $LE_k$ and $LE_{k-x}$ engaged in an order relationship at a specific time $T_2$.

Content $C_p$ is defined in section 2.1.3.2 as $C_p(DE_h;\Delta OS_i(T_1))$ with $DE_h$ as a specific disruptive event and the consequence of the disruptive event $\Delta OS_i(T_1)$. The term $\Delta OS_i(T_1)$ is determined by the changes in order attributes $OA_n$ due to a disruptive event[3]. A SNEM system requests all order attributes $OA_n$ relevant to assess a suborder's status, and it calculates deviations itself. Consequently, $C_p$ contains SNEM data types as defined in sections 3.1 and 3.2. and covers data types related to decision data types (e.g. disruptive events) as well as status data types (e.g. milestones). In addition, control data (e.g. a milestone's planned date of fulfillment) is queried, if it is not yet available for a suborder from internal data sources. An example of the content of a status request for a suborder is depicted in fig. 4-3, with variables attached to requested data types.

```
(OrderOutgoingID = 3007;.OrderType = "Warehousing"; EstimatedDateOfFulfillment = ?;
Milestones = ?; ActualQuantity = ?; DisruptiveEvents = ?)
```

Fig. 4-3. Message content of a status request (example)

The following information is provided for the recipient of the request:
- A number that identifies the suborder for which a status request is generated (*OrderOutgoingID*).
- Basic data to further characterize the suborder. This data is provided as supporting information for the recipient of the status request, e.g. the *OrderType* (possible values: warehousing, production, transportation).
- Various variables that refer to specific data types, e.g. *ActualQuantity* of an order.
- Variables that refer to a larger number of data subtypes, e.g. *Milestones* or *DisruptiveEvents*. These variables are used by the recipient to determine which specific data types are requested depending on an order's characteristics. In fig. 4-4 the variable *Milestones* (a high-level concept of the SNEM ontology) is interpreted by the recipient by using additional information on the *OrderType*. The recipient can infer from the ontology which *WarehousingMilestones* are to be checked and information on their status is to be sent as an answer to the requesting SNEM system. Relevant data types associated with these *Milestones* are both control data types (*plannedFulfillmentDate*) and status data types (*dateOfAchievement*) as attributes of a *Milestone*.

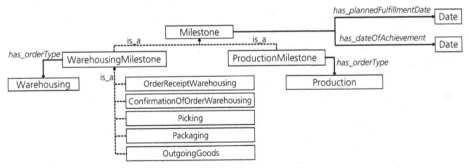

Fig. 4-4. Identification of relevant milestone types

---

[3.] $DE_h(LE_{k-x};T_1) \Rightarrow \Delta OA_n(O_i;T_1) \Rightarrow \Delta OS_i(T_1)$, see section 2.1.3.2.

#### 4.1.2.4    Generating Responses

The recipient of a query fills in data on all requested variables, as far as it is available at the time of request, and returns this information to the requestor (see fig. 4-5). In this example, the warehousing process has not yet been finished, because an out-of-stock situation has occurred and picking goods from the warehouse is not possible (=the milestone *Picking* is not yet achieved). An estimation of the currently forecasted date of achievement of the suborder is returned to the requestor. This data type incorporates consequences of the disruptive event, in that case a delay, and allows the requestor's SNEM system to calculate a deviation from the originally planned date of delivery.

```
(OrderOutgoingID = 3007; OrderType = "Warehousing"; EstimatedDateOfFulfillment =
(2004-03-20; 12:00); Milestones =

((OrderReceiptWarehousing; has_plannedFulfillmentDate(2004-03-17;13:00);
has_dateOfAchievement (2004-03-17;13.00));

(ConfirmationOfOrderWarehousing; has_plannedFulfillmentDate(2004-03-17;14:00);
has_dateOfAchievement (2004-03-17;15:20))

(Picking; has_plannedFulfillmentDate(2004-03-17;16:30); has_dateOfAchievement
(NULL))

(Packaging; has_plannedFulfillmentDate(2004-03-18;10:00); has_dateOfAchievement
(NULL))

(OutgoingGoods; has_plannedFulfillmentDate(2004-03-18;12:00); has_dateOfAchievement
(NULL)));

ActualQuantity = NULL; DisruptiveEvents = (has_description(OutOfStock);
has_disruptiveEventDate(2004-03-17;15:50); has_severity (3))
```

Fig. 4-5. Content of a response (example)

Although the supplier who receives a status request may answer it without the use of a SNEM solution, an ideal situation is characterized by a supply network where every participant has its own SNEM system and thus answers requests automatically[4]. Assuming that these systems implement the same mechanisms to gather data on suborders and to generate responses for status requests, a cascading "query tree" spreads in a supply network, determined by order relationships $OR_{ji}$ (see fig. 4-6).

At a given point in time, only part of a network defined by order relationships $OR_{ji}$ is activated by status requests: Not all fulfillment processes in a supply network are conducted at the same time and the strategy for data gathering considers these differences (see section 4.1.2.2) .

In the example of fig. 4-6 *Company 1* receives from *Company 2* SNEM data. This response considers data gathered by *Company 2* from its carrier (*Company 3*) on fulfillment of suborder $O_2$. Yet, not all information gathered from suborders is communicated in a response. Only important disruptive events and their effects on certain order attributes $OA_n$ is transmitted: Decisions on the importance of newly gathered data are made on the enterprise level, thereby adhering to the autonomy of supply network partners (see section

---

[4.] For generation of responses see also section 4.4 on generation of alerts, because responses to status requests are part of the distribution activities of a suborder recipient and thus included in its alert mechanism.

2.1.2.4). It is the task of each enterprise's SNEM system to analyze and interpret information available from its own data sources and its queries to suppliers (see section 4.3 for details). As a result, a distributed network-wide monitoring is realized.

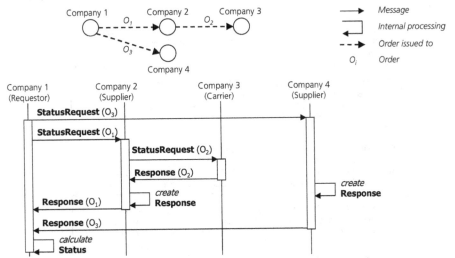

Fig. 4-6. Cascading status requests in a supply network

Every supply network partner is an expert on its own level of the supply network and is able to use its knowledge for analysis and interpretation of gathered data. Only results of this process are communicated to the next supply network level, in response to a status request or proactively as an alert in case a disruptive event with serious consequences has been identified (see section 4.4 for details). An informational overflow caused by detailed information on every related suborder in a supply network is avoided, and the primacy of local data storage as one of the requirements defined in section 2.2.2.2 is assured.

### 4.1.2.5    Handling Incomplete Information

Eventually, status requests $TE_{SR}$ will in some cases reveal only a fraction of the information requested by a SNEM system. Two mechanisms are combined in a SNEM solution to face the problem of incomplete information:
1. An additional dialog is initiated with the suborder recipient to gather further details.
2. The status of the superorder is analyzed, based on available yet incomplete information on suborders (see section 4.3).

In fig. 4-7 a dialog with a supplier is depicted in which only part of the requested data is delivered within the first response. Neither any value regarding milestones nor the actual quantity is integrated in the response. The requestor has the alternative to send the same request again or to change the content of the request. In fig. 4-7 the variable *Milestone* has been replaced with a more detailed request for specific milestone types of the warehousing process. The supplier itself no longer needs to infer which milestone types are requested, and the response is identical to fig. 4-5. This strategy of generating requests with greater detail, if data is missing, is required in heterogeneous environments encountered in supply networks, because it cannot be assumed that (automated) inference mechanisms are always available on the recipient's side.

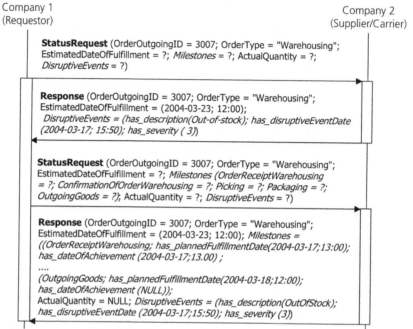

Fig. 4-7. Dialog for gathering SNEM data

Since it is not guaranteed, whether the recipient will deliver all requested data even if it is queried repeatedly, a SNEM system distinguishes between required and optional information. Required data is definitely needed to calculate at least a basic order status. Optional data allows to refine basic calculations of an order status according to section 3.1.2. Based on the top-level SNEM questions *Q1* and *Q2* defined in section 3.1.2, all data types for the first refinement level are defined as *required data types* (see fig. 4-8). As *Q3* refers to different quality measures which are often too enterprise-specific (e.g. production tolerance measures or number of picking failures), these data types are excluded from the set of *required data types*. This definition assures that every SNEM system can at least answer questions on a basic refinement level, if a minimum data set is available. All other data types, including details on disruptive events, are defined as *optional data types* and are highlighted in *italics* in the example of fig. 4-7.

| Time (Q1) | Fulfillment dates: planned; estimated; achieved |
|---|---|
| Quantity (Q2) | Delivery quantity: ordered; delivered |

Fig. 4-8. Required data types

#### 4.1.2.6    Channel Selection

Besides content $C_p$, a message $M_s$ is characterized by the location $L_r$ of its recipient. The location of a recipient determines the selection of an appropriate communication channel. Assuming that a SNEM solution is available at the supplier's site, communication is based on Internet technologies. Details of communication are determined by technical communication protocols and their realization (see chapters 5 and 6). A generalized structure of messages that is used in various technical environments adheres to the following model:

```
Performative: Request
Receiver: Company 2
Sender: Company 1
Message-ID: 40404
Content: (OrderOutgoingID = 3007; ...; DisruptiveEvents = ?)
```
Fig. 4-9. Abstract model of a message

Such a message consists of an envelope that specifies the receiver's address and the sender's reply address. The performative defines what type of message is sent (e.g. a request or a response) and what is intended with this message[5]. The *Message-ID* is required to manage various requests and responses in parallel.

Content of any message is defined independently of its message envelope, while the envelope is determined by technical communication protocols. The structure of content is derived from the SNEM ontology and enables automatic processing of the message content (see section 3.2.1).

In situations where no IT-based counterpart system is available, a status request $TE_{SR}$ is sent to a human actor. An email form or a link to a similar web form are sent by email to the recipient of the request (see section 3.3.2). To avoid misinterpretations, the use of variables for high-level concepts (especially *Milestones*) is restricted, and detailed data types are requested directly. However, it is evident that such a mechanism is only to be used as a backup-solution, because response times are prolonged and timeliness of gathered SNEM data is reduced significantly[6].

#### 4.1.2.7    Decoupled Order Relationships

Data gathering for internal suborders which are part of a decoupled order relationship $OR_{ji}$ is a special function within the SNEM concept. Assuming that internal suborders are stored according to the data scheme defined in section 3.1.1.2, any internal suborder is directed to the recipient "self".

To actively gather data on the status of an internal suborder, a status request $TE_{SR}$ is generated which is then communicated to an specific internal SNEM system. This specific SNEM system is dedicated to monitor internal suborders which are part of decoupled or-

---

[5.] Performatives are a basic concept relevant to the theory of speech acts (*Austin 1962, Searle 1969*).

[6.] Other communication channels based on manual data gathering strategies (e.g. fax forms) are even less efficient and are thus not further considered in the SNEM concept.

der relationships (see fig. 4-10). Such a system is identified by an index $D$ (=*Decoupled*) to distinguish it from the main SNEM system of an enterprise. In fig. 4-10 this $SNEM_D$ system uses the selection mechanism defined in section 3.1.1.2 to identify a relevant external suborder $O_x$. This suborder is placed with an external supply network partner (*Company 3*) to fulfill several internal suborders including $O_2$. The $SNEM_D$ system generates a status request $TE_{SR}$ to gather data on the external order $O_x$ and communicates this request to the external supply network partner (*Company 3*). Based on the response to this request the $SNEM_D$ system generates a response for the initial $TE_{SR}$ concerning the internal suborder $O_2$ of the SNEM system. In essence, the same data gathering mechanism is used to monitor direct external suborders and those internal suborders which are part of decoupled order relationships. The only step necessary for this is the introduction of an additional $SNEM_D$ layer that is able to associate internal suborders with decoupled external suborders.

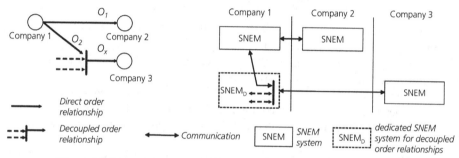

Fig. 4-10. Requesting status data for decoupled order relationships

A further extension is needed, if stocks of material or parts are held inside a company that have to be considered additionally by a $SNEM_D$ system. The $SNEM_D$ system accesses an internal data base or warehouse management system to gather data on current and projected stock levels. Gathered data concerning external orders for replenishment of stocks (e.g. $O_x$ in fig. 4-10) is then analyzed in combination with data on stock levels to create a response for the SNEM system that monitors order $O_2$.

## 4.2 Proactive and Flexible Monitoring

The functional requirement *Proactive Monitoring of Orders* as defined in section 2.2.2.3 has the objective to restrict monitoring activities to those orders that have a high likelihood of encountering disruptive events *DE* during their fulfillment. It is meant to reduce proactive monitoring efforts of a SNEM system to these orders and thus to minimize operational costs of a SNEM system. A concept which is based on the notion of *critical profiles* is presented in subsequent section. It also provides efficient adaptation mechanisms for focusing monitoring efforts thus fulfilling the requirement *Flexible Monitoring in Changing Environments* (see section 2.2.2.4).

## 4.2.1   Critical Profiles

### 4.2.1.1      Characterization

It is assumed that occurrence of *DEs* is not evenly distributed over all orders, but that certain structures of cause and effect in supply networks determine the majority of *DEs*. Causes of *DEs* are determined by characteristics of objects (e.g. resources or products), processes, organizational structures and environmental conditions. Some examples are:

- worn machines or neglected maintenance in production/transportation,
- high mechanical load, thermal stress of goods or exposure to hazardous material,
- time-critical and complex processes involving many actors and resources,
- vacation times resulting in increased traffic jams on weekends,
- unpredictable regulatory authorities (e.g. customs) at certain destinations.

An order is exposed to these objects (e.g. certain resources), processes (e.g. a picking process) and environments (e.g. the laws of a destination country) which together represent the "location" of the causes of disruptive events. This relationship between orders and the sources of *DEs* can be characterized by certain values of order attributes $OA_n$. Examples are:

- The order attribute value *Destination = Mexico* is used to hint to frequent delays during customs processes in Mexico.
- Quality deficits in specific procured materials (ID = 3322) caused by worn machines of a supplier (ID = 2341) are taken into account by using the order attribute values *Recipient-ID=2341* in combination with *Material-ID=3322* as a distinguishing feature to describe potentially critical orders.

Order attributes that characterize an order and which are used to describe sources of *DEs*, are depicted in fig. 4-11 but are not limited to these. They are already defined as data types of the SNEM data category "basic data" (see section 3.1.1.2) and do not change during order fulfillment.

| Generic order attributes for profiles | | | | |
|---|---|---|---|---|
| Order | Customer | Supplier | Product | Physical |
| • Order type<br>• Order value | • Customer-ID<br>• Priority<br>• Address | • Recipient-ID<br>• Address | • Product-/service-type<br>• Material-/product-ID | • Volume<br>• Weight |

| Process specific order attributes for profiles | | |
|---|---|---|
| Production | Transportation | Warehousing |
| • Production type<br>• Production site | • Route          • Destination<br>• Dispatch type   • Origin | • Storage location |

Fig. 4-11. Order attributes for description of *DE* sources

The following definition is used to refer to a data set that characterizes potentially critical orders:

> *Critical Profile - A Critical Profile $CCP_j$ is a set of values of order attributes $OA_n$ that characterizes a specific type of order which exhibits a high likelihood of encountering disruptive events DE during its fulfillment process.*

In the above example the single value *Destination* = *Mexico* is a simple $CCP_j$ that characterizes a group of potentially critical orders: All shipments to Mexico are prone to be delayed by customs procedures.

### 4.2.1.2    Representation

In another example many orders directed to Latvia with express shipments regardless of the shipped product type are damaged during transportation. Representation of a critical profile $CCP_j$ for this example considers two order attributes, each being mandatory. The set of attribute values is depicted in a short version as {Express delivery; Latvia}. In a formal representation a $CCP_j$ is defined as a logical term that represents a fact which describes a certain situation in a domain. Such a term is composed of various simpler terms (e.g. the elements of the set) that are connected with logic operators. The example translates into the following term:

```
CCP1 = ((Dispatch_type = "Express delivery") AND (Destination
= "Latvia"))
```

Representation of $CCP_j$ as logical terms permits to use additional logic operators such as *OR* and *NOT*. Two examples illustrate the benefits of using this additional expressive power to define $CCP_j$.

- Two product types (*Type1, Type2*) of a certain supplier (*Recipient-ID* = 8573) often fail in quality assessments regarding their physical tolerances (a reason could be that both products are manufactured in a facility with worn machines). Instead of defining two separate $CCP_j$ for *Type1* and *Type2* that both apply to the *Recipient-ID 8573*, a single rule can be defined that encompasses both:

```
CCP2 = (((Product_type = "Type1") OR (Product_type = "Type2"))
AND (Recipient_ID = 8573))
```

- Transportation orders directed to *Greece* are in most cases delayed due to the different customs procedures in the various transit countries en route from *Germany*. Only a special route (*Route21*) via Italy which employs the use of a ferry is always reliable. The resulting rule for this $CCP_j$ is:

```
CCP3 = ((Origin = "Germany") AND (Destination = "Greece") AND
(NOT (Route
    = "Route21")))
```

To represent quantitative restrictions (e.g. regarding volume or weight of an order), the use of expressions to define *larger than (>)* or *smaller than (<)* relations and variants of these is a necessary addition to define realistic $CCP_j$:

```
CCP4 = (((Weight <= 40) OR (Weight > 1500)) AND (Destination
= "China"))
```

### 4.2.1.3    Matching

Assuming that critical profiles $CCP_j$ are available (see section 4.2.2), a mechanism is needed to compare the terms of the $CCP_j$ with the characteristics of individual orders which are received over time by an enterprise in a supply network. The aim is to identify potentially critical orders based on the $CCP_j$ as early as possible, in order to initiate a proactive monitoring of these orders and thereby give monitoring activities in a supply network a focus. An illustration of the approach is given in fig. 4-12. The order characteristics of new orders are extracted e.g. from an internal ERP system. They are compared with already defined critical profiles $CCP_j$. In case a match is found, a probabilistic trigger $TE_{PT}$ is generated[7] which initiates monitoring of the order that was matched to a $CCP_j$ (*Zimmermann et al. 2003a*).

Technical realization of the matching mechanism has to be based on the values of order attributes of new orders and on the logic terms of critical profiles. Rule-based systems (also termed "expert systems") provide a mechanism to bring about a matching of these facts (*Bodendorf 2003, pp.125; Friedmann-Hill 2003, pp. 14; Luger 2001*, pp. 279). They employ rules that represent knowledge about $CCP_j$ facts and combine these with the necessary *consequences*.

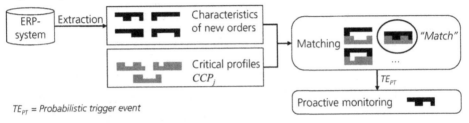

$TE_{PT}$ = *Probabilistic trigger event*

Fig. 4-12. Profile matching

For a SNEM system the *consequence* in a rule is the generation of a probabilistic trigger event $TE_{PT}$. A rule is represented by *IF-THEN* terms where the *IF* part specifies the predicate or premise of the rule (a $CCP_j$) and the *THEN* part the conclusion of the rule (e.g. generating a $TE_{PT}$). Rule-based expert systems are well-suited to solve problems where the knowledge to be represented is based on heuristic expert knowledge or incomplete information about the domain (*Luger 2001* p. 315). This can be assumed for the definition of $CCP_j$, because discovery of $CCP_j$ is not necessarily based on theoretical models about causes and effects of disruptive events. Rather, expert knowledge based on experience and heuristics points to "typical sources" of disruptive events. These can be characterized using order attributes for critical profiles (see fig. 4-11). Consequently, a SNEM system depends on the quality of expert knowledge that is coded in its $CCP_j$ rules. Both, discovery of new expert knowledge (that is new $CCP_j$, see section 4.2.2) and continuous management as well as adaptation of existing $CCP_j$ (see section 4.2.3), determine effectiveness of a SNEM system in focusing on potentially critical orders.

In fig. 4-13 an example is given with two rules and three orders to be checked against these rules. Definition of the rules adheres to the following structure: An *IF* clause follows the *defrule NAME* statement, and a *THEN* clause is preceded by the symbol *"=>"*. Facts that are compared with the rules are defined by the $OA_n$ of newly received orders of a

---

[7.] "Probabilistic trigger" refers to the high probability of an order to encounter a disruptive event which is the reason for it being proactively monitored. For details of the definition of trigger events see section 4.1.1.

company. In the example the first rule matches the orders *Order₁* and *Order₃,* and the second rule matches *Order₃*.

It is important to notice that

-   rules can only apply to a fraction of the facts (*Order₂* does not match any rule),
-   several different rules can match the same fact (*Order₃* matches two rules).

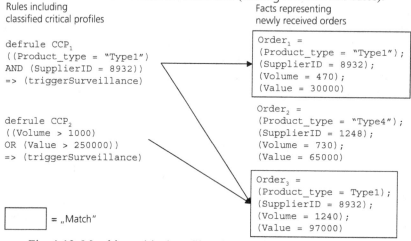

Fig. 4-13. Matching critical profile rules and facts about new orders

To assure that a single order is never monitored twice or more by a SNEM system through multiple profile matches and/or additional status requests from customers for the same order (see section 4.1.2), a SNEM system keeps track of orders that are currently being monitored.

## 4.2.2   Discovery of Critical Profiles

### 4.2.2.1     Qualitative Approach

Acquisition of knowledge from domain experts to define $CCP_j$ is conducted with a variety of techniques that are typically used in knowledge management projects. Suitability of a technique depends on the type of knowledge that is to be extracted:

-   Knowledge can be related to specific processes (e.g. a warehousing specialist has such knowledge) or to specific concepts (e.g. a product specialist has knowledge on product features).
-   Explicit knowledge is easy to document (e.g. the different steps in a process), whereas so-called tacit knowledge is by logic of a more implicit kind and cannot be articulated (e.g. the right pressure to be applied on a working piece in production) *(Nonaka 1992, pp.96)*.

Since all types of knowledge are of potential importance to identify sources of disruptive events, different techniques are applicable. For instance, interviews are well suited if knowledge is mainly explicit. Possible questions to domain experts might be:

- Which machines have the most damages and down-times? And what product groups are built on these machines?
- Are there products in the warehouse which are very difficult to handle? What problems occur during handling of these products?
- Which destination countries are known for unpredictable customs services?

Other techniques proposed by Milton (*Milton 2003*) are better suited for tacit knowledge, such as *Laddering* (used to build hierarchical structures, e.g. of problems), *diagram-based techniques* (concept maps, process mapping, state diagrams) or *sorting techniques* (used to determine rankings of, for instance, disruptive event types regarding their frequency).

These techniques are also an integral part of knowledge engineering methods such as CommonKADS (*Schreiber et al. 2000*) or MOKA (*Callot et al. 2000*) and corresponding tools for knowledge acquisition (e.g. PCPACK4 or SOPHx-PACK (*Epistemics 2004*)). Final definition of the $CCP_j$ as rules for the expert system (see section 4.2.1.2) remains a creative act to be conducted by the knowledge engineer.

### 4.2.2.2 Quantitative Approach

A quantitative approach aims at automatic discovery of $CCP_j$ in historic order data to acquire new knowledge on sources of disruptive events. Data mining algorithms such as *decision trees* or *rule induction*[8] are able to automatically select values of order attributes for inclusion in critical profiles and to rate the criticality of these profiles. Thus, a classification of orders into normal and critical ones is realized[9]. In fig. 4-14 it is assumed that a data mining algorithm has developed two sets of order attributes $S_1$ and $S_2$. A rating of criticality of their associated orders is based on the average deviation of actual fulfillment dates from planned fulfillment dates of all orders that match a certain set. Based on this criterion $S_1$ is classified as a $CCP_j$ because of its severe average delay (5.3 days).

| Set $S_i$ of order attributes selected by data mining algorithm | Average deviation from planned fulfillment date |
|---|---|
| $S_1$ = ((ProductType = Any)<br>AND (DispatchType = Express delivery)<br>AND (Destination = Latvia)) | + 5.3 days ⚡ |
| $S_2$ = ((ProductType = Books)<br>AND (DispatchType = Any)<br>AND (Destination = France)) | + 0.1 days |

Fig. 4-14. Classification of order profiles

A data mining process to identify $CCP_j$ is depicted in fig. 4-15. Three process steps are needed to prepare data before executing a data mining algorithm and validating results in the computation phase. Feedback is possible from the computation to the preparation phase. In the final phase new $CCP_j$ are defined based on data mining results.

---

[8]. Algorithms based on neural networks or instance-based learning are not considered. Since they rely on black box mechanisms, it is not possible to extract rules from their results.

[9]. A procedure of identifying groups of similar objects with data mining algorithms is termed *classification*.

In the first step of preparation (see fig. 4-15) a *class attribute* is selected which is used to separate critical profiles $CCP_j$ from non-critical sets of order attributes. In the example of fig. 4-14 the selected class attribute is the *average deviation from planned fulfillment date*. Any classification approach based on data mining algorithms requires definition of a *class attribute* (e.g. (*Kantardzic 2003*), (*Witten et al. 2001*)). The *class attribute* is used to decide whether a certain order belongs to a class or not. Since only two classes (regular orders and critical orders) are distinguished, a binary restriction on the class attribute is used: Typically, a threshold is defined above or beneath which an actual instance of the class attribute for a specific order indicates a $CCP_j$ (e.g. more than 10% delay based on the planned cycle time is defined as critical). Potential *class attributes* are e.g. deviations from planned fulfillment dates (see above), from physical tolerances, target costs or ordered quantities. This information is derived by combining *status data* and *control data* which are defined in the SNEM data model (see section 3.1.1).

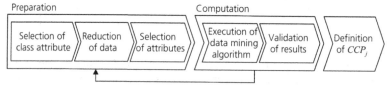

Fig. 4-15. Process for defining $CCP_j$ with data mining methods

In the second preparation step (see fig. 4-15) data input based on historic fulfillment data of orders is reduced where possible to enhance computational performance of a data mining algorithm. There are three options: a reduction of the number of data attributes, a reduction of the number of data sets, and an adjustment of single values (for details see e.g. *Kantardzic 2003, pp. 21 and pp. 40* or *Witten et al. 2001, pp. 252*).

In the third step order attributes $OA_n$ are selected that are to be considered during execution of the data mining algorithm for automatic discovery of $CCP_j$. In many cases these form a subset of the available attributes $OA_n$ which remain from the "reduction of data"-process in step 2. Since the possible combinations of $OA_n$ in critical profiles are calculated by $2^k$ with $k$ being the number of selected $OA_n$, the number of attributes should be restricted where possible to limit computation time required by a data mining algorithm. In the example of fig. 4-14 at least three $OA_n$ have been selected for computation: *ProductType, DispatchType* and *Destination,* because these have been considered by the data mining algorithm in the critical profile.

The computation process is divided into execution of a data mining algorithm and validation of the mining results. As indicated above, several types of data mining algorithms allow to classify orders as critical and identify new $CCP_j$. These are provided in standard data mining tools such as SPSS Clementine (*SPSS 2004*) or WEKA (*Weka 2005*). The generalized procedure for a typical data mining algorithm based on rule induction is illustrated in fig. 4-16. A number of orders is arranged in the left-most graph according to their volume and weight. Volume and weight are the two order attributes $OA_n$ selected for possible inclusion in the data mining computation (see above as third step of preparation). Two types of orders are assumed: some that have not encountered any problems indicated by an "a" and some critical orders marked with "x". Whether an order is critical ("x") or not ("a") depends on the class attribute which in the example is a relative *delay*: all orders more than 10% late are defined as critical.

A rule induction algorithm creates and refines rules successively. In a first step in fig. 4-16 a simple rule with only one order attribute is generated (*Weight>500*). It cannot separate all critical from non-critical orders as indicated by the class attribute of instances to which the rule applies (two orders "a" remain). Since the second order attribute available to the algorithm is not yet used, a refinement of the initial rule is calculated that optimizes the relation between critical and non-critical orders as indicated in the right-most graph of fig. 4-16. Thus the data mining algorithm proposes a new rule to identify potentially critical orders based on historic order data input:

```
Weight>500 AND Volume>200
```

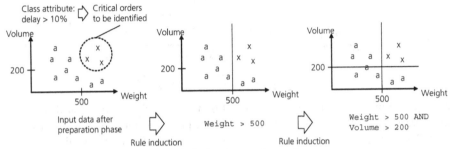

Fig. 4-16. Rule induction - schematic process

Besides rule induction algorithms (e.g. *PART* or *JRip* implemented in the *WEKA* data mining suite (*Weka 2005*)), decision tree algorithms (e.g. *J48, ADTree* (see *Weka 2005*)) are also used for classification. They successively refine an initial decision tree. Whether further refinement of the tree is necessary is decided based on the actual class attributes of orders which are separated by the intermediate version of decision tree rules into critical and non-critical ones. For an example of a decision tree applied to real-world data of a business case see fig. 4-18. Which type of data mining algorithm is actually used, depends on the quality of achievable results. Typically, several algorithms are used on the same data input, and validation of results helps to determine the most effective algorithm for a given input set.

Validation of results as the second step during computation is based on a division of the data input into two sets: a training set which is used by the data mining algorithm to determine new $CCP_j$ (see above), and a test set used to validate the performance of identified $CCP_j$ regarding correct classification of orders. For a binary class attribute - orders are critical or not - a *confusion matrix* is the standardized result of an automatic validation based on the test set. A confusion matrix is provided by data mining tools *(Freitas 2002, pp. 151)*. Calculations based on this matrix are used to determine the quality of the discovered profiles (see fig. 4-17).

In fig. 4-17 a class attribute *Deviation* indicates a $CCP_j$, if this *Deviation* is larger than some externally defined limit (see examples above). The data mining model (e.g. rules or decision trees) which results from execution of a data mining algorithm (see above) is used to predict class attributes for every instance of the test set. In the example of fig. 4-

17 the model predicts, whether an orders deviation is above or below the limit. Thus, a prediction whether an order is critical or not is generated. This prediction is compared to the eventually correct classification of an order determined by calculation of its eventually correct class attribute (its actual delay). Two possible alternatives represent correct behavior of the data mining model (see fig. 4-17): *True Positives [TP]* and *True Negatives [TN]*. Whereas an order can be assigned to the wrong class, either if it is indeed belonging to a $CCP_j$ but not classified as such by the data mining model (*False Positives [FP]*) or if it is not critical but assigned to the $CCP_j$ class (*False Negatives [FN]*) by the data mining model.

|                               |                               | Predicted class attribute | |
|                               |                               | Deviation ≤ Limit | Deviation > Limit ( → $CCP_j$) |
|---|---|---|---|
| Actual class attribute | Deviation ≤ Limit | *True Positives (TP)* | *False Negatives (FN)* |
|                               | Deviation > Limit ( → $CCP_j$) | *False Positives (FP)* | *True Negatives (TN)* |

Fig. 4-17. Confusion matrix

Two separate indicators are calculated based on the confusion matrix that denote how many percent of the classifications of the test set are predicted correctly relative to all predicted *Positives* (= order not critical) respectively *Negatives* (= order critical = $CCP_j$):

$$\text{True Positive Rate (TPR)} = \frac{TP}{TP + FN} \text{ and True Negative Rate (TNR)} = \frac{TN}{TN + FP}$$

An overall indicator of the quality of the data mining model is the combined *precision rate* calculated by the *TPR* multiplied by the *TNR*:

$$\text{Precision Rate (PR)} = TPR \times TNR$$

A *PR* with a value of zero indicates the lowest possible quality (no prediction of the data mining model is ever correct) while a value of one would indicate a perfect model.

The results of the computation process are iteratively refined by using a feedback loop to the data preparation process. These steps are repeated until sufficiently reliable outputs (e.g. based on a predefined minimum threshold of the *Precision Rate PR*) are identified. Only these are used as input for the SNEM system and coded as rules for the rule-based system in the last phase of the data mining process (see fig. 4-15). An example of a $CCP_j$ rule that is defined based on data mining results is depicted in fig. 4-18. The decision tree is generated by the data mining tool SPSS Clementine and order data of a German logistics service provider is used for the example[10].

---

[10.]For details on data mining results in real-world scenarios see section 7.2.5.1.

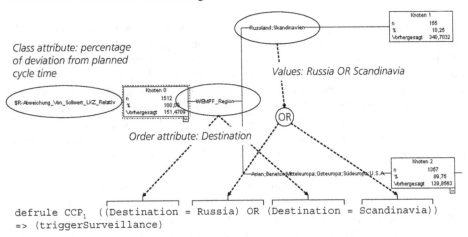

```
defrule CCP₁ ((Destination = Russia) OR (Destination = Scandinavia))
=> (triggerSurveillance)
```

Fig. 4-18. Definition of a $CCP_j$ based on data mining results (decision tree)

## 4.2.3 Continuous Assessment of Critical Profiles

### 4.2.3.1 Profile Life Cycle

A critical type of order described by a $CCP_j$ might develop over time into a reliable one. For instance, worn machines are exchanged by new ones and thus quality problems for certain products are reduced. In section 2.2.2.4 a requirement for autonomous adaptation of a SNEM system to such changes is defined. This is realized if critical profiles $CCP_j$ are continuously assessed as to their ability to identify critical orders. A life cycle model for critical profiles is proposed that assures continuous adaptation of all $CCP_j$ used in a SNEM solution (see fig. 4-19).

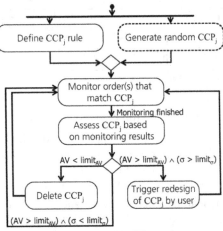

Fig. 4-19. Profile life cycle

On initialization of the profile life cycle, new critical profiles are defined according to the mechanisms presented in section 4.2.2. A random generation of $CCP_j$ is introduced additionally as a "radar" function to identify newly evolving types of critical orders automatically. Every $CCP_j$ is used for matching (see section 4.2.1.3). After an order has been finished, monitoring results that match one or more $CCP_j$ are stored in a data base, and an assessment of the related $CCP_j$ is triggered based on all available historic monitoring results related to these $CCP_j$: An *AggregatedValue AV* which integrates several profile quality measures is calculated for each $CCP_j$. It is calculated as a weighted average of four main indicators (for details see section 4.2.3.2), with $w_i$ as enterprise-specific weights:

$$AggregatedValue\ AV = w_1*IdentifiedDE + w_2*DE\_Consequences +$$
$$w_3*DegreeOfProfileUtilization + w_4*PriorityOfMonitoredOrders$$

Based on this assessment a $CCP_j$ might either be deleted, if it continuously fails to identify orders that are affected by *DEs*, or a proposal for redesign of a $CCP_j$ is generated. Redesign of a $CCP_j$ is conducted by a human actor who is for instance also responsible for discovery of new $CCP_j$ as described in section 4.2.2. A proposal is issued, if a high variation in the ability of a $CCP_j$ to identify critical orders is identified. This is indicated by a relatively high standard deviation $\sigma$ of the above mentioned indicators (for details see section 4.2.3.3). Only in case neither the aggregated value $AV$ nor $\sigma$ indicate a low quality of a profile, the evaluated $CCP_j$ is used again in the matching mechanism (see fig. 4-19).

### 4.2.3.2    Profile Quality Measures

As indicated above in section 4.2.3.1 the aggregated value $AV$ integrates four main categories of indicators to assess the quality of a critical profile $CCP_j$. Two of the indicators are further refined into sub indicators as depicted in fig. 4-20.

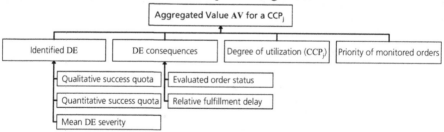

Fig. 4-20. Profile quality measures

1. *Identified DE* - The ability of a critical profile to identify disruptive events *DE* is measured by three sub indicators: a *qualitative success quota*, a *quantitative success quota* and the *mean DE severity* (see fig. 4-20):
   - A *qualitative success quota (qualSQ)* represents the average hit-rate of a critical profile which is standardized between zero and one. It is calculated for a certain $CCP_j$ by selecting all historic orders in the data base (see section 4.2.3.1) that match this $CCP_j$ and count the number of orders that encountered disruptive

events. This value is divided by the number of all matching orders for this $CCP_j$. A higher *qualitative success quota* indicates a better quality of a $CCP_j$ because monitoring efforts are less wasted on non-critical orders.

- The *quantitative success quota* (*quanSQ*) calculates the average number of *DEs* identified in those orders of the data base that matched a certain $CCP_j$ and actually encountered any disruptive events. It is standardized between zero and one (see example in table 4-1). A higher quota indicates that a profile is especially good at identifying orders with major problems, because a larger number of *DEs* per critical order is encountered on average.

- Based upon all disruptive events encountered in any historic order that match a certain $CCP_j$, an average value of severity is calculated. It employs the order attribute *DisruptiveEventSeverity* defined in the SNEM ontology (see section 3.2.3.2). The *mean DE severity* (*meanDE*) represents an average value of severity between zero and one for all identified *DEs* related to a certain $CCP_j$.

2. *DE consequences*
   An assessment of the consequences of disruptive events *DE* is measured for each order that matches a certain $CCP_j$ based on an overall *aggregated order status* (*AOS*) (see section 4.3.3). The *AOS* is standardized between zero an one with one representing perfect fulfillment of an order. Since delays in processes caused by *DEs* have a major effect on subsequent process steps in supply networks, the *relative fulfillment delay* of each such order is also taken into account[11]. Averages of both indicators are calculated for assessment of a $CCP_j$ (*meanAOS* and *meanRelDel*).

3. *Degree of utilization ($CCP_j$)*
   In case a critical profile has been used frequently in the past and the frequency of matches with new orders continuously decreases, this $CCP_j$ focuses on order types of decreasing significance to a supply network (e.g. on a product type at the end of its lifecycle). To reflect such developments the time line is considered in the *degree of utilization (util)* of a $CCP_j$ (see example in table 4-2). It offers insight into both a critical profile's absolute (how many matches per time slot) and its relative importance (compared to other $CCP_j$).

4. *Priority of monitored orders*
   Quality of a $CCP_j$ is also affected by the importance of the orders it identifies as potentially critical. Priority measures can include classification of customers into different groups (e.g. A, B, C customers), revenue generated by an order or fines for fulfillment failures (e.g. delays, product quality problems) defined in a contract. It is assumed that every enterprise determines its own priority measure (*prio*) that is to be considered in the aggregated value $AV$ of a $CCP_j$[12].

---

[11.]The delay is calculated based on achieved and planned fulfillment dates of an order defined in the SNEM data model (see section 3.1.1.3). It is divided by the planned fulfillment duration which is also calculated from SNEM data.

[12.]For details on priorities of orders see also sections 4.4.2.1 and 4.4.5.2.

As an example for calculation of one of the indicators the *quantitative success quota* is illustrated in detail. It represents an average value of the number of disruptive events encountered for each monitored order that matches a certain $CCP_j$ (see table 4-1):

| Formula | Parameters | | Example |
|---|---|---|---|
| $$quanSC = \frac{\sum\limits_{i=1}^{K} NDE_i}{k \cdot m}$$ | $k$ | Number of orders matching a $CCP_j$ | $k= 3$, $NDE_1= 3$ ; $NDE_2= 4$, $NDE_3= 1$ , $m= 4$ |
| | $NDE_i$ | Number of disruptive events of the order $i$ | |
| | $m$ | Maximum number of disruptive events encountered for an order (possibly truncated) | $quanSC = \dfrac{3+4+1}{3 \cdot 4} = \dfrac{2}{3}$ |

Table 4-1. Quantitative success quota of a $CCP_j$

The sum of all *DE* for all orders matching a $CCP_j$ is used as the numerator, while the denominator is based on the maximum number of disruptive events encountered for any order ($m$) multiplied with the number of orders matching the $CCP_j$ to be evaluated ($k$). Based on the assumption that $m$ is a realistic upper limit[13], the denominator represents a prediction of the maximum number of disruptive events possibly identifiable at all by a SNEM system. The resulting indicator *quanSC* relates all actually identified *DEs* to the potentially identifiable *DEs* defined by the upper boundary $m$. With the exception of the *degree of utilization of a* $CCP_j$, all other indicators defined above are calculated similarly as averages of various inputs, such as the *number of orders matching a* $CCP_j$, the *severity of disruptive events*, or *fulfillment delays*. In all cases a standardized value between zero and one is the result, with zero defining the lowest possible quality of a $CCP_j$ and one the highest. A high quality of a $CCP_j$ indicates its good ability to predict critical orders. The *degree of utilization* (see table 4-2) focuses on the usage of a critical profile over time where "usage" refers to the number of matches of a $CCP_j$ with new orders during the profile matching process (see section 4.2.1.3). The main indicator *util* calculates the average usage of a $CCP_j$ over the past twelve months, with emphasis on the last month and continuously decreasing importance of each preceding month[14]. This average is standardized by relating it to the maximum usage of the last twelve months indicated by $u=Max(n_j)$. In the example in table 4-2 *util* results in a value of 0.405 for a $CCP_j$ with decreasing usage. A simple average of these twelve months related to the maximum usage of the last twelve

---

[13.]The parameter $m$ can be truncated to a realistic upper bound to avoid distortions by single extreme values. An upper limit is defined for each SNEM system individually, e.g. based on historic records of disruptive events.

[14.]The term $\dfrac{13-i}{12}$ assures that the 12th month is included in the average, but weighted lowest .

months would have resulted in $util=0,556$ which overemphasizes a supply network situation that is no longer correct[15].

| Formula | Parameters | | Example |
|---|---|---|---|
| $$util = \cfrac{\sum_{i=1}^{13} \cfrac{13-i}{12} \cdot n_i}{\sum_{i=1}^{13} \cfrac{13-i}{12} \cdot u}$$ | $i$ | Index of month, $i=1$ latest month, $i=12$ one year ago | $n_1=2; n_2=3; n_3=3; n_4=2;$ $n_5=2; n_6=2; n_7=5; n_8=7;$ $n_9=8; n_{10}=9; n_{11}=8; n_{12}=9$ |
| | $n_i$ | Number of profile usages of a $CCP_j$ in month $i$ | $$util = \cfrac{\frac{12}{12} \cdot 2 + \frac{11}{12} \cdot 3 + \dots}{\frac{12}{12} \cdot 9 + \frac{11}{12} \cdot 9 + \dots}$$ |
| | $u = Max(n_i)$ | Maximum $n_i$ of the last twelve months | $= 0.405$ |

Table 4-2. Degree of utilization of a $CCP_j$

The average value $AV$ is calculated based on all seven indicators as a weighted average with different weights $w_i$ (see (A) in fig. 4-21). Each weight is configured individually for a SNEM system and reflects strategic valuations of different supply network partners (e.g. high priority orders valued higher or lower). In the example (B) of fig. 4-21 the same weights ($1/4$) are assumed for every main type of indicator (see fig. 4-20), and sub indicators are weighted in equal subparts of their main indicator's weights (e.g. $1/3*1/4=1/12$ for $qualSC$, $quanSC$ and $meanDE$). A sample calculation is depicted in (C) which indicates a medium quality of the rated $CCP_j$ ($AV=0.473$). Only 40% of all monitored orders of this critical profile encounter disruptive events ($qualSC$), but at least these orders encounter a relative high number of disruptive events ($quanSC$) with a medium average severity ($meanDE$). Consequences of these $DE$ are not too severe, since the mean $AOS$[16] is 0.6 and the average delay of orders is 14% ($meanRelDel$).The profile is still in relative intense use with $util=0.74$, and monitored orders are of medium priority ($prio=0.4$).

---

[15.]However, if a $CCP_j$ fluctuates heavily over time, $util$ underestimates the $CCP_j$'s utilization, while continuously low usage results in a high value of $util$ which in turn overestimates the importance of such a profile compared to more active $CCP_j$. A mechanism for adjustment in these cases is presented in appendix B.

[16.]The higher the $AOS$ the better an order's status. A high-quality profile will hint to orders with a low $AOS$, thus $1-meanAOS$ is used as the indicator for the average value $AV$.

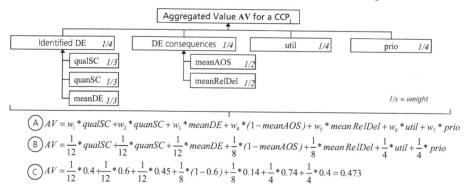

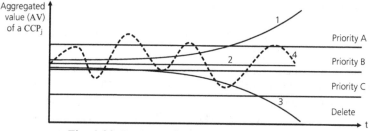

$$\textcircled{A}\; AV = w_1 * qualSC + w_2 * quanSC + w_3 * meanDE + w_4 * (1 - meanAOS) + w_5 * mean\,RelDel + w_6 * util + w_7 * prio$$

$$\textcircled{B}\; AV = \frac{1}{12} * qualSC + \frac{1}{12} * quanSC + \frac{1}{12} * meanDE + \frac{1}{8} * (1 - meanAOS) + \frac{1}{8} * mean\,RelDel + \frac{1}{4} * util + \frac{1}{4} * prio$$

$$\textcircled{C}\; AV = \frac{1}{12} * 0.4 + \frac{1}{12} * 0.6 + \frac{1}{12} * 0.45 + \frac{1}{8} * (1 - 0.6) + \frac{1}{8} * 0.14 + \frac{1}{4} * 0.74 + \frac{1}{4} * 0.4 = 0.473$$

Fig. 4-21. Calculation of aggregated value ($AV$)

### 4.2.3.3    Continuous Profile Assessment

The aggregated value $AV$ is used to define monitoring priorities associated with a $CCP_j$. Monitoring priority controls the intensity, especially the frequency, of efforts to update SNEM data (see section 4.1.2) (*Bodendorf et al. 2005*). Over time the $AV$ of a $CCP_j$ can exhibit different patterns (see fig. 4-22).

A steadily increasing $AV$ (1) in fig. 4-22 indicates a deterioration of the process performance of, for instance, a supplier with respect to the delivery of a certain product type (depending on the attributes of the $CCP_j$). Orders that match this profile have to be monitored more closely, which means that the monitoring priority is increased.

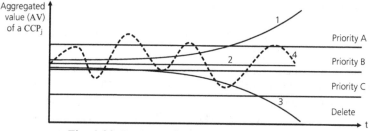

Fig. 4-22. Patterns of aggregated values ($AV$)

A more or less constant rating (2) results in a constant monitoring priority, whereas a decreasing rating (3) leads to a decreased priority and eventually to obsoleteness of the profile. In this case, the $CCP_j$ is deleted from the knowledge-base of the rule-based system (compare section 4.2.1.3), because the $CCP_j$ continuously fails to identify critical orders. A decreasing rate indicates an improvement of fulfillment processes. It might result for instance from a reengineering effort in a supplier's production facility and allows to reduce monitoring efforts. In contrast to these idealistic curves a realistic graph will fluctuate over time (4) and might follow an increasing or decreasing trend similar to (1) or (3). Thus, monitoring priorities can vary for the same $CCP_j$ over time, and the $AV$ reflects changes in the supply network environment (e.g. improved fulfillment for an order type).

A SNEM system automatically adapts to these conditions by continually assessing its critical profiles and by adapting the monitoring intensity accordingly.

The adaptation mechanism also identifies $CCP_j$ that need to be redesigned to enhance their predictive quality. This is brought about by calculating the standard deviation σ for a $CCP_j$ based on the quality measures: *meanDE, AOS, meanRelDel* and *prio*. For each of these indicators a high standard deviation indicates that in some cases a $CCP_j$ identified orders that are either extremely critical (measurements: *meanDE, AOS, meanRelDel*) or of very high importance (measurement: *prio*), while in other cases matching orders are neither critical nor important. A SNEM system flags such $CCP_j$ and induces a user of the SNEM system to redesign them (see also section 4.2.3.1).

### 4.2.3.4 Profile Generation

In the profile life cycle model (see section 4.2.3.1) a random generation of critical profiles is an additional activity which defines new $CCP_j$, besides manual creation of profiles described in section 4.2.2. The insertion of random profiles into a SNEM system has the objective to enable a SNEM system to autonomously learn new critical profiles and thus adapt to evolving critical order types: The profile life cycle model (see fig. 4-19) ensures that over time only those randomly generated $CCP_j$ will survive which are truly able to identify critical orders. All other $CCP_j$ will be deleted from the knowledge-base of the rule-based system (see section 4.2.3.1). Thus, new randomly generated profiles are automatically tested for their quality by a SNEM system, and an evolutionary selection for high-quality profiles is realized. Using randomized generation of critical profiles, a SNEM system is able to autonomously adapt to those changing conditions in a supply network which result in new critical order types[17].

A simple random generation of $CCP_j$ might result in completely unrealistic $CCP_j$, e.g. including a rule for huge quantities of goods that are never ordered. Hence, an approach is proposed which constructs profiles based on predefined profile components. These components are, for instance, defined by analyzing historic records of all orders of an enterprise and extracting attributes of these regardless of their fulfillment quality. Thus, resulting profile components hint to orders that truly exist(ed), but without any presumption on their fulfillment quality. These components are connected with logic operators to form more complex rules. A sample of such components provided in a data base is depicted in table 4-3.

All profile components are identified by an ID and defined by an attribute, an operator and an associated value, e.g. *CustomerID = 27583*. This data set represents a single component usable for definition of a critical profile. Additional data is provided by the actor who designs the profile components to assure realistic combinations of components (see table 4-3)[18]:

---

[17.]To distinguish monitoring initiated by regular $CCP_j$ from random $CCP_j$, the resulting trigger event of a random $CCP_j$ is referred to as a randomized trigger $TE_{RT}$ instead of a probabilistic trigger $TE_{PT}$ from regular $CCP_j$ (see section 4.1.1 for details).

- The *priority* of a component influences its probability to appear in a new random profile. This field is required for each profile component.
- *Component suggestions* allow the designer or a user of a SNEM system to define desired combinations of components in generated profiles. In this field an ID is defined which links to another component. The field is optional.
- *Link suggestions* are used to preselect a logical operator for connection to the next component that is selected by the profile generation mechanism. The field is optional.

| ID | Attribute | Operator | Value | Priority | Component suggestion | Link suggestion |
|----|-----------|----------|-------|----------|----------------------|-----------------|
| 1 | Destination | = | Russia | High | - | AND |
| 2 | Quantity | > | 4000 | High | 3 | OR |
| 3 | Quantity | < | 200 | Medium | - | - |
| 4 | CustomerID | = | 27583 | Medium | 7 | - |
| ... | ... | ... | ... | ... | ... | ... |

Table 4-3. Data for profile generation

Component suggestions and link suggestions are independent of each other. Consequently, a component might be suggested for addition to another component without a predefined link between these two components (see first component *ID=1*) and vice versa (e.g. *ID=4*). The two profiles $CCP_{r1}$ and $CCP_{r2}$ are examples which are generated from the components of table 4-3:

```
CCPr1 = (((Quantity > 4000) OR (Quantity < 200)) OR
         (CustomerID = 27583))
CCPr2 = ((Destination = Russia) AND (Quantity < 200))
```

The construction algorithm starts with the selection of a high priority component, e.g. *ID2* for $CCP_{r1}$. If a component suggestion exists (*ID3* for *ID2*), it is used to identify the next component. Since a link suggestion is available for *ID2* the logical connector *OR* is used. Thus, *ID3* is connected with *OR* in $CCP_{r1}$. Profiles which are generated by the construction algorithm integrate a varying number of components, but no profile exceeds an explicitly defined number of components. Thus, a wide variety of profiles is potentially available, and a SNEM system cyclically creates new random profiles to allow autonomous identification of new critical order types.

---

[18.]Note: Definition of profile components is not directly supported by a SNEM solution. A component designer has to apply its expert knowledge to create realistic components. Statistical methods can support definition of e.g. link suggestions, if typical patterns of order attributes are identified. However, such an analysis does not focus on identifying critical orders in contrast to the quantitative approach presented in section 4.2.2.2 .

# 4.3 Analysis and Interpretation of Event Data

Data that is gathered proactively by a SNEM system according to the mechanisms defined in sections 4.1 and 4.2, needs to be analyzed and interpreted automatically, if the information logistics task defined in section 2.1.3.3 is to be satisfied in a timely fashion. Such a function satisfies the requirement *Autonomous data analysis* (see section 2.2.2.5).

## 4.3.1 Basic Approach

### 4.3.1.1 Need for Heuristics

Any analysis and interpretation of event data is influenced by developments in the fulfillment processes of monitored orders. These processes are executed by a large variety of actors and resources which influence each other directly or - even more often - indirectly. An example is a disruptive event "traffic jam" which affects transportation processes. It is caused by a multitude of actors - all vehicle drivers within the congestion - and additional factors such as weather conditions or even the location of the traffic jam (e.g. large highway vs. small street). Consequently, its duration cannot be accurately forecasted with reasonable efforts. Moreover, its effects on orders transported by a certain truck which is stuck in the traffic jam cannot be predicted for certain either: The truck driver as an autonomous actor in the transportation process might be able to take a detour, to drive a little bit faster after the end of the congestion, or to shorten a scheduled break, all of which might reduce the delay of the orders.

A SNEM system that is confronted with various types of disruptive events *DE* in a multitude of environmental settings cannot model all of the influencing factors required to exactly forecast consequences of a *DE* for all affected SNEM data types. However, a human actor is able to gain important insights from SNEM information on *DEs* as well as from related status data types by generating heuristic interpretations for different aspects of an order's status. A SNEM system imitates this heuristic approach.

Another factor that underlines the applicability of a heuristic approach to SNEM data analysis and interpretation is inherent uncertainty with respect to completeness and correctness of gathered SNEM data. It is always assumed for a SNEM system that it either might not be able to gather all requested data (see section 4.1.2.5) or that received SNEM data might be inaccurate and sometimes incorrect (see alignment of physical and virtual situation in section 3.3.3.1). Thus, even if complex forecast models existed that were confronted with incomplete or incorrect SNEM data, they would generate predictions with low accuracy.

### 4.3.1.2 Analytical Perspectives

Three main analytical perspectives are proposed to heuristically interpret data which is gathered by a SNEM system[19]. Each perspective covers a different aspect of a monitored order's current situation as characterized by proactively gathered SNEM data (see fig. 4-23).

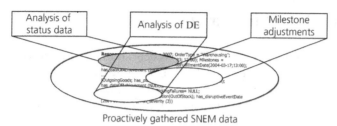

Proactively gathered SNEM data

Fig. 4-23. Analytical perspectives (schematic model)

1.  Different types of status data as defined in section 3.1.1.3 are used to calculate deviations based on control data, e.g. delays, incomplete quantities or quality measures derived from quality assessments. A human actor who assesses an order's situation considers various such indicators and generates an overall assessment of the order's status $OS_i(T_t)$. Similarly, a SNEM system integrates a variety of these inputs to form an aggregate assessment which is termed the *Aggregated Order Status AOS* (see section 4.3.3). Calculation of an *AOS* by a specific enterprise is influenced by its strategic goals: For instance, a differentiation strategy based on very high product quality makes it necessary to rate quality misses of suppliers higher than delays. A SNEM system considers these straptegic implications for its event management.

2.  Disruptive events *DE* that are identified by a SNEM system during fulfillment of either an order or one of the respective suborders, have different effects depending on the time of their identification relative to the remaining fulfillment time of an affected order. The same *DE* (e.g. a machine break-down) tends to have more serious consequences, if it takes place close to the end of a production process and thus an order's planned fulfillment date: The remaining reaction time is reduced, compared to an earlier identification of the same type of *DE,* and associated follow-up costs rise (see section 2.3.1.1). Hence, a SNEM system considers the planned timeline of a process and assesses the severity of a *DE* based on the current fulfillment situation of an affected order (see section 4.3.4). This results in an enterprise specific measurement of a disruptive event's severity, termed the *Endogenous Disruptive Event Severity EnDS*[20].

3.  Effects of disruptive events *DE* often cause delays even in case the initial *DE* primarily affects other order attributes $OA_n$: For instance, an incomplete delivery of material (affected $OA_n = DeliveredQuantity$) from a supplier might result in a delay of

---

[19.]Further perspectives are viable (e.g. refined assessments for quality and time data types according to the refinement levels defined in section 3.1.2.3) and can be realized with the Fuzzy Logic methodology proposed in subsequent sections.

[20.]Note that a general classification of a disruptive event's severity associated with a certain *DE* type is proposed within the SNEM data model (see section 3.1.3.1). To distinguish the new concept of an enterprise specific (=endogenous) interpretation of a *DE* from the general severity classification, the latter is now termed *Exogenous Disruptive Event Severity ExDS* (see also section 4.3.4.1).

production at the customer's site (affected $OA_{n+x}$ = *ActualFulfillmentDate*), because its manufacturing activities cannot be completed on time due to the missing material. Consequences are delays of several milestones at the customer's site which are identified by its SNEM system. Adjustments of milestone plans based on this data are required.

Although limitations of incomplete or incorrect input data remain, the third perspective "milestone adjustments" is the only one for which suitable forecast models exist to incorporate effects of disruptive events: Typical production (PPS) or distribution planning systems (DPS) offer capabilities to reschedule fulfillment plans on a detailed level. However, a rescheduling mechanism, which effectively changes fulfillment plans and aims at minimizing deviations from original plans, is part of a reaction $R_u$ to be triggered by a SNEM system through its messages $M_s$ (see section 2.1.3.3). A reaction $R_u$ takes place outside the limits of a SNEM system, and as such, planning algorithms and related systems are out of the focus of the SNEM concept. But a SNEM system provides interfaces to trigger rescheduling efforts within existing planning systems (see section 4.3.5.2). Besides such interfaces, a heuristic adjustment of milestones is provided as an optional add-on (see sections 4.3.5.1 and 4.3.5.3) within a SNEM system. It is meant to support initial assessments of necessary milestone adjustments before triggering external planning systems.

## 4.3.2   Data Interpretation with Fuzzy Logic

Both, input data and output data proposed for the two analytical perspectives "analysis of status data" and "analysis of DE" (see section 4.3.1.2), represent information on different data types with varying certainty regarding accurateness of the information. Simple calculations (e.g. weighted averages of input data) or simple decision rules (*If...Then...Else*) are not applicable for a heuristic interpretation which has to act similar to a human actor. Especially the vagueness of implications associated with gathered SNEM data (see section 4.3.1.1) has to be represented quite like a human actor would assess the situation. For this reason an approach based on Fuzzy Logic is chosen. In contrast to other methodologies, Fuzzy Logic is able to reason with *perceptions* (*Zadeh 1999*). Zadeh argues that a *perception* is a fuzzy evaluation of a concept such as time, distance, weight, likelihood, or truth. An example is "warm" as a *perception* of temperature. It is opposed to the concept of a *measurement* which is represented by an exact value (e.g. a temperature of 25.6 ° Celsius). SNEM data types which are the input to the analysis process are considered to be *measurements*. An assessment of a situation represented by these *measurements* has to consider both, the *perceptions* a human actor would experience regarding these *measurements* and the reasoning he would apply based on these *perceptions*. This is achieved by using Fuzzy Logic - a combination of fuzzy perceptions and mathematically grounded logic (*Friedrich 1997, pp. 161*). A short introduction to the basics of Fuzzy Logic is provided in appendix C.

### 4.3.3    Aggregated Order Status

#### 4.3.3.1    Required Status Data

The first analytical perspective to be realized with Fuzzy Logic is based on an analysis of data types that reflect the current status of a monitored order. These data types are integrated in an *Aggregated Order Status AOS* (see section 4.3.1.2). Potentially relevant status data types are defined in section 3.1.1.3. Deviations from original plans for fulfillment processes are calculated based on corresponding control data types (see also section 3.1.1.3). Thus, a variety of status assessments regarding a specific process (e.g. production) is possible that result in absolute and relative indicators. Some examples are depicted in fig. 4-24.

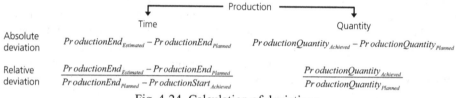

Fig. 4-24. Calculation of deviations

Depending on what types of indicators (e.g. time vs. quality) are to be considered in an *AOS* and on the characteristics of monitored orders (respectively their suborders), either absolute or relative indicators are better suited. For instance, if one suborder has a planned fulfillment duration of two weeks while another suborder has only two days, a relative indicator "%delay" is not suitable: A 10% delay of the first suborder (~1.5 days late) will affect its superorder much more than a 10% delay of the second suborder which is then only about five hours late. Relative indicators are often used in quality measurements, e.g. a percentage of defect parts in a delivery. These indicators facilitate comparison of different situations (e.g. deliveries of different size). For some status data types, calculation of deviations is not necessary at all since they are directly used as measurements of fulfillment problems (e.g. "number of picking failures").

Any indicator that is used in the automatic Fuzzy Logic analysis process is fuzzified. For each indicator a linguistic variable with different fuzzy variables is defined. An applicable membership function for fuzzy sets in this domain is the *trapezoid* function (see fig. 4-25). It is suitable for indicators that can be derived from status data types since a human actor typically perceives a deviation within a certain range as *high* or *critical* with a value of one (e.g. *critical*=1). Only the transition to the next fuzzy set (e.g. *high* to *very high*) is valued in between *one* and *zero*[21].

In the example in fig. 4-25 the linguistic variable *Delay* is defined based on five fuzzy variables within a range of 72 hours before and after the planned fulfillment date of an order (1). Depending on the strategic goals and the specific industry of a supply network partner, different definitions of delays can be configured. In fig. 4-25 two other possible definitions are depicted that spread three fuzzy sets to allow for longer delays (2) and that

---

[21.]A similar but more gradual definition of linguistic variables is achieved by using Pi fuzzy sets.

add a sixth fuzzy set to further differentiate delays (3). Which indicators are chosen and how these are considered by a SNEM system in the assessment of the *AOS*, remains an individual decision of each supply network partner. The various refinement possibilities proposed in section 3.1.2 provide a pool of potential data inputs which is to be selected individually.

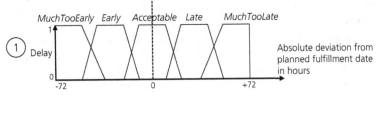

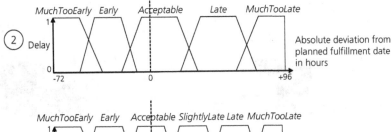

Fig. 4-25. Alternative fuzzy sets

### 4.3.3.2    Order Status Rules and Results

To assess fuzzified input values a fuzzy rule set is required which allows creation of an *Aggregated Order Status AOS*[22]. The *AOS* is standardized in the range between zero and one. It is defined as a linguistic variable with fuzzy sets *VeryHigh* for fulfillment that is as planned and *VeryLow*, if large problems are identified. Three intermediate fuzzy sets complete this linguistic variable. For two basic input values - absolute delay of an order (*ProcessTimeAbs*) as defined in section 4.3.3.1 and absolute deviation from ordered quantity (*ProcessQuantAbs*)[23] - part of a possible fuzzy rule set is depicted in fig. 4-26.

```
IF ProcessQuantAbs = MassiveShortage AND ProcessTimeAbs = MuchTooLate THEN AOS = VeryLow
  :
IF ProcessQuantAbs = Shortage AND ProcessTimeAbs = Acceptable THEN AOS = High
  :
IF ProcessQuantAbs = Correct AND ProcessTimeAbs = Acceptable THEN AOS = VeryHigh
```

Fig. 4-26. Fuzzy Logic rule set for order status (example)

---

[22.]See appendix C for details.

In fig. 4-27 a graphical representation of two possible rule sets for the two input values is given. The first rule set (*Strategy 1*) reflects a typical just-in-time strategy of a manufacturer that depends on timely deliveries from its suppliers and has (nearly) no capacities for safety stocks. Both, late or incomplete deliveries result in high follow-up costs for the manufacturer, because his production lines are halted soon, if input material is not delivered continuously. Thus, every kind of late delivery and every type of incomplete delivery is rated very critical and results in a low *AOS*. The second rule set (*Strategy 2*) is characteristic for an enterprise with stock capacities and large buffers of time in its fulfillment processes. Neither a quantitative shortage nor a late delivery is a very critical event for this enterprise. On the other hand, too many delivered goods and too early delivery are rated relatively positive, because costs of capital resulting from higher stocks are not considered critical for fulfillment.

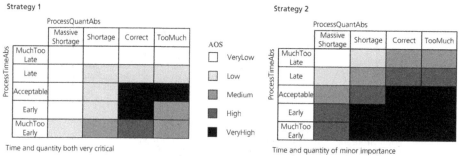

Fig. 4-27. *AOS* - definition of fuzzy rules

By comparing the fuzzy rule base to the *perceptions* associated with the input values, a number of evaluations is generated for each *perception*[24]. These evaluations are aggregated, and a single value for the *AOS* is calculated using a defuzzification method (e.g. the *Center of Gravity*). This *AOS* allows to characterize a monitored order's status. For instance, a value of 0.23 with a possible interval of the *AOS* between zero and one indicates a relatively high current criticality of a monitored order.

The large variety of potential input values provided by the SNEM data gathering mechanism to calculate an *AOS* may eventually result in very complex fuzzy rule sets, if every possible combination of perceptions is to be considered (see fig. 4-28).

A reduced rule set is possible, if analysis steps are sequenced. This is depicted by the stacked analysis design in fig. 4-28. For each analysis step only two variables are considered, with rule sets similar to those in fig. 4-27. This analysis design reduces the number of rules significantly. Such an approach is well suited for linguistic input variables without strong interdependencies. An example is the additional inclusion of a quality index (e.g. tolerance measures of material or parts) in the *AOS*. Even in case a delivery is on time and complete, a low quality index can result in severe consequences for following fulfill-

---

[23.]Four fuzzy sets are assumed for *ProcessQuantAbs*: *MassiveShortage, Shortage, Correct, Too-Much*.

[24.]For details on the mechanism see appendix C.

ment activities. For instance, a production lot cannot be produced, if higher product quality is required than received from a supplier. In this case, a second Fuzzy Logic assessment that combines an initial analysis which results in a linguistic variable $LV_4$ (see fig. 4-28) and a quality index ($LV_3$) is appropriate.

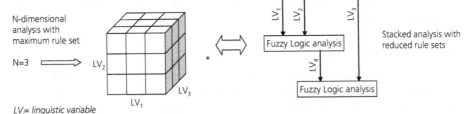

Fig. 4-28. Complex fuzzy rule sets

Integration of different linguistic variables is realized by a Fuzzy Logic approach, but a SNEM system provides the same data types for data on an order as well as its suborders. Thus, a number of sets with similar data inputs have to be aggregated and then autonomously interpreted by a SNEM system, which is depicted in fig. 4-29 (basic scenario).

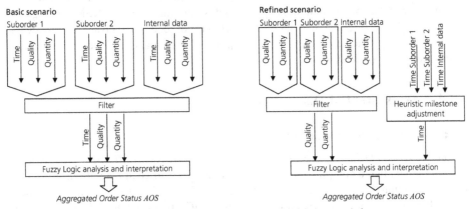

Fig. 4-29. Aggregation of suborders with internal data

A SNEM system relies on a general heuristic mechanism that allows coping with a varying number of input sets as well as incomplete information (see section 4.1.2.5). A filter is used to select the most important SNEM data inputs and forward these to the fuzzy analysis component. Depending on how this filter is configured, the SNEM system reflects individual strategies of supply network partners. A typical strategy is to select worst cases for each type of indicator and forward these to Fuzzy Logic analysis. This constitutes a very precautious strategy. Another possibility is to calculate weighted averages for each indicator (with weights depending on priority of (sub)orders) and thus consider all incoming information at once. In the following, it is assumed that worst cases reflected in separate indicators (e.g. the largest delay or the largest quality deficit) will eventually affect follow-up processes the most. Consequently, a filter for worst cases is proposed for the SNEM concept.

One refinement regardless of the type of filter function is available for aggregation, if data on delays of processes is preprocessed by the optional heuristic milestone adjustment function as proposed in section 4.3.5 (see fig. 4-29, *refined scenario*). This function provides initial forecasts on required milestone adjustments and calculates delays of a monitored order based on estimated delivery dates of its suborders. Results of the heuristic are used as input to calculation of the *AOS*.

### 4.3.3.3    Interpretation                              •

The *AOS* is an individual assessment of a monitored order's situation which incorporates different status aspects of an order and its relevant suborders. The *AOS* is calculated whenever new SNEM information becomes available and thus changes over time. The assessment reflects individual valuations and strategies that vary for each supply network partner. It allows to consider heterogeneity of supply network partners regarding their relevant data types (see section 2.1.2.5) as well as their individual strategies which result from their autonomy (see section 2.1.2.4). The *AOS* is one input for deciding on generation of alerts (see section 4.4). An alert represents a message $M_s$ to satisfy the implicit demand $D_q$ which is needed to solve the SNEM problem (see section 2.1.3.3). The *AOS* can be a part of the content of a message $M_s$ and is thus added to the SNEM ontology. A recipient might use it for his own interpretation but is not required to do so, because every supply network partner gathers status data types on his own and analyzes this input according to his own rule systems.

## 4.3.4    Assessment of Disruptive Events

### 4.3.4.1    Disruptive Event Data

Disruptive events *DE* have to be analyzed as to their effect on fulfillment processes, in spite of the fact that a complex model of cause-and-effect for each type of *DE* is not feasible (see section 4.3.1.1). As requested in section 4.3.1.2 a *DE* is analyzed with respect to the planned timeline of the fulfillment processes it affects. Two input values are needed, based on the SNEM data types defined in section 3.1:

- An external classification of a disruptive event's severity is a measurement of severity which is assumed to be defined for each type of *DE* and which is derived for instance from a ranking list with associated severity values (see also section 3.1.3.1). As an example, a machine failure is rated lower than a power outage. For each *DE* a classification value between zero and one is assumed which is referred to as the *Exogenous Disruptive Event Severity (ExDS)*. This severity is independent of the time of occurrence of a *DE* and is fixed.

- The *RemainingTime (RT)* to a planned fulfillment date is considered under the assumption that a *DE* has a larger negative impact on an order's fulfillment the later it occurs in a fulfillment process and the less time for reaction remains. It is defined as the difference between the planned end date of fulfillment of an order and the date of identification of a *DE* by a SNEM system.

In fig. 4-30 these two input values are represented as *linguistic variables* with five *fuzzy sets* each. As in section 4.3.3.1 trapezoid *membership functions* are chosen, and similar arguments as to individual configuration of these *fuzzy sets* apply. In fig. 4-30 cases for *RT* larger than 72 hours or less than -5 hours[25] are considered to be completely true (=1) for the fuzzy set *VeryMuch* (> 72) or respectively *VeryLittle* (< -5).

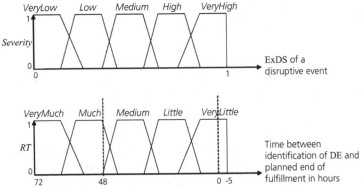

Fig. 4-30. Input variables for disruptive event analysis

### 4.3.4.2 Assessment Rules and Results

Both linguistic input variables *Severity* and *RT* (see fig. 4-30) are assessed by a fuzzy rule set with one resulting linguistic variable, the *Endogenous Disruptive Event Severity (EnDS)*[26]. A part of a potential rule set is depicted in fig. 4-31 (left side).

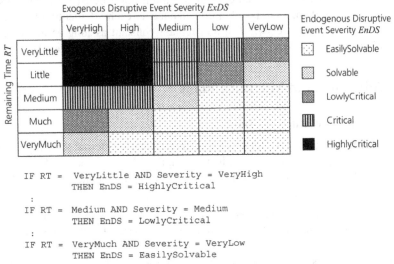

```
IF RT =  VeryLittle AND Severity = VeryHigh
         THEN EnDS = HighlyCritical
  :
IF RT =  Medium AND Severity = Medium
         THEN EnDS = LowlyCritical
  :
IF RT =  VeryMuch AND Severity = VeryLow
         THEN EnDS = EasilySolvable
```

Fig. 4-31. Fuzzy rules for *DE* assessment

---

[25.] A negative *RT* implicates that a process is already delayed when the DE occurs.

Definition of fuzzy rules is affected by the ability of an enterprise to react to disruptive events *DE* (e.g. management skills, flexibility of processes). The rule set defined in fig. 4-31 indicates that an enterprise with this configuration has a very good ability to react to a *DE*, if it has enough time for reaction (based on fig. 4-30 approximately more than 48 hours). However, it has severe problems to take counter measures even for relatively unimportant *DE*s, if these occur very late in a fulfillment process when little time is left for reaction. As mentioned before in section 4.3.3.2, individual constraints and strategies of supply network partners will result in individual rule sets for each network partner's SNEM system.

The final step in the assessment of a disruptive event is calculation of a defuzzified value for the endogenous severity *EnDS*. A value of zero indicates an easily solvable situation, and one a highly critical situation that cannot be coped with.

### 4.3.4.3      Interpretation

The endogenous severity *EnDS* of a disruptive event *DE* reflects a heuristic assessment of the probability to solve the problem that is caused by a *DE* in the remaining planned fulfillment time of an order. A high *EnDS* indicates that propagation of a *DE* to the next supply network level is highly likely, whereas a low *EnDS* characterizes a *DE* that is solvable within an enterprise. Consequently, *EnDS* is used to determine whether a specific *DE* has to be communicated by a supply network partner in a message $M_s$ to its customer, to satisfy the implicit demand $D_q$ [27]. Disruptive events with a low *EnDS* are not communicated, in order to avoid an information overflow on following supply network levels through irrelevant data[28]. *EnDS* is added as an additional concept to the SNEM ontology (see section 3.2.3) and is thus usable in automated communication between SNEM systems. Calculation of an *EnDS* for a *DE* is only initiated once for each *DE* identified by a SNEM system, because its parameters (*ExDS*, *RT*) remain constant as long as no corrections (such as a revision of *ExDS*) occur, in which case a recalculation is initiated.

## 4.3.5    Adjustment of Milestone Plans

### 4.3.5.1      Required Milestone Data

Adjustment of milestone plans, either by using an interface to external scheduling systems (see section 4.3.5.2) or by employing a heuristic approach integrated in a SNEM system (see section 4.3.5.3), have to fulfill similar tasks. They build upon the basic model of pro-

---

[26.]This severity is termed "endogenous" because it is generated within a SNEM system, in contrast to the exogenous severity *ExDS* of a disruptive event which is an external input (see also section 4.3.1.2).

[27.]Since disruptive events will often affect more than one order, though to a varying degree, the *EnDS* concept offers a method to assess implications of *DE*s for specific orders.

[28.]Note, that the requirement for "primacy of local data storage" is also supported by this function (see section 2.2.2.2).

curement, internal fulfillment, and distribution, which sequences external and internal activities (see fig. 4-2 in section 4.1.2.2).

Adjustment of milestone plans focuses on recalculation of start and end dates of processes. Each milestone represents a planned result of an enterprise's internal fulfillment process. As depicted in fig. 4-32 milestones of suborders that are achieved in sourcing activities affect internal fulfillment, for instance $O_2$ as a sourcing order of the manufacturer. However, a suborder for distribution (e.g. $O_3$) only affects the completion date of the superorder ($O_1$) with respect to its final delivery to the customer.

Both, delay of start time and prolonged duration of a sourcing suborder result in the same consequence for internal fulfillment milestones: a later end date of the suborder as depicted in fig. 4-32 (right side) and a later start date for internal processes. All changes in milestones of the sourcing suborders have to be calculated by suborder recipients, in this case the supplier of $O_2$. The manufacturer itself recalculates its own milestones and requests its carrier to reschedule order $O_3$ based on these results. The carrier adjusts its milestones as necessary and communicates changes in the order's end date to its customer (the manufacturer in fig. 4-32).

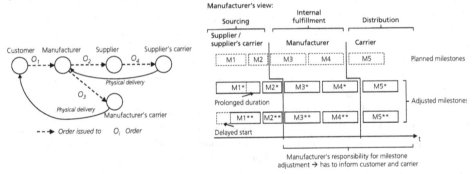

Fig. 4-32. Basic scenario for milestone adjustment

This basic pattern for milestone adjustment relies on several input data types already defined in the SNEM ontology and thus available from a SNEM system (their use is demonstrated in section 4.3.5.3):

- Planned start and end date of a milestone (initial plan)[29]
- Predicted or actual start and end date of a milestone (after milestone adjustment or milestone achievement)
- Flag "finished" that is either true or false for any milestone
- Rank of a milestone - indicates the sequence of milestones within a fulfillment process (e.g. production)
- Planned duration of a milestone (the standard duration that is associated with a milestone and used for forecasts and scheduling can be derived from planned start/end dates)

---

[29.]For simplicity, the term "milestone" is also used as a reference to its associated activities or processes.

It is assumed that disruptive events *DE* are reflected in deviations of these time-oriented data types. Due to the complexity of potential interdependencies between processes and *DE* (see section 4.3.1.1)[30], no explicit link is made between a specific *DE* and a certain delay.

### 4.3.5.2    Interface to Planning Applications

Specialized scheduling applications exist that are focused on certain process types, e.g. production or transportation scheduling. Information as defined in section 4.3.5.1 is provided by a SNEM system for rescheduling. For each scheduling domain different constraints have to be considered by these systems to generate realistic schedules. For instance, production planning considers capacity information (e.g. available resources, setup times of machines) as well as situation dependent information (e.g. work-in-progress, other scheduled orders) (*Stadtler 2002, pp. 182*) for rescheduling an order's production process (*Stadtler 2002, pp. 186*)[31]. This information is managed by each scheduling application individually and need not be provided by a SNEM solution. Typical supply network management tools that integrate planning applications for demand-, production- and distribution-planning are summarized within the term *Advanced Planning Systems (APS) (Fleischmann et al. 2002)*. They rely on data from *Enterprise Resource Planning (ERP)* systems, cover planning aspects such as long-, mid- and short-term planning and offer capabilities to optimize plans within an enterprise and (partly) beyond. An overview of different products from *I2 Technologies, SAP* and *J.D. Edwards* is provided by Meyr (*Meyr et al. 2002*).

To connect a SNEM system to specific planning applications, existing interfaces of these applications have to be used. Typically, a variety of connectors are provided that are based on proprietary message formats, XML-formatted interfaces, or various forms of remote procedure calls. For instance, SAP provides its *BAPI* technology to access functions of its APS system via messages sent by an external system (e.g. a SNEM solution) to the *APO* tool (*SAP 2002, pp 114*). To trigger rescheduling of an order, the business object *ManufactOrderAPS* for instance provides a method *SaveMultiple* that allows changing an order's attributes and initiates rescheduling[32]. Although vendor-specific connectors clearly require definition of individual interfaces to planning applications for each SNEM system, the basic data types relevant for adjusting milestones, as defined in section 4.3.5.1, are main input to define such interfaces. For instance, in the SAP example of the business object *ManufactOrderAPS* a changed start date derived from a delayed milestone for a

---

[30.]Consequently, a disruptive event's effect on a certain milestone will often be identified in a data gathering round later than the *DE* itself. Thus, reactions to a *DE* are triggered, as soon as the *DE* becomes known although the exact consequences of the *DE* are not yet completely observed.

[31.]Constraints for transportation planning are e.g. available transportation resources, routes to be used, or legal restrictions (e.g. holidays). For planning warehouse processes, availability of goods and optimized picking routes are constraints to be considered.

[32.]For details see the *Interface Repository* of SAP (*SAP 2005a*).

certain activity triggers rescheduling when used as a parameter for the *ChangeActivities* method (for details see *SAP 2005a*).

Since rescheduling with an external planning system is considered to be a reaction $R_u$ that is triggered by a message $M_s$ (see section 4.3.1.2), initiation of such a message is part of distributing event management information which is discussed in section 4.4. Consequently, alert mechanisms decide whether rescheduling mechanisms are triggered. This prevents expensive activities for rescheduling in case only small deviations to milestone plans are identified by a SNEM system.

### 4.3.5.3    Heuristic Adjustments

The heuristic to adjust milestones within a SNEM system assumes that all milestones for a process type are defined in one sequence which applies to the generic supply network processes as defined in section 3.1.1.3 and considered in the SNEM ontology[33]. It does not consider constraints that are used by scheduling applications (e.g. resource capacities) for effectively replanning the fulfillment activities as part of their reaction $R_u$. In fig. 4-33 the overall process of heuristic adjustments for one enterprise is depicted. It provides an intuitive assessment of the impact of delays in fulfillment processes on an order's fulfillment, similar to what a human actor can derive from SNEM data without considering further planning constraints. As long as no adjustments have been conducted for an order, the initially planned start and end dates are used. Otherwise, predicted and/or actual start/ end dates as defined in section 4.3.5.1 are utilized.

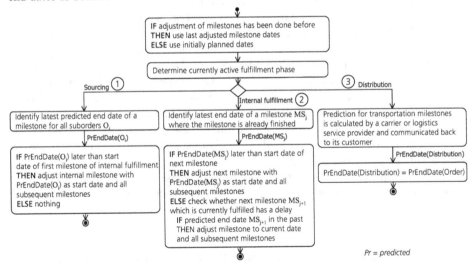

Fig. 4-33. Milestone adjustment based on fulfillment phase

---

[33.]Alternatives modeled in the transportation process are neglected, since they effectively result in one sequential flow of milestones with multiple instances of similar milestones.

The heuristic distinguishes between the three fulfillment phases *Sourcing, Internal fulfillment* and *Distribution*:

1. *Sourcing* - For all sourcing suborders of an order the latest predicted end date is determined. This is compared with the predicted start date of the first internal milestone of the order. In case this start date is before the predicted end of any sourcing order, all internal milestones are shifted, based on the predicted end of the sourcing phase. An example can be derived from fig. 4-32.

2. *Internal fulfillment* - During internal fulfillment[34] the latest internal milestone $MS_j$ already finished is identified, and its achieved end date is compared to the predicted start date of the next milestone $MS_{j+1}$. For a start date of $MS_{j+1}$ before the predicted end of its predecessor $MS_j$ a similar adjustment as above for *Sourcing* is conducted. In the other case, it is still possible that the currently active process associated with milestone $MS_{j+1}$ encounters a disruptive event which delays its achievement. This is definitely the case, if the predicted end of $MS_{j+1}$ is already in the past. In that case, since no other information is available, the new predicted end date of $MS_{j+1}$ is set to the current date[35].

3. *Distribution* - During the last phase of distribution any delay is considered by the responsible carrier or logistics service provider himself and is communicated to the SNEM system of the customer who issued the distribution suborder.

Shifting of start and end dates of a milestone is in reality constrained by daily working hours and holidays[36]. The SNEM heuristic can consider working hours, if it implements an algorithm as depicted in fig. 4-34. For any milestone to be adjusted, the working time $WT$ is calculated for the start day ($WT_{StartDay}$) based on the start time of the milestone and the end of work at this day. If this time span is larger than the planned duration of the milestone, the new predicted end date of the milestone is calculated by adding its planned duration to its start time. Otherwise, a remaining working time $WT_{Remaining}$ for this milestone is calculated, and a day counter $DC$ is increased by one. The currently remaining working time for the milestone $WT_{Remaining}$ is then compared to the standard working time $WT_{Standard}$ available each day. A positive difference repeats calculating a new remaining waiting time $WT_{Remaining}$ for the milestone and an additional increase of $DC$ (see cycle in fig. 4-34). Else, a new predicted end of the milestone is calculated based on $DC$ and $WT_{Remaining}$ (see fig. 4-34).

This algorithm can also consider holidays, if the increase of the day counter $DC$ is always followed by a validation mechanism that checks whether the date indicated by $DC$

---

[34] Internal fulfillment depicts the situation where all sourcing suborders are finished (data flag "Finished", see section 4.3.5.1) and distribution has not yet begun.

[35] This underestimates the delay but is corrected in a later monitoring cycle when the milestone is actually achieved. Note that the SNEM system cannot identify a delay in a currently active process for an internal milestone, if the predicted end date of the milestone is not yet achieved.

[36] Note that further restrictions such as availability of resources or conflicts with other orders are not considered in this heuristic planning algorithm.

is a holiday. If a holiday is encountered $DC$ is increased once more and the validation conducted again.

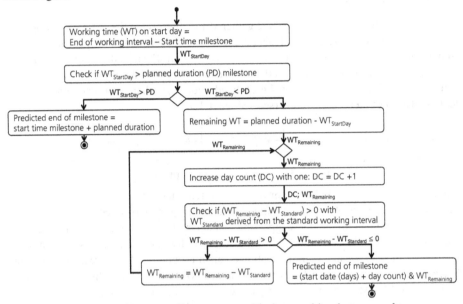

Fig. 4-34. Milestone adjustment considering working hours per day

Concluding, the proposed heuristic enables to assess required milestone adjustments based on available SNEM data. However, it does not provide true managerial reactions that change for instance production schedules. This is only provided as a reaction $R_u$ which can be triggered by a SNEM system through an alert message $M_s$ as described in section 4.4. Thus, the heuristic is considered as an optional add-on not required to provide basic SNEM capabilities.

## 4.4  Distribution of Event Data

SNEM data that has been analyzed as proposed in section 4.3 is distributed to actors within a company and to partners in supply networks to satisfy the SNEM requirement for flexible distribution of SNEM data (see section 2.2.2.6). This is the final activity to satisfy the implicit demand $D_q$ identified in section 2.1.3. By satisfying this demand with proactive alert messages $M_s$, reactions $R_u$ are triggered to reduce the negative effects of identified disruptive events $DE$[37].

---

[37.]Reactions which are triggered by such messages are conducted outside of the boundaries of a
  SNEM system and are not part of the information logistics task fulfilled by a SNEM solution.

## 4.4.1    Alert Management Process

### 4.4.1.1    Overview

A basic process to proactively distribute gathered and interpreted SNEM data is proposed in fig. 4-35. Results of the data analysis functions (see section 4.3) for a specific order are used as input to decide whether an alert is necessary at all. Besides the actual situation of an order, further information (e.g. on the importance of a customer or priority of an order) influences this decision (see section 4.4.2). In addition, a mechanism for situation-dependent escalation of alerts is included (see section 4.4.3).

Fig. 4-35. Alert management process

Any alert is to be directed to an actor or an IT-system that is able to react upon the alert information it receives. As part of communication management (see section 2.2.2) receivers are identified that are able to trigger and manage reactions to minimize the effects of disruptive events $DE$ (see section 4.4.4). For every individual recipient a selection of an appropriate media type and communication channel is conducted. Before an alert is sent, the content of the alert is selected from potentially available content which is defined by the available SNEM data for an order (see section 4.4.5). The communicated content is mainly restricted by the selected media type (e.g. a short message to a mobile phone is based on a reduced set of SNEM data types) and an enterprise-specific information policy.

### 4.4.1.2    Internal and External Alerts

For any SNEM system a distinction between alerts to internal recipients inside the enterprise and to network partners on other levels of a supply network is relevant. Internal alerts are directed to human actors (e.g. transportation managers, production planners) or IT-systems (e.g. scheduling systems, see section 4.3.5.2) that can react to critical incidents identified by a SNEM system. Regarding human actors, various recipients at different organizational levels and departments have an interest in SNEM alerts, depending on the criticality of an order, the severity of a disruptive event, and the actors' abilities to trigger reactions $R_u$. A SNEM system utilizes knowledge on organizational hierarchies and chooses recipients (including IT-systems) autonomously, based on the current situation of an order (see fig. 4-36).

The objective of internal alerts is to prevent propagation of negative effects of disruptive events $DE$ to customers and further levels within a supply network. Use of different media types as indicated in section 4.4.1.1 is an integral part of this strategy. For instance, major alerts are sent based on media types such as mobile communication technologies which assure faster reception of an alert than a normal email.

To satisfy the implicit demand $D_q$ of supply network partners for information on disruptive events $DE$, external alerts are required. These are communicated in the same way as responses to status requests (see section 4.1.2.4)[38]. Another SNEM system at the customer's site (*manufacturer*) analyzes incoming alert information with respect to the customer's processes. Hence, the customer receives an alert trigger $TE_{AT}$ as defined in section 4.1.1.

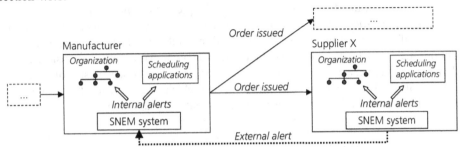

Fig. 4-36. Internal and external alerts

Each supply network partner is responsible for relating external alert information to its internal personnel if necessary. For this task it can use the same structures required for internal alerts (see fig. 4-36). This architecture respects the autonomy and heterogeneity of supply network partners (see sections 2.1.2.4 and 2.1.2.5), because every partner is responsible to individually configure its internal organizational responsibilities without any need to publish this information for use by other network partners[39]. Interaction between two companies regarding the exchange of alerts is reduced to an exchange of messages $M_s$ between two SNEM systems. Consequently, interfaces between supply network partners are minimized since only one standardized interface to each SNEM system (or similar applications) at customers' sites is required.

## 4.4.2  Alert Decision Management

### 4.4.2.1  Alert Index

The first step in the alert management process in fig. 4-35 requires a decision whether to generate any alert for a certain order. Data considered in this decision encompasses results of the Fuzzy Logic data analysis proposed in section 4.3 and further information such as the priority of an order. Similar to the heuristic approach to data analysis, this decision process - if conducted by a human actor - is based on *perceptions* of an order's situation and the current situation of its environment. Therefore, the same arguments as in section 4.3.2 apply and an approach based on Fuzzy Logic is proposed. The basic mechanism em-

---

[38.]Essentially every response to a status request is created the same way as an alert, with the difference that an alert is sent depending on the criticality of an order while a status request always has to be answered. However, the same mechanisms e.g. for information policy are applied to both (see section 4.4.5.2).

[39.]In case external alerts would have to be directed to specific actors or organizational units, each supply network partner would have to model at least parts of the organizational hierarchy of its customers.

ploys a two-step Fuzzy Logic process (see fig. 4-37). It results in an abstract metric value termed *Alert Index AI* that is used in subsequent steps to decide on generation of an alert and to determine recipients and media types.

Input values for the *AI* as depicted in fig. 4-37 represent examples of potential inputs: the *Aggregated Order Status AOS* and the maximum *Endogenous Disruptive Event Severity EnDS* of all new disruptive events *DE* identified in the last data gathering round (see sections 4.3.3 and 4.3.4). Additional data types that a company wants to consider for its alert generation (e.g. a customer's rating) are incorporated in the second step of the Fuzzy Logic analysis. Every enterprise is free to decide which analytical results from SNEM data and which additional data types it integrates in its alert decision.

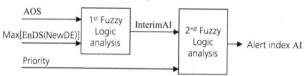

Fig. 4-37. Calculation of an alert index

Fuzzy sets for these input values are represented for instance by trapezoid membership functions similar to those in sections 4.3.3.1 and 4.3.4.1: For all linguistic variables it is feasible that the values of each input variable can be exclusively attributed to a specific type of perception within a certain range (e.g. an *AOS* between 0.45 and 0.55 is *medium*, with a value of 1.0 and all other fuzzy sets with 0.0). The output linguistic value (both the interim result and the final result) for the alert index *AI* is categorized into five classes with respective fuzzy sets for a base variable between zero and one. Definition of these classes is based on a standard definition for event notification messages in computer networks (*Lonvick 2001*)[40]. An adaptation of the definition to the supply network domain is depicted in fig. 4-38.

| Alert | Action must be taken immediately |
|---|---|
| Critical | Critical fulfillment condition with high impact |
| Error | Significant fulfillment problems with medium impact |
| Warning | Slight fulfillment problems with low impact |
| Notice | Mainly normal fulfillment without negative impact |

Fig. 4-38. Categories for alert index

A two-step stacked Fuzzy Logic process is chosen to limit the complexity of the fuzzy rule sets[41]. A fuzzy rule set for the first step is depicted in fig. 4-39 on the left side. It represents

---

[40] In the BSD syslog protocol described by Lonvick (*Lonvick 2001*) three more levels are suggested. Two deliver standard messages for debugging and regular process fulfillment. A third indicates a complete breakdown of the computer system. These levels are not considered for SNEM because neither standard messages are required nor is an alert realistic, if a company "breaks down" completely (e.g. induced by a natural disaster).

[41] This is possible because integration of additional data such as an order's priority is mainly independent of an order's current alert status, as represented by the *InterimAI*.

a very precautious strategy regarding the condition of an order. Primarily, it considers severe disruptive events (*VeryHigh EnDS*) as very important and thus raises the alert index *AI* to the highest level (*Alert*), even if the corresponding aggregated order status *AOS* is very high.

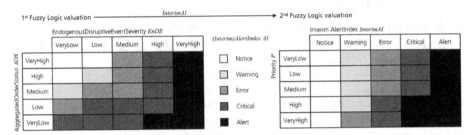

Fig. 4-39. Rule set for alert index (first step)

The strategy is justified under the assumption that a newly discovered severe disruptive event *DE* has not yet affected an order's status data, and its negative consequences thus have not yet been measured. However, effects on status data will be reflected in future data gathering rounds, but the *AI* is raised instantaneously to a very high level which allows to consider reactions $R_u$ even before any negative consequences of the *DE* are encountered. Calculation of an *InterimAI* also has to cope with the case where no new *DEs* are identified by a SNEM system in a data gathering round. In this case the *Aggregated Order Status AOS* solely characterizes the situation of a monitored order. Thus, the first step of the analysis is reduced to a simpler calculation of an *InterimAI*, with $InterimAI = 1 - AOS$ [42].

The second Fuzzy Logic step is independent of the first step. In fig. 4-39 (right side) a strategy is depicted where a company values some orders higher than others, depending on their priority. Combined with the first step in fig. 4-39 any *InterimAI* that is at least rated with *Error* is promoted to the next *AI* level for all orders the *Priority P* of which is at least *High*. For orders with *Medium* or even lower priority the *InterimAI* is not adjusted. The data type *Priority P* of an order is a value that can be defined in numerous ways. It is determined outside a SNEM system by each supply network partner. Important sources for definition of an order's priority are e.g. marketing and sales departments that have data and strategies in place to define order priorities. Some possible input values that can be considered in an order's priority are: sales revenues with a customer, profit margin of an order, service level agreements with customers, or duration of a relationship with a customer (long-term vs. ad-hoc). Ideally, a standardized value for an order's priority is provided that is for instance calculated based on a multi-dimensional scoring model (see also section 4.4.5.2).

---

[42.] The *AOS* is defined between zero and one with one being a perfect order. An alert index *AI* between zero and one, where larger values reflect an increased necessity to generate alerts, is thus the inverse value *1-AOS*.

After the second Fuzzy Logic step a defuzzification mechanism provides a metrical value between zero and one. This final result of the Fuzzy Logic mechanism represents the alert index before escalation which is termed $AI_{BeforedEsc}$.

### 4.4.2.2    Alert Decision

The decision whether an alert is generated at all - either internal or external - requires rules that set global minimum thresholds for the alert index $AI_{BeforedEsc}$. Two possible rules with *Threshold2 > Threshold1* are:

```
IF AIBeforeEsc > Threshold1 THEN send internal alert
IF AIBeforeEsc > Threshold2 THEN send external alert
```

Based on this configuration, internal alerts are generated in more cases than external alerts, which reflects an attitude that many minor problems during fulfillment can be handled without affecting and alerting external partners. Consequently, customers are only informed of major problems. Depending on the frequency of data gathering rounds (see section 4.1.2.2) an alert index *AI* is calculated quite often. However, if an order's situation has not changed, alerts are not to be sent for every update round, in order to prevent repeated alerts. Thus, an *Allowed Reaction Time ART* is considered by a SNEM system that guarantees a certain time for taking reactions on a previous alert before an update of an alert is sent (see fig. 4-40). In the example an alert index *AI* calculated at $t_1$ does not trigger a new alert, as long as neither a new disruptive event nor a significant change in the alert index compared to the last update round has been identified.

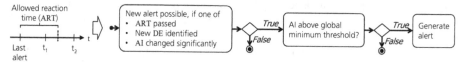

Fig. 4-40. Allowed reaction time and alert decision

However, at time $t_2$ a new alert is created as long as the *AI* is above a global minimum threshold (see fig. 4-40). This alert is considered to be a reminder that some serious situation has obviously not improved and has probably not been managed yet.

To realize this alert decision process, *ART* has to be calculated which requires information on historic alert index calculations for an order (e.g. date of last generated alert). A specific historic record of an order is in the following referred to as an *Alert History Item* $AHI_j$. An $AHI_j$ with its attributes is depicted in table 4-4: Each $AHI_j$ is identified by the $AHI\_ID$ and associated with a specific order $O_i$ (*OrderID*) and referred to as $AHI_j(O_i)$. Multiple $AHI_j(O_i)$ for the same order $O_i$ with $j = 1...n$ for $n$ different points in time form a sequenced story of an order's alert history. An *AHI* is only created, if an alert is generated.

Within an *AHI* the attributes *DateOfCalculation* and *TimeOfCalculation* indicate when the $AHI_j(O_i)$ has been generated. This information is used to calculate the *Allowed Reaction Time ART* based on the last *AHI* of an order and a predefined duration of *ART*. The attribute *NewDE* is set to *True*, if any new disruptive events which affect order $O_i$ have first been identified in the update round which resulted in this $AHI_j(O_i)$.

| AHI_ ID | Order ID | DateOf Calculation | TimeOf Calcula- tion | New DE | $AI_{BeforeEsc}$ | $AI_{Fin}$ | Reci- pient list |
|---------|----------|---------------------|----------------------|--------|------------------|-----------|------------------|
| 1 | 7593 | 2004-07-22 | 14:55 | True | 0.77 | 0.82 | ... |

Table 4-4. Alert history item

Two alert indices $AI$ are stored in an $AHI_j(O_i)$: the $AI_{BeforeEsc}$, which is the result of the fuzzy analysis steps presented in section 4.4.2.1, and a final alert index $AI_{Fin}$ that is increased, if an escalation is necessary (see section 4.4.3.1). In the example an escalation of 0.05 has been added to $AI_{BeforeEsc}$. To determine whether an alert index $AI$ has changed significantly (see fig. 4-40), the $AI_{BeforeEsc}$ of the last known $AHI_j(O_i)$ is compared to the current alert index $AI$ after Fuzzy Logic analysis. The alert index $AI$ is used to determine recipients of an alert and media types to transmit alerts (see section 4.4.4). All selected recipients are stored in an additional attribute of the $AHI$.

## 4.4.3   Escalation Management

### 4.4.3.1   Rationale for Escalation Management

A SNEM system regularly gathers updates of SNEM data for each of its monitored orders as well as the respective active suborders (see section 4.1.2.2), and alert management is initiated for each update. Thus, the alert history of an order can be taken into account because it reflects an order's development over time. For instance, if no improvement of an order's status after identification of a disruptive event is realized in due time, previous alerts influence decisions to warn higher organizational levels and initiate additional managerial reaction. Escalation mechanisms also provide the ability to choose other more direct communication channels to contact human actors. An initial alert might for instance be based on an asynchronous channel such as email while an escalated alert is sent as a short-message or even a call to a mobile phone which assures fast reception of the alert.

Two escalation types are distinguished: implicit and explicit escalation both of which increase the alert index $AI$ (see fig. 4-41). Finally, the escalated alert index $AI_{Fin}$ is used to identify recipients of an alert based on the following rule: The higher $AI_{Fin}$, the higher is a recipient's organizational level and/or the more direct is a chosen communication channel (for details see section 4.4.4):

- *Implicit escalation:* A deterioration of an order's situation that calls for an escalation is represented for instance by a lower $AOS$ or new and severe $DEs$. They result in an automated increase of interim values of the alert index $AI$ (*InterimAI* and $AI_{BeforeEsc}$) due to the Fuzzy Logic calculations (see section 4.4.2.1). Thus, escalation is implicitly realized by the Fuzzy Logic algorithms.
- *Explicit escalation:* The historic context of an order is analyzed and compared with its current situation. In case certain conditions apply (e.g. a low order status has not

improved), different escalation levels are defined that increase the alert index $AI_{BeforeEsc}$ with predefined values to a final alert index $AI_{Fin}$. This is not covered by the Fuzzy Logic calculations, and an additional mechanism is required to explicitly escalate $AI_{BeforeEsc}$. Explicit escalation is only conducted, if the alert decision (see section 4.4.2.2) is positive (see fig. 4-41).

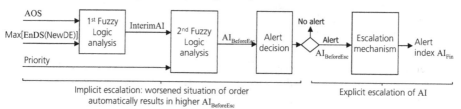

Fig. 4-41. Variants of escalation

### 4.4.3.2 Escalation Mechanism

The escalation mechanism indicated in fig. 4-41 is not based on Fuzzy Logic because escalation levels and corresponding increases of $AI_{BeforeEsc}$ are defined in discrete steps. A discrete mechanism assures that escalation to another organizational level is definitely realized. An algorithm is proposed that consists of several steps which define whether an alert history item $AHI_j(O_i)$ is considered for escalation of a certain order or not (see fig. 4-42).

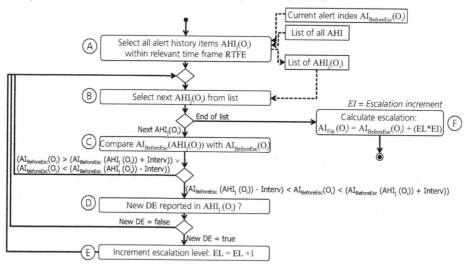

Fig. 4-42. Escalation algorithm

A few parameters illustrated in fig. 4-43 are required which are subsequently used in the escalation algorithm. Besides the *Allowed Reaction Time (ART)* that is introduced in section 4.4.2.2 a second time interval termed *Relevant Time Frame for Escalation (RTFE)* is defined. *RTFE* ensures that very old alert history items *AHI* are not considered for escalation. It is assumed that after a longer period of time (e.g. a couple of days) the probability is very high for a critical situation to have been taken care of already. Thus, the *AHI* can no longer be directly related to any current critical *AOS* and shall not be considered for escalation[43].

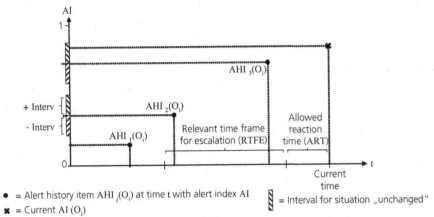

Fig. 4-43. Parameters for escalation management

This selection in step (A) of the algorithm (see fig. 4-42) is also illustrated in fig. 4-43 where two alert history items $AHI_2(O_i)$ and $AHI_3(O_i)$ are further considered for the escalation algorithm and $AHI_1(O_i)$ is omitted. The resulting list of *AHI* is iteratively assessed in steps (B) to (E) of the algorithm.

In step (B) an alert history item is selected from the list of $AHI_j(O_i)$. Subsequently in steps (C) and (D) two conditions are checked (see fig. 4-42). If both conditions apply, a counter for an *Escalation level EL* is increased by one:

1. The relative change of the historic unadjusted $AI_{BeforeEsc}$ (of the *AHI*) to the current $AI_{BeforeEsc}$ is minimal. This is defined by the interval *Interv* that is set around the historic $AI_{BeforeEsc}$ (step (C)). In fig. 4-43 this applies solely to $AHI_3(O_i)$.
2. In the currently selected alert history item *AHI* an identification of a new *DE* is documented (step (D)) based on the *AHI* attribute *NewDE* (see table 4-4). In the example of fig. 4-43 this is assumed for $AHI_3(O_i)$, and the escalation level *EL* for $O_i$ is increased by one, in compliance with step (E) of the algorithm in fig. 4-42.

For the first condition (step (C)) the following reasoning applies: If the current $AI_{BeforeEsc}$ is very different from a historic $AI_{BeforeEsc}$ no need for an explicit escalation is found. Either an improvement has taken place which forbids escalation or a severe deterioration is reflected in an increased $AI_{BeforeEsc}$ and an implicit escalation has already been realized (see section 4.4.3.1). Only relatively small changes in a situation require consideration of historic situations for escalation.

---

[43.]In case a severe *DE* has a very long lasting effect on an order, this will be reflected in the order's aggregated status (*AOS*). The *AOS* will decrease over time, because follow-up process steps are continuously affected. As a result the *AI* for the order will decline which leads to an implicit escalation as defined in section 4.4.3.1.

However, not all of the $AHI_j(O_i)$ which indicate a relatively stable critical situation are allowed to increase the escalation level $EL$. Otherwise, a simple update of SNEM data would always result in an escalation. Since different and sometimes frequent data gathering cycles are possible in a SNEM system, escalation would solely depend on the number of update rounds and the allowed reaction time $ART$. This problem is taken care of by the second condition (step (D)). Only those $AHI$ where a new disruptive event is identified are considered for escalation. The reasoning behind this is that a critical situation of an order due to a specific disruptive event, which was identified in the past and which required managerial reactions, should have improved. Thus, the current $AI_{BeforeEsc}$ had to be lower but this is not the case (see condition in step (C)). Consequently, some other reaction has to be initiated which occurs by sending an alert e.g. to a higher organizational level. The escalation level $EL$ is increased by one (step (E) in fig. 4-42).

After all alert history items in the selected list have been tested, a final adjustment of the current $AI_{BeforeEsc}$ to $AI_{Fin} = AI_{BeforeEsc}(O_i) + (EL \times EI)$ is conducted. The Escalation increment $EI$ is a predefined increment which represents the increase in an alert index $AI$ associated with a single escalation level.

In fig. 4-44 an example is presented for the use of the escalation algorithm. The first row contains the first alert history item for order 8473 for which no historic data is yet available but a $DE$ is identified. Thus no escalation is possible: $AI_{Fin}$ is identical to $AI_{BeforeEsc}$. A day later a SNEM data update is created but no new $DEs$ are identified. However, the situation has neither improved nor deteriorated much: It remains within the interval $Interv$. Because of the previous $AHI$ ($ID$=234) where a $DE$ was identified both conditions for step (C) and (D) of the escalation algorithm apply, and the escalation level $EL$ is increased by one. Consequently, $AI_{BeforeEsc}$ is increased according to $EL \times EI = 1 \cdot 0.05$ by 0.05 and results in $AI_{Fin}$= 0.76 . On the third day (2004-07-19) a second $DE$ is identified with the escalation level $EL = 1$ as before. On day four the $AI_{BeforeEsc}$ is escalated two levels, because the situation has still not improved, with all $AHI_j(O_i)$ in the $RTFE$ range. Since two of the $AHI$ have identified new $DEs$ ($NewDE$=True), the escalation level $EL = 2$ results in an alert index $AI_{Fin}$ of 0.82.

| | AHI_ID | OrderID | DateOfCalculation | TimeOfCalc. | NewDE | $AI_{BeforeEscal}$ | $AI_{Final}$ | ... |
|---|---|---|---|---|---|---|---|---|
| ① | 234 | 8473 | 2004-07-17 | 12:14 | yes | 0.7 | 0.7 | ... |
| ② | 253 | 8473 | 2004-07-18 | 13:23 | no | 0.71 | 0.76 | ... |
| ③ | 269 | 8473 | 2004-07-19 | 12:35 | yes | 0.73 | 0.78 | ... |
| ④ | 286 | 8473 | 2004-07-20 | 13:11 | no | 0.72 | 0.82 | ... |

ART = 12 hours
RTFE = 4 days
Interv = 0.05
EI = 0.05

Fig. 4-44. Example for escalation

## 4.4.4    Selection of Recipient and Media Type

### 4.4.4.1    Recipient Hierarchy

Following a positive alert decision and the escalation mechanism (see sections 4.4.2 and 4.4.3), the selection of recipients for an alert is triggered. This selection requires a model of available recipients in an organization[44]. The notion of "roles" allows defining responsibilities in an organization without directly specifying actors for these responsibilities. An actor is either a human actor or an IT-system (e.g. a scheduling application). Actors are assigned to roles as depicted in the data model in fig. 4-45.

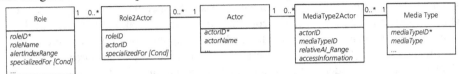

Fig. 4-45. Data model for selection of recipients and media type

Each actor in a company can have various roles (e.g. a person can be responsible for distribution planning and for hiring new personnel)[45]. An organizational role is more stable over time than the assignment of actors to a specific role, because new assignments of actors to a job are common. These organizational changes are easily reflected in the data model (relation *Role2Actor*). For each role an applicable interval of the alert index *AI* (*alertIndexRange*) is defined (e.g. [0.4; 0.7]). The interval is interpreted by a SNEM system as a rule of the following type:

```
IF AI within alertIndexRange(Role(i)) THEN Role(i) = recipient
```

A role that applies to this rule is used to find applicable actors that fulfill this role by searching in the relation *Role2Actor*. Hierarchical levels of an organization are represented on the role level by different values for the *alertIndexRange* of each role.

Table *Role*

| roleID | roleName | alertIndexRange | specializedFor |
|---|---|---|---|
| R1 | Production planner | 0.2; 1.0 | OrderType = production |
| R2 | Production director | 0.7; 1.0 | OrderType = production |
| R3 | Transportation planner | 0.35; 1.0 | OrderType = transportation |
| R4 | PPS function | 0.5; 1.0 | OrderType = production |
| ... | | ... | ... |

Table *Role2Actor*

| roleID | actorID | specializedFor |
|---|---|---|
| R1 | A2 | - |
| R2 | A1 | - |
| R3 | A3 | Destination = Asia |
| R3 | A4 | Destination = America |
| R4 | A5 | - |
| ... | ... | ... |

Table *MediaType*

| mediaTypeID | mediaType |
|---|---|
| M1 | Website (HTML) |
| M2 | Filetransfer (XML) |
| M3 | Email |
| M4 | Mobile phone |
| M5 | Fax |
| ... | ... |

Table *MediaType2Actor*

| actorID | mediaTypeID | relativeAI_Range | accessInformation |
|---|---|---|---|
| A2 | M3 | 0.0; 1.0 | Miller@produc.com |
| A2 | M4 | 0.5; 1.0 | +491713423421 |
| A1 | M5 | 0.0; 1.0 | +49911345-54 |
| A1 | M4 | 0.5; 1.0 | +49911345-73 |
| A5 | M2 | 0.0; 1.0 | BAPI_APO@Comp |
| ... | ... | ... | ... |

Table *Actor*

| actorID | actorName |
|---|---|
| A1 | Smith |
| A2 | Miller |
| A3 | Baker |
| A4 | Parker |
| A5 | APS tool |
| ... | ... |

Fig. 4-46. Example for data on recipients and media types

[44.]Note that only internal recipients of a company are modeled within a SNEM system, because for external alerts it is assumed that a corresponding SNEM system receives the alert and distributes it within its organization (see section 4.4.1.2). External alerts are sent in the same format as responses to status requests as defined in section 4.1.2.4. For technical details see section 5.3.2.2.

[45.]Additional attributes are possible for relations *Role, Actor* and *MediaType* but not of importance to the selection process. Possible additions are e.g. documentation, address/location of an actor or basic technical configurations for a media type such as a server address.

In the example in fig. 4-46 the superior role *Production director* is only warned if the *AI* is larger than 0.7, whereas the *Production planner* is warned beginning with 0.2. This role model does not require explicit representation of hierarchical interdependencies which limits its complexity. However, basic hierarchical structures can be represented (see above) and further refinement is achieved based on specific features of an order for which an alert is to be generated: The condition *specializedFor* allows to restrict applicability of a role for an alert, based on individually configurable conditions that refer to certain order attributes $OA_n$. An example in fig. 4-46 is the role *Transportation planner* which only applies to orders of the *OrderType transportation*. Conditions may be defined upon all available SNEM data types, but data types used to define critical profiles $CCP_j$ are especially well suited since they point to sources of a disruptive event *DE* (see section 4.2.1.1). Thus, a role that is responsible for an organizational unit where a *DE* has occurred, is selected for an alert. In fig. 4-46 the roles *R1* to *R4* are differentiated by the *OrderType* into production and transportation related roles.

In the *Role2Actor* relation a *spezializedFor* condition is used to further restrict selection to actors who are specialized on certain subtypes of orders. In the example in fig. 4-46 the two actors *Baker (A3)* and *Parker (A4)* both are assigned to the role of a transportation planner responsible for transportation orders, but one is responsible for the region Asia and the other for America. For a transportation order where SNEM data on a destination is available, the SNEM system automatically selects the actor responsible for the appropriate region[46]. Besides human actors, IT systems for rescheduling might be available in an enterprise, and a SNEM system relates information for planning and scheduling tasks to such systems (see section 4.3.5.2). If direct communication via file-transfer or remote function call (RFC) with such systems is possible (e.g. an *Advanced Planning System APS* with a defined interface for triggering a rescheduling task as described in section 4.3.5.2), these systems are represented as specific actors and related to applicable roles. Technical details of alert communication between a SNEM system and another IT system is defined by the associated media type of this IT system which is for instance based on an XML file-transfer (see below).

### 4.4.4.2   Media Type Hierarchy

Following the selection of recipients an appropriate media type is chosen by a SNEM system (see fig. 4-35) based on the *MediaType2Actor* relationship (see fig. 4-45). Various media types can be associated with an actor, and each actor defines its individual hierarchy of media types with the attribute *relativeAI_Range*. In fig. 4-46 actor *Miller (A2)* chooses *Email* as the basic media type which is applicable for each alert directed to him (*relativeAI_Range*: [0.0; 1.0]). The mobile phone used to send short-message alerts is only to be used in addition, and only for severe alerts[47] with an alert index $AI > 0.6$.

---

[46.]The SNEM system ensures that an actor receives only one alert per SNEM data gathering and analysis update round for each order, even if the actor covers multiple roles for which multiple *alertIndexRanges* exist that are covered by the alert index.

Some basic media types are depicted in fig. 4-46 which incorporate traditional tele-communications (Fax), Internet-based channels, and mobile communication. Further media types can be integrated into a SNEM system with the single restriction that an interface for the communication channel has to be integrated into the SNEM system.

## 4.4.5  Selection of Content

### 4.4.5.1   Media Type Constraints

The final step before transmitting an alert is to select content $C_p$ for the alert message $M_s$ (see fig. 4-35) from available SNEM data which was gathered and analyzed as described in previous sections 4.1 to 4.3. Main restrictions for internal alerts arise from media types and their requirements regarding scope and format of content $C_p$. External alerts are not further considered here, because alerts use the same mechanisms as responses to status requests (see section 4.1.2.4). Since SNEM data is defined in the SNEM ontology and stored in a machine-readable format, a conversion into other formats required for internal alerts is possible as indicated in fig. 4-47.

Mobile communication often restricts the amount of information that can be transmitted in one message. For instance, a short-message template only considers selected data types to characterize an order's status such as the current alert index $AI$, aggregated order status $AOS$ and number of newly identified disruptive events (see fig. 4-47). Definition of templates is also needed to define email messages or other text-based media types (e.g. websites). Integration with other IT-systems, for instance to reschedule activities and milestones, requires tool-specific data templates into which SNEM data types are inserted and which are transmitted to the IT-systems interface. A schematic example is indicated by the XML-file in fig. 4-47.

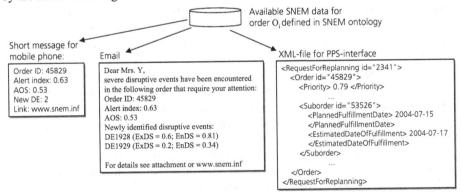

Fig. 4-47. Content for various media types

---

[47.]The relative interval of the media type is applied to the absolut *alertIndexRange* of the respective role. In the example the relative interval [0.5;1.0] is applied to the *alertIndexRange* [0.2;1.0] which results in an effective interval for use of a mobile phone between 0.6 and 1.0.

#### 4.4.5.2      Information Policy

External alerts as well as responses to status requests (see section 4.1.2.4) are directed to supply network partners' SNEM systems (see section 4.4.1.2). Each supply network partner retains its ability to control information it communicates to other external partners as part of its security strategy. A SNEM system supports such a strategy by enabling an information policy which restricts clearance for information transmission depending on the external recipient[48]. To select data, two dimensions are proposed for a SNEM system: First, "importance" of a customer is considered which might be reflected in an order's priority as presented in section 4.4.2.1, because a plausible strategy is to offer higher-value information to important customers. Second, a certain level of trust among partners is necessary to freely communicate potentially sensitive information. These two dimensions are calculated outside a SNEM system since input data is primarily gathered within marketing and sales departments. Related analytical tasks are fulfilled within these departments. In fig. 4-48 possible data inputs for calculation of both indices are depicted:

1.  Typical data inputs for calculation of customer importance are ABC-analyses on revenues or profit contribution generated by a customer. Examination of a customer's lifecycle is also used to determine importance, e.g. for early lifecycle stages an increase in future sales is predicted. For further details on these concepts see e.g. Hunsel (*Hunsel et al. 2000*) and Cornelsen (*Cornelsen 2000*).

2.  Measuring levels of trust is complex, because trust is primarily a qualitative and at most ordinally measurable concept for which reliable data is hardly available. Some approaches consider buying patterns of customers and their willingness to cooperate. They measure available customer feedback and intensity of communication with a customer. Any relationship between the level of trust and these indicators is assumed to be as follows: The more regular and intense buying patterns are, the more dependent is a customer on a supplier and the higher is the trust level for a customer. Regarding communication with customers and feedback intensity, a higher level indicates better knowledge of the customer and therefore a sound basis for a higher level of trust. For details see Thelen (*Thelen et al. 2000*) and Tomczak (*Tomczak et al. 2001*).

An operationalized indicator set is for instance based on a multi-dimensional scoring model and provided externally to a SNEM system (see above). A SNEM system defines a portfolio based on these indicator inputs. All potentially available SNEM data types are located according to their associated minimum levels of customer importance and trust (see fig. 4-48). These thresholds are defined individually by every enterprise and reflect its information policy. Given specific indicators for a customer, a portfolio as indicated in fig. 4-48 is created that defines all SNEM data types possibly transmitted to a customer in case of an alert or a response to a status request (see section 4.1.2.4). In the example *Esti-*

---

[48.]This information policy also applies to responses on status requests of network partners discussed in section 4.1.2.4. An integrated approach for these functions is presented in section 5.4.2.3.

*matedMilestoneDates* are not to be communicated to the specific *customer X*, presumably to prevent giving him insight into internal fulfillment processes.

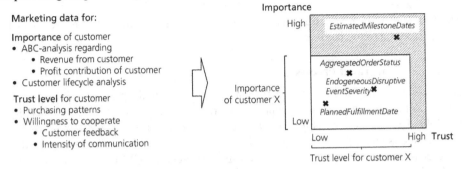

Fig. 4-48. Information policy

The information policy feature of a SNEM system is an element that supports autonomy of supply network partners and increases acceptance of SNEM systems. Each partner can individually define its degree of transmitted data and thereby adhere to possible concerns within a company when implementing a SNEM system.

## 4.5 Event Management Process

The basic information logistics functions of gathering, interpreting and distributing SNEM data are the basis for all event management functions defined in sections 4.1 to 4.4. An integration of these separate SNEM functions in an overall SNEM process is presented in the following. The SNEM process is shown to provide a mechanism that is reusable by every enterprise in a supply network thus forming a flexible and distributed network of event management activities. Network-wide emerging event management is the result.

### 4.5.1 Event Management Functions

#### 4.5.1.1 Trigger Events Revisited

All trigger events defined in section 4.1.1 that initiate monitoring of orders by a SNEM system have been considered by the main SNEM functions defined in sections 4.1 to 4.4:

- *Status requests* $TE_{SR}$ are triggered by queries on the status of an order received from external partners (see section 4.1.2).
- *Alert triggers* $TE_{AT}$ are consequences of external alerts generated by a SNEM system of a supplier (see section 4.4.1.2) and are received by customers from their suborder recipients.
- *Probabilistic triggers* $TE_{PT}$ are created by using critical profiles $CCP_j$ for identification of potentially critical orders and initiate monitoring of these (see section

4.2.1).

- *Randomized triggers* $TE_{RT}$ result from random generation of new $CCP_j$ (see section 4.2.3.4).

All of these triggers are considered as potential start events for the SNEM process which is defined in the following section.

#### 4.5.1.2    Integrated Process

The integration of all event management functions defined in the previous sections 4.1 to 4.4 results in a generic process for supply network event management. This is depicted in fig. 4-49. The first activity is the *Monitoring decision* that is based on different triggers (queries, alerts and $CCP_j$ including random $CCP_j$). Since it is possible that more than one type of trigger requires monitoring of a specific order, a SNEM solution assures that the SNEM process is only initiated once for each order and that later triggers are related to the instance of the process concerned with the order in question. Profile matching as defined in section 4.2.1 is integrated in the activity *Monitoring decision*.

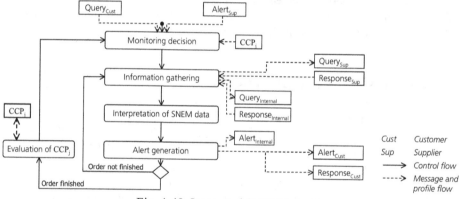

Fig. 4-49. Integrated SNEM process

The strategy for proactively gathering SNEM data in supply networks (see section 4.1.2) is used within the activity *Information gathering* that is cyclically initiated as long as a monitored order is not finished. Data is gathered both from internal sources and from external supply network partners to assess suborders, as indicated by the two query variants. *Interpretation of SNEM data* (see section 4.3) and *Alert generation* (see section 4.4) follow in the next process steps. After an order is finished and monitoring is terminated, results of monitoring activities are evaluated to improve existing critical profiles $CCP_j$, as proposed in section 4.2.3, and enhance the focus of SNEM efforts on potentially critical orders.

## 4.5.2 Distributed Event Management in Supply Networks

### 4.5.2.1 Distributed Architecture

Autonomy and heterogeneity of supply network partners are two of the main characteristics identified to affect a SNEM solution (see sections 2.1.2.4 and 2.1.2.5). For the various SNEM functions proposed before, it is argued that autonomy of a supply network partner is not affected negatively. Furthermore, aspects of heterogeneity regarding organizations, products and strategies are considered in a SNEM system, for instance through specific data types or individual Fuzzy Logic rule sets. The result is a network of individual SNEM systems that reflect different enterprises in a supply network and that interact by exchanging messages - specifically queries, responses and alerts as depicted for two enterprises in fig. 4-50. Interfaces between different SNEM systems are very limited and consistent semantic definitions for message content are assured by the SNEM ontology proposed in section 3.2.3.

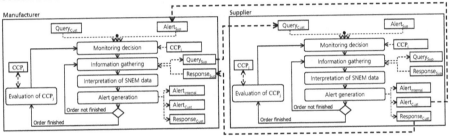

Fig. 4-50. Distributed SNEM systems

### 4.5.2.2 Implications for Supply Network Event Management

Given that a distributed architecture as presented above exists within a supply network, the SNEM monitoring process spans a complete network of enterprises and at the same time a limited complexity for each individual system is assured. Queries for suborder information and integration of this data in interpretations of monitored orders' current situations assure that disruptive events $DE$ on all levels of a supply network are identified and considered, but only to the extent where they really affect orders of customers. Everything that can be handled within a company is managed locally, and proactive external alerts are only generated when necessary or if status requests have to be answered. Use of critical profiles $CCP_j$ reduces the amount of required inter-organizational communication to a low level. This occurs under the assumption that $CCP_j$ with a high quality are defined on each supply network level.

Interactions between SNEM systems are very limited and addition of new supply network partners is realized seamlessly: As soon as a new partner initializes its SNEM system and makes itself known to its customers and suppliers, it is integrated in the distributed monitoring process. This is a major benefit for the dissemination of SNEM systems in existing supply networks where eventually only a small number of partners will start to use event management and other partners might join over time. Since each partner's autonomy is supported and individual configuration is possible (e.g. critical profiles, fuzzy rules, alert generation rules and information policy), potential barriers for implementing a SNEM solution are relatively low.

# Chapter 5

# Agent-based Concept

In chapter 3 a *Supply Network Event Management (SNEM)* data model and ontology have been defined while in chapter 4 main functions to be realized by a SNEM solution are proposed. An integrating technological approach for the realization of a SNEM system is presented in the following. It is based on software agent technology as an innovative technology for the realization of autonomous and distributed software solutions.

## 5.1  Software Agents and Supply Network Event Management

Before an agent-based SNEM concept is developed in subsequent sections, suitability of agent technology for event management is discussed in section 5.1 and an appropriate software engineering approach is adopted in section 5.2 to design an agent-based SNEM system.

### 5.1.1  Introduction to Software Agents

#### 5.1.1.1    Agent Characteristics

There is not one all-encompassing definition of the term "software agent", but some aspects are agreed upon as being fundamental to the notion of a software agent (*Wooldridge et al. 1995, Jennings 2001*)[1]:

- *Autonomy*: A software agent has control over its own actions. It derives these actions from its internal state and acts without intervention by a human actor (at least in most cases).

---

[1.] Other characteristics attributed to certain types of agents are mobility (migration of agents), rational behavior, ability to learn.

- *Reactivity*: Changes in the environment of a software agent are perceived by the agent (e.g. information is received from a user or a physical sensor), and it generates a reaction to the new information in due time (e.g. it sends a message).
- *Proactiveness*: Besides reactions to environmental changes, a software agent pursues individual objectives and takes the initiative by exhibiting activities that are not directly triggered by changes in its environment.
- *Social ability*: The ability to communicate with other agents (or humans) is fundamental to the definition of a software agent.

Although a software agent is still a computer program that is based on the same set of computable functions any program can use, the characteristics (see above) and the techniques offered by agent technology for the design of software systems (see subsequent sections) are fundamentally different from traditional functional programming and even from the object-oriented paradigm (*Jennings 2001*)[2].

In agent theory two main architectures for software agents are distinguished: *deliberative* and *reactive* agent architectures (see fig. 5-1). *Deliberative agents* (*Genesereth et al. 1987, pp. 325*) stem from symbolic *Artificial Intelligence (AI)* and require an explicit symbolic representation of their environment (*Wooldridge 1992, p.36*). They apply logical reasoning mechanisms based on symbolic manipulation and inference mechanisms to explicitly decide on necessary actions to achieve their goals (e.g. *Ferber 1999, pp. 204*). An example of such an architecture is the *Belief-Desire-Intention (BDI)* architecture proposed by Rao and Georgeff. It is the prevalent theoretical model to describe deliberative agents and the way they plan their actions (*Rao et al. 1992, Rao et al. 1995*)[3].

A counter-proposal based on early work by Brooks (*Brooks 1986*) suggests that many activities an agent has to conduct consist of simple routines and do not require complex abstract reasoning[4]. Ferber terms this type of agent *reactive (Ferber 1994, p. 9)*. It implements simple reflex rules that act according to sensor data it perceives (see fig. 5-1). No memory on past experiences or situations is stored and execution of actions is solely based on the current situation of an agent's environment. Even though a single agent only has a limited set of rules that govern its behavior, it is able to cope with a variety of situations. In addition to these two conceptual extremes, *hybrid architectures* with layered approach-

---

[2] Although software agents are often implemented using object-oriented programming languages, a software agent is different from an object (*Jennings 2001, p. 39*): An object's behavior is invoked via publicly available methods and it is not able to refuse to act on a method invocation. In this sense, it cannot act autonomously and cannot exhibit proactive behavior either, since it has no objective. In addition, interactions between objects are primitive and not flexible compared to the communicative abilities software agents are endowed with.

[3] An agent's sensory input is considered to be its *believes*, the agent's goals are its *desires*, and *intentions* are plans an agent devises to satisfy its desires. Plans depend on the current situation of an agent's environment as it is perceived by the agent and described in its believes.

[4] In the subsumption architecture proposed by Brooks, an agent has different layers of goals which it tries to achieve by reacting to its perceptions. For instance, "find food" might be a top-level goal and "move around" is a lower level goal for a reactive agent needed to find food.

es have been proposed that integrate both: fast reactions from reactive architectures and longer-term strategic decisions made by deliberative structures (e.g. the *INTERRAP* approach by *Müller 1996*)[5].

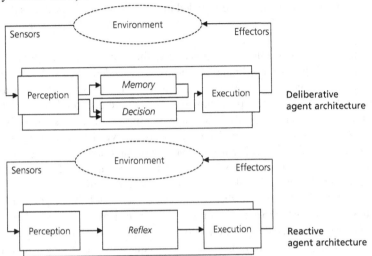

Fig. 5-1. Basic agent architectures (based on *Ferber 1999, p. 193 and p. 206*)

Applications of agent technology for real-world problem domains often use elements of both architectural alternatives. The theoretical models are interpreted in a pragmatic fashion, and the extent to which *AI* methods are used is limited (*Jennings 2004*). The agent-based SNEM concept proposed in subsequent sections follows this approach and combines both proactive and reactive elements in its software agents.

### 5.1.1.2    Multi Agent Systems

An agent's capability to actively communicate provides the basic means to exhibit social behavior (see section 5.1.1.1). This facilitates the design of *Multi Agent Systems (MAS)*. A *MAS* consists of a group of agents that interact with each other by exchanging messages which are defined in a specific *Agent Communication Language (ACL)*. A standard for an *ACL* has been adopted by the *Foundation for Intelligent Physical Agents (FIPA)*[6] (*FIPA 2002a*), which is the relevant standardization body for agent technology issues[7]. The FIPA-ACL is composed of a message body and a message header. In the header a performative is declared such as *Request* or *Inform*[8] which expresses the basic intention the sender wants to communicate to the receiver. In addition, the header identifies sender and receiver, provides data for communication management (e.g. message identifiers) and meta-information about the content of the message (e.g. the ontology used for defining

---

[5.] An in-depth overview of theoretical aspects of agent technology and agent architectures can be found e.g. in *Wooldridge et al. 1995, Wooldridge 1999, Müller 1996* or *Ferber 1999*.

[6.] http://www.fipa.org

the message). The message body contains the content of the message which specifies the topics of the conversation, for instance *what* is requested in a message. An agent that receives a message needs both performative and message content to correctly assess a message. The content of an agent message is coded in terms of an ontology that is defined for a specific domain (e.g. the SNEM ontology defined in section 3.2.3). For examples of agent messages see section 5.3.2.2.

Communication between software agents allows for coordination of activities that are pursued by different agents. Coordination is for instance needed when software agents are negotiating prices for goods or services on behalf of a human actor. Another aspect of *MAS* is their potential for solving problems in a cooperative fashion that is based for example on delegation of subtasks to different agents. Besides other tasks in a SNEM system, cooperative behavior is required during the proactive data gathering phase (see section 4.1) where a subtask - gathering SNEM data on suborders - is delegated to a supplier by requesting information on its suborders. Assuming that a supplier's agents are not cooperating, they will not deliver the desired response although they understand the request. This illustrates the difference between software agents and object-oriented systems: The latter have no choice but to act according to their specification, if one of their methods is invoked. Coordination and cooperation among agents is realized through agent communication in multi-step dialogs (e.g. negotiating or requesting something which requires several message exchanges). Such interaction sequences are summarized in interaction protocols. Several standardized interaction protocols are provided by the *FIPA* (*FIPA 2001*) which - under the assumption that messages themselves are understood - allow different agents to facilitate coordination or to cooperate.

### 5.1.1.3    Agent Platforms

Software agents are implemented in different programming languages. To facilitate communication among agents either direct agent-to-agent communication with proprietary communication protocols is realized (which is very flexible but induces control and security problems) or standardized basic communication services are used. The latter resolve control and security problems but require a division of logical communication between agents and physical communication based on a standard platform. The *FIPA* has proposed a set of standards for communication management, message transportation and basic services that are integrated into an agent platform (for an overview see (*Willmott et al. 2004*))[9]. An agent platform serves as the standard "habitat" of a software agent (see fig.

---

[7.] Other standardization bodies also influence the development of agent technology. The *Object Management Group OMG* considers agent-specific aspects for object-oriented technologies and cooperates with the FIPA (*OMG 2005a*). For the definition of content-related semantic issues the *World Wide Web Consortium (W3C)* pursues the development of the *Ontology Web Language (OWL)* which is developed based on the *DAML+OIL* ontology definition language. It is one main option to define message content for agent communication (*W3C 2005*).

[8.] Performatives define the intention of a message (also termed the illocutionary act). They are a basic concept derived from the theory of speech acts (*Austin 1962, Searle 1969*).

5-2) and allows the system developer to focus on functional aspects of the domain problem to be solved by an agent system. It represents middleware between existing basic network resources or the operating system of a host and the application layer represented by specific software agents.

The *Message Transport Service (MTS)* of a FIPA platform ensures secure and reliable transportation of messages between agents. It also ensures that agents on different agent platforms which are located for instance at different enterprises can exchange messages (see fig. 5-2). Two standard types of services are provided by every platform: An *Agent Management Service (AMS)* supervises instantiation and termination of software agents on a platform. Every agent is required to register upon its initialization with the AMS. The second service is a *Directory Facilitator (DF)* which provides yellow-pages where software agents can publish their own services to enable identification by other agents, for instance to facilitate cooperation among agents.

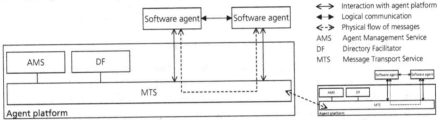

Fig. 5-2. FIPA standard agent platform (*FIPA 2004, p. 5*)

## 5.1.2    Benefits of Agent Technology for Event Management

### 5.1.2.1    Proactivity of Agents

In section 2.2.1.1 the first general requirement for a SNEM solution is *proactivity* in gathering event-related data and communicating information on disruptive events across a supply network. Unlike any other software technology software agents are characterized by their ability to exhibit proactive behavior which is realized through autonomous decision-making. The ability to endow an agent with a goal it pursues (see section 5.1.1.1) and its advanced capabilities to engage in dialogs with other software agents (see section 5.1.1.2) enables an agent to proactively gather SNEM data and to decide on the necessity of proactively generating alert messages.

---

9. The specifications of the FIPA define an abstract architecture of an agent platform and refine various services. Different implementations of these standards exist (e.g. JADE (*JADE 2005*), FIPA-OS (*FIPA OS 2005*), JACK (*JACK 2005*)) which are used to implement FIPA-conform software agents.

#### 5.1.2.2    Institutional Rules

A need for definition of institutional rules is identified as a second major requirement in section 2.2.1.2. Since each supply network partner pursues its individual goals and strategies, some basic agreements are required to guide individual behavior towards the objective of a SNEM solution to proactively provide information on disruptive events. As mentioned in section 2.2.1.2 definition of roles, hierarchies, allowed statements and vocabulary in messages or predefined types of dialogs is required for an effective solution to the SNEM problem. The definition of roles and hierarchies is natural to the notion of an agent, because any society (artificial or human) consists of different actors (the agents) which fulfill various roles during their "lifetime". Communication between agents is based on a standardized agent communication language (see section 5.1.1.3), and the "vocabulary" is explicitly defined in an ontology for the SNEM domain (see section 3.2.3). Therefore, agent technology inherently supports the definition of institutional rules required for a SNEM solution.

#### 5.1.2.3    Distributed Systems for Supply Networks

Event management in supply networks has an inherent distributed character since all partners act as autonomous entities and pursue their own goals (see section 2.1.2.4). Interaction during proactive data gathering and alert communication calls for a distributed solution where every partner can govern its own area of responsibility according to its individual strategy. This results in different rule sets for analyzing data and generating alerts (see sections 4.3 and 4.4). These rule sets have to be integrated in a SNEM solution. One of the main benefits of agent technology is its support for designing distributed systems which are founded on the concept of individual agents that act as delegates for certain actors (humans or legal entities). Jennings generalizes the applicability of agent technology to all those problems that are characterized by independent roles of different actors where these have to interact in order to solve the problem (*Jennings 2001, pp. 36*). This characterization applies to the SNEM problem on an abstract level where legal entities try to satisfy their implicit demand $D_q$ for SNEM information on disruptive events by interacting with each other (see section 2.1.3).

#### 5.1.2.4    Alternative Technologies

Alternative architectures for applications that cover aspects of event management in supply networks have been introduced in section 2.4 - namely tracking-and-tracing (T&T) systems as well as SCEM systems. The centralized architecture of T&T-systems is not suited for an implementation in a complex supply network environment that spans several enterprises. It neither respects autonomy of partners nor their heterogeneity which is characterized by their need for individual configurations of SNEM functions. A centralized system cannot cope with the complexity of partners, data types and configurations encountered in a supply network whereas a distributed system consisting of many autonomous software agents that are specialized for enterprise-specific SNEM tasks can iteratively grow with every new partner included for the event management in a supply network.

Current SCEM systems have centralized event management servers at their heart (see section 2.4.2), but allow integration of data from disparate sources which might compensate some of the problems of centralized T&T-systems. Their main drawback is to be found in a lack of autonomy which is required to exhibit the proactive behavior requested in section 2.2.1.1. An additional lack of advanced communicative abilities to participate in flexible dialogs with changing communication partners (e.g. for data gathering and alert exchange) is a second major drawback of these systems. However, some SCEM vendors are beginning to use agent-technology (or at least proclaim certain functions to be agent-based) (*Barrows 2003, PSI 2005*). This is an additional indicator for the suitability of agent technology to implement a SNEM system.

Summing up, agent technology provides the necessary ability for distributed problem solving and the autonomy to realize proactive system behavior. In addition, flexible communication abilities are a basic feature of agent technology. Existing technological approaches which are based on state-of-the-art server technologies do not provide these features.

## 5.1.3 Related Work in Agent Technologies

As was predicted early by Jennings et al. (*Jennings et al. 1998*) an increasing number of application areas is currently being explored by agent researchers and agent technology enterprises. Numerous concepts, prototype implementations and few business applications are found. Although none explicitly confronts the SNEM problem, research in related areas of supply chain management and information management exist. An overview of potential future application fields for agent technology is provided by a roadmap of the *AgentLink* initiative (*Luck et al. 2005*) which predicts for instance that *Ambient Intelligence, Grid Computing* and *Electronic Business* are key fields for development. Another overview of current issues in agent research is provided by Klügl (*Klügl 2004*). Overall, market forecasts for agent technology are extremely positive for the mid-term future: sales-volume is predicted to reach approximately 250bn $ in 2010 (*SAP 2004b*).

### 5.1.3.1 Agents for Supply Chain Management

In supply chain management, agent technology is at the brink of being integrated in full-fledged industrial applications. One of the most successful examples is a prototypical industrial implementation at *Daimler-Chrysler* where agents negotiate in order to control a manufacturing process in cylinder production (*Bussmann et al. 2000; Bussmann et al. 2004, pp. 44*). In the context of transport optimization *Whitestein Technologies* (*Dorer et al. 2005*) provides a product (*LS/ATN*) for scheduling trucks to routes and tours. Benefits result from reduced transportation costs which average at about 3% to 6% of overall transportation costs in a transportation network (*Calisti et al. 2005*).

Research regarding application of software agents in the supply chain domain often focuses on optimizing schedules with decentralized coordination mechanisms such as negotiation for resource capacities (e.g. *Wagner et al. 2002b*). Typical resources which are allocated during supply chain processes are machines in production environments, transportation media such as trucks (see above) or network and computer resources in telecommunication networks (*Haque et al. 2005*).

Other approaches to supply chain management propose an array of different types of software agents that cover planning and execution of fulfillment actions (e.g. *Fox et al. 2000*). Specialized on machine control are concepts of *Holonic Manufacturing Systems (HMS)* that have been extensively studied in many research projects (e.g. *van Brussel et al. 1998*). A *Holon* represents a *system* (e.g. an agent) which itself may be made of smaller systems and/or is also part of a larger system (e.g. a multi-agent-system). A hierarchical dependency among all these *systems* is the main distinguishing characteristic of a *Holon* as compared for instance to a system made of equal peers which cooperate. Holonic agent-concepts are an active research area: Current trends focus on larger systems such as complex supply chains (*Többen et al. 2005*), aspects of transportation management (*Basra et al. 2005*) and validation of concepts in realistic environments (e.g. *Maturana et al. 2005, Soundararajan et al. 2005*).

To provide support for administrative business processes, agents are used for process management in the *ADEPT* project with *British Telecom* (*Jennings et al. 2000a*; *Jennings et al. 2000b*). In telecommunication networks, agent technology is e.g. used for seamless provision of services to customers with respect to switching between locally available communication technologies. For instance, agents allow to switch from UMTS to WLAN, if the latter is available locally without disconnecting existing communication flows (*Calisti et al. 2004*). Optimized usage of computer networks based on GRID technologies increasingly leverages agent technology to provide efficient allocation of GRID resources. Main topics are service detection, selection and agreement procedures (e.g. *Reinicke et al. 2005*) and allocation mechanisms such as GRID markets (e.g. *Eymann et al. 2005, Lang 2005*).Further examples of agent applications to industrial problems are provided by Parunak (*Parunak 2000*).

In contrast to more complex agents implemented in the concepts above, approaches based on simple reactive agents that replicate natural mechanisms of swarm intelligence are pursued in production optimization (*Brueckner 2000*) or automated vehicle control (*Parunak et al. 2005*). An overview of other application areas for swarm intelligence is given by Bonabeau (*Bonabeau et al. 2001*). An enterprise which specializes in the application of swarm intelligence to industrial problems is *Icosystems* (*Icosystems 2005*).

Another type of agent-based solutions for supply chain management is dedicated to marketplaces where software agents sell and buy products or services on behalf of their users. An example for a spot market where electricity contracts are bought and sold is provided by Eymann (*Eymann 2003, pp. 86*). Other examples are auction platforms such as *Ebay* where (simple) agents provide services like proxy-bidding (*Eymann 2003*, pp. 105). An overview of other potential types of agents in electronic commerce especially in the consumer-to-consumer (C2C) environment is provided by Moukas et al. (*Moukas et al. 2000*). Marketplaces are often based on auction mechanisms. Different such mechanisms are explored in order to design (allocative) efficient auctions (e.g. *Sandholm et al. 2003, Conen et al. 2004, Rogers 2005*). Uncertainty in opponents' behaviors is often analyzed using game theoretic approaches (e.g. *Sandholm et al. 2005*). A provider of agent-based marketplaces which employ auction mechanisms is e.g. LostWax (*LostWax 2005*).

### 5.1.3.2 Information Agents

For an agent-based SNEM system insights on information gathering agents in supply networks can be of interest although they are primarily concerned with searching for information in Internet resources especially to prepare a transaction (e.g. comparing and combining offers) (*Wagner et al. 2001; Chun et al. 2000*). A series of workshops on *Cooperative Information Agents (CIA)* is regularly organized since 1997 by Klusch (*Klusch 2005*). Latest results have focused on aspects of information gathering based on the semantic web, interactive and mobile agents, agents in peer-to-peer computing and recommender agent systems. Agent systems based on the *Holon* paradigm (see above) are also used for providing information to process management, e.g. in the KARMEN system which monitors complex industrial production processes (*Bunch et al. 2005*). However, any focus on SNEM like problems in multi-level supply networks has not been identified.

### 5.1.3.3 Further Fields of Research on Agent Technology

Agent technology is also used to simulate and forecast dynamic behavior in business environments, such as multi-level supply networks. A basic introduction to agent-based simulation is provided by Klügl (*Klügl 2000*). Simulations of industrial problems have been conducted e.g. by Swaminathan (*Swaminathan et al. 1998*) or Parunak (*Parunak et al. 1999*). However, simulation of supply networks is no feature a SNEM system has to provide.

New identification technologies as discussed in section 3.3.3 as potential data sources (e.g. RFID technology) are increasingly combined with agent-based concepts. This combination is one major aspect in the evolving field of *Ambient Intelligence*. Both approaches - agents and advanced identification technologies - focus on distribution of knowledge and activities within processes. Combined, they allow for the creation of autonomous smart objects termed *Object Chips* (*Wacker 2001*) or *Smart-Active-Labels* (*SAL-C 2005*) (see also section 3.3.3.3). However, current research on ambient technologies (e.g. *Ambient Networks 2004*) focuses on development of basic infrastructures that provide security mechanisms, context awareness (e.g. *Sashima et al. 2005*) and mobile communication channels (*Helin et al. 2005*). Thus, integration with agent technology is at most in a conceptual phase. Although the SNEM concept does not focus on the use of ambient technologies, an outlook for potential integration is provided in section 8.2.

Practical relevance for industrial agent applications is attributed to security and robustness aspects of agent systems that are influenced by data base management mechanisms such as transaction security (*Nimis et al. 2004*) and cryptographic techniques (e.g. *Hannotin et al. 2002*). In physically distributed and mobile environments aspects of agent mobility and related security aspects are additional important constraints for a practical solution (*Bryce 2000*). However, such aspects are not considered in detail in the basic SNEM concept although they are important for future developments towards integration of ambient technologies in SNEM scenarios (see also section 8.2).

## 5.2 Agent Oriented Software Engineering

To develop an agent-based SNEM concept an appropriate software engineering methodology is needed. In the following, specific characteristics of agent-oriented software engineering are presented (see section 5.2.1) and a suitable methodology is selected and adapted to the needs of agent-based event management in supply networks (see section 5.2.2).

### 5.2.1 Approaches

#### 5.2.1.1 Macro- and Micro-Perspective

Software engineering for agent-based systems is a major field of current research in agent technologies (e.g. documented by numerous proceedings of conference workshops on *Agent-oriented Software Engineering (AOSE)* (e.g. *Giorgini et al. 2003*; *Odell et al. 2004*). It is generally agreed upon that methodologies for structured programming and even for object-oriented programming cannot be transferred directly to the design of agent systems because of agent-specific characteristics:

- The autonomy of a software agent which allows proactive behavior to achieve an objective (goal) is in contrast to the simple method invocation characteristics of object-oriented software engineering (*Odell et al. 2001, p.4*).
- Interactions between agents are complex, compared to simple message exchange within conventional object-oriented systems. They provide agents with the ability to coordinate and cooperate their behavior according to their individual goals (*Jennings 2001, p.39*).

However, basic engineering steps (e.g. analysis, design, implementation) are commonly applied to the design and development of multi agent systems. A major distinction is made between the design of an agent society as a whole, where each agent type is considered as a black-box, and subsequent refinement of each individual agent type (e.g. *Wooldridge et al. 2000*). The first is referred to as the *macro-perspective* of AOSE while the second is termed the *micro-perspective* of AOSE (see fig. 5-3).

In the analysis phase as part of the macro-perspective three aspects are commonly considered (e.g. *Wooldridge et al. 2000, Bauer et al. 2004*):

1. The environment of an agent system is analyzed. For instance, the domain, the problem for which an agent system will provide a solution and environmental constraints are identified, and objectives for the agent system are defined based on system requirements.
2. Important roles that are responsible for major functions of a system are identified[10]. These functions have to be performed to achieve the objectives of an agent solution (see above).
3. Interactions between functions respectively their associated roles are identified and modeled. These interaction models define for instance which roles have to cooperate

to achieve an objective.

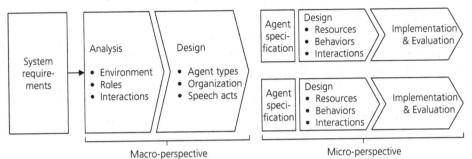

Fig. 5-3. Macro- and micro-perspective of AOSE

The results of the analysis phase are used in the design phase to define agent types that assume one or more of the identified roles. Structural dependencies between agent types are defined that establish a society of agents (e.g. how many agents of a certain agent type are instantiated in an agent system). Within such an agent society the interactions identified in the analysis phase are designed as structured agent interactions based on speech acts. The design phase provides a holistic model of a multi agent system (MAS) that describes agent types, their roles, and the primary interactions between agents.

One result of the design of the agent society are specifications for each agent regarding its roles, which in turn define primary functions and duties of an agent. In the design phase of the micro-perspective these agent specifications are refined with respect to the following aspects (*Bauer et al. 2004, pp. 125*):

- *Resources:* Each agent requires several types of resources it can use to conduct activities. These consist of its internal knowledge assets, its goals, and the external resources it can employ. External resources either provide sensory input (e.g. access to data bases, user inputs) or represent effectors which are used to influence an agent's environment (e.g. communication channels or control interfaces of machines).
- *Behaviors*: How a single agent achieves its goals by employing activities that utilize its available resources (see above), is described within an agent's behaviors. A behavior combines several activities that are triggered, if certain preconditions apply, and that result in a specific outcome (e.g. a change in an agent's knowledge assets or in the agent's environmental situation).
- *Interactions:* A detailed description of how an agent interacts with other agents in an agent society as well as how these interactions are initiated and controlled by an

---

[10.]The term "role" in the context of agent technology does not have an agreed upon definition, but it is mostly used based on a sociological notion. A broad definition is provided by Bahrdt (Bahrdt 1994) whereas Weiss focuses on a cognitive notion of agents' roles (Weiss 1999). In the following, the definition by Lind is used: "A role is a logical grouping of atomic activities according to the (physical) constraints of the operational environment of the target system" (Lind 2001, p. 140).

agent's behaviors, is summarized in an interaction model.

The final step of AOSE is implementation of the detailed concept and an evaluation of the multi agent system.

Regarding the development of an agent-based SNEM solution, a macro-perspective analysis has been conducted in chapters 2, 3 and 4. In the following sections of chapter 5 a specific methodology for the design of the agent society and for the micro-perspective design of individual agent types is selected and applied to the SNEM concept. Prototypical implementations are discussed in chapter 6, and an overall evaluation of the agent-based SNEM concept with respect to its ability to realize the potential benefits identified in section 2.3 is provided in chapter 7.

### 5.2.1.2    Existing Methodologies for Agent-Oriented Software Engineering

As Bauer notes (*Bauer et al. 2004, p. 78*) a multitude of software engineering methodologies is proposed by the agent research community for designing software agent systems. Two major types of methodologies are distinguished: Some are founded directly on theoretical foundations of software agents while others build upon object-oriented software engineering methodologies and add agent-specific mechanisms (*Weiß et al. 2005, p. 15*)[11].

The most prominent representative of the first methodology type is *GAIA* proposed by Wooldridge (*Wooldridge et al. 2000; Zambonelli et al. 2003*). Its focus is on a generic mechanism to design agents. It considers both macro- and micro-perspectives but remains very abstract regarding the implementation of agents. In an evaluation of several methods Weiß concludes that none of the existing approaches is superior. Their suitability depends on individual specifics of the given software development project (*Weiß et al. 2005, pp. 182*).

A close relationship between designing software agent systems and object-oriented software engineering is agreed upon by agent researchers (e.g. *Burmeister 1996* (cited by *Bauer et al. 2004*)). This is documented by a number of approaches which include aspects of object-oriented design mechanisms such as the methodologies *Massive (Lind 2001)*, *MaSe (DeLoach et al. 2001)* or PASSI (*Cossentino et al. 2002*). An overview of these methodologies is provided by *Bauer et al. 2004* and in part by *Weiß et al. 2005*. None of the methodologies is clearly superior as noted by Bauer (*Bauer et al. 2004, pp.110*), but most of them are more or less based on extensions to the *Unified Modeling Language UML*. UML is an object-oriented modeling standard proposed and maintained by the *Object Management Group OMG* (*OMG 2005b*). This methodology is widely accepted for object-oriented design in industrial software development practice.

For the design of an agent-based SNEM concept an AOSE methodology is chosen that builds upon UML. Several agent-specific additions have been proposed over time that constitute the *Agent Unified Modeling Language (AUML)* (e.g. *Odell et al. 2001, Bauer*

---

[11.]Older methodologies have foundations in knowledge engineering (*Bauer et al. 2004, pp. 80*) which is a major aspect of agent design (see e.g. ontology design in section 3.2.3). However, these methodologies do not model roles, resources and behaviors of an agent in greater detail.

*2001, Huget 2002, Bauer et al. 2004).* Consequently, an intuitive understanding of AUML models for actors accustomed to UML is guaranteed. Another indicator for the relevance of AUML is its adoption as the preferred modeling method for defining interaction protocols in the FIPA standards (e.g. *FIPA 2001*) and an established working group at FIPA for development of AUML. Since the design of the SNEM agent concept, a new approach based on UML2.0 is under development which is termed *Agent Modeling Language (AML)*. AML is inspired by different AOSE concepts such as Gaia or Passi and also considers FIPA's communication architecture as well as semantic-related aspects of ontology description languages (e.g. OWL) (*Whitestein 2004*, pp. 11). It provides a holistic metamodel for describing agent systems. However, AUML is selected since AML was not available at the time of development of the agent-based SNEM concept.

## 5.2.2  AUML for Supply Network Event Management

### 5.2.2.1  Agent Society

In the design phase of the *macro-perspective* two main types of AUML diagrams are proposed to give a formalized overview of the structure of an agent society and its dynamic interactions. An example of a simple scenario in which one seller and multiple potential buyers negotiate prices is used to present and illustrate the different model types (see fig. 5-4).

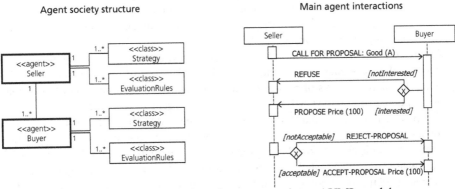

Fig. 5-4. Macro perspective of an agent society - AUML models

Definition of roles and interactions between roles as a result of the analysis phase (see section 5.2.1.1) is assumed. In the example, it results in two main roles that are to be realized by two different agent types: *Seller* and *Buyer* agents. On the left hand side of fig. 5-4 an agent-specific type of a class diagram (*Bauer 2001; Huget 2002*) is used to depict a one-to-many relationship between a *Seller* agent and multiple *Buyer* agents. In this view additional classes (not agents!) are integrated. They represent important knowledge resources which an agent needs to fulfill its tasks. In the example the *Seller* needs knowledge on strategies for optimal bargaining and evaluation rules that allow to assess a proposal of a buyer with respect to its goals (e.g. maximize profit). These resources are termed "knowledge assets" of an agent[12].

The AUML class diagram depicts all relevant agent types and their structural relationships within an agent society. Their interactions are depicted in a sequence diagram, syntactic of which has been adapted to model agent interactions based on FIPA-conform speech acts (see fig. 5-4). In particular, parallel aspects in dialogs can be modeled in an AUML sequence diagram (*Odell et al. 2001*). In the example a Buyer agent can answer a *call-for-proposal*, which it receives from the *Seller* agent, with either a *refuse* message or a *proposal* in which it bids for the good the *Seller* agent offers. This exclusive *OR* is indicated by the "x" in the decision box whereas an empty box would represent a logic *OR*. A logic *AND* is represented by a straight line connecting the parallel communicative acts without any decision box (not depicted in the example of fig. 5-4).

### 5.2.2.2    Internal Models of an Agent

Modeling internal aspects of an agent which are neglected in the macro-perspective's design phase of the AOSE process requires various diagram types as depicted in fig. 5-5. Diagrams of the micro-perspective of AOSE build on AUML model types described by Huget (*Huget 2002*), Bauer (*Bauer 2001*) and Odell et. al. (*Odell et al. 2001*), but have been modified to focus on main aspects of agents' resources, functions and interactions within the SNEM concept, while minor details primarily relevant for implementation are omitted[13]. Agent design is initiated with an extended class diagram of the agent that depicts several aspects relevant to the structure of an agent (see fig. 5-5).

- *Role:* All roles that have been assigned to an agent type in the preceding design phase of the macro-perspective are represented.
- *Knowledge Asset:* Primary types of knowledge assets relevant to an agent type are listed in the class diagram. Depending on the complexity of an agent society, additional knowledge assets of minor relevance are added in the micro-perspective that are not depicted in the AUML class diagram of an agent society (see fig. 5-4).
- *Behavior:* Similar to methods in object-oriented class diagrams the various behaviors an agent can apply to achieve its goals are depicted. As common for agent activities each behavior is characterized by a precondition (in parentheses) that has to apply for the behavior to be activated and a postcondition that characterizes the goal which is achieved, if the behavior is executed successfully. Such a design guarantees high

---

[12.]The notion of these additional classes is that of believes or goals that are represented as classes (*Huget 2002*). This design simplifies manipulation and assment of specific instances of a believe or goal since an instance of the class is assessed in an implementation using get- or set-methods. For the SNEM concept a more general perspective is chosen with the notion of "knowledge assets".

[13.]Some attributes are not included although proposed initially by Huget and Bauer in their papers on AUML class diagrams (*Bauer 2001, Huget 2002*). Among these are for instance basic agent attributes such as an agent-identifier or capabilities that are registered with a directory facilitator to publish available services which an agent can provide.

flexibility for controlling an agents behavior, because behaviors can be executed in parallel, if preconditions are found to be true for multiple behaviors[14]. Three different types of behaviors are differentiated according to (*Huget 2002*).

- *Proactive behaviors (Pro)* are initiated by an agent upon its own decision and not as a response to any external trigger event which an agent might receive from its environment. The agent decides based on its internal knowledge and assessment of its current situation on the necessity to initiate such a behavior.
- *Reactive behaviors (Reac)* are used when an agent reacts directly to an external signal it receives with its sensors. It interprets the input in a predetermined fashion by initiating an applicable reactive behavior (determined by the precondition of the behavior).
- *Internal behaviors (Int)* are triggered due to preconditions that are the result of other agent behaviors and that are identified within the agent. Another possibility is the direct call of such a behavior by another behavior.
- *Perception*: Since every agent has some kind of sensors (at least for receiving agent messages from other agents), the various types of inputs an agent can receive are summarized in the last field of the AUML class diagram.

Details on behaviors an agent can exhibit are modeled outside the AUML class diagram in separate diagrams based on UML activity diagrams which are adapted from a proposal of Huget (*Huget 2002*) (see fig. 5-5, top-right). To structure all behaviors of an agent, a diagram type is proposed here that separates behaviors which realize sensors and effectors of the agent from all other behaviors. Thus, behaviors for receiving (= sensors) and sending agent messages (= effectors) are depicted on the outer sides. All other behaviors within the agent are arranged in between, and control flows indicate on an abstract level possible sequences as well as parallelism of behaviors. Another variant is the direct call of a behavior which is indicated by a directed *<<use>>* relationship between two behaviors (see fig. 5-5).

In a second step conventional activity diagrams are used to depict details of a behavior with its various tasks, potential alternatives and required inputs and outputs. In the example three steps are designed for the proactive *SendCallForProposal* behavior. This behavior determines on its own when to start a new selling process, selects potential buyers and creates a *call-for-proposal* that is distributed by an internal *SendMessage* behavior which realizes the effector of the *Seller* agent in the example of fig. 5-5.

---

[14.] In addition, high-level control mechanisms such as planning algorithms from *Artificial Intelligence* rely on formalized models of *precondition-activity-postcondition*. Planning algorithms are used to realize advanced deliberative agents. A typical planning algorithm is *Graphplan* and subversions of it, and they are used to devise feasible plans for agent behavior (*Hofmann 2000*). However, in the current prototypes a simpler autonomous control with tests on preconditions of behaviors is implemented (see section 6.1).

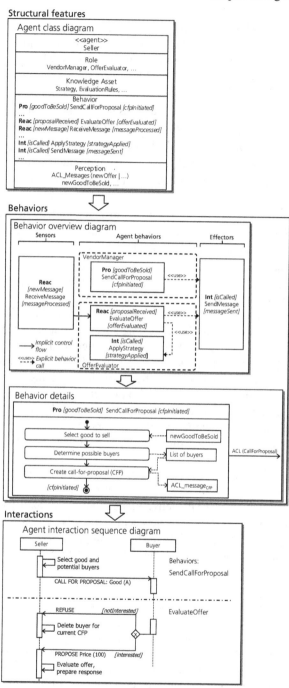

Fig. 5-5. Micro perspective of an agent - AUML models

A final aspect to describe a single agent type is the relationship between its internal behaviors and its external interactions with other agents. This is depicted in an AUML sequence diagram similar to the one in fig. 5-4 but with a different focus: Not all agent types of an agent society are necessarily depicted but only those directly in contact with the agent type to be modeled. Each behavior that either acts upon incoming agent messages or triggers messages to other agents is depicted separately with the respective agent messages modeled as FIPA speech acts. Traceability of the relationship between internal behaviors and agent interactions is ensured.

# 5.3 Agent Society for Supply Network Event Management

According to the design phase in the macro-perspective of AOSE an agent society for event management in supply networks is proposed. The society is derived from main roles in the SNEM process and basic interaction patterns are presented which emerge from the agents' behaviors in a supply network (see sections 5.3.1 and 5.3.2). Institutional agreements which are required to facilitate a stable agent society are defined in section 5.3.3.

## 5.3.1   Roles and Agent Types

### 5.3.1.1     Roles in the Event Management Process

The event management process in supply networks (see section 4.5) is associated with different roles which realize different functions in this process. Main roles can be directly derived from the primary activities of the event management process (see section 4.5.1.2), e.g. information gathering or alert generation (see fig. 4-49). Within an agent-based SNEM system two roles need to be considered additionally: They are responsible to provide interfaces to (1) the internal data sources of an enterprise (see section 3.3) and (2) to external supply network partners. The second type of interface requires mechanisms to handle communication security[15].

In principle, each role associated with the event management process could be implemented as a specific agent type. However, in the following, four clusters of roles are proposed that define a preferable design of the agent society (see fig. 5-6):

1. All external communication with supply network partners is conducted via one dedicated interface. This ensures e.g. consistent encryption/decryption of messages, management of contact information on external recipients and reception of messages from external partners. External messages are related to appropriate internal systems which can act on the received information. The interface also ensures that received data conforms to a predefined syntax and is understood by all other agents of a

---

[15.]In the SNEM concept it is assumed that only external communication has to be secured, while security risks for internal communication is assumed to be of minor relevance. Eventually, security aspects can be added to every internal communication, if needed.

SNEM system (semantic correctness). Thus, no faulty external information (e.g. an ontology which is not supported by the agent system is used in a received message), except content-related failures that cannot be checked by the interface (e.g. an unrealistic quantity of a product), is related to internal SNEM functions. These functions are realized by the SNEM roles *CommunicationManager* and *SecurityManager*, and they are aggregated in the cluster *external communication*.

| Basic SNEM roles | Cluster of roles | Agent type |
|---|---|---|
| CommunicationManager | External communication | Discourse agent |
| SecurityManager | | |
| SurveillanceManager | Coordination of event management | Coordination agent |
| AlertManager | | |
| ProfileManager | | |
| InformationGatherer | Order surveillance | Surveillance agent |
| DataAnalyzer | | |
| DataRetriever | Wrapper layer | Wrapper agent |
| DataTransformer | | |

Fig. 5-6. Role clusters and agent types

2. All trigger events (e.g. status requests or profile matches with $CCP_j$ (see section 4.5.1.1)) that initiate the event management process are managed by one role. This role ensures that no order is monitored redundantly (role *SurveillanceManager*). Closely related to initiation of monitoring activities is the completion of incoming status requests with responses to customers, and the management of proactive alerts. Alerts are directed both to internal actors and to external supply network partners (see section 4.4.4). The management of alerts ensures that no additional alert is sent to a customer, if a request for information on the same order was received in parallel and has already been answered (role *AlertManager*). An additional function which is needed to adapt monitoring decisions to new developments in a supply network, is the evaluation of critical profiles $CCP_j$ (see section 4.2.3). This is realized by the role *ProfileManager*. All three roles are included in the cluster *coordination of event management*.

3. Proactive gathering of SNEM data based on internal and external requests for SNEM data (see section 4.1) is realized by the SNEM role *InformationGatherer*. It provides the basis to the process step of analyzing and interpreting SNEM data (see section 4.3) which is the duty of the role *DataAnalyzer*. Both process steps represent activities in which new information is produced through searching, selecting and interpreting data. These activities are related to the basic information logistics function of *content management* as defined in section 2.2.2. An information product is created that illustrates an order's status represented by a set of SNEM data types. This cluster of roles is termed *order surveillance* cluster.

4. Access to various internal data sources requires individually configured interfaces for each data source. Maintainability of these interfaces without affecting other functions of a SNEM agent society is an important requirement. A specific type of interface

integrates the individual specialties of different data sources and provides a standard-ized access for other roles of a SNEM system. It requires (1) a data-source-specific function for data retrieval which is realized by the role *DataRetriever,* and (2) a map-ping of the selected source data to the terms of the SNEM ontology (role *DataTrans-former*). This group of interfaces and their corresponding roles are referred to as the *wrapper layer,* because data sources are "wrapped" with a standardized interface for access.

For each cluster of roles a different agent type is defined:

1. A *discourse agent (DA)* provides the interface to external supply network partners. Its roles are: *CommunicationManager* and *SecurityManager.*

2. The *coordination agent (CA)* coordinates initialization of monitoring processes and distributes their results. Its roles are: *SurveillanceManager, AlertManager* and *Profi-leManager.*

3. A *surveillance agent (SA)* is responsible for creating an information product by gath-ering and interpreting SNEM data. It has the roles *InformationGatherer* and *Data-Analyzer.*

4. A *wrapper agent (WA)* hides heterogeneous data sources from a SNEM system and allows standardized access to these sources with its roles *DataRetriever* and *Data-Transformer.*

In fig. 5-7 a mapping of the four agent types to the different activities of the integrated event management process (see section 4.5.1.2) is depicted. As defined above in the role cluster, a discourse agent covers all external messages, while the coordination agent is re-sponsible for monitoring decisions, alert generation and evaluation of critical profiles. Gathering new SNEM data and interpreting this data is conducted by a surveillance agent. Data gathered from internal data sources is provided by a wrapper agent, while external SNEM data on suborders is requested and received via the discourse agent.

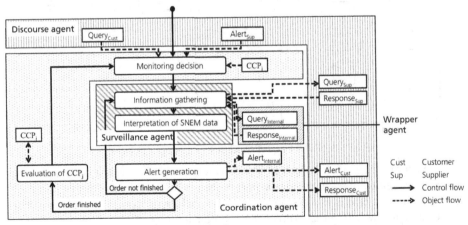

Fig. 5-7. Agent types in the event management process

### 5.3.1.2    Structural Design of the Agent Society

To realize the SNEM concept within a supply network, each supply network partner provides one agent society with a discourse and a coordination agent, as well as various surveillance and wrapper agents (see fig. 5-8) (*Zimmermann et al. 2003b*). Two main
dimensions of communication are distinguished in the agent-based SNEM concept:

1. Interaction between enterprises which is referred to as *inter-organizational communication*: It is facilitated by discourse agents of the enterprises which exchange messages via the Internet. Every SNEM agent society has one discourse agent that serves
   as the single point-of-contact for external communication of SNEM data in an enterprise.

2. *Intra-organizational communication* within one enterprise: It refers to the interactions within one agent society between the various agent types that realize a SNEM
   system of a single enterprise. The interactions among all agents in the agent society
   and among agent societies are described in detail in section 5.3.2.

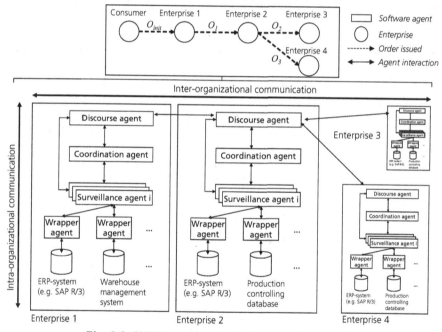

Fig. 5-8. SNEM agent societies in a supply network

A single coordination agent in each enterprise is responsible for the tasks covered in the
cluster *coordination of event management* (see section 5.3.1.1). It assures that initialization of monitoring efforts and management of external status requests and alerts is handled consistently within an enterprise. The coordination agent also allows gaining an
overview of all monitored orders of an enterprise. This input is required for the continuous
evaluation of critical profiles $CCP_j$ (see section 4.2.3).

For each monitored order of an enterprise a dedicated surveillance agent is triggered by the coordination agent which realizes *order surveillance* roles (see section 5.3.1.1). Varying priorities of orders (see section 4.2.3.3) result in different data gathering strategies to be enforced by the surveillance agents (see section 4.1.2). Managing such strategies by a single agent for various orders would require at the same time additional scheduling procedures. To avoid these complexities, an encapsulation of the data gathering and analysis functions in dedicated surveillance agents for each monitored order are proposed here for the SNEM agent society.

Wrapper agents provide a standard interface to internal data sources for the surveillance agents (see section 5.3.1.1). An integration of theses abilities in surveillance agents would require a replication of all access details for each available data source in every surveillance agent. This redundancy is avoided by introducing wrapper agents. They also prevent that multiple agents (e.g. surveillance agents) access the same data source simultaneously which might have a negative effect on availability of data sources for other IT-systems in an enterprise. However, a wrapper agent can handle multiple requests from different surveillance agents at the same time and thus manages access to its data source. Such mechanisms are standard features of agent development frameworks (e.g. FIPA-OS (*FIPA OS 2005*), JADE (*JADE 2005*)) which can be used to implement a SNEM agent system (see also section 6.1.1.2).

Wrapper agents can also be used to query external Internet resources. For instance, carriers regularly allow customers to track their shipments via the carrier's own website (see section 3.3.2). Manual access of a user to these systems can be substituted by an automatic query mechanism provided by a wrapper agent. In this way supply network partners that own proprietary tracking systems without event management capabilities can be integrated into a customer's SNEM system by means of wrapper agents. However, the ideal situation for event management in supply networks is achieved, if every supply network partner implements a SNEM system. This facilitates data gathering and analysis over all levels of a supply network (see section 4.5.2)

An AUML class diagram (see section 5.2.2.1) as an abstract model of a SNEM agent society illustrates the structural interdependencies between the agents (see fig. 5-9). It also gives an overview of the main types of knowledge assets upon which the agents act. The discourse agent has a one-to-one relationship with the coordination agent. It forwards incoming status requests and alerts from external partners to the coordination agent and receives responses and alerts addressed to external network partners. Since the coordination agent initiates monitoring activities, a one-to-many relationship with the surveillance agents exists. Each surveillance agent has access to various wrapper agents and each wrapper agent can be used by every surveillance agent depicted by the many-to-many relationship. To create queries for external SNEM data on suborders, each surveillance agent has a direct link to the discourse agent (many-to-one relationship) which in turn serves as the gateway to external supply network partners. An additional agent is introduced which serves as a directory for the discourse agents where they can query address information to access SNEM systems of other supply network partners: a global directory facilitator (*GlobalDF*)[16]. Since the SNEM process is applicable for every supply network partner which results in multiple SNEM systems connected in a supply network (see section 4.5.2 and fig. 5-8) a many-to-many recursive relationship between enterprises' agent societies is modeled.

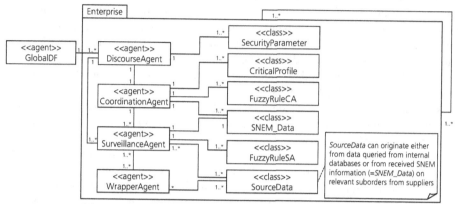

Fig. 5-9. AUML class diagram of a SNEM agent society

Main knowledge assets of the agent types as their major internal resources (see section 5.2.2.1) are depicted in the diagram in fig. 5-9. The discourse agent has parameters for security functions (e.g. passwords) as knowledge assets (*SecurityParameter*). To realize the different activities for coordination of event management, the coordination agent needs critical profiles $CCP_j$ (*CriticalProfile*) for proactive monitoring of orders and fuzzy-rule-sets (*FuzzyRuleCA*) for its alert management. Alert management is based on the surveillance results a surveillance agent provides to the coordination agent. The results consist of SNEM data on monitored orders (*SNEM_Data*) . Any surveillance agent has exactly one knowledge asset of the *SNEM_Data* type, because it is dedicated to a single order and cyclically updates this knowledge asset. Data received during its data gathering activities is stored in the knowledge asset type *SourceData* which it gathers from internal sources (wrapper agents). To analyze *SourceData* and update its *SNEM_Data* asset a surveillance agent requires a set of Fuzzy Logic rules defined based on the class *FuzzyRuleSA*.

## 5.3.2    Agent Interactions

### 5.3.2.1    Basic Interaction Protocol

Interactions among all SNEM agent types are based on requests for SNEM data and requests for activities to be performed for gathering or manipulation of this data. A suitable basic interaction protocol is depicted in fig. 5-10: the standardized FIPA "Request" interaction protocol[17] (*FIPA 2002b*). After a *request* has been sent from the initiator the participant can send an *agree* to indicate it accepts the *request*, but this step is optional[18]. In case it does not accept the *request* a *refuse* is sent[19].

---

[16.]The *GlobalDF* is not further considered because directory facilitator agents are a standard infrastructure of agent platforms provided in agent development kits.

After activities triggered by the *request* are conducted by the participant it either has to admit it has failed and a *failure* message is sent or an *inform* is sent as a final response. This *inform* either includes the result of the actions (*inform-result*) or a simple confirmation of a successful completion of the request (*inform-done*) is sent to the initiator. In a SNEM agent society the standard response to a request includes communication of the results. In the following subsections a simple *inform* is depicted to reduce the complexity of the graph but an *inform-result* is intended.

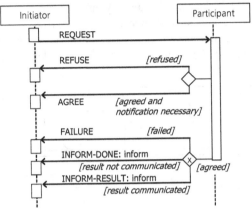

Fig. 5-10. FIPA "Request" interaction protocol (*FIPA 2002b*)

The content of the messages is defined based on the SNEM ontology (see section 3.2.3), and each agent type decides, based upon the message type, the sender and the content of a message, on an appropriate action, in order to fulfill its duties within the SNEM process (e.g. analysis of received *SourceData* (see section 5.3.1.2)). Besides reactions to messages, every agent can decide proactively to take or initiate further actions in the event management process (e.g. send an alert).

### 5.3.2.2    Intra-organizational Communication

A SNEM system within a single enterprise is realized by different agent types as defined above (see section 5.3.1). Communication is based on the FIPA "Request" interaction pro-

---

[17.]The "Query" interaction protocol defined by the FIPA (*FIPA 2002c*) would be a viable alternative but it implies a restriction to queries for data and does not demand any action be taken on the data. For instance a query for data to a supplier requires a whole set of actions that is requested from the different agents (e.g. data analysis on selected data) which is not directly implied by a query. To reduce the complexity of the agent interaction concept only the "Request" interaction protocol is used.

[18.]This is indicated by the empty decision box in the AUML diagram which implies a non-exclusive "OR".

[19.]In older versions of the FIPA protocol a "not understood" is part of the interaction protocol. This has been abandoned by FIPA because a failure to understand a message can be sent at every time in any interaction protocol and therefore is not depicted (*FIPA 2002b*, p.5).

tocol (see section 5.3.2.1). In fig. 5-11 an overview of the main interactions in a single SNEM system (*Enterprise 2* in the example) is depicted. Two possible external triggers (a *request* from *Enterprise 1* on $O_1$ or a supplier's *inform(alert)* (e.g. on $O_2$)) might be received by the discourse agent[20]. Both are forwarded to the coordination agent[21]. Within the activity *monitoring decision* the coordination agent considers external triggers that it might have received and checks whether any critical profiles $CCP_j$ map to the order $O_1$. If it identifies a need to proactively monitor order $O_1$ because of one of the trigger types (see also section 4.5.1.1), it checks for an already initiated surveillance agent dedicated to $O_1$. In case none exists, a new surveillance agent is initialized and a *request* for SNEM data on order $O_1$ is sent to the surveillance agent. Otherwise the *request* is sent to the appropriate surveillance agent. An example of such a *request* defined as a FIPA message is depicted in fig. 5-12.

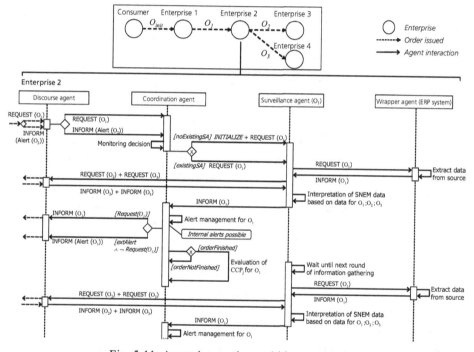

Fig. 5-11. Agent interactions within a enterprise

---

[20.]Other external messages sent from or received by the discourse agent are only indicated without message types in fig. 5-11, since details on external communication are presented in section 5.3.2.3.

[21.]Note that the AUML notation (=empty decision box) indicates that none, one, or both triggers can occur.

```
(request
  :sender CoordinationAgent@Enterprise2
  :receiver SurveillanceAgent_Order1@Enterprise2
  :content
    (OrderOutgoingID = 1; OrderType = "Warehousing"; EstimatedDateOfFulfillment = ?;
     AggregatedOrderStatus = ?; Milestones (OrderReceiptWarehousing = ?;
     ConfirmationOfOrderWarehousing = ?; Picking = ?; Packaging = ?;
     OutgoingGoods = ?); ActualQuantity = ?; NoOfPickingFailures= ?;
     DisruptiveEvents = ?)
  :ontology SNEM_Ontology
  :conversation-id 8694043)
```

Fig. 5-12. Request for SNEM data to surveillance agent (FIPA-message)

The conversation initiated by the *request* for SNEM data is identified by means of a *conversation-id* which is created by the initiator of a *request* (in this case the coordination agent). A response to be created by the surveillance agent will use the same *conversation-id* (see fig. 5-13). The identification number is used by the coordination agent to map incoming *informs* to already existing conversations and identify when a *request* has been satisfied. Content of the *request* is based on the SNEM ontology and follows the syntax introduced in section 4.1.2. Various status data types and information on disruptive events is requested. This data represents a knowledge asset of the type *SNEM_Data* as defined in section 5.3.1.2.

While the coordination agent can receive further *requests* or *alerts* and initiate other surveillance agents, the surveillance agent dedicated to order $O_1$ begins to actively gather data from internal data sources. It requests data from a wrapper agent that has, for instance, access to the enterprise resource planning (ERP) system of *Enterprise 2*. Based on SNEM data that the surveillance agent receives in the corresponding *inform* message from the wrapper agent, it extracts knowledge on all related suborders. The data gathering strategy (see section 4.1.2) of a surveillance agent requires that it requests information from suppliers or carriers which have received suborders that are currently active and not finished. Requests for suborders $O_2$ and $O_3$ are sent to the discourse agent which will identify the relevant supply network partners' discourse agents and forward the messages to these (for details of the external communication see section 5.3.2.3). When the suborder recipients send their replies *(inform ($O_2$); inform ($O_3$))*, the discourse agent transmits these to the surveillance agent. To identify the internal surveillance agent that waits for the response, the discourse agent uses a mapping table that consists of *conversation-ids* of forwarded *requests* to suppliers and associated *request* messages sent to the discourse agent by surveillance agents (for details see section 6.1.2.3).

After the surveillance agent has received all data (knowledge asset type: *SourceData*, see section 5.3.1.2) it analyzes and interprets this input with the help of its Fuzzy Logic rule system (see section 4.3) and creates for instance an aggregated order status *AOS* or an assessment of the criticality of a disruptive event (endogenous severity *EnDS*). Results which represent new information created by the surveillance agent, are stored in its knowledge asset *SNEM_Data*. The updated knowledge asset is communicated in an *inform* message to the coordination agent. This reply to the coordination agent's *request* is illustrated in fig. 5-13.

```
(inform-result
  :sender SurveillanceAgent_Order1@Enterprise2
  :receiver CoordinationAgent@Enterprise2
  :content
    (OrderOutgoingID = 1; OrderType = "Warehousing";
    EstimatedDateOfFulfillment = (2004-03-23; 12:00); AggregatedOrderStatus = 0.64;
    Milestones = ((OrderReceiptWarehousing; has_plannedFulfillmentDate(2004-03-17;13:00);
    has_dateOfAchievement (2004-03-17;13.00)) ;
    ....
    (OutgoingGoods; has_plannedFulfillmentDate(2004-03-18;12:00);
    has_dateOfAchievement (NULL))); ActualQuantity = NULL; NoOfPickingFailures= NULL;
    DisruptiveEvents = (has_disruptiveEventID (342); has_description(OutOfStock);
    has_disruptiveEventDate(2004-03-17;15:50); has_ExogenousSeverity (3);
    has_EndogenousSeverity (0.43))
  :ontology SNEM_Ontology
  :conversation-id 8694043)
```

Fig. 5-13. Monitoring result - FIPA-message to coordination agent

In the example order $O_1$ is not yet finished, it is characterized by various SNEM data types, the aggregated order status *AOS* is 0.64 (medium level) and a disruptive event with an endogenous severity *EnDS* of 0.42 (medium severity) is identified. The last two values are calculated by the surveillance agent based on currently available SNEM data on the orders $O_1$, $O_2$ and $O_3$.

Based upon the SNEM data provided by the surveillance agent the coordination agent initializes the alert management activities defined in section 4.4. Besides internal alerts to actors (see section 4.4.4), three possible outcomes of these activities with respect to external alerts can occur:

1. Neither an alert needs to be sent because the alert index *AI* is too low (see section 4.4.2.2), nor any request from the customer who issued $O_1$ is currently pending[22].
2. A *status request* of *Enterprise 1* for $O_1$ has to be answered. Even if it is determined by the coordination agent that an external alert has to be sent to *Enterprise 1*, this alert is integrated in the response to the *request*. A redundant transmission of SNEM data can be prevented.
3. No *request* of *Enterprise 1* is pending and an external alert is required for order $O_1$. The alert is sent as a proactive *Inform(Alert)*[23] to *Enterprise 1*. Note that this *inform* is not associated with any *request,* and a new *conversation-id* is defined by the coordination agent for this message[24].

The possibility to apply an information policy to the content of the *inform* which is directed to the customer of *Enterprise 2* is realized by the coordination agent. The policy is based on the concept defined in section 4.4.5.2. After any alerts or responses to *requests* have been sent by the coordination agent, it checks whether the monitored order $O_1$ has

---

[22] This is indicated by the empty decision box which represents a simple *OR* and not an *XOR*.

[23] An alert has a very similar content with respect to fig. 5-13. It can contain an additional identifier to mark it as an alert. This is justified because an alert is considered as a response to a request that was never generated by a customer but that satisfies the demand for the information on disruptive events. The implicit demand $D_q$ is satisfied by a proactive alert message $M_s$.

been finished yet. If so, it uses the gathered SNEM data to evaluate any $CCP_j$ that have matched this order according to the mechanism described in section 4.2.3.

However, as long as order $O_1$ is not finished (except if the coordination agent terminates the surveillance agent due to some monitoring policy that might be additionally implemented by *Enterprise 2*) proactive monitoring of order $O_1$ is continued by the surveillance agent (see fig. 5-11). Data gathering from internal and external data sources is cyclically reinitiated by the surveillance agent (e.g. influenced by the priority of the order), and update information is interpreted by the Fuzzy Logic rule system. The updated knowledge asset *SNEM_Data* is sent to the coordination agent as an *inform* message, and the coordination agent initiates alert management for $O_1$ again, as described above. As soon as the knowledge asset *SNEM_Data* gathered by the surveillance agent indicates that order $O_1$ has been finished, the coordination agent will terminate the surveillance agent and use the last update of *SNEM_Data* to evaluate any $CCP_j$ that matched $O_1$ (see above).

As illustrated in fig. 5-11 coordination within the distributed agent society is based on the communication of SNEM data. Each instance of an agent type acts autonomously with respect to its proactive capabilities and the messages it receives from other agents[25]. A highly parallel behavior of the distributed agents is the result that realizes the event management processes within a supply network.

### 5.3.2.3    Inter-organizational Communication

Direct interaction between SNEM agent societies of different supply network partners is facilitated through their discourse agents. Messages directed from the coordination agent and the surveillance agents to the discourse agent of an enterprise (see section 5.3.2.2) are intended for external receivers. Two main interaction patterns evolve across a supply network which are depicted in fig. 5-14. They illustrate proactive behavior that is achieved by the agent-based SNEM approach: proactive gathering of SNEM data within a supply network and proactive distribution of alerts in case disruptive events are identified. Both patterns satisfy the implicit demand $D_q$ for information on disruptive events *DE* with

---

[24.] The single use of an inform is a valid instrument to send information between agents if no further interaction in this dialog is intended. In this case the alert will trigger monitoring activities in the customer's SNEM system but no reply to the alert is required. The supplier's sole intention is to forward the information it has gathered to satisfy the implicit demand $D_q$ of its customer regarding information on disruptive events that have been identified in one of its orders. Reactions are taken by the customer, and in subsequent SNEM data gathering rounds the customer will eventually request update information from the supplier. This is discussed in section 5.3.2.3.

[25.] An implementation will have to consider the possibility of "Cancel" messages that can be triggered by agents in case of execution failures. Since different requests are nested within each other, an implementation has to make sure that all related and pending nested requests are cancelled, too.

messages $M_s$ that are exchanged between supply network partners (see definition of the SNEM problem in section 2.1.3.3).

Proactive monitoring of orders is initiated within an enterprise by the coordination agent, based on critical profiles $CCP_j$. The monitoring activities result in *requests* of a surveillance agent to suborder recipients (see fig. 5-11). In fig. 5-14 *Enterprise 1* begins to proactively monitor order $O_{init}$ and sends a *request* to its supplier *Enterprise 2* regarding suborder $O_1$. The *request* is similar[26] to the one illustrated in fig. 5-12. Consequences of this initial *request* are cascading *requests* to the two suppliers of *Enterprise 2* which return SNEM data on the suborders $O_2$ and $O_3$ to *Enterprise 2*. After *Enterprise 2* has interpreted all available data (including its internally gathered data according to fig. 5-11) it returns an *inform* to *Enterprise 1*. In this *inform* SNEM data on order $O_1$ is communicated which integrates relevant information on all currently active suborders of the supply network, as defined in the data gathering concept in section 4.1.2.

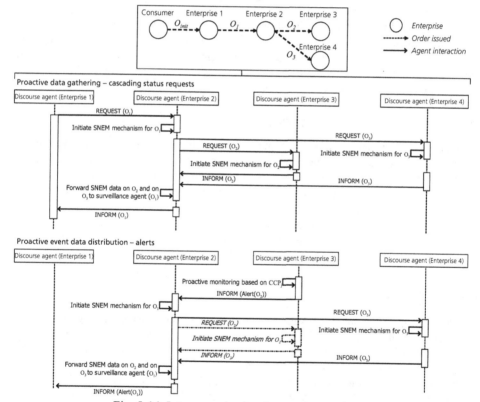

Fig. 5-14. Inter-organizational agent interactions

---

[26.] A restricted set of message types in different situations reduces the complexity of agent interactions. This simplifies the design, implementation, and maintenance of the agent society.

The second aspect of proactivity in event management is concerned with the active distribution of important SNEM data to supply network partners who will be negatively affected by the consequences of disruptive events in the near future. In fig. 5-14 the supplier *Enterprise 3* has identified a disruptive event based on its own proactive monitoring of order $O_2$, assuming that in this scenario neither *Enterprise 1* nor *Enterprise 2* are proactively monitoring order $O_1$. *Enterprise 3* sends an *inform(Alert)* to *Enterprise 2* which acts on this information by initiating a new surveillance agent for the affected superorder $O_1$ (for details see section 5.3.2.2). In this case monitoring activities of *Enterprise 2* may omit the request to *Enterprise 3* in the first data gathering round, because *Enterprise 3* has already sent its most current information in the *inform(Alert)*.

After *Enterprise 2* has gained knowledge on all relevant suborders of its order $O_1$, it can decide whether it has to send an alert to its customer. This might be necessary because the disruptive event at *Enterprise 3* might have such severe effects that the propagation along the path depicted by the order relationships will eventually affect *Enterprise 1* and the *Consumer*. In the example of fig. 5-14 such an alert is necessary, and *Enterprise 1* will eventually initiate monitoring of its own order $O_{init}$ of which order $O_1$ is a relevant suborder. At this point, it is evident to all network partners that some serious situation in this specific network of orders has occurred and further monitoring of the orders is necessary. After a waiting interval a new round of proactive data gathering will eventually be triggered by *Enterprise 1*. This request results in cascading status requests in the whole supply network. However, at any time the supply network partners may identify new critical situations based on their own update cycles and inform other partners based on the alert interaction mechanism.

The result is a system for monitoring critical orders across a supply network with a combination of proactive SNEM data gathering (*pull* mechanism) and proactive distribution of alerts (*push* mechanism). The effectiveness (Are *DEs* identified?) and efficiency (How much communication is necessary?) of the distributed network of SNEM agent societies depend on the ability of the supply network partners to focus their proactive monitoring activities with the help of critical profiles $CCP_j$. It is apparent that partners further downstream in a supply network (that is "near" the *Consumer*) should restrict their proactive monitoring and rely on the proactive monitoring of their suborder recipients and associated alert generation where possible to reduce monitoring efforts in the supply network. An assessment of the impact on efficiency and effectiveness of the mixed *pull/push*-approach of the agent-based SNEM system is presented in section 7.2.5.1.

### 5.3.3 Institutional Agreements

In section 2.2.1.2 the definition of basic institutional agreements to define the rights and obligations in a SNEM solution (that is now to be realized by an agent-society) is requested. Some relevant aspects of such agreements have already been addressed by introducing roles of agents, dependencies between agent types (see section 5.3.1) and main agent interactions (see section 5.3.2). To facilitate execution of an agent-based SNEM solution and to promote dissemination and acceptance of the approach in supply networks some further aspects are considered regarding semantics of interactions, behavior of agents in general, and rules for providing SNEM services to other supply network partners.

### 5.3.3.1    Commitment to an Ontology

Importance of semantics for communication is identified in section 3.2 and an ontology has been designed to model relevant semantic concepts and their relationships for the SNEM domain (see section 3.2.3). To realize agent interactions as proposed in section 5.3.2 each agent has to use an ontology to define the meaning of its messages. To facilitate interaction among all agents in a SNEM society an agreement on the same ontology is necessary which in this case is supposed to be the SNEM ontology. For the purpose of inter-organizational interaction between SNEM systems use of the SNEM ontology is also requested, because conversions between different semantic representations of content can be omitted and implementation of such systems is eased. Therefore, the basic agent concept of a SNEM solution proposed here assumes that all agents commit themselves to the use of the same ontology in order to provide seamless interactions without the need for conversion mechanisms.

However, within realistic inter-organizational supply network settings this assumption may not hold and an integration of other IT-based event management solutions (e.g. an existing T&T or SCEM system of a network partner) might be desired. In this case matching mechanisms between different semantics which are represented by specific ontologies are required. Interfaces to solve this problem are discussed in section 5.6 as part of the discourse agent's design.

### 5.3.3.2    Benevolent Agents

In section 2.1.2.4 the autonomy of an enterprise is a constraint which a SNEM solution has to observe. Although a SNEM system must not interfere with individual strategies of an enterprise, some basic rules are defined to ensure proper execution of a SNEM system. Above all, the objective of proactivity with respect to data gathering and alert generation has to be supported. This results in the following rules that each agent in a SNEM system and thereby each SNEM agent society has to adhere to:

- Each agent exhibits cooperative behavior regarding the requests it receives. If any incoming request is understood by an agent, a trustworthy answer is generated and sent to the requesting agent. Only the scope of the information which is provided may vary due to the application of an information policy as defined in section 4.4.5.2.
- Proactivity regarding the provision of newly acquired knowledge on disruptive events is the common goal for all coordination agents in the various agent societies of a supply network. If the assessment of an enterprise, which is influenced by an individually configured Fuzzy Logic rule-set (see section 4.4.2), indicates the necessity to generate alerts to external partners, no strategic hiding of this information is allowed. The coordination agent communicates this information to affected supply network partners as soon as possible.
- A SNEM system is not used by an enterprise to spy on other agents respectively supply network partners which host these agents. Each enterprise is supposed to commit

itself to this rule. However, to restrict opportunistic behavior which may result in abuse of data by non-trustworthy network partners, each enterprise has the ability to constrain the extent to which it answers requests (see above).

### 5.3.3.3    Free Information Services

Assuming that the benefits of a SNEM solution (see section 2.3) can largely outweigh the costs of implementation and operation of such systems no charges apply for status requests to external supply network partners. This assumption facilitates dissemination and acceptance in supply networks and reduces administrative activities and associated costs of monitoring, compared to the situation when status requests were charged.

## 5.4   Coordination Agent

While descriptions of the agent society focus on organizational structures and interactions among all agents (macro-perspective of AOSE, see section 5.3), a detailed concept for each agent type is provided within the micro-perspective of AOSE in sections 5.4 to 5.7. This detailed concept describes internal resources, behaviors of an agent and related agent interactions with AUML models as proposed in section 5.2.2.2. The coordination agent's design is detailed in subsequent sections. This agent has a central role in the SNEM concept: It decides on initiation of monitoring activities and on generation of alerts thus providing main proactive features for event management.

### 5.4.1   Structure

An overview of structural features of a coordination agent is provided in the AUML class diagram in fig. 5-15. As defined in section 5.3.1 a coordination agent incorporates three roles: *SurveillanceManager*, *AlertManager* and *ProfileManager*. Its main resources encompass several knowledge assets: For decisions on proactive monitoring of orders it relies on critical profiles $CCP_j$ which it also evaluates (see section 4.2). To avoid redundant monitoring of orders by multiple surveillance agents, the coordination agent in a SNEM agent society employs a list of all currently active surveillance agents (*ListOfActiveSA*). Monitoring results are provided by surveillance agents to the coordination agent as instances of the *SNEM_Data* knowledge asset. Based on these results the coordination agent initiates its alert management behaviors. These require Fuzzy Logic rule-sets to determine an alert index *AI* (*FuzzyRuleCA*). For generation and communication of alerts potential receivers (*AlertRecipient*) and media types (*MediaType*) are required (see section 4.4). Alerts which a coordination agent sends to its customers or receives from suborder recipients consist of *SNEM_Data:* This knowledge asset consists of results from the order monitoring process of a suborder (for details on *SNEM_Data* see section 5.5.1).

The behaviors a coordination agent employs to fulfill its roles are analyzed in section 5.4.2 and simply listed in fig. 5-15. A coordination agent relies on several perceptions of its sensors that provide information on its environment. Five agent message types are received by the agent: status requests from customers (*newRequest*), alerts from suborder recipients (*alertReceived*), monitoring results from its surveillance agents (*newStatusUpdateFromSA*). Two message types are received from an internal wrapper agent: a list of newly accepted orders of an enterprise (*newOrders*) and information on a specific order identifier (*orderIncomingID*). The context in which these messages are received is detailed in subsequent sections. The last perception concerns the provision of new critical profiles by a user (*newCCPj*), for instance as the result of profile discovery mechanisms (see section 4.2.2) or by random generation of profiles (see section 4.2.3.4).

| <<agent>> CoordinationAgent |
|---|
| **Role** SurveillanceManager, AlertManager, ProfileManager |
| **Knowledge Asset** CriticalProfile, ListOfActiveSA, SNEM_Data, FuzzyRuleCA, AlertRecipient, MediaType |
| **Behavior** **Reac** *[newRequest]* ManageCustomerRequest *[requestProcessed]* **Reac** *[alertReceived]* ManageIncomingAlert *[alertProcessed]* **Reac** *[newStatusUpdateFromSA]* ManageStatusUpdate *[monitoringStatusUpdated]* **Reac** *[newMessage]* WaitForMessages *[messageProcessed]* **Pro** *[cyclic | newCCPj]* ManageProactiveMonitoring *[monitoringInitiated]* **Pro** *[cyclic]* GenerateProfiles *[newCCPj]* **Int** *[monitoringStatusUpdated]* AlertGeneration*[alertSent | noAlertSent]* **Int** *[monitoringStatusUpdated ∧ orderFinished ]* ManageProfiles *[profilesAssessed]* **Int** *[isCalled]* CheckForExistingSA *[returnAID | startSA ∧ returnAID]* **Int** *[isCalled]* MapSuborderToIncoming *[returnOrderIncomingID]* **Int** *[isCalled]* SendMessage *[messageSent]* |
| **Perception** ACL_Messages (newRequest | alertReceived | newStatusUpdateFromSA | newOrders | orderIncomingID) newCCPj |

Fig. 5-15. AUML class diagram of a coordination agent

## 5.4.2 Behaviors

### 5.4.2.1 Overview

An overview of behaviors associated with the roles of a coordination agent and interdependencies between these behaviors is presented in fig. 5-16. Two basic behaviors realize functions of sensors and effectors of a coordination agent:

1. The reactive behavior *WaitForMessages* acts upon newly received agent messages, extracts their content and makes it available to other behaviors of the agent[27].
2. A *SendMessage* behavior is triggered by other behaviors and thus defined as internal (*Int*). It is able to influence the environment of a coordination agent by sending messages based on an agent communication language[28].

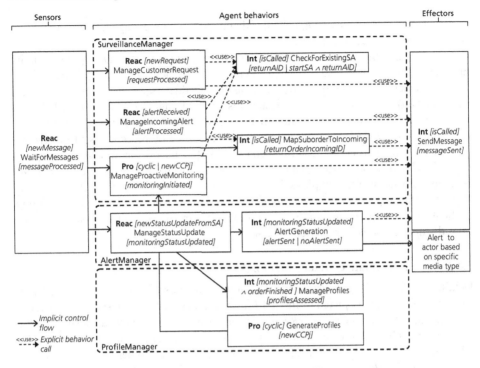

Fig. 5-16. Behaviors of a coordination agent

Within a coordination agent's role as *SurveillanceManager* three behaviors are reactively or proactively initiated: The behaviors *ManageCustomerRequest* and *ManageIncomingAlert* react to perceived agent messages, namely the perception types *newRequest* or *alertReceived,* as indicated in the preconditions of these behaviors. Besides, *ManageProactiveMonitoring* is cyclically initiated by the coordination agent or in case new critical profiles are available. Hence, it is a proactive behavior whose initiation is controlled internally by the agent. Before a new surveillance agent is launched, each of these three behaviors tests for existing surveillance agents, and this is conducted by a separate behavior *CheckForExistingSA*. An additional task arises, if an alert is received from a suborder recipient, because this alert refers to a specific suborder of a supplier. Before the coordination agent is able to check for any existing surveillance agents due to the alert, it has to identify the customer's order to which this suborder belongs. This information is retrieved

---

[27.]Notice that the *WaitForMessages* behavior does not necessarily trigger other operations. Instead, other behaviors decide autonomously as defined by their preconditions when to act on certain new information that is made available by the *WaitForMessages* behavior. This architecture realizes flexible behavior of an agent and offers a hot spot for future integration of high-level planning mechanisms for agent activities (see also section 5.2.2.2).

[28.]Additional communication with actors, e.g. via email as a result of the alert generation, is a further effector type of the coordination agent indicated in fig. 5-16.

by the *MapSuborderToIncoming* behavior that queries a wrapper agent to gain the information (details in section 5.4.2.2).

As part of the *AlertManager* role a coordination agent receives status updates from its surveillance agents with results of their monitoring activities. The *ManageStatusUpdate* behavior reacts by updating corresponding knowledge assets on monitored orders (*SNEM_Data*). As soon as an order's status is updated, the *AlertManagement* behavior acts upon new status data and decides on alerts as described in section 4.4.

The third role *ProfileManager* is not directly triggered by perceptions of the agent's sensors. Only if an order has been finished (indicated by the precondition *monitoringStatusUpdated AND orderFinished*) a profile evaluation mechanism in the *ManageProfiles* behavior activates itself. It employs the mechanisms described in section 4.2.3. Additionally, new critical profiles are randomly generated by the *GenerateProfiles* behavior on a cyclical basis to support autonomous adaptation of the monitoring activities to new sources of disruptive events (see section 4.2.3.4).

### 5.4.2.2    Surveillance Management Behaviors

Detailed AUML activity diagrams for each of the behaviors relevant to the *Surveillance-Management* role are depicted in fig. 5-17. In case a new status request from a customer is received, the *ManageCustomerRequest* behavior becomes active and uses the *CheckForExistingSA* behavior to determine the responsible surveillance agent's identifier (*AID*) which it needs to request a status update. A response to the customer request is managed separately by the *AlertManagement* role (see section 5.4.2.3). The behavior *CheckForExistingSA* returns the required agent identifier (*AID*) and initiates a new surveillance agent, if none exists yet for the order mentioned in the status request.

An alert which is received from a suborder recipient to inform the coordination agent's enterprise of a disruptive event in a suborder's fulfillment represents a second type of perception for the coordination agent (see also fig. 5-15). As indicated in section 5.4.2.1 the supplier's suborder has to be matched with an order of the alert recipient. This is realized by the *MapSuborderToIncoming* behavior. It extracts the *SuborderID* from the alert message and sends a request to a wrapper agent that is responsible for an enterprise resource planning (ERP) system (or a similar data source). The wrapper agent is able to identify the relevant superorder which was issued by a customer of the coordination agent's enterprise: In the terms of the SNEM ontology an *OrderIncoming* is searched that originally triggered the suborder (= *OrderOutgoing*). This result is returned in an agent message, received by the *WaitForMessages* behavior (see fig. 5-16), and processed by the *MapSuborderToIncoming* behavior. Finally, the *OrderIncomingID* is returned to the *ManageIncomingAlert* behavior, and the next steps are identical to those of the *Manage-CustomerRequest* behavior.

Besides these two reactive behaviors, the coordination agent provides a proactive behavior that governs its decisions on orders to be monitored proactively (*ManageProactiveMonitoring*). This behavior relies on the use of critical profiles $CCP_j$ as defined in section 4.2.1. It is initialized cyclically or in case new $CCP_j$ are generated randomly or externally by a user (see fig. 5-17). First, information is gained on newly received orders of the enterprise. This is achieved by sending a request for a list of all new orders to a wrapper agent responsible for the ERP system. It returns the knowledge asset *ListOfNewOrders* which consists of *SNEM_Data* instances distinguished in fig. 5-17 by an index *NewOrders* (see fig. 5-17). These orders are used as the facts that are compared during profile matching by the expert system with all currently available $CCP_j$. All orders that match at least one $CCP_j$ are selected (instances of *SNEM_Data* with index *MatchingOrders*) and subjected to checking whether any surveillance agents already exist. As above for requests and alerts, an agent message to the relevant surveillance agents concludes the execution of this behavior.

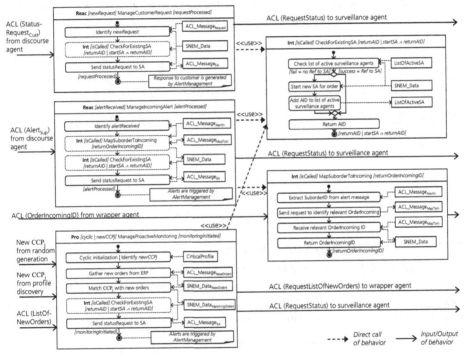

Fig. 5-17. Surveillance management behaviors

### 5.4.2.3  Alert Management Behaviors

Since the coordination agent creates all surveillance agents, each surveillance agent returns its monitoring results to the coordination agent. Even if no explicit request for an order's status is sent from the coordination agent to surveillance agents, status updates are returned proactively as they become available (see also section 5.5.2.2). These ACL agent messages are received by the *WaitForMessages* behavior (see fig. 5-16). The *ManageStatusUpdate* behavior (see fig. 5-18) acts upon this information and updates the knowledge asset *SNEM_Data* that corresponds to the monitored order. For instance, new status data types such as milestone information or quality measurements are stored in the *SNEM_Data* asset as they become available. The postcondition *monitoringStatusUpdated* is the precondition of the *AlertGeneration* behavior with all its functions as defined in section 4.4: Monitoring results for a newly updated order are assessed with Fuzzy Logic, and a new alert index *AI* is calculated for this order. Based on the *AI* a decision is made whether an alert is necessary. Assuming that an alert is necessary, the escalation mechanism is initiated as described in section 4.4.3. In the next steps recipients as well as appropriate media types are chosen, and content is selected from the available *SNEM_Data* of the order. Finally, alerts are sent either as an agent message, if this is directed to the customer's SNEM agent system, or via other channels such as email or mobile phone to actors within the enterprise of the coordination agent. In case a customer request for status data is still unanswered for this order (see section 5.4.2.2), the *AlertGeneration* behavior answers this request regardless of whether an alert is necessary or not (see *Response$_{Cust}$* in fig. 5-18 and section 5.4.3).

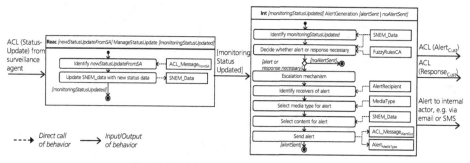

Fig. 5-18. Alert management behaviors

### 5.4.2.4 Profile Management Behaviors

After an order which is monitored by a surveillance agent has been finished, a final status update is received by the coordination agent before the surveillance agent is terminated. The precondition *monitoringStatusUpdated AND orderFinished* applies and the *ManageProfiles* behavior assesses any critical profiles $CCP_j$ that matched the finished monitored order (see fig. 5-19).

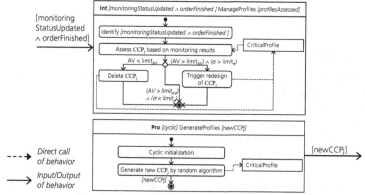

Fig. 5-19. Profile management behaviors

An aggregated value $AV$ is calculated as defined in section 4.2.3.2, and the standard deviation of selected quality measures is assessed. In case neither the $AV$ nor the standard deviation indicate a low quality of a $CCP_j$, it is used again for further profile matching by the *ManageProactiveMonitoring* behavior. If the $AV$ indicates a quality below a predefined quality, the $CCP_j$ is deleted from the knowledge base of the coordination agent and no longer used for profile matching. For a standard deviation above a predefined limit a user is triggered to redesign the $CCP_j$, before it is used again for profile matching.

Another behavior relevant to the role *ProfileManagement* generates new profiles randomly (*GenerateProfile*). These are used for profile matching and are subsequently evaluated by the *ManageProfiles* behavior when they have matched orders in the profile matching mechanism of the *ManageProactiveMonitoring* behavior. Details of the profile generation mechanism are described in section 4.2.3.4.

## 5.4.3 Interactions

Main interactions between different agent types are presented in section 5.3.2.2. The AUML sequence diagram in fig. 5-20 illustrates how different behaviors of a coordination agent participate in interactions with other agent types. For instance, mapping of a suborder to its superorder through a request to a wrapper agent is a specific detail that is not incorporated in the overview in section 5.3.2.2. The same applies to the request to a wrapper agent for a list of all newly arrived orders; this request is triggered by the *ManageProactiveMonitoring* behavior.

The behaviors that initiate monitoring of an order (*ManageCustomerRequest*, *ManageIncomingAlert*, *ManageProactiveMonitoring*) depend all on the *CheckForExistingSA* behavior that initializes a new surveillance agent, if none yet exists for order $O_1$ in the example. As soon as the surveillance agent is known to the coordination agent, a request for status information is sent to the surveillance agent. In fig. 5-20 the difference between the two reactive behaviors *ManageCustomerRequest*, *ManageIncomingAlert* and the proactive behavior *ManageProactiveMonitoring* is apparent: In the first two cases an external agent message is sent via the enterprise's discourse agent to the coordination agent. The coordination agent has to react to both messages, whereas in the last case monitoring is initiated without external triggers autonomously by the coordination agent itself by means of the profile matching mechanism.

Cyclically, surveillance agents gather and analyze status data on the orders they are responsible for and send messages with status updates to the coordination agent, e.g. *Inform(O1)* in fig. 5-20 (bottom). Depending on whether a request is still unanswered and on the decision to generate alerts, either a response to the request, an alert or nothing is sent to the customer via the discourse agent. Internal alerts are not further depicted since they do not rely on agent messages but on other communication channels. In case a monitored order has been finished, the *ProfileManagement* behavior evaluates relevant $CCP_j$ as described above in section 5.4.2.4.

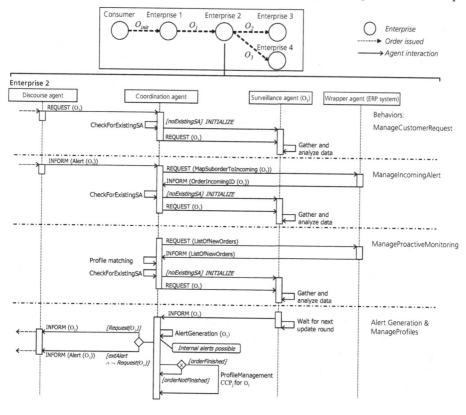

Fig. 5-20. Agent interactions of a coordination agent

## 5.5 Surveillance Agent

A surveillance agent is responsible for proactively creating the content $C_p$ of a message $M_s$ which is needed to satisfy the implicit demand $D_q$ of a customer for event-related information (see section 2.1.3). Structural features such as knowledge about SNEM data of monitored orders and behaviors for data gathering and data analysis determine the interactions of a surveillance agent with other agent types. These are detailed in the following sections.

### 5.5.1 Structure

As defined in section 5.3.1.1 two major roles are associated with this production process: gathering SNEM data from internal and external sources by the role *InformationGatherer* and automated analysis of this data performed by the role *DataAnalyzer* (see fig. 5-21).

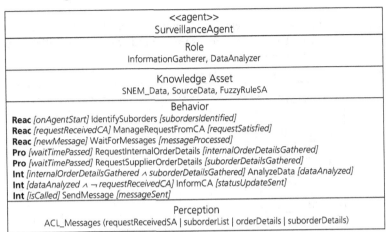

Fig. 5-21. AUML class diagram of a surveillance agent

Three types of knowledge assets are used by the different roles of a surveillance agent:

1. Any surveillance agent has exactly one knowledge asset of the *SNEM_Data* type, because it is dedicated to a single order (*OrderIncoming* as the ontological concept). It cyclically updates this knowledge asset which represents content $C_p$. This knowledge asset consists of all data types defined in the SNEM ontology (see section 3.2.3). Its content is gathered by the *InformationGatherer* role (e.g. milestone data, data on disruptive events, quality measures), but it also contains results of the data analysis performed by the *DataAnalyzer* role (e.g. an aggregated order status *AOS* (see section 4.3.3)).

2. To distinguish the content $C_p$ from data which a surveillance agent receives during its data gathering activities, a knowledge asset type *SourceData* is introduced. For each suborder and for the monitored superorder separate *SourceData* assets are generated. Basically, they consist of the same data types as the *SNEM_Data* asset, but without analysis results of the *DataAnalyzer* role. *SourceData* assets are updated when a surveillance agent receives agent messages from either internal sources (wrapper agents) or external SNEM agent systems of suborder recipients.

3. The various *SourceData* assets which a surveillance agent manages are used by the *DataAnalyzer* role. It analyzes these knowledge assets and updates the single *SNEM_Data* asset with analysis results. For these actions the *DataAnalyzer* relies on a set of fuzzy-rules (see sections 4.3.3 and 4.3.4) which are stored in the knowledge asset type *FuzzyRuleSA*.

Surveillance agents distinguish four main types of agent messages they perceive with their sensors. One is sent by the coordination agent and requests status information on the monitored order from the surveillance agent (*requestReceivedSA*) while the other three are responses a surveillance agent receives during its data gathering activities. Upon its initialization the agent identifies all relevant suborders with the help of a wrapper agent: It receives a *suborderList*. During its data gathering cycles *orderDetails* from internal sources are provided by wrapper agents and *suborderDetails* by suborder recipients (external supply network partners). All response messages which a surveillance agent receives contain *SourceData* knowledge assets (see above).

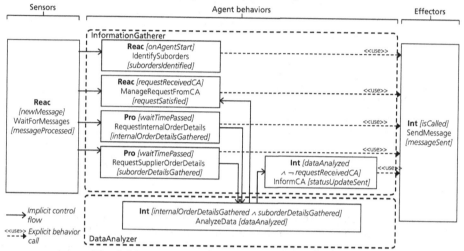

Fig. 5-22. Overview behaviors of a surveillance agent

## 5.5.2    Behaviors

### 5.5.2.1    Overview

Every surveillance agent is started by a coordination agent (see section 5.4.2.2)[29]. During its initialization an identification number (ID) for the order to be monitored is provided to the surveillance agent. The reactive behavior *IdentifySuborders* is triggered only once during an agent's life cycle: upon its initialization (see fig. 5-22: precondition *onAgentStart*). It identifies all relevant suborders of the order to be monitored and provides a list of suborders to the other behaviors of the surveillance agent.

Based on the ID of the order to be monitored and on the list of its suborders, both proactive behaviors for gathering status data from internal data sources of the enterprise (*RequestInternalOrderDetails*) and requesting data from suborder recipients (*RequestSupplierOrderDetails*) act according to their own schedules: Data gathering is reinitiated by these two behaviors cyclically. Update cycles are determined by waiting times between data gathering rounds. SNEM data gathered by these behaviors is input to a complex internal behavior *AnalyzeData* that realizes the *DataAnalyzer* role and is based on the functions defined in section 4.3. Two behaviors manage the communication of monitoring results to the coordination agent:

---

[29.]Every surveillance agent possesses the same behaviors for sensors and effectors as a coordination agent: *WaitForMessages* and *SendMessage*. These behaviors are standard features of all agents in a SNEM agent system and are therefore not discussed repeatedly.

1. In case the coordination agent explicitly requests an update from a surveillance agent[30], the reactive *ManageRequestFromCA* behavior assures that a response to this request is sent as soon as new information is gathered, analyzed and provided by the other behaviors described above.
2. Once a surveillance agent is initialized it is supposed to monitor an order until this order has been finished. Therefore, status updates that are generated cyclically become available without explicit requests for information from the coordination agent. Each surveillance agent is responsible for forwarding its newest findings to the coordination agent proactively, which is realized by the *InformCA* behavior. *InformCA* becomes active, if no request from the coordination agent remains unanswered for the reason that otherwise update information will be provided by the *ManageRequestFromCA* behavior to the coordination agent. Thereby, redundant communication activity is prevented.

### 5.5.2.2 Information Gathering Behaviors

Details on the behaviors of the *InformationGathering* role of a surveillance agent are depicted in fig. 5-23. On initialization of the agent the *IdentifySuborders* behavior sends a request for a list of all relevant suborders to a wrapper agent that provides access to the ERP system of the enterprise. The list is provided in an agent message from which the behavior extracts relevant information on suborders (primarily suborder identifiers (ID) and supplier IDs)) and adds this data to its knowledge asset *SNEM_Data*. This knowledge asset stores all information on the monitored order and is regularly updated by different behaviors whenever new information becomes available.

The behavior *ManageRequestFromCA* identifies any requests for status updates from the coordination agent and waits for the end of the next status update cycle. This is determined by the condition *dataAnalyzed* as the relevant postcondition of the *AnalyzeData* behavior (see fig. 5-24), because update rounds are scheduled independently of any status requests from a coordination agent (see below). As soon as the update cycle is finished, a status update is sent as a response to the request. It contains the *SNEM_Data* knowledge asset with any new data on the monitored order, e.g. milestones achieved, changed quality measures, new disruptive events. At all other times, whenever a status update is available but no request is currently pending, the behavior *InformCA* acts upon the updated *SNEM_Data*: It sends a proactive inform to the coordination agent[31].

---

[30]. A coordination agent will request status information from a surveillance agent when it receives a request from a customer, or an alert from a supplier, or when a (new) critical profile $CCP_j$ matches the monitored order for which a specific surveillance agent is already responsible.

[31]. A similar mechanism is used for generating inter-organizational alerts (see section 5.3.2.3).

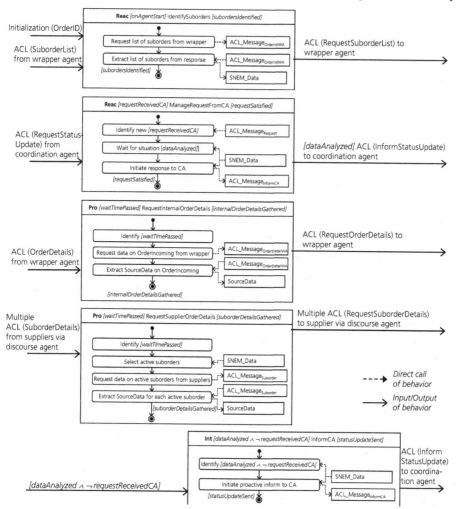

Fig. 5-23. Information gathering behaviors

The two proactive behaviors which schedule their data gathering activities autonomously, both request SNEM data from other agent types:

1. *RequestInternalDetails*: This behavior queries a wrapper agent that has access e.g. to the ERP system of the enterprise to gather internal data on the monitored order. A *SourceData* knowledge asset is created by the behavior when it receives the response. This knowledge asset provides the most current information available from internal data sources on the monitored order and is used as one input for the *Analyze-Data* behavior (see section 5.5.2.3).

2. *RequestSupplierOrderDetails* as the second proactive behavior first identifies all currently active suborders from the list of relevant suborders of the monitored order. It uses the data gathering strategy defined in section 4.1.2.2 that distinguishes procure-

ment and distribution suborders. Based on progress of the monitored order's fulfillment, the behavior only selects a subset of all suborders. It generates requests to the suborder recipients' agent-based SNEM systems which are sent via the discourse agent to external supply network partners (see section 5.3.2.3). Responses are treated similar to the *RequestInternalDetails* behavior: For each suborder a *SourceData* knowledge asset is created and all these *SourceData* assets represent input on external suborders to the *AnalyzeData* behavior.

### 5.5.2.3    Data Analysis Behavior

A surveillance agent analyzes the various data inputs it gathers from internal and external data sources and thereby establishes an assessement of the current situation of its monitored order. For each update round it has exactly one *SourceData* knowledge asset that represents the most current information available from internal data sources (e.g. ERP systems) and possibly a number of *SourceData* assets according to the number of currently active suborders. The *AnalyzeData* behavior waits for these inputs (see precondition), before it starts its analysis and interpretation (see fig. 5-24).

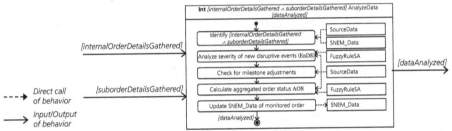

Fig. 5-24. Data analysis behavior

Three analysis steps are realized within the behavior, according to the three different analytical perspectives identified in section 4.3.1.2:

1.  Newly identified disruptive events are evaluated with respect to the current situation of the monitored order's situation. Based on Fuzzy Logic a so called *Endogenous Disruptive Event Severity EnDS* is calculated for each disruptive event (see section 4.3.4). The knowledge asset *FuzzyRuleSA* provides knowledge for data analysis to this part of the behavior.

2.  Assuming that effects on planned fulfillment dates of milestones are identified, a heuristic adjustment of the milestone plans is conducted (see section 4.3.5). However, this step can be omitted, if data is not available (e.g. incompleteness of gathered SNEM data as discussed in section 4.1.2.5).

3.  In a final analysis step an overall *Aggregated Order Status AOS* is calculated based on Fuzzy Logic rules coded in another instance of the knowledge asset type *FuzzyRuleSA*. The *AOS* integrates various indicators of status data such as delays, delivery shortages or quality measures into one abstract measure to rate the status of an order (see section 4.3.3).

All results of the various analysis steps, along with selected data types gathered from external sources (e.g. new important disruptive events in suborders), and updates of SNEM data types for the monitored order are integrated in the *SNEM_Data* knowledge asset of the surveillance agent. Typical updates are for instance new estimated fulfillment dates of milestones, a new *AOS* or newly discovered disruptive events along with their respective *EnDS*. The updated *SNEM_Data* knowledge asset is then sent according to the mechanisms described in section 5.5.2.2 to the coordination agent, which in turn will decide on the generation of alerts (see section 5.4.2.3).

## 5.5.3 Interactions

All interactions with other agent types that result from behaviors of a surveillance agent are depicted in fig. 5-25. In the example a surveillance agent for order $O_1$ is initialized by the coordination agent. Subsequently, it issues a request for the list of relevant suborders of order $O_1$ to the wrapper agent which retrieves this data and sends an inform message including the requested list.

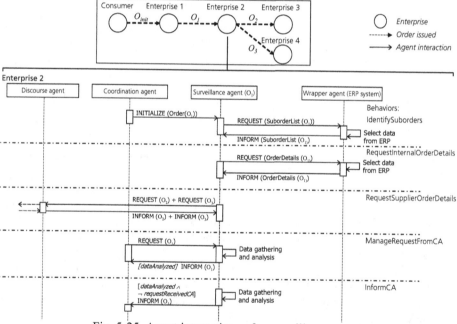

Fig. 5-25. Agent interactions of a surveillance agent

Proactive data gathering is directed to the wrapper agent by the *RequestInternalOrderDetails* behavior: A request for new information on $O_1$ is sent. Similar requests regarding currently active suborders $O_2$ and $O_3$ of order $O_1$ are sent to the discourse agent by the *RequestSupplierOrderDetails* behavior. For both types of requests responses are received as inform messages.

In case the coordination agent actively requests a status update from the surveillance agent (either because *Enterprise 1* has sent a request for information or because one of the suppliers has sent an alert to *Enterprise 2* or some critical profile has matched order $O_1$), the surveillance agent answers as soon as the next status update is available (*ManageRequestFromCA* behavior). For situations where no request from the coordination agent exists the *InformCA* behavior sends an inform message to the coordination agent when a new status update is available.

## 5.6  Discourse Agent

An enterprise's discourse agent serves as the interface to other supply network partners as far as inter-organizational event management activities are concerned. Hence, security issues and mechanisms to ensure quality of data exchange (e.g. semantic consistency of messages) are vital to a discourse agent. Both are specifically reflected in the structure and behaviors of this agent type.

### 5.6.1  Structure

A discourse agent is responsible for managing all external communication of a SNEM agent society with supply network partners. This includes management of communication processes in especially issues of syntactic and semantic quality of external messages. These responsibilities are inherited by the *CommunicationManager* role defined in section 5.3.1.1 and depicted in the AUML class diagram of a discourse agent in fig. 5-26. Every software agent uses the SNEM ontology to create its messages but the discourse agent requires this ontology and eventually other ontologies as explicit knowledge assets to check for semantic correctness of external messages and translate content as required (see also section 5.6.2). The same applies to content languages that provide the syntax to define propositions based on an ontology - they define the "grammar" of the content of an agent message (*Willmott et al. 2004, pp. 140*).

A second major aspect of a discourse agent's responsibilities is security of communication with external partners. This is managed by the *SecurityManager* role as proposed in section 5.3.1.1. Various parameters such as logins, passwords and encoding/decoding parameters are subsumed in a knowledge asset type *SecurityParameter*. It is required by the *SecurityManager* role to fulfill tasks of securing or decoding agent messages that are directed to or received from external supply network partners[32].

Two main perceptions of a discourse agent are distinguished: inbound messages from supply network partners directed to an agent within the enterprise and outbound messages from internal agents to external network partners. A third perception is a response re-

---

[32]For the SNEM concept, communication security within an enterprise is assumed to be given and it is therefore not further addressed.

ceived from a global directory facilitator where discourse agents request address information on other network partners' agent systems.

| <<agent>><br>DiscourseAgent |
|---|
| Role<br>CommunicationManager, SecurityManager |
| Knowledge Asset<br>Ontologies, ContentLanguages, SecurityParameter |
| Behavior<br>**Reac** *[inboundMessage ]* ManageInboundMessage *[inboundMessageHandled]*<br>**Reac** *[outboundMessage]* ManageOutboundMessage *[outboundMessageSent]*<br>**Reac** *[newMessage]* WaitForMessages *[inboundMessage | outboundMessage]*<br>**Int** *[isCalled]* DecodeEncode *[messageDecoded | messageEncoded]*<br>**Int** *[isCalled]* CheckContentLanguage *[languageChecked]*<br>**Int** *[isCalled]* CheckOntology *[ontologyChecked]*<br>**Int** *[isCalled]* SendMessage *[messageSent]* |
| Perception<br>ACL_Messages (inboundMessage | outboundMessage | requestGlobalDF) |

Fig. 5-26. AUML class diagram of a discourse agent

## 5.6.2  Behaviors

### 5.6.2.1    Overview

A discourse agent does not provide proactive behaviors, because it acts as an interface between external supply network partners and the internal agent types of a SNEM agent society. Hence, it receives messages from both kinds of actors and reacts upon these, but has
no need to proactively create new messages. In fig. 5-27 two reactive behaviors manage
inbound messages received from supply network partners (*ManageInboundMessage*) and
outbound     messages     received     from     internal     SNEM     agent     types
(*ManageOutboundMessage*). In each case, messages are assessed within other behaviors
(see <<*use*>> relationships in fig. 5-27) and then forwarded to either internal agents of
the agent society (inbound message) or to external partners (outbound message)[33].

Two behaviors for assessing the quality of inbound messages from external partners
are provided by the *CommunicationManager* role: one for checking the content language
and a second for assessing the ontological representation within an agent message. A content language defines the syntactic structure of a message, that is how different terms are
arranged to form a logic proposition. For instance, different order attributes are separated
by a colon (":"), and details of attributes are clustered in parentheses. An example in the
FIPA  Semantic  Language  (*FIPA  2002d*)  for  a  SNEM  data  object  is    *(Order*

---

[33.]Note: The perspective of a discourse agent is that of an enterprise which receives messages from
external partners (*inbound*) or sends messages to these (*outbound*) via the "interface" represented by the discourse agent.

*:has_OrderType (ProductionOrder) :has_OrderStatus (OrderStatus :has_Value 0.56))*
with order attributes separated by colons and an order status refined in parentheses.

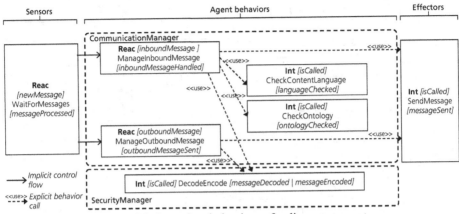

Fig. 5-27. Overview behaviors of a discourse agent

Besides the syntactic structure of a message defined by a content language, semantic meanings of terms are defined in an ontology (see section 3.2.3). Potentially, a translation between different ontologies is required. Although on a conceptual level syntactic and semantic quality of external messages can be assumed as long as every supply network partner implements the same type of SNEM agent system (see section 5.3.3.1), this assumption does not always hold in realistic environments. A multitude of partner systems is thinkable, and neither syntactic nor semantic characteristics can be guaranteed beforehand in a supply network. Therefore, a discourse agent acts as a filter for a SNEM agent society and assures that only messages are forwarded to internal agent types (coordination and surveillance agents) which can be understood and interpreted by these.

For outbound messages received by the discourse agent a correct syntactic and semantic format is assumed, because these messages are created by SNEM agent types. Thus, these messages are forwarded as such to external supply network partners after encoding. A possible extension to the concept is a translation into another ontology and/or content language, if that is required by a recipient (reverse mechanism of *CheckContentLanguage* and *CheckOntology*). However, it is assumed that other supply network partners manage their inbound messages accordingly and that necessary translation is conducted on the receiver's side. This reduces implementation efforts for each supply network partner to the realization of matching algorithms for inbound messages.

### 5.6.2.2    Communication Management Behaviors

Each behavior of the *CommunicationManager* role is detailed in fig. 5-28. The *ManageInboundMessage* behavior identifies messages from those supply network partners that have been received by the *WaitForMessages* behavior (see fig. 5-27).

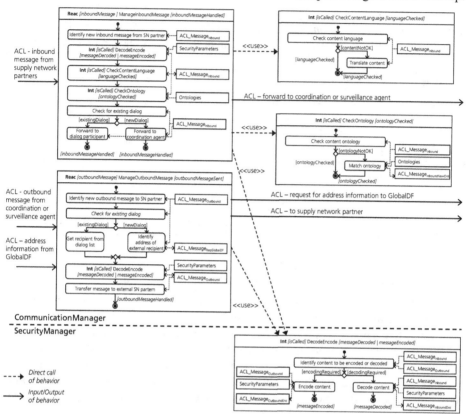

Fig. 5-28. Behavior details of a discourse agent

In a first step the content of the message is decoded by the *DecodeEncode* behavior (for details see section 5.6.2.3). The next steps check content language and ontology. This is realized by the internal behaviors *CheckContentLanguage* and *CheckOntology* which are called by the *ManageInboundMessage* behavior. The behaviors check whether a received message conforms to syntax (content language) and semantics (ontology) used by the SNEM agent society (for details see also section 6.1.2.2)[34]. For cases where conformance is not given, a translation approach to a different content language respectively matching to another ontology is conducted[35]. Finally, the behavior searches for an existing dialog and the respective internal dialog participant: This can only be a surveillance agent which has sent a request for information to a supplier (see section 5.5.2.2 for details). If a dialog participant is identified, the processed message is forwarded to this agent. In the other

---

[34.]It is possible that syntactic or semantic checks fail and a message is not understood. In that case a "not-understood" message as defined in FIPA interaction protocols (see section 5.3.2.1) is returned to the sender (a supply network partner). This case is not depicted in fig. 5-28 since such robustness aspects are relevant for implementation but not for the concept itself.

case, the coordination agent receives the message, since it can either be an alert from a supplier or a status request of a customer. Both types of messages are handled by the coordination agent (see section 5.4).

Outbound messages from the coordination agent or any surveillance agent of an outside enterprise are processed in the *ManageOutboundMessage* behavior. In its first activity it checks for an existing dialog within a list of active dialogs. If one exists, the recipient of the message is directly extracted from the list. Otherwise, the behavior identifies the address of the external supply network partner. For this purpose the global directory facilitator agent *GlobalDF* (introduced in section 5.3.1.2) is queried with, for instance, an enterprise name or an enterprise identification number as a parameter. It returns address information required to send an agent message to the intended recipient. The address is composed of details about the agent platform of the recipient and the agent identifier of the discourse agent at the recipients platform[36]. Before the message is forwarded to the supply network partner via the *SendMessage* behavior, it is encoded by the *DecodeEncode* behavior.

### 5.6.2.3    Security Management Behavior

Encoding and decoding of external messages is conducted in the *SecurityManagement* behavior which is also depicted in fig. 5-28. Depending on parameters provided by the calling behavior, a message is either encoded based on implemented security methods or decoded. For instance, if a public-key-infrastructure is used, the discourse agent encodes the message with the public key of the recipient which it receives from the global directory facilitator (see above). The recipient decodes the message with its private key (e.g. *Bodendorf 1999, pp. 34*). During decoding of a message a similar process as for encoding is conducted, assuming that necessary keys are available to the discourse agent. If the message cannot be decoded, a failure is generated and the discourse agent sends a "not-understood" message to the sender of the message (not depicted in fig. 5-28).

## 5.6.3    Interactions

Both reactive behaviors of a discourse agent act upon interactions with other agents inside the enterprise and externally with supply network partners' discourse agents as depicted in fig. 5-29. In the example the discourse agent of *Enterprise 2* receives three types of inbound messages (from top to bottom):

1.  A status request from its customer *Enterprise 1* regarding order $O_1$ is received.
2.  Each suppliers may send alerts to its customer *Enterprise 2* regarding orders $O_2$ or

---

[35.]Especially ontology matching is a complex problem not yet solved. Constant research efforts are made, e.g. in the DFG project on *Adaptive Agent Applications and Autonomy (A4)* as part of the German priority research program on *Intelligent Agents in Realistic Business Scenarios (1083)*.

[36.]All agent platforms of different enterprises are required to register with the *GlobalDF*.

$O_3$ which are suborders of $O_1$ . Only an alert from *Enterprise 3* is depicted in fig. 5-29.

3. Both suppliers respond to status requests of *Enterprise 2* (only *Enterprise 3* depicted) which have been initiated by a surveillance agent responsible for $O_1$ .

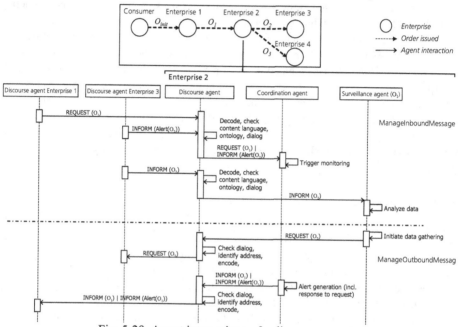

Fig. 5-29. Agent interactions of a discourse agent

In each case the discourse agent decodes the messages if necessary and checks content language and ontology as defined in section 5.6.2.2. Depending on whether a dialog exists, messages are forwarded to the coordination agent (= no existing dialog) or to a surveillance agent (= unfinished dialog of a status request).

Similar to inbound messages different types of outbound messages are distinguished (from top to bottom in fig. 5-29 (lower half)):

1. A surveillance agent for order $O_1$ requests status data from a supplier regarding a relevant suborder (in the example a request to *Enterprise 3* concerning $O_2$ ) which is forwarded to the external recipient's discourse agent after initiating a new dialog, identifying the recipient's address and encoding the message. A new dialog is initiated because a new request is issued by the surveillance agent. Logging the dialog is needed to determine the surveillance agent as the intended recipient of a response to be received by the discourse agent in the future (see above),

2. The coordination agent either responds to a former status request of a customer with an *Inform($O_1$)* message, or it has received update information on a monitored order that requires an alert of its customer while no status request of this customer is pending (*Inform(Alert($O_1$))* in the example of fig. 5-29). Both cases are very similar since the message content is the same and only the type of message differs slightly (see

section 4.4.1.2). In each case, the discourse agent forwards the message to its counter part at *Enterprise 1*.

Not depicted in the sequence diagram of fig. 5-29 is the query to the *GlobalDF* for address information which is realized as a simple *Request* interaction protocol within the *ManageOutboundMessage* behavior (see section 5.6.2.2).

## 5.7 Wrapper Agent

A wrapper agent is a dedicated agent that serves as an interface to proprietary data sources such as data bases. Types of data sources that are accessed by a SNEM agent system and are thus relevant to the concept of a wrapper agent are described in section 3.3 while the design of a wrapper agent is detailed below.

### 5.7.1   Structure

Two basic roles are assumed by a wrapper agent (see fig. 5-30): Upon request it extracts data from a data source, for which it is responsible (*DataRetriever*). As soon as data is extracted from the source, it is transformed into a standardized format according to the SNEM ontology (*DataTransformer*). Thus, other agent types receive data in a standardized format, and heterogeneous data sources are hidden from them.

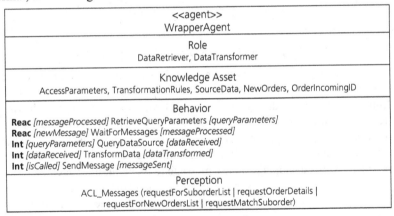

Fig. 5-30. AUML class diagram of a wrapper agent

Main knowledge assets associated with these tasks are access parameters for the specific data source, to which a wrapper agent is dedicated (*AccessParameters*), as well as rules for mapping this basic data to the semantics of the knowledge asset type *SourceData* (*TransformationRules*). *SourceData* is sent in response to a request of a surveillance agent (see also section 5.5.2.2). To satisfy requests of a coordination agent, a list of all newly accepted orders needed for profile matching (*NewOrder*) and an identifier for a monitored order to handle incoming alerts (*OrderIncomingID*) are provided additionally (see also section 5.4.2).

Perceptions of a wrapper agent are determined by all types of data requests issued by other agents to retrieve data from a proprietary data source. A surveillance agent requests a list of all suborders at its initialization and subsequently order details in each update cycle. The coordination agent primarily requests a list of new orders for its profile matching mechanism and in case it receives alerts it requests the wrapper to match a suborder to a superorder.

## 5.7.2 Behaviors

### 5.7.2.1 Overview

The overall behavior of a wrapper agent is structured in a simple manner, because only a single reactive behavior (*RetrieveQueryParameters*) acts upon other agents' requests that are received by the *WaitForMessages* behavior (see fig. 5-31).

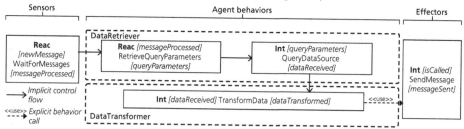

Fig. 5-31. Overview behaviors of a wrapper agent

*RetrieveQueryParameters* is responsible to identify what kind of request is received and what parameters are used to filter data from the wrapper agent's data source. Extraction of data from the source is conducted by the *QueryDataSource* behavior which is activated by the precondition *queryParameters*. *DataReceived* as the postcondition, after data is returned from the source, is applicable as the precondition to the *TransformData* behavior. It maps retrieved data to the terms of the SNEM ontology and initiates the *SendMessage* behavior which returns data in a response message to the requesting agent.

The possible complexity of a wrapper agent is not found in the basic types of behaviors, but in the configuration of each specific agent for its data source. The configuration task is twofold:

1. To retrieve desired data from a data source, the structure of the source and its data formats are considered. As indicated in the examples on data base sources in section 3.3.1, data to be retrieved is often distributed over a variety of data base tables. In an ERP system such as SAP R/3 the information is provided by several business objects or similar interfaces that have to be accessed by a wrapper agent as defined in section 3.3.1.2. Knowledge on where to find the desired information is part of the wrapper agents knowledge asset *AccessParameters*.
2. Transformation of retrieved data into concepts of the SNEM ontology is required.

Besides changing formats of data types (e.g. changing date formats), the wrapper agent has knowledge (*TransformationRules*) to assign retrieved data to corresponding concepts in the ontology. For examples of source data types matched to ontological concepts see sections 3.3.1.1, 3.3.2.1 and 3.3.2.2.

A wrapper agent realizes functions for a SNEM agent society, which *Enterprise Application Integration (EAI)* tools provide in other business contexts. Wrapper agents can benefit from existing EAI applications that provide access to a variety of data sources in an enterprise, because the number of necessary wrapper agents is reduced significantly. Ideally, only one wrapper agent provides access to the *EAI* layer/system of an enterprise.

### 5.7.2.2    Data Retrieval Behaviors

Incoming requests from other agents are handled by the reactive *RetrieveQueryParameters* behavior. This behavior distinguishes four basic types of requests as indicated in section 5.7.1 (see fig. 5-32):

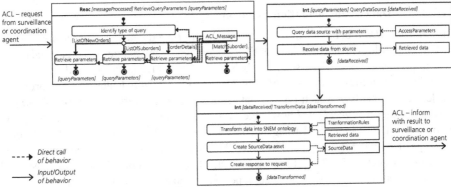

Fig. 5-32. Behavior details of a wrapper agent

1. A request for a list of all newly arrived orders is received from the coordination agent. This list provides new facts to the expert system of the coordination agent, which in turn compares them to its critical profiles $CCP_j$ during profile matching (see section 5.4.2.2).

2. Requests for a list of suborders related to a specific *OrderIncoming* (a customer order) are issued by newly started surveillance agents. They have to identify all relevant suborders of the order they are responsible for (see section 5.5.2.2).

3. While gathering data, surveillance agents request order details for their monitored orders. These details provide an update on internally available SNEM data types for this order (see section 5.5.2.2).

4. A relatively simple request is generated by a coordination agent in case it receives an alert: It identifies which of its orders is affected by a disruptive event in one of its suborders. Thus, the wrapper agent has to match a received suborder ID from the alert message with its suborders stored in the ERP system. It then extracts the *OrderIncomingID* of the related superorder (see section 5.4.2.2).

In all cases query parameters (e.g. selection criteria such as an order ID) are retrieved from the message. For instance, a request for order details may only contain the identifier of the order for which all available SNEM data types are extracted. Or a more detailed request defines specific SNEM data types and thus overrules the general retrieval mechanism (see also sections 4.1.2.3 and 4.1.2.5). These parameters are input for the data source specific retrieval mechanism implemented in the *QueryDataSource* behavior. For a typical data base this behavior translates query parameters into a SQL statement that selects requested data from all tables of the data base relevant to this query (for an example see section 6.1.6.1). The data source returns data which is input to the behavior *TransformData* (see below). Other data sources are e.g. HTML- or XML-based Internet sources such as web pages or web services (for an example see section 6.3.4). As RFID-based process monitoring will increase, it will also provide SNEM data (see section 3.3.3). Such information requires access of wrapper agents to reader hardware or middleware that manages RFID readers in a facility (e.g. a warehouse - see section 8.2 for a scenario).

### 5.7.2.3    Data Transformation Behavior

The *TransformData* behavior in fig. 5-32 matches retrieved data types to the concepts of the SNEM ontology. An example is an ERP system where milestones are organized based on enterprise-specific number sets: The behavior matches for instance a milestone *M340* to the SNEM ontology's concept *MilestoneOrderArrivedAtHub*. Rules for transformation are defined manually for each type of data source. After conversion, the *TranformData* behavior creates a *SourceData* knowledge asset, the content of which is understood by every other agent type in the SNEM agent society, since it is defined in the SNEM ontology. This type of asset is explicitly used by surveillance agents as an input to their *AnalyzeData* behavior (see section 5.5.2.3). Requests for lists of new orders or suborders are answered by creating lists of this knowledge asset type so as to ensure semantic consistency and reuse of the existing data structures. The same applies to an abbreviated answer where only an *OrderIncomingID* is returned to the coordination agent (see section 5.7.2.2).

## 5.7.3  Interactions

As depicted in fig. 5-33 four different types of requests are received from other agent types which are identified by a wrapper agent (see section 5.7.2.2). Two originate from the coordination agent (request for *ListOfNewSuborders* and for *MatchSuborder*), the others are sent from surveillance agents, in the example from the agent responsible for monitoring $O_1$. Initially, it requests a list of relevant suborders for $O_1$, and in subsequent data gathering rounds it requests order details for $O_1$. An enterprise resource planning (ERP) system with an underlying data base is assumed in the example. It is accessed by the wrapper agent with a SQL statement which it defines based on query parameters that it has retrieved from the various data requests (see section 5.7.2.2).

After transformation of retrieved data into a *SourceData* knowledge asset, the *TransformData* behavior triggers responses to requests it has received and it provides the appropriate type of data (order details or lists of orders) as depicted in fig. 5-33 and presented in section 5.7.2.3.

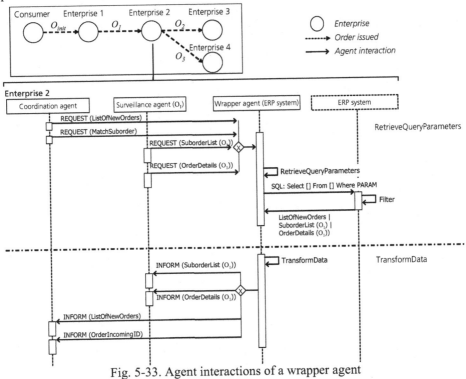

Fig. 5-33. Agent interactions of a wrapper agent

# Chapter 6

# Prototype Implementations

Agent-based supply network event management (SNEM) as proposed in chapters 3 to 5 is realized in two prototype implementations. The SNEM process with its four associated agent types, which communicate based on the SNEM ontology, is the basis for a generic prototype that has the objective to provide an initial proof-of-concept (see fig. 6-1). The prototype is embedded in a supply network testbed which is designed for conducting experiments within a defined environment. It allows an assessment of the basic characteristics and abilities of an agent-based SNEM system.

To facilitate acceptance of the general SNEM concept and its realization based on agent technology a showcase with a business partner is conducted (*Zimmermann et al. 2003a, Bodendorf et al. 2005*). Objective of the showcase is to demonstrate the integration of an agent-based SNEM system into the fulfillment processes of a business partner and into existing IT-infrastructures in a real-world environment.

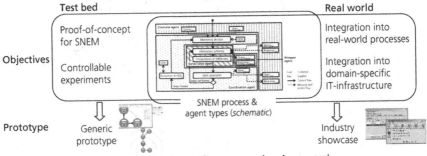

Fig. 6-1. Objectives of prototype implementation

## 6.1 Generic Prototype

The technological basis of the prototype as well as some basic design patterns which are used by all agent types to employ the SNEM ontology and to manage agent communication are presented first in section 6.1.1. Secondly, implementation of the four agent types is described in sections 6.1.2 to 6.1.6, but details are restricted to SNEM specific implementation details[1].

## 6.1.1  Overview

### 6.1.1.1    Architecture

Within the generic prototype all variants of agents as defined in chapter 5 are realized: Each enterprise in a supply network hosts an agent society which consists of a discourse agent, a coordination agent and several surveillance agents (see fig. 6-2). A single wrapper agent per enterprise is required to access a database that simulates an ERP system which provides all internal SNEM data on orders. The main focus of the implementation is on SNEM features provided by coordination and surveillance agents, whereas only basic mechanisms of discourse and wrapper agents are realized. Every agent society is realized on its own instance of a FIPA-conform agent platform (for details see section 6.1.1.2). As in a realistic supply network, agent platforms can be hosted on different computers to realize a physical distribution of SNEM systems.

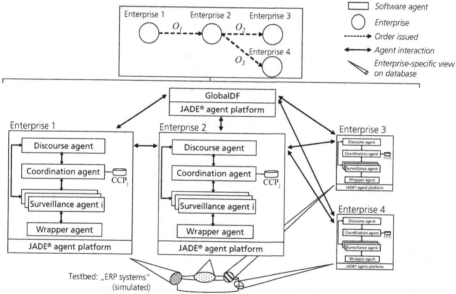

Fig. 6-2. Architecture of the generic prototype

[1]. Implementation of the generic prototype is realized in a research project under the title *Agent-based Tracking and Tracing* which is funded by the *Deutsche Forschungsgemeinschaft (DFG)* as part of the *DFG*'s priority research program *1083*.

In section 5.3.1.2 an additional agent type is introduced that provides white and yellow pages services to all discourse agents of a supply network: a global directory facilitator (*GlobalDF*). This agent is also depicted in fig. 6-2. Such an agent type is provided by every standard FIPA agent platform. It resides upon its own platform on a host-server and provides address information to discourse agents which need to send agent messages to other supply network partners' discourse agents that they do not yet know (see section 5.6.2.2).

The data base which provides the testbed for the prototype implementation stores data on all orders of each enterprise within the simulated supply network (for details see section 6.2.1). Each wrapper agent responsible for accessing internal data from its enterprise's ERP system has a restricted view on this database. These enterprise-specific views of wrapper agents are indicated in fig. 6-2. They allow the use of a single database on a separate host that is centrally controlled during experiments. In section 6.2.2 a simulator is presented that manipulates orders and related suborders: It triggers disruptive events and changes dates of order fulfillment to simulate a dynamic multi-level supply network. It manipulates data directly within the database and thereby mimics ERP-systems of all supply network partners simultaneously.

### 6.1.1.2    Technological Basis

The implementation of the generic prototype is based on the Java programming language which guarantees platform independency of the implementation. Popular agent platforms that conform to the FIPA standards are Java-based, e.g. JADE (*Bellifemine et al. 2003*), JACK (*JACK 2005*) or FIPA-OS (*FIPA OS 2005*). For this prototype the *Java Agent Development Framework JADE* is selected. It is based on a peer-to-peer model which facilitates interaction between peers that have equal rights regarding provision and usage of services (*Bellifemine et al. 2003*). Such a peer is able to take autonomous action, govern its own behavior and pursue goals: It is thus considered to be a software agent (*Bellifemine et al. 2003, pp. 9*). Since JADE is based on FIPA standards, interactions between agents are based on the exchange of messages in the FIPA-ACL format and structured according to FIPA interaction protocols (see sections 5.1.1.2 and 5.3.2.1). JADE provides a middleware architecture and a framework for realizing agents. It allows concentrating on solution-specific functions while providing basic infrastructure services such as message format and transport or white and yellow pages services (*Bellifemine et al. 2003, pp. 10*).

An overview of packages and main classes of the generic prototype is depicted in fig. 6-3. On the left side the top-level package $ATT^2$ integrates seven packages. For instance, the *attAgent* package contains basic classes of each agent type. As every agent has various behaviors and visualizations of its behaviors, relationships with the packages *attBehavior* and *attGUI* exist. Packages *attTest* and *attTool* integrate supporting classes such as data

---

2. The generic prototype of an agent-based SNEM system is developed within a research project funded by the *Deutsche Forschungsgemeinschaft (DFG)* called *Agent-based Tracking and Tracing (ATT)*. Therefore, many names of implementation details make use of the abbreviation *ATT*.

base interfaces. All ontological concepts used within the generic prototype for agent communication and representation of SNEM data are defined in the *attOntology* package (see section 6.1.2). The package *attEnterpriseOntology* is a second ontology used within the specific context of a research program[3] but not considered here further.

In fig. 6-3 two packages are presented in greater detail: *attAgent* and *attBehavior*. The connection to the JADE framework is realized by extensions of the core agent class and the core behavior class of JADE[4]. Every specific agent type is a subclass of the *AttAgent* class which provides basic mechanisms for each agent such as data structures (from the *dataStructure* package) for managing its incoming and outgoing messages. To configure an agent's capabilities, an agent type's class defines links to agent-specific behaviors of the *attBehavior* package.

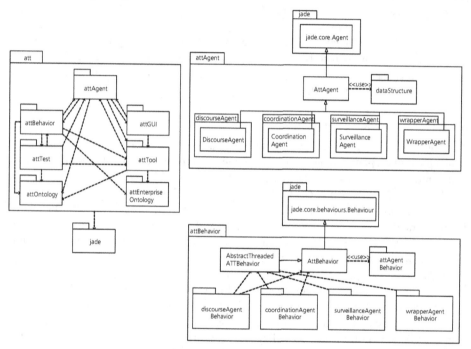

Fig. 6-3. Packages and main classes of generic prototype

Besides the *AttBehavior* class a second class is defined that provides the ability to execute a behavior in a separate Java thread: *AbstractThreadedAttBehavior*. Thus, truly parallel

---

[3.] The *attEnterpriseOntology* is used to connect the generic prototype of a SNEM system to other multi-agent-systems (MAS) within the *DFG* priority research program 1083. These MAS provide production planning capabilities in a complex scenario of a supply network. For details see *Frey et al. 2003a*.

[4.] The difference in spelling the term "behavior" is caused by JADE which uses British spelling whereas the SNEM prototype implementation is based on US spelling.

behaviors of a single agent are realized, because several threads in Java are executed in parallel which is ensured by the Java runtime environment (multiple *Java Virtual Machines (JVM)* are used). Threading of behaviors prevents that other agent behaviors are blocked, if one agent behavior requires extensive computation or waits for some response. For instance, each *WaitForMessages* behavior of an agent is started within a separate thread because this behavior is always active and it may otherwise block execution of SNEM functions conducted in other agent behaviors[5]. Depending on the type of agent behavior the simpler *AttBehavior* or the threaded variant is chosen as indicated in fig. 6-3.

### 6.1.1.3    System Visualization

To support the understanding of interactions among agent systems in a multi-level supply network a central visualization is provided. Although such a visualization is not very realistic in a real-world environment of multiple autonomous enterprises, it is possible in a laboratory environment: In fig. 6-4 (left side) an overview of a supply network with eight partners and their related SNEM agent societies is given. An initial customer is depicted in the center as a circle with several related suppliers and/or carriers which are positioned on surrounding meridians. The metaphor of orders and suborders (see section 2.1.2.2) is applied to this illustration: Every directed graph between two enterprises represents placement of an order respectively a suborder.

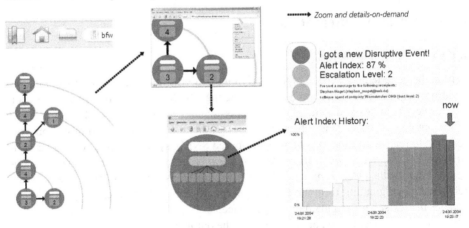

Fig. 6-4. System visualization of generic prototype

Since visualization of a distributed system which consists of a varying number of agent societies (e.g. new network partners) and individual agents (e.g. varying number of sur-

---

[5.] Threading is necessary because a JADE agent registers its behaviors with an internal scheduler. Every active behavior is added to a queue and waits for processing. The scheduling mechanism decides, based on a round robin algorithm, which behavior is executed at what time. Since interruption of long-running behaviors is not predictable, additional threading ensures parallel execution of behaviors.

veillance agents over time) cannot be defined up-front, each agent is responsible to provide its representation within the visualization (*Eller et al. 2005*). For instance, each discourse agent is responsible to draw a circle for its enterprise and position it on one of the meridians of the central GUI in fig. 6-4. The visualization allows to zoom into structural details of each agent society (see fig. 6-4, screenshots in the middle). Topmost, the discourse agent is visualized as a rectangle with rounded corners, below is the coordination agent of an enterprise, and in the lowermost rectangle a number indicates how many surveillance agents are currently active. In a more detailed view a single enterprise is represented with each separate surveillance agent. By using links from these top-level views to individual agents, details are provided on-demand within each enterprise's agent society. A sample visualization is depicted in fig. 6-4. It represents a view of the coordination agent and in particular a view provided by the *AlertBehavior* (see section 6.1.3.2). It depicts the alert history of a specific order, which has continuously worsened, and the calculated current alert index *AI* of the order as well as its escalation level.

Visualization is based on technologies that are displayed in a typical Web browser: HTML (Hyper Text Markup Language) and SVG (Scalable Vector Graphics). The latter is used to draw figures that can be scaled seamlessly, whereas HTML provides the ability to display text and text-related elements such as tables. For details on the concept of agent visualization in the prototype see (*Eller et al. 2005*).

## 6.1.2    Ontology Integration

### 6.1.2.1    Ontology Subset

Within the generic prototype all agents rely on the SNEM ontology as defined in the institutional agreements in section 5.3.3.1. Since the SNEM ontology presented in section 3.2.3 is very complex and some of the concepts are not necessary for a prototype, a subset of the ontology is used. This subset encompasses the most important and basic concepts required to realize all functions of an agent-based SNEM system (see fig. 6-5): *LegalEntity* types, *DisruptiveEvents*, various *Measurement* types, *Milestones* and the central concept *Order* with *OrderType* and *OrderItem* are considered. In fig. 6-6 relevant relationships originating from the *Order* concept are illustrated to exemplify interdependencies that exist between main ontology concepts.

The following concepts are not considered in the ontology subset:

- *Activities* and their *Effects*: A detailed description of *Activities* derived from process models of the supply network domain in section 3.1.1.3 is used in the SNEM ontology to define *Milestone* types (see section 3.2.3.2). This definition is needed to assure unambiguous semantic meanings of *Milestone* concepts in realistic environments where a matching of enterprise-specific milestone definitions to the SNEM ontology's *Milestone* concepts is required. However, in a prototype implemented within a virtual testbed agreed-upon definitions of *Milestones* are assumed. Thus, *Milestones* are only defined by a name, a relationship with an order type, and a rank that indicates the predefined sequence of *Milestones* for an order type (see section 3.2.3.2).

- *Measurements* of monetary dimensions: In the SNEM ontology concepts for different types of costs are primarily defined, These are considered to be too critical for communication in inter-organizational settings.
- *Measurements* for defining the dimensions, volume and mass of products: They are too domain-specific for a generic prototype.

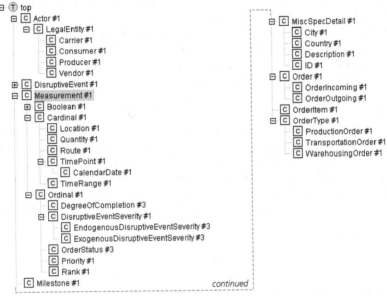

Fig. 6-5. Hierarchy of SNEM concepts - subset for generic prototype

| Restrictions | | |
|---|---|---|
| type | property | filler |
| min 0 | has #1 | DisruptiveEvent #1 |
| exact 1 | has #1 | OrderType #1 |
| exact 1 | has #1 | ID #1 |
| exact 1 | has_plannedFulfillmentDate #1 | CalendarDate #1 |
| max 1 | has_orderReceiptDate #1 | CalendarDate #1 |
| max 1 | has_dateOfAchievement #1 | CalendarDate #1 |
| exact 1 | is_receivedBy #1 | (LegalEntity #1 and (not Consumer #1)) |
| exact 1 | is_finished #1 | Boolean #1 |
| exact 1 | has #1 | Priority #1 |
| min 1 | has #1 | OrderItem #1 |
| min 1 | has #1 | Milestone #1 |
| exact 1 | is_triggeredBy #1 | LegalEntity #1 |
| exact 1 | has #1 | Location #1 |
| exact 1 | has #1 | OrderStatus #3 |

Fig. 6-6. Attributes of the order concept

### 6.1.2.2 Implementation

The JADE agent platform selected for implementation of the generic prototype supports a special representation of ontologies based on *Java Beans (JB) (Caire et al. 2004)*. A *Java Bean* is a simple Java class that provides set- and get-methods to change and retrieve values of attributes. Information on a certain instance of an ontological concept (e.g. a specific order) is represented as an instance of a *JB* class *Order*. Instantiation of ontological concepts define knowledge facts of an agent's knowledge base. These facts represent a certain type of knowledge asset, for instance the concept *Order* is part of the *SNEM_Data* knowledge asset type (see section 5.3.1.2).

Besides creating, accessing and manipulating an agent's knowledge base with *JBs*, this representation is used by the JADE platform to define content of FIPA-ACL messages. Thus, knowledge is standardized among agents in a SNEM system, easily exchanged between agents, and always accessible through Java programming instructions.

The ontology subset (see section 6.1.2.1) which is represented in the *DAML+OIL* format is transformed into a *JB* representation by means of a software tool: A plug-in to the ontology tool *Protégé* called *Bean-Generator (Aart 2005)*. It provides an automatic transformation from the *Ontology Web Language (OWL)* format to the JADE-conform *JB* representation. Since *DAML+OIL* and *OWL* are both supported by the *OilEd* editor (see section 3.2.3.3), an automatic transformation from *DAML+OIL* to *JB* is possible. An excerpt of the resulting class diagram and an excerpt of the Java code produced by the *Bean-Generator* for the concept *DisruptiveEvent* is depicted in fig. 6-7. Indicated are various set- and get-methods to define for instance the exogenous and the endogenous severity of disruptive events (see section 4.3.4.2) depicted as *ExoSeverity* and *EndoSeverity*.

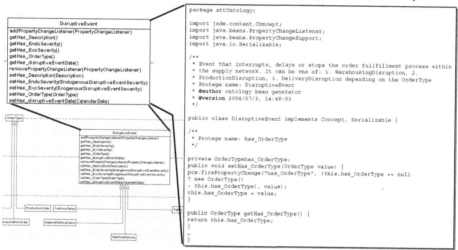

Fig. 6-7. Ontology based on *Java Beans (JB)*

The JADE agent-platform has a built-in mechanism that transforms an ontological *JB* representation into a FIPA-SL0 statement. FIPA-SL0 is a content-language proposed by the FIPA to define the syntax of an agent message's content (see section 5.6.2.1). An example of FIPA-ACL messages based on the SNEM ontology's *JB* representation transformed into FIPA-SL0 statements is provided in fig. 6-8. A *REQUEST* message is for instance sent from a surveillance agent to a wrapper agent. The corresponding *INFORM* message provides the desired information (e.g. a *plannedFulfillmentDate*) in a response to the requesting agent. JADE provides a mechanism that checks all incoming agent messages upon reception whether they conform to the ontology defined in the message-header. This integrated mechanism assures that no agent receives a message it cannot understand due to semantic problems. However, it does not provide any mechanism to correct such problems as is intended within the discourse agent of a SNEM agent society (see section 5.6). Both, transformation of content-language as well as ontology matching remain to be implemented in a discourse agent, because these problems cannot be avoided in realistic inter-organizational settings.

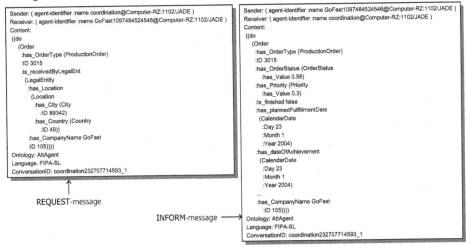

Fig. 6-8. FIPA-ACL message by JADE

### 6.1.2.3    Data Structures

All agents within the generic prototype utilize three basic types of data structures for coordinating their dialogs and storing order information in the ontology format (see fig. 6-9). Each data structure is termed "Map" because it is based on a so called *Hash-Map* which is a Java concept of a list where the index is represented as a hash number for performant search and where its content is flexibly defined in a second column. Within the prototype the content of each map (second column) is filled with an instance of an object that itself has various variables, e.g. the *ATTConvMapEntry* with agent identifier (*AID*), conversation identifier (*ConvID*) and further variables (see fig. 6-9). Within the *Hash-Map* class (e.g. *AttConvMap*) several methods are defined that allow selecting and sorting of the map's content according to various parameters (e.g. obtain all conversation identifiers for a specific order ID). The data structure types are:

- *AttConvMap + AttConvMapEntry*
  For every received agent message the sender agent's identifier is stored along with conversation identifier, performative, order identifier and a time stamp.
- *AttForwardMap + AttForwardMapEntry*
  In case a message is received and has to be forwarded to another agent, this data structure provides a table for mapping inbound messages to their related outbound (that is the forwarded) message. Both agent identifiers, for sender of the inbound and

receiver of the outbound message, are stored with the relevant conversation identifiers. Since a message is simply forwarded, the relevant performative as well as order identifier are constant and only stored once. A time stamp is added when the message is forwarded.

- *AttOrderMap + AttOrderMapEntry*
  Each agent requires knowledge management capabilities to store instances of SNEM data in its knowledge base: Each such instance characterizes a single order based on the SNEM ontology in the *JB* format presented in section 6.1.2.2. The *AttOrderMap* is the knowledge base for each agent regarding its knowledge on specific orders (SNEM data). The *AttOrderMapEntry* as the content of the *AttOrderMap* includes an order identifier and an instance of the SNEM ontology that stores the specific values associated with this order. In addition, an agent identifier is stored in the variable *CorrespondingSurvAgentId*, if an active surveillance agent for this order is known.

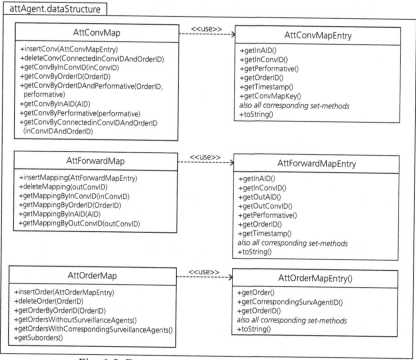

Fig. 6-9. Data structures within generic prototype

As soon as a message is received by the *WaitForMessages* behavior which all agents implement (see agent concepts in chapter 5), the *AttConvMap* is updated with data relevant to dialog management (see above), and content of the message is stored within the *AttOrderMap*. Update mechanisms are employed by each agent type, if SNEM data on a certain order is already available within the *AttOrderMap*. This makes sure that only the newest and most detailed version of SNEM information is available for an order. The knowledge base of an agent regarding SNEM information is always updated, if new information is received from the agent's environment or information is created by the agent itself (e.g. during data analysis).

## 6.1.3 Coordination Agent

A coordination agent assumes roles for managing monitoring activities as well as alert generation and profile management (see fig. 6-10). All classes are discussed in detail in subsequent sections[6].

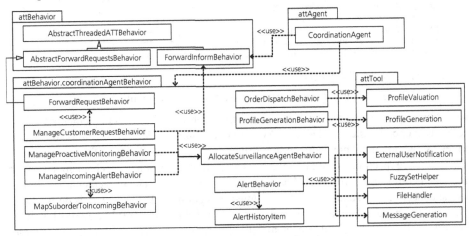

Fig. 6-10. Class diagram of a coordination agent

### 6.1.3.1 Surveillance Management

All trigger events as defined in section 4.1.1.1 are considered by the coordination agent in the generic prototype: status requests from customers $TE_{SR}$, incoming alerts $TE_{AT}$ from suppliers, and proactive monitoring of orders $TE_{PT}$ and $TE_{RT}$ based on critical profiles $CCP_j$. Within the *ManageCustomerRequestBehavior* every *REQUEST* agent message received by the coordination agent is processed after it has been received by the *WaitFor-Messages* behavior class[7]. In case a status request $TE_{SR}$ on a certain order is received from a customer the *AllocateSurveillanceAgentBehavior* is invoked. It checks with a method called *isLocalOrder* whether a surveillance agent for this order is already active. This information is extracted from the coordination agent's knowledge base which stores all information about orders (the *AttOrderMap* in section 6.1.2.3). If the variable *correspondingSurvAgentID* of the *AttOrderMapEntry* is empty, a new surveillance agent is invoked (see fig. 6-11). The agent identifier of the new surveillance agent is stored with the order identifier in the *AttOrderMapEntry* of the coordination agent. After the (new)

---

[6.] Methods and variables of classes are not depicted, but are addressed in the text where appropriate.

[7.] This class which is used by every agent type is not depicted in the class diagram.

surveillance agent is either identified or started, the status request is forwarded to the surveillance agent by the *sendMessage* method of the *ForwardRequestBehavior* class. For a received alert, the *ManageIncomingAlertBehavior* identifies the relevant superorder by querying the wrapper agent as defined in section 5.4.2.2 and then proceeds similar to the *ManageCustomerRequestBehavior*.

```
jade.core.Runtime rt = jade.core.Runtime.instance();
PlatformController container = this.callingAgent.getContainerController();
//arguments for the new agent
  Object[] args = {"orderIncomingID:" + orderID, "agentCompanyName:" +
  callingAgent.getAgentCompanyName()};
//create a new agent
  String agentName = callingAgent.getAttAgentType() + cnt++;
  AgentController surAgentControl = container.createNewAgent(agentName,
  "attAgent.surveillanceAgent.SurveillanceAgent", args);
//fire up the agent
  surAgentControl.start();
```

Fig. 6-11. Start of a new surveillance agent

Initiation of proactive monitoring based on critical profiles $CCP_j$ is implemented with a rule-based expert system called *Java Expert System Shell (JESS)* (*JESS 2005*). JESS provides its own internal knowledge base for rules and facts as well as an inference machine. The inference machine is based on the *Rete* algorithm, an efficient mechanism suited for the "N:M comparison problem" (*Forgy 1982, Winston 1992*). The implementation realizes the concept for matching profiles presented in section 4.2.1: Each $CCP_j$ is defined as a *JESS* rule. An example of a profile is defined as a JESS rule in LISP-like syntax below. It considers all orders received from a specific customer (*isTriggeredBy* relation of an *OrderIncoming* concept) and an *OrderedQuantity* larger than 6500 as potentially critical:

 *(defrule LargeQuantityAtCustomerYX (OrderIncoming (and (and (> OrderedQuantity 6500) (= isTriggeredBy 1020)) (OrderIncomingID ?id))) => triggerSurveillance)*

All profiles are stored persistent in an extra profile data base as indicated in fig. 6-2. Facts on newly accepted orders of the enterprise are gathered by the coordination agent through a request to the wrapper agent (see section 5.4.2.2). All orders are received as instances of the *Java Beans (JB)* ontology format described in section 6.1.2.2 and asserted as *shadow-facts* to the knowledge base of the JESS engine. Shadow-facts are a feature of JESS that allows direct usage of *Java Beans* as facts in the rule-based expert system (*Friedmann-Hill 2003, pp. 87*). A seamless integration of the SNEM ontology into *SNEM_Data* knowledge assets of a software agent and into facts of the expert system is realized.

 For all orders where a $CCP_j$ matches a shadow-fact of a specific order, the *ManageProactiveMonitoringBehavior* initiates a check for a surveillance agent (see above) and stores information on what order matched which profile(s). No specific visualization is available for this behavior.

### 6.1.3.2 Alert Management

Alert management within the generic prototype is based on the concepts introduced in section 4.4. Classes relevant to realize the corresponding agent role *AlertManager* as designed in section 5.4.2.3 are depicted in fig. 6-10: The central class *AlertBehavior* uses several classes that implement specific functions such as Fuzzy Logic calculations (*FuzzySetHelper*), selection of recipients, media types and content of alerts (*MessageGeneration*) as well as transmission of alerts via email or short-message-service (SMS) (*ExternalUserNotification*). The *FileHandler* class implements basic methods for manipulation of files needed by the *AlertBehavior* (e.g. create, read or delete files).

Within the *AlertBehavior* a method *processDisruption* requires an order object as input parameter which means that a *SNEM_Data* knowledge asset is required. Only updates of *SNEM_Data* on a monitored order that are received by the coordination agent from some surveillance agent, are appropriate (see section 5.4.2.3). A two step Fuzzy Logic assessment is conducted to determine an *alert index AI* for each order where new *SNEM_Data* is available (see section 4.4.2). The open-source Fuzzy Logic application programming interface (API) *FuzzyJ-API (NRC 2004)* for Java is used to realize Fuzzy Logic calculations within the generic prototype. It provides a flexible interface to design and configure Fuzzy Logic applications. Configuration is realized by a *Microsoft-Excel* file: It specifies all fuzzy variables and fuzzy rules of the application. A *Java-Excel-API (Khan 2005)* is integrated in the prototype that extracts this configuration data from the *MS-Excel* file and provides it to the Fuzzy Logic system controlled by the *FuzzySetHelper* class. An excerpt of a configuration file is depicted in fig. 6-12.

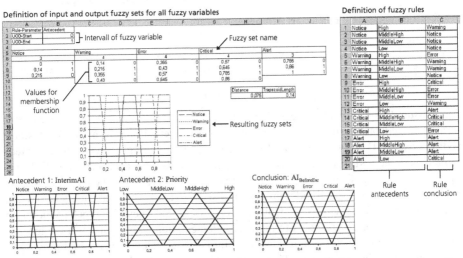

Fig. 6-12. Configuration of fuzzy sets and rules

For each order assessed by the *AlertBehavior* an interim alert index *InterimAI* considers the maximum severity of any identified disruptive event (*Max(EnDS)*) and the aggregated order status *AOS* of the order (see section 4.3.4). The result - a defuzzified value - is calculated in the *FuzzySetHelper* class by the *getDefuzzifiedValues* method which is called by the *AlertBehavior* from within the *processDisruption* method. In a second step an order's priority is considered to realize appropriate behavior for orders that have a varying importance to an enterprise (for details see section 4.4.2). The resulting $AI_{BeforeEsc}$ is input to the escalation mechanism (see section 4.4.3) realized in the *processDisruption* method. In the prototype implementation an alert history item *AHI* is created for each order during an alert generation process as an instance of the *AlertHistoryItem* class (see fig. 6-10). Only those *AHI* are selected for consideration in the escalation mechanism that belong to the currently processed order and which were created within the *relevant time frame for escalation* (*RTFE*) (for details see section 4.4.3). Each of these *AHI* increases the escalation level of the order, if all of the following conditions apply:

- *AHI* is newer than a specified escalation date but older than reaction time (that is within the time frame *RTFE*).
- The attribute *escalationFlag* of the *AHI* is set to true. It means a new disruptive event *DE* was identified in the historic alert management process and this *DE* was considered for alert generation.
- The new alert index $AI_{BeforeEsc}$ (not yet escalated) is within the range of the old - not escalated - alert index stored in the *AHI*.

These conditions ensure that an escalation only takes place, if no improvement of a situation is achieved although disruptive events have been identified in the past (also see section 4.4.3). The Java code responsible for this escalation decision is depicted in fig. 6-13.

```
for (int i = 0; i < oldAHIVector.size(); i++) {
AlertHistoryItem oldAHI = (AlertHistoryItem) oldAHIVector.elementAt(i);
try {
    if (oldAHI.getDateOfOccurrence().after(escalationDate)
    && oldAHI.getDateOfOccurrence().before(reactionDate)
    && oldAHI.isEscalationFlag()
    && (alertIndexFinal[0] > oldAHI.getAlertIndexNotEscalated() - escalationRange
    && alertIndexFinal[0] < oldAHI.getAlertIndexNotEscalated() + escalationRange))
    {escalationLevel++;}}}
```

Fig. 6-13. Escalation mechanism

The *MessageGeneration* class (see fig. 6-10) decides in its method *getRecipients* whether an alert is generated either to internal actors or to external supply network partner's SNEM systems. Based on the final alert index $AI_{Fin}$ (which might have been escalated) and all available SNEM data, that is stored in the *AttOrderMap* (see section 6.1.2.2), recipients are selected. Configuration of potential recipients is also defined in an *MS-Excel* file. It implements the data model proposed in section 4.4.4 which considers actors and media types associated with these. However, organizational roles of actors have not been introduced in the prototype so as to reduce implementation complexity. But the mechanism for selecting an actor or a role is very similar. A *getRecipients* method provides a *vector* with all recipients of alerts for the currently processed order.

This vector is used as input by several other methods that define the content of alert messages, e.g. the *sendMessages* or *createSVGFile* methods of the *MessageGeneration* class. Within the *sendMessages* method an information policy as requested in section 4.4.5 is implemented. For each supply network partner a trust level is defined in the *MS-*

*Excel* configuration file for recipients (see fig. 6-14 ). To illustrate the information policy, the following data types are provided for a supply network partner in an agent message according to its trust level:

- *Trust level = 1*: The current aggregated order status *AOS* and all available SNEM data on the order are sent as an agent message to the supply network partner (e.g. *PlannedFulfillmentDate, DisruptiveEvents, Milestones*). Only an order's priority is kept secret because such information usually is considered confidential by an enterprise.
- *Trust level = 2*: Besides the aggregated order status *AOS* only newly discovered disruptive events are considered in an alert message to the supply network partner.
- *Trust level = 3*: Only the aggregated order status *AOS* is provided to the affected network partner.

| | A | B | C | D |
|---|---|---|---|---|
| 1 | CompanyName | AlertIndexBegin | AlertIndexEnd | TrustLevel |
| 2 | CompressorMan Inc. | 0 | 1 | 1 |
| 3 | ChassisSup Inc. | 0,8 | 1 | 2 |
| 4 | AlwaysRun Inc. | 0 | 1 | 3 |
| 5 | GoFast Plc. | 0,6 | 1 | 1 |
| 6 | | | | |

Fig. 6-14. Configuration of recipients

Two types of visualizations provide information on an order's status (order information view) and on the history of its alerts (see fig. 6-15). They are available through the generic prototype's visualization (see section 6.1.1.3) by selecting a coordination agent of a network partner. Furthermore, Email or short-messages (SMS) to a mobile phone are used for alerts to human actors.

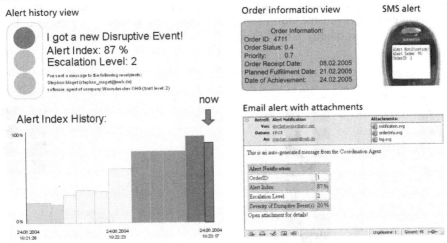

Fig. 6-15. Alert visualizations

### 6.1.3.3    Profile Management

Continuous assessment of critical profiles $CCP_j$ as defined in section 4.2.3 is realized by two classes depicted in fig. 6-10. The *OrderDispatchBehavior* is initialized, if a monitored order has been finished and the final assessment of the respective surveillance agent has been received by the coordination agent. In this case a *readOrder* method is invoked. This method extracts part of the SNEM data from the *SNEM_Data* knowledge asset of the monitored order and writes this information to the dedicated profile data base indicated in fig. 6-2. In addition, information on what profile matched this order is stored in the data base which provides a persistent basis for profile assessment.

This data is input to the *ProfileValuation* class (see fig. 6-10). A number of indicators are calculated for each profile, based on all orders found in the data base which match a certain critical profile (see section 4.2.3). Finally, the aggregated value $AV$ is calculated as a mean average of all indicators by the *aggregatedCharacteristics* method. The $AV$ is used to determine whether a profile remains in the knowledge base of the *JESS* expert system (see section 6.1.3.1) or is deleted from it. However, no monitoring priorities are currently distinguished in the prototype.

A visualization of the profile assessment results is available to a user (see fig. 6-16). In the example a profile with *ID 2* is rated with a medium quality. The various basic indicators are symbolized with traffic lights (from left to right: green, yellow, red). Profile 2 has identified orders that mostly did encounter severe disruptive events as indicated by high values for *Exogenous Severity* and *Fuzzy Severity* (which is based on the *EndogenousSeverity* measurement of section 4.3.4) while other indicators only have a medium to low value. In the graph the $AV$ of the profile is depicted over the last twelve month, showing large variations in profile quality. This is also indicated by a large average standard deviation regarding the priority of monitored orders which may be a reason for fluctuation of the $AV$. Consequently, the coordination agent suggests that the profile is redesigned by a user and split to better focus on either low or high priority profiles. On the right side, a ranking of currently available profiles with their aggregated values $AV$ is presented. It allows to identify low-quality $CCP_j$ for redesign or removal of these profiles from the JESS rule-engine.

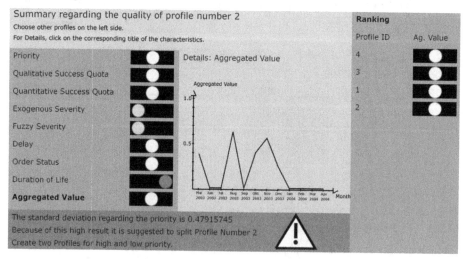

Fig. 6-16. GUI for profile management

The *ProfileManagement* role of a coordination agent (see section 5.3.1.1) is also responsible to randomly create new critical profiles $CCP_j$ and thus support automatic identification of new sources of disruptive events (see section 4.2.3.4). High quality profiles will "survive" the continuous assessment process whereas others will be deleted automatically. Within the generic prototype a random generation of $CCP_j$ is realized by the *Profile-GenerationBehavior* and the *ProfileGeneration* class (see fig. 6-10). The latter creates $CCP_j$ whereas the behavior class proactively triggers new generation sessions at certain times.

Generation of a new critical profile requires two variables that determine the average number of elements within a profile (*meanNumberOfElem*) and an average deviation from the *meanNumberOfElem* (*deviation*). These variables determine the complexity of a random generated $CCP_j$. According to the concept presented in section 4.2.3.4, predefined components as basic elements for new profiles are selected from the *MySQL* data base which in turn also stores profile evaluation data (see above). Selection of components is made as defined in section 4.2.3.4. After all terms for a new profile have been selected, the *combineProfileElements* or the *combineProfileElementsInPairs* method is triggered at random and a new profile is generated: either by sequenced concatenation or by selecting pairs of components up-front and later coupling these pairs. For instance, the components *c1, c2, c3, c4* and three logic operators *op1, op2, op3* can result in two types of rules written in the syntax required by the JESS rule engine:

1. *combineProfileElements* method:         *(op3 (op2 (op1 c1 c2) c3) c4)*
2. *combineProfileElementsInPairs* method:  *(op3 (op1 c1 c2) (op2 c3 c4))*

## 6.1.4   Surveillance Agent

The main classes which are relevant to a surveillance agent in the generic prototype are depicted in fig. 6-17. The *AnalysisBehavior* uses tool classes such as a class for Fuzzy Logic (*FuzzySetHelper*) or a date converter. It also relies on an additional data structure that is detailed in section 6.1.4.2. All other behaviors are concerned with proactive gathering of SNEM data (see section 6.1.4.1).

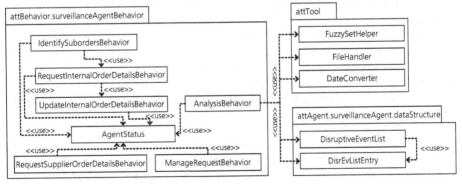

Fig. 6-17. Class diagram of a surveillance agent

#### 6.1.4.1    Gathering Information

A surveillance agent is responsible for gathering all information needed to assess an order's current situation. This includes requesting SNEM data from those suppliers and carriers which have received suborders related to the monitored order to which a surveillance agent is dedicated. In the generic prototype all behaviors except the *AnalysisBehavior* are associated with the role *InformationGatherer* as defined in section 5.5.2 (see fig. 6-17).

To realize synchronization of all behaviors an additional class *AgentStatus* is introduced which represents the current internal status of a surveillance agent, for instance whether it waits for any responses to data gathering requests or is currently analyzing gathered data.[8] Every behavior of a surveillance agent accesses the agent's status and decides on its own, whether to become active or not. An activation decision within a behavior depends on additional constraints; for instance data gathering requests for update information are of no use, if the last requests have just been answered. Thus, a waiting time is considered by behaviors responsible for data requests (e.g. *RequestInternalOrderDetailsBehavior*, see also section 5.5.2.2). In table 6-1 different states of a surveillance agent are listed.

| AgentStatus | Description |
|---|---|
| NOT_INIT | Surveillance agent started, not fully initialized: relevant suborders not known |
| INIT | Relevant suborders known, data gathering allowed |
| REQUEST | Data gathering initiated, requests not yet answered |
| INFORM | Data received due to data gathering requests, data analysis allowed |
| STABLE | Stable order status, SNEM data can be communicated to coordination agent |

Table 6-1. Agent status of a surveillance agent

Upon start of a surveillance agent the agent status is set to *NOT_INIT*. The *IdentifySubordersBehavior* reacts upon this agent status, tests that the order to be monitored has a valid order identifier (method *isValidOrderIncoming*) and no suborders have yet been identified (method *suborderUpdateable*). It uses the *RequestInternalOrderDetailsBehavior* to gather an initial set of data on the monitored order from the enterprise's internal data source (in this case from the simulated ERP system). The response from the wrapper agent is accepted and made available to the surveillance agent by the *UpdateInternalOrderDetailsBehavior*. Only then does the *IdentifySubordersBehavior* extract all relevant suborders of the monitored order from a list within the now available *SNEM_Data* knowledge

---

[8.] An explicit synchronization mechanism is introduced within a surveillance agent, because the preconditions for behaviors such as the *AnalyzeData* behavior would otherwise require multiple tests on conditions of various other behaviors (e.g. the status of several data gathering requests generated in parallel). The agent status clarifies the agent's internal status at a given point in time and reduces implementation complexity.

asset (see section 5.5.2.2), creates a separate list of suborders to be used by the other behaviors (method *buildSuborderList*) and sets the agent status to *INIT*.

All agent states except the *NOT_INIT* state are cyclically achieved by a surveillance agent, because monitoring of an order is always continued until finalization of the order's fulfillment. As soon as the agent status is set to *INIT*, the *RequestInternalOrderDetails-Behavior* and *RequestSupplierOrderDetailsBehavior* activate themselves at the next point in time where the agent's scheduler provides processing time to these behaviors[9]. Both behaviors implement parts of the *InformationGatherer* role and set the current agent status to *REQUEST*[10]. The *RequestInternalOrderDetailsBehavior* generates a request to the wrapper agent of the internal ERP system, and the *RequestSupplierOrderDetailsBehavior* is responsible for gathering data from suborder recipients. The latter generates requests for SNEM data that are forwarded via the coordination agent and discourse agent to external supply network partners. First, this behavior generates a list of suborders for which requests are to be generated, and second, uses the general *SendMessages* behavior - which is part of every agent within the prototype - to create an ACL message based on the SNEM ontology. This message mainly contains a suborder identifier and information on the recipient of the request (for an example see fig. 6-8). A visualization of agent interactions is available with the *Sniffer-Tool* provided by the JADE platform. An excerpt of a surveillance agent's data gathering is depicted in fig. 6-18.

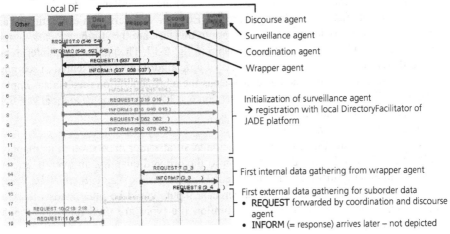

<hr />

[9] Every JADE agent has an internal scheduler where every active behavior is registered. Cyclically, each behavior is granted access to the processor. The design of the prototype's behaviors allows these to autonomously check whether their preconditions apply and otherwise give way to the next behavior.

[10] Since internal and external requests are managed by two separate autonomous behaviors, two subtypes of an agent status are considered within the implementation - one for internal data gathering (*OrderIncomingStatus*) regarding the monitored order and one for external data gathering on suborders (*OrderOutgoingStatus*). These subtypes are considered in parallel by all other behaviors to check on preconditions, but they are not further detailed here.

Fig. 6-18. *JADE* Sniffer-tool

As long as requests to other agents are pending the agent status is not changed. To enhance robustness of the system a time-out mechanism ensures that a surveillance agent is not blocked forever, if a request is not answered (e.g. due to communication infrastructure problems). The agent status is changed to *INFORM* either, if all responses are received and processed, or if a time-out is encountered. The *AnalyzeData* behavior (see section 6.1.4.2) acts upon this agent status by analyzing all gathered data and sets the agent status to *STABLE* after finishing its interpretations.

A surveillance agent is only allowed to provide a new *SNEM_Data* knowledge asset to its coordination agent, if data is available that has undergone all analytical tasks, because only then is the newest information guaranteed. This situation is encountered during an agent's *STABLE* phase: Both, a response to any request from the coordination agent or a proactive INFORM message with new *SNEM_Data*, are created by the *ManageRequest-Behavior* and sent to the coordination agent. To realize a cyclical update behavior, the agent status is again set to *INIT* after a predetermined waiting time, and the data gathering mechanisms start again.

### 6.1.4.2    Analysis of Data

To realize the role *DataAnalyzer* (see section 5.5.2.3) the surveillance agent implements mechanisms to automatically assess gathered SNEM data and derive an evaluation of an order's current situation. Main classes relevant to this task are the *AnalysisBehavior* and classes associated with a $<<use>>$ relationship in fig. 6-17. The analysis and interpretation of gathered SNEM data is based on Fuzzy Logic algorithms as presented in sections 4.3.3 and 4.3.4. It uses the same basic classes as the alert generation mechanism implemented within the coordination agent (see section 6.1.3.2). Assessments are realized that calculate two different indicators:

1. *Aggregated Order Status AOS*
   Based on two inputs that characterize the delay of an order in relation to its planned fulfillment date and shortages in relation to the ordered quantity, an overall assessment of an order's fulfillment is calculated. The result is the *Aggregated Order Status AOS* as defined in section 4.3.3. Further data inputs could be integrated with little effort, since the same *MS-Excel* configuration file types are used for Fuzzy Logic analysis as described in section 6.1.3.2.

2. *Endogenous Disruptive Event Severity (EnDS)*
   Every identified disruptive event *DE* is analyzed with respect to the remaining *Reaction Time RT* of an order (see fig. 6-20) and the *DE*'s severity which is depicted by a general severity measure. This assessment results in the so-called *Endogenous Disruptive Event Severity EnDS* (see section 4.3.4).

Both assessments rely on the *FuzzySetHelper*, *FileHandler* and *DateConverter* classes within the *attTool* package. The *AnalysisBehavior* has control over the analysis process and initiates the process as soon as the agent status indicates an *INFORM* (see section 6.1.4.1) for both internal and external data gathering activities. This is assessed by means of a method called *informationComplete*. Results of the analysis are depicted in two visu-

alizations (see fig. 6-19), provided by the *AnalysisBehavior* and accessible for each surveillance agent by details-on-demand in the central visualization (see section 6.1.1.3).

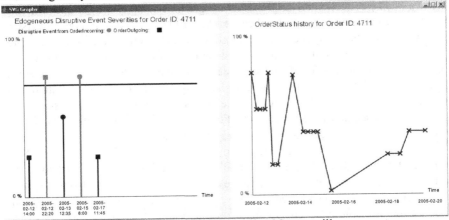

Fig. 6-19. Visualization of *EnDS* and *AOS* - surveillance agent

Besides the basic analytical tasks the *AnalysisBehavior* assures that existing analytical results on monitoring data from previous analysis rounds is considered correctly during update of the *SNEM_Data* knowledge asset of a surveillance agent. At all times, the
*SNEM_Data* knowledge asset represents the most current version of a monitored order's
status (see section 5.3.1.2). It is assured that no disruptive event, which has been identified
in an earlier update round, is assessed again. However, results of a previous assessment
need to be accessible within the current version of the *SNEM_Data* knowledge asset. An
example depicted in fig. 6-20 clarifies this task.

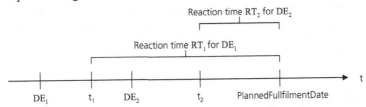

Fig. 6-20. Data consistency during analysis of disruptive events

As defined in section 4.3.4 each disruptive event that is identified by a SNEM system is
assessed with a Fuzzy Logic mechanism (see above). In the example two disruptive
events occur, where $DE_1$ is identified at time $t_1$ and $DE_2$ at time $t_2$. An assessment by
the *DataAnalyzer* role is only needed once at the time of identification, because it is assumed that as a consequence of a *DE*'s identification a reaction $R_u$ is triggered to minimize negative consequences of the disruptive event in the remaining reaction time (see
section 2.1.3.3). However, knowledge of the previous identification and assessment of
$DE_1$ is still of interest to any actor involved in the fulfillment process at time $t_2$. Provision of this knowledge is ensured by the *AnalysisBehavior* class.

A specific data structure is provided by the *DisruptiveEventList* with a content object
named *DisrEvListEntry* (see fig. 6-17). It is designed according to the data structures

which every agent uses (see section 6.1.2.3). Within this data structure the ontological concept of a disruptive event *DE* and related data types (e.g. *ExDS* and *EnDS*) are stored as a Java Bean (see section 6.1.2.2). Furthermore, a timestamp of the *DE*'s identification as well as two flags indicating, whether the *DE*'s *EnDS* exceeds an enterprise-specific limit and whether the disruptive event occurred within the enterprise, are stored in this list.

Every disruptive event that is identified at some point in time by a surveillance agent is added to the *DisruptiveEventList*. During each update round the surveillance agent creates a new *SNEM_Data* knowledge asset which integrates the most current data from internal data sources (the ERP system) and the newest *AOS* from analysis. A surveillance agent decides based on two criteria which of the known disruptive events contained in its *DisruptiveEventList* is added to this new *SNEM_Data* asset:

1. Any disruptive event that is characterized by an *Endogenous Disruptive Event Severity EnDS* which exceeds some configurable threshold, is considered worth to be communicated to actors within the enterprise and potentially to external supply network partners. This selection is based on the *exceedsLimit* attribute of the *DisrEvListEntry*.
2. Since minor disruptive events of suppliers might not affect an enterprise or even its customers, this assumption does not hold for events identified within the own enterprise. Thus, all disruptive events indicated by the *fromOrderIncoming* flag are always added to the new *SNEM_Data* object. This procedure assures that all internally identified disruptive events are communicated to the coordination agent which will eventually decide whether to send an alert (either internal or external) or not (see section 6.1.3.2).

All selected disruptive events are added to the *SNEM_Data* knowledge asset as further instances of the *Java Bean (JB)* classes of the SNEM ontology (see section 6.1.2.2).

Finally, the *AnalysisBehavior* sets the agent status to STABLE, thereby indicating that a new stable version of the monitored order's status is available for communication to the coordination agent (see section 6.1.4.1). At this point in time the surveillance agent has autonomously created a new information product that is the content for messages $M_s$, to solve the SNEM problem as defined in section 2.1.3.3.

## 6.1.5 Discourse Agent

A discourse agent as defined in section 5.6 is responsible for managing all inbound and outbound agent messages of a SNEM agent society which pertain to other supply network partners. It is the sole gateway to other supply network partners' SNEM systems. As such, its focus is on message forwarding mechanisms and dialog management, but in the prototype implementation is kept simple.

### 6.1.5.1    Management of Inter-Organizational Messages

Specific behaviors of a discourse agent necessary to fulfill the role as an interface to external supply network partners are depicted in fig. 6-21. Only two relevant performatives are distinguished within a SNEM agent system as defined in section 5.3.2.1: *REQUEST* and *INFORM* messages. Although content of both message types and thereby their specific statement or intention vary depending on sender and intended receiver of a message (for details see section 5.3.2), some general activities are always applied to each type separately. Consequently, generic behaviors are defined in the *attBehavior* package available to all agent types, and extended subclasses exist for the discourse agent. Within the *AbstractForwardRequestsBehavior* a *runBehavior* method gathers all *REQUEST* messages an agent has stored in its *AttConvMap* (see section 6.1.2.3) on a periodical basis. Only those requests for information not yet forwarded (regardless whether they are received from a customer or an internal surveillance agent that requests SNEM data from a supplier) are selected by the *determineRequests-ToForward* method. In the following, a *determineReceiver* method is used to identify a recipient to forward the message to. This method is not specified further in the abstract class but in its extension *ForwardMessagesBehavior* which is a discourse agent specific class. Its *determineReceiver* method distinguishes whether the request is made by an external supply network partner or an internal agent. The distinction is realized based on the SNEM ontology concept *Legal Entity* (see section 6.1.2.1) and results in two possible actions:

1. If an inbound *REQUEST* message from a supply network partner is received (that is from a *Legal Entity* other than the enterprise to which the discourse agent belongs), it is forwarded to the coordination agent.

2. An outbound *REQUEST* message can solely be generated by a surveillance agent that belongs to the same enterprise as the discourse agent. The intended receiver (a supplier's discourse agent) is identified via a request to the *GlobalDF* agent (see section 6.1.1.1).

Finally, the data structure *AttForwardMap* (see section 6.1.2.3) is updated with information on the forwarding process, and the *sendMessage* method of the *ForwardMessagesBehavior* calls a *SendMessageBehavior*[11] to finish forwarding the request.

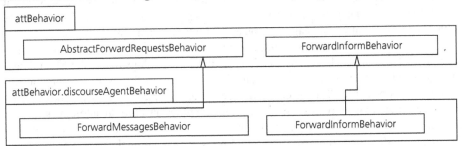

Fig. 6-21. Class diagram of a discourse agent

Reception of *INFORM* messages by the discourse agent induces a different behavior that is mainly based on the *ForwardInformBehavior* of the *attBehavior* package. Similar to receiving *REQUEST* messages, all *INFORM* messages are extracted from the agent's *AttConvMap* first. Again, only messages not yet forwarded are selected, and a check is made based on the *AttForwardMap* whether the *INFORM* belongs to an already existing dialog.

---

[11.]This behavior is implemented by every agent as part of the *attAgentBehavior* package (see section 6.1.1.2).

This check is based on the conversation identifier that is created for every *REQUEST* message and used in the corresponding response message (*INFORM*). If a match is found, the *INFORM* is forwarded to the original requestor as stored in the *AttForwardMap*. However, two cases exist where an *INFORM* is received without any corresponding *REQUEST* having been found (see section 5.6.3):

1.  An external *INFORM* message from a supply network partner is received. This is always a proactive alert generated due to identification of a disruptive event somewhere within the supply network. According to the design specified in section 5.3 only suborder recipients issue such alerts to their customers, if necessary. The *INFORM* is forwarded to the coordination agent for further treatment.

2.  An internal *INFORM* message from the coordination agent is received but no external *REQUEST* exists. This represents an alert that is to be sent to a customer who is specified in the message's content. The customer in turn will receive this *INFORM* as described above.

After forwarding the *INFORM* message, corresponding entries in the *AttForwardMap* are deleted, if any existed, because the dialog has been completed correctly.

### 6.1.5.2      Hot Spot for Reasoning Support

In section 5.6.2.2 two tasks are defined within the *CommunicationManager* role of a discourse agent that ensure syntactic and semantic quality of any messages received from external partners: *CheckContentLanguage* and *CheckOntology*. Within the generic prototype these are not considered, because only SNEM agent systems exist which adhere to the SNEM ontology and which are based on an automatic message encoding mechanism provided by the *JADE* agent platform which employs the *FIPA-SL0* content language (see section 6.1.2.2). This mechanism ensures that every agent of a SNEM agent society can rely on the quality of any received message, because *JADE* checks conformity to the *FIPA-SL0* content language and the SNEM ontology automatically.

However, in future scenarios an implementation of higher-level mechanisms is desirable, for instance to match content encoded in a different ontology to the SNEM ontology. Openness of the prototype implementation allows to integrate for instance automatic reasoning software such as *RACER* or *FACT* (see section 3.2.3.3) and to perform reasoning or ontology matching activities. Reasoning software relies on a formal ontology definition as is provided by the *DAML+OIL* definition and its transformation into the *Ontology Web Language (OWL)*. Since the *Java Bean (JB)* representation within the prototype is directly generated from an *OWL* format of the SNEM ontology, any SNEM data stored within an agent might be translated into an *OWL* representation and thereby made available to reasoning mechanisms.

## 6.1.6    Wrapper Agent

Only a simple wrapper agent type is required for the generic prototype. This agent provides access to the simulated ERP database. For each enterprise one wrapper agent exists that is accessed by all those surveillance agents of this enterprise which request data updates for their monitored orders. In addition, it receives special queries from the coordination agent of its enterprise. The coordination agent requests either a list of newly arrived orders for its profile matching mechanism or identification of a customer order in case an alert is received that indicates fulfillment problems within a specific suborder[12].

### 6.1.6.1    SQL Wrapper

To retrieve data from the *MySQL* data base (see section 6.2.1) two main classes are implemented: The *GetOrderFromDBsBehavior* is the wrapper's main behavior class. It uses a general database connector (*MySqlDatabaseConnector*) that can open and close a database connection and execute SQL statements, which are provided as parameters for its methods (e.g. a method *execQuery* requires a parameter *sqlquery*). As soon as a wrapper agent receives a *REQUEST* message, the *runBehavior* method of the *GetOrderFromDBs-Behavior* class extracts the order ID from the content of the message and calls the method *transferDBData2OrderObject*. Since the generic prototype is based on one single database, where each wrapper agent has a limited view on data relevant to its enterprise (see section 6.1.1.1), the company's name is provided as a second parameter to ensure adherence to this restriction. Subsequently a SQL statement is created by the wrapper agent that is used as the input parameter to a method in a class called *MySQLDatabaseConnection*. A template of such a SQL statement is depicted in fig. 6-22. The order ID is added as a variable, whereas the restricted view on the specific company's data is assured beforehand in the *isLocalOrder* method. This method checks whether the order ID is a valid identifier created by the enterprise itself.

```
"SELECT OrderIncomingID, isReceivedBy, isTriggeredBy,
OrderFinished, PromisedDeliveryDate, PlannedDeliveryDate,
TypeOfOrder FROM `orderincoming` WHERE
OrderIncomingID="+ orderID + " UNION SELECT OrderOutgoingID,
isAddressedTo, isTriggeredBy, OrderFinished, PromisedDeliv-
eryDate, PlannedDeliveryDate, TypeOfOrder
FROM `orderoutgoing` WHERE OrderOutgoingID=" + orderID
```
Fig. 6-22. SQL statement within a wrapper agent

The data set returned by the data base as a result of the query is further processed in the *transferDBData2OrderObject* method (see below).

### 6.1.6.2    Transformation to Ontology

Before the wrapper agent returns gathered data to the requestor, it transforms the retrieved data into the ontological representation that is based on Java Beans (see section 6.1.2.2). First, it creates a new order object and subsequently selects data from the query result as depicted in fig. 6-23. In the example the query result as a whole is stored in a variable *row*

---

[12.]An alert always contains SNEM data on a suborder. The receiving enterprise (respectively its coordination agent) has to find out to which of its orders a suborder mentioned in an alert belongs. A wrapper agent provides this insight by searching in the ERP system for the suborder and retrieving the related superorder.

which is accessed to set a variable *receivedByLegalEntity*. This is used as the parameter to set the attribute of the order object by means of the *setIs_receivedByLegalEnt* method. Similar mechanisms are implemented for each retrieved SNEM data type. The transformation of the query result into an ontological representation is always specific to the underlying data model of a data source. For this reason, a wrapper agent as the interface to this data source needs transformation knowledge regarding the ontological concepts. In the generic prototype this knowledge is coded in transformation rules (see fig. 6-23).

```
LegalEntity receivedByLegalEntity = getLegalEntity(new
Integer(row[1][2]).intValue());
order2fill.setIs_receivedByLegalEnt(receivedByLegalEntity);
```
Fig. 6-23. Transformation to ontology

As soon as data transformation is finished, the *runBehavior* method calls the *SendMessage* behavior available to every agent type and creates a reply to the initial request (*INFORM* message) the content of which is filled with the newly created order object that contains information derived from the data base.

# 6.2    Supply Network Testbed

The testbed for the generic prototype consists of a data base that simulates enterprises' ERP systems (section 6.2.1). Dynamic changes in fulfillment processes of every enterprise are simulated and reflected in this data base by a Java-based simulator which allows to conduct and monitor experiments (see section 6.2.2).

## 6.2.1    Simulated Enterprise Data Base

The subset of the SNEM ontology which is used in the generic prototype is the basis for the testbed's data base. In fig. 6-24 the data model of this "ERP" data base is depicted. As introduced in section 6.1.1.1 the same data base is used for every enterprise in the testbed, while enterprise-specific views realize virtual ERP systems for every supply network partner.

Data types are closely associated to concepts defined within the SNEM ontology. This facilitates transformation of data (see section 6.1.6.2). Main tables are *OrderIncoming* and *OrderOutgoing*. They represent orders received by a company from its customers (*incoming*) and related suborders which it issues to its suppliers and carriers (*outgoing*). Milestones and disruptive events associated with an order are termed in a similar fashion. The various columns in each table are derived from the SNEM ontology, for details on the definition of concepts see section 3.2.3. The data base is implemented as a *MySQL* data base. It is accessed with SQL statements as illustrated for the wrapper agent in  section 6.1.6.1.

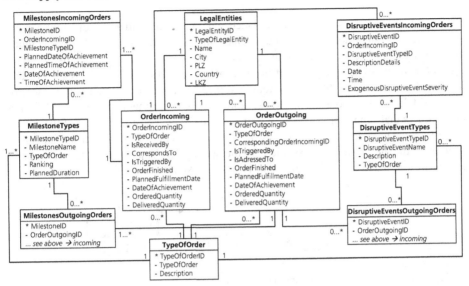

Fig. 6-24. Data model of the testbed

## 6.2.2 Simulator

A simulator is required to reflect changes in fulfillment processes in the ERP system. These changes are to be identified by agents of the SNEM system. The architecture in fig. 6-25 shows a simulator which is integrated in the testbed. It provides several functions relevant to conduct experiments with the prototype:

1. Disruptive events and their consequences on cycle times (= delays) are inserted by the simulator into the ERP systems of supply network partners.
2. To accelerate experiments the simulator manipulates the system time of the IT-system upon which the generic prototype is realized. Thus, it is able to simulate faster advancement of time.
3. A generalized reaction mechanism provides the ability to simulate reactions $R_u$ after identification of disruptive events by the agent system and thus simulates benefits achieved through event management.
4. A specific data base is used to store data on an experiment's design and results. Defined variations of experiment parameters are controlled by the simulator, and automated start and termination of experiment runs are possible.

The functions are integrated in a special agent type: a simulator agent which has direct access to both the ERP and the experiments data base (see fig. 6-25). This agent initiates new experiments by starting all agent societies and initiates monitoring through requests to *Enterprise 1* which it transmits via an additional discourse agent. During execution of fulfillment processes it generates disruptive events for selected orders of the supply network. It stores these disruptive events in the ERP system for discovery by the agents of the SNEM systems. As soon as a surveillance agent has identified a new disruptive event and its corresponding delay, a reaction mechanism is triggered that calculates how much of the delay can be reduced depending on the remaining reaction time. Details of the reaction function are discussed as part of the evaluation in section 7.3. The results of this reaction $R_u$ are stored in the ERP system, and measurements (e.g. time point of identification of DE, reaction consequences) are stored in the experiments data base. All delays in suborders that cannot be coped with propagate to the next customer level of the supply network. Such propagation is assured by the simulator agent. In case several suborders are delayed, a maximum delay is assumed for the superorder. Thus, propagating disruptive events are simulated and effects of agent-based SNEM are measurable.

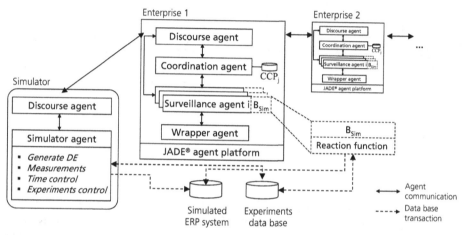

Fig. 6-25. Simulator architecture

The simulator agent terminates an experiment when all orders of the experiment are finished. To realize robust experiments that can be conducted automatically, the simulator agent implements a time-out function: If any of its requests are not answered after a certain time interval, it assumes that some computational problem has occurred (e.g. a severe program exception). It then terminates the ongoing experiment and starts the same experiment again. This feature allows to define a set of experiments up-front (e.g. with varying parameters) and to automatically execute experiments.

In fig. 6-26 an overview of main classes of the simulator is depicted. Since many data base operations are required for logging experiments, the *MySqlDatabaseConnection* in the *attTool* package is used by most classes. The *SimulatorSendAgent* extends the general *AttAgent* class, and the *SimulationRunner* class provides the functions for starting and terminating new experiments. The classes *TimeTakeTool* and *DateConverter* provide supporting functions. For instance, *TimeTakeTool* is used for changing agents' parameters depending on experiment parameters and logging experiment results. *LocalSimulatorComponent* contains the reaction function that is triggered within the *AnalysisBehavior* of a surveillance agent, because in this behavior a surveillance agent recognizes any new disruptive events and their consequences. The *LocalSimulatorComponent* has direct access to the ERP system for writing consequences of reactions $R_u$ and to the experiments data base for logging experiment results (see above).

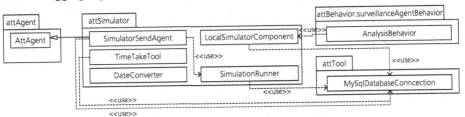

Fig. 6-26. Class diagram of the supply network simulator

## 6.3  Industry Showcase

A second prototype of an agent-based SNEM system called PAMAS[13] is realized as a showcase within a real-world environment of a logistics service provider (LSP). It provides insight into the ability to integrate agent-based SNEM concepts into existing fulfillment processes and IT-infrastructures. The showcase is implemented in cooperation with the LSP that has been introduced in section 2.4.1.3 and is documented in *Paschke et al. 2003, Zimmermann et al. 2003a, Bodendorf et al. 2005.*

### 6.3.1  Overview

Within this industrial setting the same generic agent architecture as presented in section 5.3 is employed. However, carriers integrated in this agent-based SNEM solution do not have their own SNEM agent societies, but only provide conventional web-interfaces for their customers. These interfaces offer status information on transportation orders (see tracking systems in section 2.4.1). To integrate these external network partners in the inter-organizational event management, dedicated wrapper agents for web interfaces of different carriers are implemented. Thus, no discourse agent is needed for dialogs between SNEM agent societies of supply network partners (see fig. 6-27).

The implementation of PAMAS is based on a FIPA-compliant agent platform which is implemented in Java: The *FIPA-OS* platform (*FIPA OS 2005*). A focus of the showcase is on integration of real-world data sources and on realization of the proactive monitoring of orders based on critical profiles $CCP_j$ as defined in section 4.2. The latter results from requirements of the LSP which wanted to focus the showcase on its main problems: large amounts of irrelevant and outdated data that it gathers in its data bases but that nobody uses for proactive event management (see section 2.4.1.3). Hence, profile-based proactive monitoring is the key element to increase efficiency of monitoring efforts, whereas the

---

[13.]PAMAS = Proactive Order Monitoring Multi-Agent System (= "Proaktives Auftragsüberwachungs Multi-Agenten-System")

limited scope of the domain of the LSP allows to use simpler rules and calculations for data analysis as well as for alert generation. Consequently, to restrict the complexity of the prototype, an implementation of the enhanced Fuzzy Logic analysis and alert generation concepts (see sections 4.3 and 4.4) was not intended.

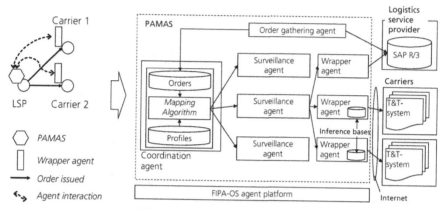

Fig. 6-27. PAMAS architecture

PAMAS is connected to the enterprise resource planning (ERP) system *SAP R/3* of the LSP by two types of wrapper agents (see fig. 6-27): A conventional wrapper agent is used by surveillance agents to access internal data sources, and an order gathering agent proactively provides updates on newly arrived orders to the coordination agent. These updates are inserted into the profile matching mechanism.

An overview of main packages and classes of the PAMAS system is depicted in fig. 6-28. All agent types are derived from the *FIPAOSAgent* class except the *CoordinationAgent*. This is derived from a specialized *JESSAgent* class that integrates the JESS rule engine (*JESS 2005*) required for the profile matching mechanism (also see section 6.1.3.1). *ECTLAgent* and *LZFAgent* represent wrapper agents to internal data sources of the LSP. These agents are connected to the *SAP R/3* system (*LFZAgent*) and to a second data base where order-related data received from carriers in EDI-messages is deposited (*ECTLAgent*). Since the second data base is often incomplete and outdated (see section 2.4.1.3), it is primarily used by surveillance agents to retrieve tracking identification numbers required to access the tracking systems of carriers. These tracking systems are accessed by PAMAS through dedicated wrapper agents: In the showcase a connection to the FedEx website has been realized (*FedExAgent*).

Similar to "behaviors" in *JADE,* the *FIPA-OS* agent platform provides "tasks" to encapsulate certain activities of an agent. Every task in *FIPA-OS* is processed within a separate Java thread. This assures parallel execution of agent activities. Corresponding to the generic agent prototype in section 6.1 information on the status of an order and its milestones is stored in instances of Java classes called *Order* and *Milestone*. Possible attributes are for instance planned and estimated/achieved fulfillment dates, order items or order volumes. To reduce implementation complexity of the showcase only selected attributes relevant for the LSP's processes and defined in the SNEM ontology are integrated in these ontological classes. To facilitate definition and manipulation of critical profiles $CCP_j$, an additional class *Profile* is integrated in PAMAS. It stores meta information on a $CCP_j$ such as its lifetime and further data required for permanent evaluation of a profile[14].

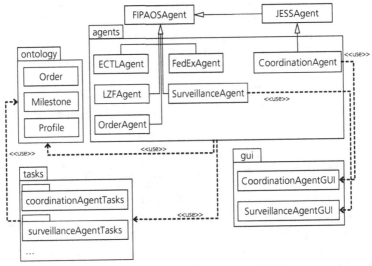

Fig. 6-28. Class diagram PAMAS

Various graphical user interface (GUI) classes provide visualizations for the coordination agent and surveillance agents. In this prototype the visualization primarily aims at supporting actors within the LSP to promote usage of a SNEM system in contrast to the generic prototype in section 6.1. There, visualization is a means to oversee experiments within the testbed environment.

## 6.3.2   Coordination Agent

### 6.3.2.1   Management cockpit

The coordination agent offers a graphical user interface (GUI) which allows a user to monitor and manage the SNEM agent society of the LSP (see fig. 6-29)[15]. A user can manually start surveillance agents to monitor certain orders, access detailed information of a specific surveillance agent, and terminate observation tasks. The GUI provides a short overview of all currently active surveillance agents with their monitored order's identifier, predicted duration of the order, and an aggregated status that indicates whether the order is *on time, late, critical,* or *finished.* Configuration and management of critical profiles is also managed by this GUI (for details see section 6.3.2.3). All wrapper agents that are

---

[14.]The same function is realized by a separate profile database in the generic prototype in section 6.1.

[15.]Since the LSP is based in Germany, the user interface had to be implemented in German.

currently active and known to PAMAS are featured, and some further parameters regarding SNEM functions of the PAMAS system are controlled on this level, as indicated in fig. 6-29 and detailed in fig. 6-30.

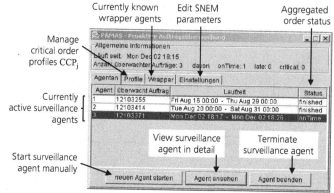

Fig. 6-29. Graphical user interface of a coordination agent

In fig. 6-30 parameters are defined that determine how often the order base of the coordination agent is deleted. This order base contains all newly accepted orders of the LSP and is used for profile matching (see section 6.3.2.3). To prevent accumulation of deprecated orders, a regular process for clearing the order base is provided. The same applies to surveillance agents whose orders have been finished and that are no longer required. How soon these are terminated after finalization of an order is determined by a separate parameter[16].

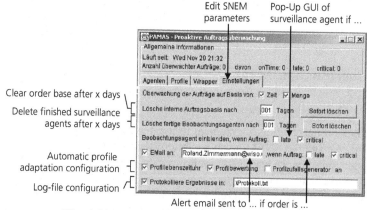

Fig. 6-30. Configuration of SNEM parameters

---

[16.]In case information is required for an already finished order, a manual start of a surveillance agent is possible. This agent will gather all available data from relevant data sources and provide a quick overview of the historical situation of an order.

Further parameters control alert generation by the SNEM agent system (see fig. 6-30). Two main features are provided: First, a pop-up feature displays a surveillance agent to the user of PAMAS in case a monitored order is either late or critical, depending on the configuration. Second, an alert email is sent to one or more predefined email-addresses[17]. Finally, continuous profile evaluation and adaptation mechanisms (see section 6.3.2.3) are activated or deactivated by the user.

### 6.3.2.2 Initialization of Surveillance Agents

If a user decides to monitor a specific order or if an order is identified as potentially critical (see section 6.3.2.3), the coordination agent instantiates and initializes a surveillance agent. The surveillance agent monitors the fulfillment process across the entire supply network from order reception to order delivery. The system uses a series of milestones, which divide the entire fulfillment process into individual sub-processes defined by the LSP (see fig. 6-31).

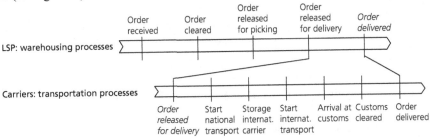

Fig. 6-31. Processes of a logistics service provider

Milestones to be monitored and their planned dates of achievement are communicated by the coordination agent to a surveillance agent as part of a surveillance agent's initialization. In fig. 6-32 the Java class *CoordinationAgent* with its primary methods and associated tasks of the coordination agent are depicted. Instantiation and initialization of a new surveillance agent is realized by the *startWatchAgent* method that requires two parameters: The order and the milestone types to be monitored. Planned dates for predefined milestones are calculated based on standard durations (with consideration of weekends[18]) and communicated to the newly initialized surveillance agent. Quality of planning data regarding durations of each milestone is essential to the performance of the whole SNEM system, because this is the basis for assessing the current status of an order. A set of standard durations for different types of fulfillment processes considered in the PAMAS system (e.g. varying destinations) has been defined together with experts of the LSP.

---

[17.]Additional order-specific adresses may be defined for each surveillance agent (see section 6.3.3.2).

[18.]Holidays might be added but pose complexity to the implementation since they differ in various destinations. An integration of specialized web services that provide such information is a possible extension to the prototype.

The *getWatchAgent* method returns all currently active surveillance agents to display these in the coordination agent's GUI, and the *finishWatchAgent* method is used to terminate surveillance agents either through manual intervention of a user or through finalization of the monitored order.

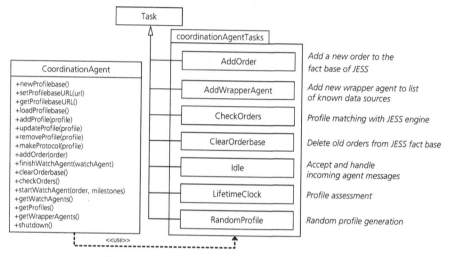

Fig. 6-32. Class diagram of a coordination agent

### 6.3.2.3    Profile Management

The coordination agent uses critical profiles $CCP_j$ as proposed in section 4.2 to manage proactive monitoring of orders. The implementation is very similar to the generic prototype: The rule-based system JESS (*JESS 2005*) is integrated within the coordination agent, $CCP_j$ are stored in the rule base and characteristics of new orders in the fact base. Mapping is conducted with the *Rete* algorithm, and new surveillance agents are initialized as described in section 6.3.2.2. The fact base which is termed *OrderBase* within the prototype implementation (see fig. 6-32) is updated with new orders in the *AddOrder* task received from the *OrderAgent* (see fig. 6-28) periodically. The mapping algorithm is executed in the *CheckOrders* task as soon as new order data is inserted into the fact base or new $CCP_j$ are added to the rule base.

New profiles are defined with a graphical user interface depicted in fig. 6-33. Besides a name for each profile, a profile's priority and an initial profile rating are defined. Profile priority determines how often a surveillance agent tries to gather update information on an order[19], and a profile's rating is input to the evaluation mechanism that assesses the quality of a $CCP_j$ over time. Profile parameters selected from available data types of the LSP and suited as profile attributes (see section 4.2.1.1) are proposed in editable input

---

[19.]A maximum waiting time is divided by an integer value. The larger this value (= the priority) the shorter the update cycle for gathering new information. Priority of a profile is also adjusted dynamically by the evaluation mechanism which is detailed in section 6.3.2.3.

fields (see fig. 6-33). Input to any of these fields is translated into a JESS rule which is automatically updated in the window below the input fields. All inputs with the editor result in conjunctive rules (logic *AND* between rule terms). In the editable window below, further additions and changes to the JESS rule can be made. Consequently, complex $CCP_j$ are definable, if such knowledge is available e.g. from expert interviews or data mining results (see section 4.2.2).

In addition to manual definition of $CCP_j$, a dedicated task *RandomProfile* (see fig. 6-32) creates simple random profiles, if this feature is activated. The implemented method is less complex than the methods which are proposed in section 4.2.3.4 and implemented in the generic prototype. The method randomly considers profile attributes with a numeric value (e.g. a postal code or a country identifier) and generates random numbers to fill these attributes into a JESS rule. This mechanism may well lead to profiles that never fit any order, but an evaluation mechanism automatically deletes these profiles after a certain time.

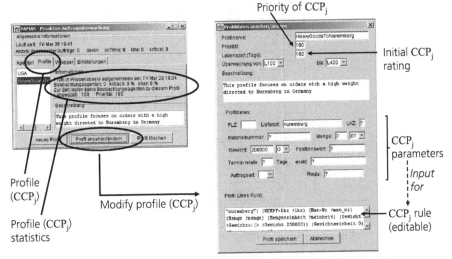

Fig. 6-33. Profile management menu of a coordination agent

The profile assessment mechanism introduced in section 4.2.3 is realized in a simpler version in PAMAS. A lifetime concept for profiles is implemented: If disruptive events arise during monitoring of orders, the respective $CCP_j$'s lifetime is increased otherwise reduced[20]. Profiles which are seldom used or do not help to identify disruptive events are removed as soon as the lifetime counter is zero. For each profile a separate *LifetimeClock* task (see fig. 6-32) is initiated that periodically checks whether matches to new orders were found. In case no matches are found the lifetime is decreased, otherwise an increase/decrease depends on whether the monitored orders were critical or not during fulfillment.

---

[20.]Each profile has an initial value for the lifetime which is defined in the profile management GUI.

## 6.3.3　Surveillance Agent

Fig. 6-34 depicts an overview of a surveillance agent's main class and its associated tasks. Two primary types of tasks are distinguished: The five top-most tasks are concerned with managing proactive data gathering, while all "update" tasks perform analysis of gathered data and create updates of graphical user interfaces to present a monitored order's current status. The final task realizes an organized termination of a surveillance agent after finalization of a monitored order. Within this task activities such as proper deregistering from the agent platform and termination of any remaining active tasks of a surveillance agent is realized.

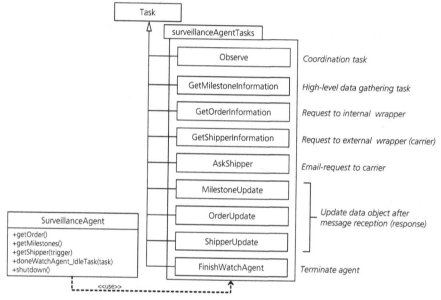

Fig. 6-34. Class diagram of a surveillance agent

### 6.3.3.1　Data Gathering

A surveillance agent implements the data gathering strategy presented in section 4.1.2.2 and restricts its gathering activities to those data sources currently involved in the fulfillment process of an order. To determine which data source is to be queried, each surveillance agent acts according to the decision matrix illustrated in fig. 6-35: As long as only milestones of the LSP's internal warehousing activities are identified by the surveillance agent[21], queries are restricted to the wrapper agent responsible for the internal *SAP R/3* data source (*LZFAgent*). As soon as the transfer of physical goods to a carrier is realized (indicated by the milestone "Order released for delivery"), the second internal data base

---

[21.]This includes the situation that no information on milestones is available at all. This is the case at the beginning of proactive monitoring (surveillance agent's initialization).

is queried via the wrapper *ECTLAgent*. This returns the identification number required for accessing information on the monitored order within a carrier's tracking system. The surveillance agent determines the relevant wrapper agent for a carrier and begins gathering data from the tracking system of the carrier.

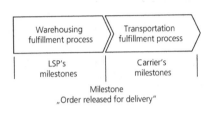

| Last milestone completed | Query strategy |
|---|---|
| LSP's milestones | Query wrapper (internal data source) |
| Milestone „Order released for delivery" | 1. Query wrapper (internal data source) for *TrackingID* 2. Query wrapper (carrier's tracking system) |
| Carrier's milestones | Query wrapper (carrier's tracking system) OR Email-query |

Fig. 6-35. Data gathering strategy of a surveillance agent

All following milestones are transportation milestones which indicate to the surveillance agent, that only external information from supply network partners (= a carrier) is to be gathered.

An example of interactions that evolve between a wrapper agent and a surveillance agent is depicted in fig. 6-36. The wrapper agent has access to a carrier's tracking system, hence the monitored order is already within the transportation fulfillment process and the *GetShipperInformation* task is used to gather new information. It generates a FIPA-conform *REQUEST* message with content that contains the *TrackingID* of the monitored order. Assuming that the wrapper agent retrieves desired update information, an *INFORM-RESULT* is sent which integrates data directly gathered from the tracking system ("*Information (08-20...*") and data on achieved milestones ("*MilestoneReached(...*"). The latter is the result of the wrapper agent's ability to match retrieved data of a carrier with the milestone concepts of the LSP (which correspond to the SNEM ontology). This ensures that a surveillance agent can calculate deviations from the planned milestone dates which it has received from the coordination agent upon initialization (see section 6.3.2.2).

In a real-world environment it cannot be ensured that every carrier provides a tracking system with a web interface. And even if a system is available, it may have down-times. In the latter case the wrapper agent will return a *FAILURE* message, otherwise no wrapper exists at all. As a backup solution surveillance agents can send an email form to a human actor who serves as a contact person to the LSP within a carrier's limits. The email form has a rigid format very similar to that presented in section 3.3.2.3 (fig. 3-29). The format has to be adhered to by the contact person who fills in requested data. Each data element is separated by a semicolon. This allows the surveillance agent to parse the response email automatically and extract information from the completed form. This mechanism ensures robustness of proactive order monitoring even in the face of missing or disabled wrapper agents. However, semi-automatic data gathering increases the time between occurrence of a disruptive event and its detection significantly, because responses to emails have to be generated manually.

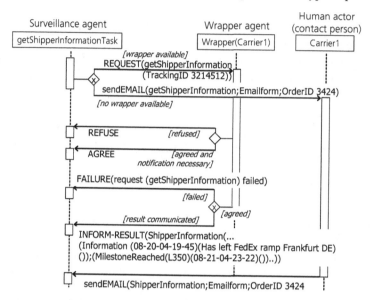

Fig. 6-36. Agent interaction: data gathering by surveillance agent

Results of proactive data gathering for each surveillance agent are presented in a special user interface depicted in fig. 6-37.

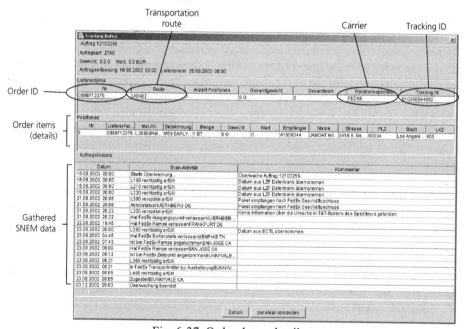

Fig. 6-37. Order data - details

Besides basic information on an order which is gathered from the internal ERP system of the LSP (e.g. the order's ID and its order items), information on the route, the carrier employed and the *TrackingID* are displayed as soon as this information is retrieved. Gathered information on the development of the monitored order's fulfillment processes are depicted in the lower part of the GUI. All information which is gathered from the various data sources is displayed in this view:

1. Data is visualized without any interpretation as it is gathered from a data source. For instance the information *"Hat FedEx Rampe verlassen..."* (= has left FedEx station) is a *FedEx*-specific remark provided within the *FedEx* tracking system and displayed to the user by PAMAS after retrieval.

2. Data is mapped to the milestone definitions of the LSP. For instance *"L300 verspätet erfüllt"* (=L300 fulfilled late) indicates that a milestone was fulfilled after its planned fulfillment date.

### 6.3.3.2    Status Calculation and Alerts

Based on the order's milestone plan (see section 6.3.2.2) which defines when a milestone is supposed to be completed, each surveillance agent identifies any deviations. This is achieved by the *Observe* task (see fig. 6-34) which employs an internal timer to compare current time, predicted progress defined by the milestone plan and actual progress indicated by achieved milestones. Any deviation is registered by the agent and displayed to the user, if a serious deviation is identified (see fig. 6-38).

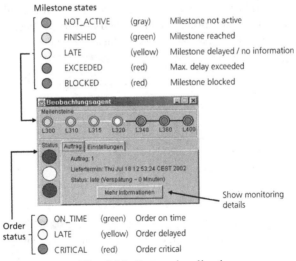

Fig. 6-38. Status visualization

The main graphical user interface (GUI) provided by each surveillance agent to a user upon request employs a traffic light metaphor. To indicate the status of a monitored order PAMAS differentiates between states of single milestones and an aggregated status of an order. All states are defined based on the traffic-light metaphor (see fig. 6-38). Within the sequence of milestones individual states of already achieved milestones form a history, which is used for calculation of an aggregated status. This order status indicates, whether an order is fulfilled *on time*, is *late*, or *critical*.

Proactive alerts to actors are provided by PAMAS in two ways:

1.  If a maximum delay is exceeded, a surveillance agent automatically sends a warning email to a person specified by the user of the PAMAS system (configuration see section 6.3.2.1).

2.  In addition, the GUI of the surveillance agent is automatically displayed to the user at the LSP ("pop-up").

Further configurations of a specific surveillance agent are shown in fig. 6-39. A selection is possible whether ordered quantity and/or time-related attributes are monitored. Regarding quantities, PAMAS checks whether an order is delivered in full or only in part and integrates this information in its assessment of an order's status. Time is considered as described above, based on the achievement of milestones and on comparisons with a milestone plan. Different variants to assess the severity of delays can be chosen. Simple thresholds consider absolute or relative deviations from plan, for instance x% after planned achievement is critical. The variant *"Verzug/Restzeit"* (=Delay/RemainingTime) considers the relation between delay and remaining time for fulfillment until the planned fulfillment date of the order. As soon as this relation reaches a threshold (in the example in fig. 6-39: limit=1), an order is considered to be *critical*, otherwise any delay only results in a *late* status (see fig. 6-38).

To enable order specific email-alerts in addition to the generally defined recipients (see section 6.3.2.1), email-addresses can be added/changed for each surveillance agent as necessary. Email alerts provide information on planned fulfillment date, current status of the monitored order (e.g. critical) and an up-to-date history of the order's fulfillment.

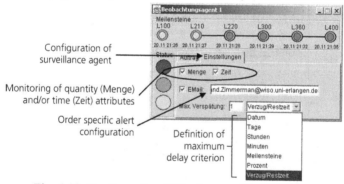

Fig. 6-39. Configuration GUI of a surveillance agent

## 6.3.4   Wrapper Agent

Various types of wrapper agents are realized in PAMAS to enable data gathering from several data sources. Internal data sources represent data bases that are accessed in a similar fashion as described for the wrapper agent in the generic prototype (see section 6.1.6).

Since supply network partners of the logistics service provider do not provide their own agent-based SNEM systems (see section 6.3.1), wrapper agents provide an interface to existing tracking systems of these partners. Depending on the kind of data source the extraction of data and its transformation into a uniform output format pose different problems. Transformation requires interpretation of retrieved information in order to map e.g. the definition of milestones of a carrier to that of the LSP. This is relatively simple if source documents retrieved from a carrier's tracking system are based on XML or described by other kinds of meta data. However, most tracking systems only provide purely text based documents (HTML) without tags that structure the content[22]. In this case a wrapper agent must have exact knowledge concerning the structure and semantics of the retrieved document. With this information, it analyzes the HTML code and searches for desired information. For instance, it maps the following information retrieved from the HTML code of a *FedEx* tracking response to milestones of the LSP:

```
"abgeholtNUERNBERG DE" = Order picked up by carrier
    --> milestone L300
"zugestellt"           = Order delivered to customer
    --> milestone L400
```

These transformation rules are stored in an internal inference basis of a wrapper agent as indicated above in fig. 6-27.

---

[22]·For instance, at the time of implementation of PAMAS *FedEx* only provided simple HTML documents. In the meantime XML-based data is available to large customers if these implement specialized interfaces (*FedEx 2005*).

# Chapter 7

# Evaluation

An evaluation of the SNEM concept and its related prototype implementations has to consider specifics of the supply network domain, especially its structural complexity. In the following, an approach to evaluation is selected which permits to consider benefits and constraints of agent-based SNEM from different analytical perspectives. The primary focus of all evaluation activities is on economic benefits to be achieved by an agent-based solution to the SNEM problem.

## 7.1 Concept

Several constraints exist which prevent realization of a large-scale field trial for agent-based SNEM and thus to provide a single evaluation activity. Hence, three different perspectives ranging from a theoretical model to laboratory experiments and an assessment of an industry showcase are used to provide an overall assessment of the economic potential for agent-based event management in complex supply networks.

### 7.1.1 Constraints to an Evaluation

#### 7.1.1.1 Complexity of the Domain

Evaluation of the SNEM concept is restricted by the inherent complexity of the supply network domain. The multitude of partners who cooperate in a realistic supply network and the autonomy of each of these partners (see section 2.1.2.4) prohibit testing a prototypical system in a realistic setting. A typical situation in a network consists of at least several suppliers for each single manufacturer. Each manufacturer himself is again part of an even larger supply network not to speak of logistics service providers. This results in a multitude of relationships between supply network partners. Aside from prohibitive costs of implementing prototypes in such an environment for a large number of enterprises it is likely that most partners will not agree beforehand to participate in a large-scale trial without any initial indication which realistic benefits a SNEM solution can provide. This sit-uation precludes field trials that would cover multiple levels of a supply network, because empirical data on the fulfillment processes of all levels is hardly available. Only data on a limited scope (e.g. the business case depicted in section 2.4.1.3) is available for an eval-uation.

### 7.1.1.2    Planning of Reactions

A second constraint that adds additional complexity to the evaluation of the SNEM con-cept is the fact that economic benefits measured in monetary units are achieved only in-directly. The following argument uses the formal specification (see section 2.1.3) of the problem: A SNEM system satisfies the implicit demand $D_q$ for information on disruptive events $DE$ by a message $M_s$. $M_s$ is the input for any reaction $R_u$ that is supposed to min-imize the consequences $CSQ$ of the disruptive events $DE$. These negative consequences and their reduction through event management can be measured in monetary terms, as il-lustrated by the calculation of potential benefits in section 2.3. But realizing a managerial reaction as a result of a message $M_s$ is not part of the information logistics task and out-side the boundaries of SNEM systems. Typical reactions consist of recalculating existing plans and schedules of activities. These calculations are conducted in dedicated planning systems or manually by operational experts. Execution of revised plans is the second part of a reaction $R_u$. However, the complexity of the planning and scheduling tasks prohibits their direct integration into a SNEM system. Instead, interfaces to these systems are de-fined (see sections 4.4.4 and 4.4.5).

In a realistic field trial benefits of the SNEM concept can only be proven, if reactions $R_u$ are truly realized and consequences $CSQ$ can be measured. The required interaction of a SNEM system with existing planning systems (e.g. production planning systems (PPS) or advanced planning systems (APS)) in a prototypical implementation is not fea-sible in a large industrial context. The impact on operational performance of network part-ners, for instance in the case of initial problems in the SNEM system, is prohibitive to any company. An enterprise cannot risk consequences of a (semi-)automatic change of its pro-duction or transportation schedules based on information that is provided by an early-stage prototype system, if its customers depend on these goods and services. In addition, costs of integrating existing planning systems with SNEM systems are prohibitive in this initial stage of development.

## 7.1.2    Multi-dimensional Evaluation

### 7.1.2.1    Perspectives

A multi-dimensional evaluation approach is chosen that encompasses three different per-spectives with separate evaluation approaches (see fig. 7-1). Each approach offers a dif-ferent view on the main question to be answered: *By how much can follow-up costs*[1] *of disruptive events DE be reduced by a SNEM system?*

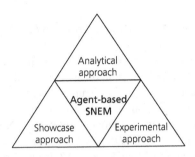

Fig. 7-1. Perspectives of evaluation

The three evaluation perspectives offer the following views on this question:

- *Analytical approach*
  A cost-benefit analysis for event management is conducted. For this analysis a formal model is proposed which quantifies the benefits of agent-based event management. In addition, benchmarks are defined that characterize existing systems for event management. It is shown that conceptual differences between agent-based SNEM and other systems result in different monetary benefits.

- *Experimental approach*
  Based on the generic prototype presented in section 6.1 experiments in a simulated supply network are conducted to validate the hypotheses developed in the analytical approach. A mechanism is introduced in the testbed that simulates the ability of an enterprise to react to disruptive events as soon as these are identified by the SNEM prototype (see section 6.2.2). Thus, benefits in multi-level supply networks are quantified in an experimental setting, and constraints to the agent-based SNEM concept are identified.

- *Showcase approach*
  The prototype developed in cooperation with a logistics service provider (LSP) (see section 6.3) is assessed with respect to its potential to reduce costs that are related to disruptive events in the LSP's supply network. This showcase complements the analytical and experimental evaluation: It establishes realistic parameters which are required in the cost-benefit model. An outlook on potential benefits of agent-based SNEM and on constraints to be encountered in industrial settings is given.

### 7.1.2.2 Analytical Approach

A cost-benefit-model is developed which integrates the cost model of the follow-up costs of disruptive events proposed in section 2.3 and a model for event management costs. The main parameter to be influenced by event management is the time between occurrence of

---

[1.] Follow-up costs of disruptive events are considered in a broad sense. They incorporate direct costs such as costs for expediting orders and indirectly related costs such as loss of sales due to dissatisfied customers (see section 2.3.1.2)

a disruptive event $DE$ and its identification, termed $\Delta T = T_{IdentInfo} - T_{DE}$ in section 2.3.

Any type of event management relies on updates of monitoring information to establish a new status assessment, based on which alerts are generated if necessary. The time span between occurrence and identification of a disruptive event ($= \Delta T$) is determined by the number of update-cycles per time frame. In the following, each update-cycle is referred to as a *SNEM cycle*. For each monitored order a number of SNEM cycles is realized, and the higher this number is the faster any $DE$ will be discovered and the lower $\Delta T$ will be. A direct relationship between SNEM cycles and $\Delta T$ is used in the cost-benefit-model to quantify $\Delta T$ (see section 7.2.1).

To achieve a large number of SNEM cycles and thus reduce $\Delta T$ significantly, an automation of the monitoring process is required as intended by the agent-based SNEM concept. Besides the prototypes presented in chapter 6 which illustrate the ability to automate the SNEM process (see section 4.5), some additional results from tests document this ability (see section 7.2.2.1). Operational costs associated with automated event management are quantified (see section 7.2.2.2) and serve as input to the aggregated cost-benefit model of event management (see section 7.2.3).

The cost-benefit-model results in a cost function which allows an optimal number of SNEM cycles to be calculated, if the parameters of cost functions are known (see fig. 7-2). This model is used to characterize three benchmark situations: (1) without any event management, (2) manual event management with a traditional *Tracking and Tracing (T&T)* system (see section 2.4.1) and (3) state-of-the-art *Supply Chain Event Management (SCEM)* systems (see section 2.4.2).

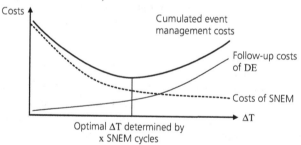

Fig. 7-2. Minimal event management costs

The benefits realized in the benchmark situations are compared to benefits which are achievable with agent-based SNEM. Two conceptual differences to existing systems are analyzed in detail: Effects due to inter-organizational communication in supply networks and effects of critical profiles $CCP_j$ are quantified. For inter-organizational communication the propagation of disruptive events in multi-level supply networks is considered, based on the theoretical model of section 2.3. Critical profiles $CCP_j$ are assessed based on empirical results obtained from data of the business case (see section 2.4.1.3): Realistic critical profiles are identified and validated with data mining mechanisms. Effects of these $CCP_j$ on monitoring efficiency in supply networks are predicted with a separate model.

These results are subsequently used as input to the cost-benefit-model, and differences between situations with and without critical profiles are quantified.

### 7.1.2.3    Experimental Approach

Based on the generic prototype presented in section 6.1 and the supply network testbed with its simulation component (see section 6.2) experiments are conducted in a multi-level supply network. These experiments are used to substantiate the forecasts provided by the analytical evaluation perspective. In particular, the influence of SNEM cycles on the performance of event management is analyzed. In addition, disruptive events that occur at different times in a fulfillment process are examined regarding their effects on supply network performance.

Delays as consequences of disruptive events are at the heart of the experiments. These delays spread to customers, if no reaction is possible (see fig. 7-3 top). In the example without event management a delay occurs in a suborder, but it is neither identified within the enterprise nor communicated to the customer. Thus, the remaining reaction time $RT$ until the planned fulfillment of the order is negative and the delay is completely propagated to the customer.

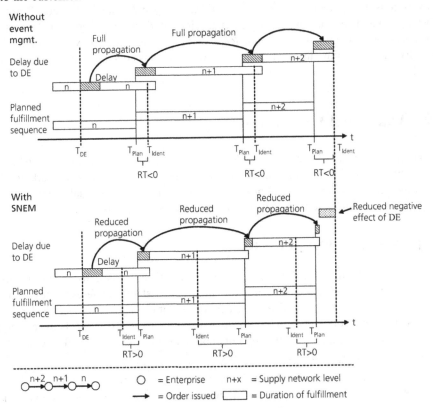

Fig. 7-3. Analytical scenarios

The simulator presented in section 6.2 provides a simple reaction mechanism which realizes reactions $R_u$ to reduce delays, if information on delays is available before the planned end of fulfillment (see fig. 7-3 bottom). Consequently, reaction time $RT$ is positive[2], and an overall reduction of the consequences of disruptive events $DE$ is measured. Details on the reaction mechanism within the testbed are presented in section 7.3.1.

Experimental results on the ability to reduce delays with event management are rated with costs. A comparison with the results of the analytical evaluation approach concludes the experimental perspective.

#### 7.1.2.4    Showcase Approach

The industrial showcase (see section 6.3) serves as a proof-of-concept for integration of agent-based event management in a real-world environment and to substantiate findings of the analytical and experimental evaluation perspectives. The assessment of the showcase and associated data retrieved from the business case is twofold: First, some direct measurements are provided for characterization of the prototype (e.g. reduction in search times, scalability). Second, a cost analysis is conducted for a certain type of reaction which is conducted in the case of a severe disruptive event during transportation. The analysis considers potential variants of the reaction $R_u$ and related activities. Resource consumption and costs attributed to these activities are identified. A cost function which depends on the remaining reaction time $RT$ of an order is determined. A discussion of the cost curve and the ability to generalize the showcase results concludes this evaluation approach.

## 7.2    Analytical Evaluation

The analytical evaluation approach is based on a theoretical cost-benefit model which is iteratively developed in subsequent sections. It is used to assess three benchmarking situations for agent-based SNEM and provides an evaluation of conceptual differences between these situations and the agent-based event management approach.

### 7.2.1    Effects of SNEM Cycles

In section 2.3.1.2 a linear cost model for calculating effects of disruptive events (follow-up costs) is presented. It is argued that this model consistently underestimates realistic benefits to be gained from any event management solution. Thus, any analytical evaluation based on this model tends to be conservative. The time interval $\Delta T$ between occurrence and identification/notification of a disruptive event is the major influencing factor

---

[2.] Reaction time $RT$ is closely linked to $\Delta T$ (time between occurrence and identification of a $DE$) since $RT$ is measured as the time between identification of a $DE$ and the planned fulfillment date of an order. Thus, an increase in $RT$ corresponds to a decrease of $\Delta T$.

among these follow-up costs. The first step in the analytical evaluation is therefore to determine the influence of SNEM cycles on $\Delta T$ (see fig. 7-4).

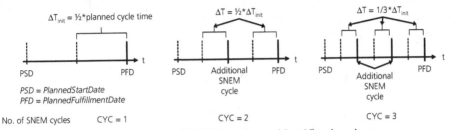

Fig. 7-4. Influence of SNEM cycles on identification time

If no explicit event management mechanisms are in place, disruptive events $DE$ are identified at some late point in time after the *PlannedFulfillmentDate* of an order, namely when some human actor realizes, that either an order has not yet arrived due to a delay or some quality deficit is identified (e.g. incomplete delivery or product failures). In these cases, a manual event management process is begun and data will be gathered by human actors to identify the reason for the problem and to react to it. Therefore, a single (manual) SNEM cycle is assumed ($CYC=1$), even if no explicit event management techniques are in place (see fig. 7-4). It is further assumed that identification of any disruptive event $DE$ is realized at the *PlannedFulfillmentDate*, although in reality later identification is common (see section 7.2.3.2). Consequently, parameter $\Delta T$ for any order is in the range between zero and *PFD-PSD*. For the analytical model an average value for all monitored orders is used: As long as no indication of statistical distributions of disruptive events during fulfillment is available, the same probability of encountering a disruptive event is assumed. If all disruptive events are discovered at the *PlannedFulfillmentDate* and disruptive events $DE$ are evenly distributed over the duration of an order's fulfillment, the average value of $\Delta T$ is one half of the planned duration (=cycle time) of an order (see fig. 7-4). This initial value of $\Delta T$ is termed $\Delta T_{init}$.

Based on the notion of a constant probability of disruptive events during fulfillment, influence of additional SNEM cycles on $\Delta T$ is determined: If the probability of encountering a disruptive event is the same at every point in time during fulfillment, then a rational strategy to maximize the monitoring success is to evenly distribute SNEM cycles over the whole duration of a fulfillment process. The effect for one ($CYC=2$) and two ($CYC=3$) additional SNEM cycles is depicted in fig. 7-4. It is based on the same principle as for $CYC=1$, with the first SNEM cycle covering the first 50% of *DEs* and the second SNEM cycle at *PFD* the last 50% of *DEs* encountered on average in all monitored orders for $CYC=2$. The average time between occurrence of a single disruptive event $DE$ and its identification and notification by a SNEM system is thus reduced to $\Delta T_{init}/CYC$. The influence of SNEM cycles on follow-up costs of a single disruptive event $DE$ is integrated into the cost model[3] presented in section 2.3.1.2 as:

(1) $CO_{DE}(CYC) = \alpha S + \beta \dfrac{\Delta T_{init}}{CYC}$

The first term considers the severity $S$ of such a disruptive event and determines associated costs that cannot be reduced with operational reactions. The second term consists of the cost parameter $\beta$ and the truly realized $\Delta T$ depending on $CYC$. Parameter $\beta$ varies for different types of disruptive events $DE$ (see section 3.1.3.2) and it depends on the time of occurrence of the $DE$.

## 7.2.2 Costs of Event Management

### 7.2.2.1 Automation of Event Management

Proactive data gathering in inter-organizational environments is one main feature required for automated event management. In the testbed of section 6.2 multiple enterprises are simulated as depicted in fig. 7-5. The generic prototype (see section 6.1) implements the data gathering strategy proposed in section 4.1: Every surveillance agent queries suppliers about suborders, if these are related to the monitored order to which a surveillance agent is dedicated. In the experiments an initial request for order information is triggered at enterprise $E1$ which gathers information on a suborder from $E2$ which in turn has to query $E3$ and $E4$ for its suborders. The overall response time from the initial request of $E1$ to the final response received by $E1$ is measured (see fig. 7-5). These experiments indicate that on average responses based on this strategy arrive within a matter of seconds if SNEM agent societies are available on every network level.

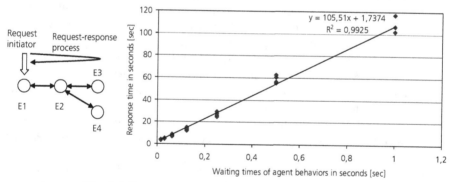

Fig. 7-5. Response times in multi-level supply network

This observation also holds in the event that computational times are increased for each enterprise: For instance, complex data retrieval mechanisms may take additional time in reality. This situation is simulated through additional waiting times for every agent behavior in the prototype[4]. Although computational time for a response is increased significant-

---

[3.] Note: This cost model measures effects of an average disruptive event $DE$ that occurs early during fulfillment. Whether effects are similar for later $DEs$ is analyzed in the experimental approach (section 7.3).

ly (see also fig. 7-5), resulting response times technically permit data gathering cycles at least every few minutes.

Both, analysis of gathered SNEM data as well as decisions on alerts rely on Fuzzy Logic assessments (see sections 4.3 and 4.4). In fig. 7-6 results of tests with the Fuzzy Logic module, which is integrated in the coordination agent, are depicted[5]. In these tests several test data sets are analyzed by the coordination agent's Fuzzy Logic behavior. Different strategies are reflected by different Fuzzy Logic rule sets which are defined as MS-Excel sheets that are used as configuration files for the behavior (see section 6.1.3.2).

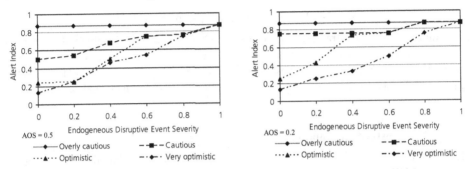

Fig. 7-6. Influence of Fuzzy Logic rule sets

Results of the tests regarding the aggregated order status $AOS$ and the endogenous disruptive event severity $EnDS$ which are both integrated in the alert index $AI$ are depicted in fig. 7-6. Input parameters and further results of tests are provided in appendix D. In fig. 7-6 $AOS$ is fixed and $EnDS$ is variable. The same alert index $AI$ is calculated with four different Fuzzy Logic rule sets that represent different strategies: Cautious strategies tend to generate alerts even for less severe problems and thus produce higher $AI$ than optimistic strategies in the same situation. This behavior is illustrated in fig. 7-6. For instance, with a medium $AOS$ of 0.5 and low $EnDS$ an optimistic strategy results in a low $AI$, while a cautious strategy leads to a significantly higher $AI$. This difference increases, if $AOS$ is lowered (0.2 in fig. 7-6, right side), because cautious strategies value $AOS$ higher than $EnDS$ and raise $AI$ for every disruptive event to a very high level. Optimistic strategies value small disruptive events less, even though the $AOS$ is lower.

In fig. 7-7 further test results are depicted for input values at the limits of the defined intervals of each parameter. The results indicate plausible behavior of the Fuzzy Logic components even for these extreme inputs. For instance, a disruptive event with $EnDS=1$ (highest possible severity), the lowest possible $AOS=0$ and the highest priority[6] of an order ($=1$) is rated with $AI=1$.

---

[4.] Every agent type in the SNEM society has several behaviors (see chapter 5) that are often active more than once to satisfy a single status request. Thus, an additional second of waiting time for each activation of a behavior has a very large impact on response times while processing times themselves can be neglected in the prototype as depicted by the results in fig. 7-5.

[5.] Since the same mechanism is implemented within the surveillance agent type, the results are also applicable to data analysis by surveillance agents.

| Endogeneous Disruptive Event Severity (EnDS) | Aggregated Order Status (AOS) | Priority | AlertIndex AI (cautious strategy) |
|---|---|---|---|
| 0 | 0 | 0 | 0.75 |
| 0 | 0 | 1 | 1 |
| 0 | 1 | 0 | 0 |
| 1 | 0 | 0 | 0.75 |
| 1 | 1 | 1 | 1 |
| 1 | 1 | 0 | 0.5 |
| 1 | 0 | 1 | 1 |
| 0 | 1 | 1 | 0.25 |

Fig. 7-7. Results for extreme parameter values

Summing up, different strategies for evaluating SNEM data are realizable with different Fuzzy Logic rule sets which are used for configuration of the Fuzzy Logic behaviors implemented in the SNEM agent types: coordination and surveillance agent. These strategies provide plausible results and enable automatic SNEM data analysis and alert decisions.

### 7.2.2.2 Costs of Automation

The notion of "automating SNEM cycles" is important to define potential costs associated with each SNEM cycle, because direct labor costs related to event management can be neglected[7]. Operational costs of IT technology and communication that are only indirectly affected by labor costs (e.g. personnel for maintaining servers) are considered. For the analytical evaluation approach it is assumed, that IT resources and communication network capacities are provided by third-party service providers to all enterprises that conduct event management. Enterprises' SNEM systems are hosted by service providers: Infrastructure - hardware and communication network resources - are provided and priced on a pay-per-use basis. Consequently, fixed costs are not considered in the cost-model for SNEM usage, and an aggregated cost parameter $\vartheta$ is introduced to calculate costs of monitoring a single order. These costs are determined by the number of SNEM cycles $CYC$ which are conducted for one order[8]:

(2) $CO_{SNEM}(CYC) = \vartheta \cdot CYC$ with $\vartheta > 0$

The cost parameter $\vartheta$ integrates two major types of costs[9]:

---

[6.] Priority of an order is considered in the second step of the Fuzzy Logic assessment (see section 4.4.2).

[7.] Note: Automated event management solely considers the SNEM process as defined in section 4.5, but not human interventions during execution of reactions $R_u$.

[8.] A linear model is chosen, because it overestimates potential costs of monitoring, if it is assumed that economies-of-scale apply to the monitoring of orders. Such effects occur for instance when prices decrease, if IT infrastructure is utilized more intensely by one customer (e.g. increased storage requirements). Overestimation of event management costs with the linear model ensures conservative estimates of potential benefits of a SNEM solution when compared to the follow-up costs of disruptive events (see section 7.2.3).

- *IT resource consumption*
  Under the assumption of hosted applications, costs for providing IT infrastructure are determined by actual consumption of storage and processing capacities. These are provided on a flexible basis, and prices charged for these services are directly linked to consumption. Typical costs for these services range at around 1 US-Dollar for one hour of CPU-time or for 1 Gigabyte of storage capacity including storage management (e.g. *Sun 2005*, *Gray 2003*). Execution of a SNEM cycle includes access to data bases and agents' computations but these are well below an hour CPU-time and a Gigabyte of gathered data. Thus, resource consumption is at the highest in the range of single US-Cents per SNEM cycle.
- *Communication volume*
  One major aspect of the agent-based SNEM concept is inter-organizational communication during proactive data gathering and alert distribution. Every SNEM cycle results in communication activities between companies. Bandwidth used by SNEM systems is assumed to be priced according to a pay-per-use contract. Since prices for communication bandwidth have decreased severely in the last years, it is assumed, that costs of communication per SNEM cycle tend to be lower than those for consumption of other IT resources: About 1 US-Dollar per Gigabyte communication volume is a realistic price according to *Gray 2003*. Each exchanged agent message in the SNEM context contains a few Kilobytes of data which results in a price per message of significantly less than one US-Cent per SNEM cycle.

Although monitoring costs are relatively low per SNEM cycle with an assumed maximum of around five US-Cent (sum of costs defined above), an increase of monitoring costs is associated with every additional SNEM cycle. Hence, the maximum number of SNEM cycles which is technologically possible is not necessarily reasonable from an economic point-of-view: For instance, updates every five minutes for an order with a five day cycle time would result in monitoring costs of up to 72 US-Dollar. These costs cumulate, if every order of an enterprise is to be monitored this intensely.

## 7.2.3    Cost-Benefit-Model and Benchmarks

### 7.2.3.1    Formal Model

To answer the question by how much follow-up costs of disruptive events are reduced with the SNEM concept (see section 7.1.2.1), an overall assessment of potential cost reductions and induced costs of event management as depicted in fig. 7-2 is conducted with an integrated cost-benefit-model. This model cumulates both cost types $CO_{DE}$ and $CO_{SNEM}$ in a new cost type $CO_{cum}(CYC)$ that is determined by the number of SNEM cycles

---

[9.] Further cost types can be considered in the cost parameter, if appropriate, as long as prices vary with each SNEM cycle. Fixed costs might be integrated into the model by shifting the linear cost curve upwards, but are omitted here for simplicity reasons.

conducted $(CYC)$. $CO_{cum}(CYC)$ integrates formula (1) (see section 7.2.1) and formula (2) (see section 7.2.2) in one cumulative model:

$$(3) \quad CO_{cum}(CYC) = \alpha S + \beta \frac{\Delta T_{init}}{CYC} + \vartheta \cdot CYC \cdot w$$

An additional parameter $w$ is introduced in formula (3) which considers costs of event management for monitoring activities that are conducted but do not identify any disruptive events $DE$. However, two different types of "wasted" monitoring efforts need to be distinguished and only the second type is considered by parameter $w$:

1. The cost-benefit-model concentrates on follow-up costs of a single disruptive event $DE$ which affects a specific order. Since the time between occurrence and identification $(\Delta T)$ of this $DE$ is determined by the number of SNEM cycles realized for this order, all data gathering rounds except the one which identifies the $DE$ are essentially conducted without "success". Nonetheless, all SNEM cycles are required to achieve $\Delta T$ and associated costs of these monitoring efforts are covered by formula (2) with $CO_{SNEM}(CYC) = \vartheta \cdot CYC$.

2. For every monitored order that is affected by a single disruptive event a certain number of orders is monitored although no $DEs$ are identified for these orders. Monitoring activities for these orders result in additional event management costs which are not considered in formula (2) for $CO_{SNEM}$. However, these costs need to be considered in a cost-benefit-model that confronts benefits from identification of a single $DE$ with all costs required for identification of this $DE$. For instance, if every order of an enterprise is monitored and only 5% of all orders are affected by disruptive events, for every monitored order with a disruptive event, 19 others are monitored although no problems occur. Since all 20 orders are monitored with the same number of SNEM cycles to identify a single disruptive event, event management costs $CO_{SNEM}(CYC) = \vartheta \cdot CYC$ have to be multiplied by 20 which is the corresponding value of $w$ in formula (3). In the following the parameter is referred to as the *Monitoring Efficiency w* of an event management system.

In fig. 7-8 a typical situation is depicted with all three cost functions, namely event management costs $(CO_{SNEM})$, follow-up costs of $DE$ $(CO_{DE})$ and cumulated costs $(CO_{cum})$. All cost functions depend on the number of actually realized SNEM cycles $(CYC)$. In this scenario the severity cost parameter $\alpha$ is 100 monetary units [MU] which is multiplied with the disruptive event's severity $S=0.4$. $\Delta T_{init}$ is 60 time units[10] [TU] and the time between occurrence and identification of a $DE$ is valued with a cost parameter $\beta$ of 6 MU per time unit. The cost parameter $\vartheta$ for event management costs is significantly lower with 0.1 MU per SNEM cycle. Since only every 20th monitored order is affected by a $DE$[11] the monitoring efficiency parameter $w$ is 20.

---

[10.] A time unit is an abstract measurement of time in the cost-benefit-model. In fulfillment processes time is mostly measured in hours.

[11.] Parameter $w=20$ in the scenario indicates, that all orders are monitored, but only 5% encounter disruptive events which corresponds to empirical observations on important deviations in fulfillment processes (see section 2.4.1.3).

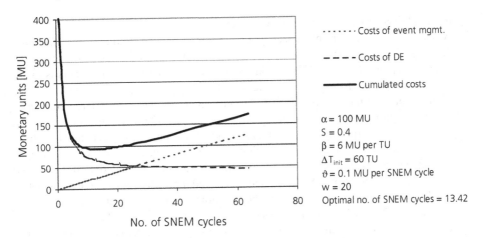

Fig. 7-8. Cost functions in event management

The optimal number of SNEM cycles is calculated as follows:

$$(4)\frac{\partial CO_{cum}(CYC)}{\partial CYC} = -\frac{\beta \Delta T_{init}}{CYC^2} + \vartheta w = 0 \Leftrightarrow CYC^2 = \frac{\beta \Delta T_{init}}{\vartheta w} \Leftrightarrow CYC = \sqrt{\frac{\beta \Delta T_{init}}{\vartheta w}}$$

An increase in the cost parameter $\beta$ or in the cycle time of an order (which determines $\Delta T_{init}$) results in an increase of the optimal number of SNEM cycles. This behavior is plausible, because higher follow-up costs provide greater potential for reduction of costs and longer cycle times require an increased number of monitoring cycles, if disruptive events are to be detected early. In contrast, increased monitoring costs or more wasted monitoring efforts reduce the number of economically optimal SNEM cycles in a given situation.

### 7.2.3.2    Benchmark Situations

Three basic situations are associated with different numbers of SNEM cycles. Each situation characterizes a certain realistic scenario with or without some type of event management system:

1. For $CYC=1$ no proactive event management is assumed, and disruptive events are never identified before a planned fulfillment date of an order (see fig. 7-4). $\Delta T_{init}$ determines an initial cumulated cost level $CO_{cum}(1)$. Costs for $CYC=1$ are very high (see fig. 7-8, in the example 402 MU). However, this situation is realistic for many enterprises that do not regularly try to gain insight into the current status of order fulfillment but rely on manual identification and communication of disruptive events, often by customers themselves (see e.g. business case in section 2.4.1.3). $CO_{cum}(1)$ calculated with formula (3) underestimates the realistic cost level for these situations since gathering of information in case of disruptive events is conducted by human actors whose associated costs tend to be much higher than auto-

mated IT-based data gathering and analysis.

2. A realistic scenario for enterprises that have implemented traditional *Tracking-and-Tracing (T&T)* systems without proactive event management methods (see section 2.4.1) is represented for *CYC=2*. Some important data on an order's status is available upon request from a T&T system, but interpretation and distribution of this information is a manual task delegated to human actors. Thus, for a large number of orders a high number of monitoring cycles is not feasible, if a human actor has to select orders, interpret their current status and decide on possible reactions[12]. However, supported by automated gathering of data through the T&T system (that is restricted to internal information, because no suborders are considered), it is assumed that at least one additional SNEM cycle is realized manually for every order which is monitored by the T&T system. In the example of fig. 7-8 costs $CO_{cum}(2)$ are reduced to 224 MU which represents a decrease of about 44% compared to $CO_{cum}(1)$. However, in reality benefits of using a T&T system are smaller, because no labor costs are integrated in $CO_{cum}(2)$, and they would increase the event management cost level significantly.

3. Assuming that automation of SNEM cycles is possible, as illustrated for the SNEM concept in section 7.2.2.1, the optimal number of cycles is realizable. In the example of fig. 7-8 costs $CO_{cum}(OPT)$ are 93.66 MU[13]. The reduction compared to a traditional T&T system is about 58% and about 77% compared to the situation without event management. Depending on the choice of parameters in the analytical model, different reductions apply that vary in magnitude but remain significant (see below).

In fig. 7-9 a variety of scenarios are depicted for different $\Delta T_{init}$ and varying cost parameters $\beta$. The optimal number of SNEM cycles grows both with an increase of $\Delta T_{init}$ and $\beta$ but below a linear function.

For *CYC=2* which represents a T&T system (see above) a linear development of costs is identified whereas optimal costs increase less, due to an increase in *CYC* that affects costs of disruptive events in the denominator of formula (3). In conclusion, a reduction of costs with an optimal number of SNEM cycles ranges from nearly zero to 90% compared to a T&T system. This is due to the wide range of parameter $\beta$ in the scenarios which is not entirely realistic: Zero reduction only occurs, if costs of a single SNEM cycle are the same as follow-up costs of disruptive events. However, realistic costs of automated event management will tend to be in the range of Cents per SNEM cycle (see section 7.2.2.2), whereas costs of disruptive events in most cases add up to at least several Euro (see also section 7.4.2.1). In the scenarios of fig. 7-9 a realistic ratio of at least 1:50 is depicted[14] by a value of $\beta = 5$. Reduction of costs for $\beta > 5$ is between 20% and 70% depending on $\Delta T_{init}$ which is determined by the duration of order fulfillment. Thus, the longer the fulfillment durations of an order are and/or the higher potential follow-up costs are, the

---

[12.]See section 7.4.1.1 for an example of realistic manual search times.

[13.]Note that this is a theoretical measurement of an average value since in reality only complete SNEM cycles are possible for monitoring an order. However, both 13 or 14 cycles result in about 93.7 MU which is a minimal difference.

greater is the potential of an automated event management as provided by the agent-based SNEM concept.

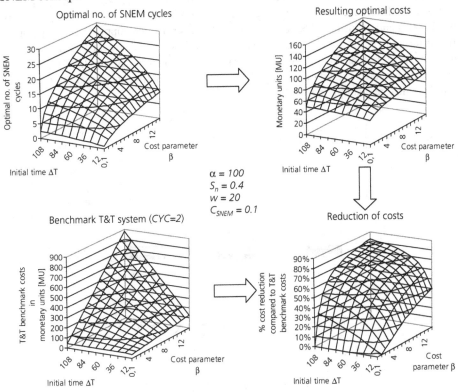

Fig. 7-9. Scenarios for cost reduction

In section 2.4.2 existing approaches for *Supply Chain Event Management (SCEM)* software systems are analyzed. It is concluded that existing SCEM systems have a similar objective as SNEM systems, but they neither focus explicitly on multi-level supply networks nor can they fulfill the requirements of SNEM systems. However, assuming that on a single-enterprise level a SCEM system is able to provide at least automatic data gathering and alert generation based on business rules, it is presumed that an optimal number of SNEM cycles can be achieved by advanced SCEM systems, too. This assumption establishes a third benchmark for agent-based SNEM solutions. Further analytical evaluation focuses on differences in performance regarding the reduction of follow-up costs of disruptive events *DE* between traditional SCEM and agent-based SNEM concepts.

---

[14.]The ratio 1:50 refers to 1 MU monitoring costs per SNEM cycle compared to 50 MU disruptive event costs per additional time unit TU (e.g. hours, although no explicit metric is required in the model) - in the example 0.1 MU are costs of one SNEM cycle and thus the cost parameter $\beta$ can be 5 MU.

## 7.2.4    Supply Network Effects

According to the arguments of section 7.2.3.2 regarding $CO_{cum}(OPT)$ for a single enterprise, no difference between the benefits of a traditional SCEM system (= highest benchmark) and agent-based SNEM exists[15]. However, from a supply network perspective differing benefits are encountered as illustrated in fig. 7-10. Agent-based SNEM reduces costs more than SCEM systems, because it is shown in section 2.4.2 that SCEM systems do not have a standard concept for proactively gathering and integrating information from different supply network levels.

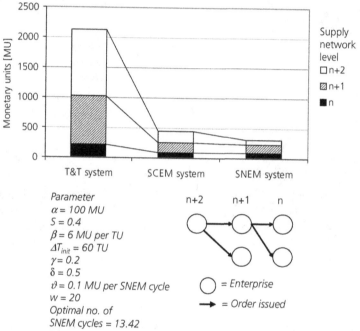

Fig. 7-10. Cost reduction at supply network level

Based on the cost model for multi-level supply networks proposed in section 2.3.3 the following characteristics are relevant and determine the two different cost levels[16]:
-    Every SCEM system is able to realize optimal identification times with the optimal number of SNEM cycles on its own supply network level. However, a lack of inter-

---

[15.]This statement only holds as long as critical profiles $CCP_j$ are omitted (see section 7.2.5)

[16.]Parameters are identical to the scenario of section 7.2.3.1 except for two additional parameters that determine the propagation of a disruptive event in a supply network. Parameter $\gamma$ represents the intensity of propagation due to a $DE$'s severity which is between zero and one and $\delta$ is a measurement of an enterprise's ability to react to disruptive events, if event information is available. In the scenario a relatively small propagation intensity ($\gamma = 0.2$) and a medium ability to react is assumed ($\delta = 0.5$). For details on parameters' characteristics see section 2.3.2.

organizational integration of SCEM systems characterizes current implementations (e.g. *Masing 2003*). This deficit prevents exchange of advance notices on disruptive events between network partners. Thus, follow-up disruptive events that propagate to supply network levels of customers (levels $n+x$) are identified by the first update cycle of a SCEM system but never before this point in time. Consequently, $\Delta T$ is the same on all supply network levels, and cumulated costs are calculated based on the cost model of section 2.3.3 with additional consideration of event management costs $CO_{SNEM}$[17]. Compared to the situation with T&T systems ($CYC=1$) on all supply network levels, a substantial reduction of costs in a supply network is realized (78% in the example of fig. 7-10)[18].

- In contrast to SCEM systems, the agent-based SNEM concept explicitly considers information from network partners and communicates event information along the path of any potential event propagation. Thus, $\Delta T$ is reduced to zero on all supply network levels $n+x$, because disruptive events are known to a customer before the start of the customer's internal fulfillment processes[19]. Only effects attributed to the severity of a propagating disruptive event and monitoring costs for the affected order are incurred at a customer's level. The costs due to a propagating disruptive event tend to be overestimated, because very early warnings may permit the effects of disruptive events to be contained within a single enterprise and thus to stop propagation of disruptive events in a supply network. This restriction of the analytical model supports a conservative estimation of SNEM benefits. In the example of fig. 7-10 an additional reduction of costs compared to the cost level of SCEM systems of 31% is realized. It adds up to an additional 7% reduction compared to the difference between T&T- and SCEM systems.

## 7.2.5 Event Management with Profiles

### 7.2.5.1 Efficiency of Proactive Monitoring

Effects of automated event management with proactive data gathering in supply networks have been evaluated above. However, automated monitoring of all orders of every enterprise wastes resources and raises event management costs: This is reflected in the high monitoring efficiency parameter $w=20$ which is used in sections 7.2.3 and 7.2.4. The results are an unnecessarily high communication load among partners in a supply network and an even more costly use of IT resources (see section 7.2.2.2) by surveillance agents. These agents realize the monitoring efforts but in most cases do not identify any disruptive events. Associated operational costs for every enterprise are higher than necessary. The concept of critical profiles $CCP_j$, as proposed in section 4.2, has the objective of sig-

---

[17.]The same parameters for costs are used for all supply network levels in this analysis.

[18.]Specific reduction rates depend on parameters which are selected in the model.

[19.]Effectively, $\Delta T$ is even negative, but this is omitted in the analytical model to avoid "negative costs".

nificantly reducing the amount of required monitoring activities and focusing event management on potentially critical orders. An assessment of the effectiveness of the critical profile concept (see below) precedes an analysis of its effects in the cost-benefit-model (see section 7.2.5.2). The concept of critical profiles is evaluated for two aspects:

1. Whether critical profiles $CCP_j$ are truly identifiable in realistic settings is analyzed based on a data mining analysis with historic data of a business case. This includes an assessment of data mining results with respect to the effectiveness of identified $CCP_j$ in focusing monitoring efforts on critical orders.

2. The effectiveness of critical profiles in reducing the communication load and IT resource consumption for proactive SNEM data gathering in a supply network is analyzed with a forecast model that is fed results of the data mining analysis.

Quantitative profile discovery, which implements the data mining approach proposed in section 4.2.2.2, has been conducted for a data set of the logistics service provider (LSP) who participates in the business case of section 2.4.1.3. The data set covers three months of orders (more than 4000 orders) fulfilled from the LSP's warehouse and sent with subcontracted carriers to international customers. Delay of an order compared to its anticipated fulfillment duration, which depends on its specific destination, is chosen as the class attribute (see section 4.2.2.2) . It results in 11.7% critical orders. Several data mining algorithms have been tested on the data set, and results are mostly the same. The best algorithm is the decision tree algorithm *J48*. All tests have been conducted with the WEKA data mining tool (*Weka 2005*). Results of the three algorithms best suited for the test data set are depicted in appendix E. The analysis reveals that several critical profiles $CCP_j$ can be extracted from the historic data set of the LSP as depicted in fig. 7-11..

```
Example: defrule Australia  (Destination = Australia) => (triggerSurveillance)

1.  Destination = Australia (J48)
2.  Destination = Bulgaria AND NOT (Weekday = Tuesday) (J48)
3.  Destination = Estonia (J48)
4.  Destination = Norway (J48)
5.  Destination = Poland AND ((Weekday = Tuesday) OR (Weekday = Wednesday) OR
    (Weekday = Thursday) OR (Weekday = Friday)) (J48)
6.  Destination = Russia (J48)
7.  Destination = South Africa (J48)
8.  Destination = Sweden AND Weekday = Tuesday (J48)
9.  Destination = Turkey AND NOT (isAdressedTo = carrier J) (J48)
10. Destination = United Arab Emirates (J48)

11. Destination = Greece (PART)
12. FreightTerms = FCA and isAddressedTo = carrier K (JRip)
```

Fig. 7-11. Critical profiles discovered with data mining

The order attribute *Destination* has the highest impact within the test data set. This may hint to country-specific problems such as customs procedures or non-standardized transportation processes to these destinations. Some critical profiles incorporate specific carriers or weekdays. The latter may indirectly hint to country-specific regulations that can delay transportation processes, e.g. weekend-regulations for trucks in certain countries. As depicted in fig. 7-11 most rules have been identified by the *J48* algorithm which provided the most detailed rules, although other algorithms provided very similar results. Two further critical profiles ((11) and (12), see fig. 7-11) are suggested by two other algorithms. Definition of critical profile rules from data mining results is mostly intuitive, but specialties such as *NOT* relations are introduced by human actors during interpretation of the data mining results (see e.g. (2) in fig. 7-11)

Quality of the data mining results is measured by means of a confusion matrix that is provided for each analysis automatically. In fig. 7-12 the results for the best algorithm (decision tree, *J48*) are depicted. Considering the ten critical profiles it identifies (see fig. 7-11), the results require to monitor 5.3% of all orders[20] and thus 36.6% of all critical orders are identified (measured by *TPR*). This empirical finding supports the assumption defined in section 4.2.1.1 that disruptive events do not occur completely at random, but primarily at certain sources, and this allows critical profiles to be defined. A critical profile's quality is described by its hit-rate: For 100 monitored orders an average of 81 orders is truly critical for the profiles identified here[21], i.e. the hit-rate is 81%.

Confusion matrix

| | | Predicted class | |
|---|---|---|---|
| | | Positive (=CCP_j) | Negative |
| Actual class | Positive (=CCP_j) | 177 True positives (TP) | 306 False negatives (FN) |
| | Negative | 41 False positives (FP) | 3598 True negatives (TN) |

$$TruePositiveRate(TPR) = \frac{TP}{TP+FN} = \frac{177}{177+306} = 0.366$$

Fig. 7-12. Confusion matrix for *J48* data mining algorithm

The results indicate that realistic critical profiles can be discovered using a data mining approach and that the quality of these profiles, as described by their hit-rate, is high. However, in the experiment only about 37% of all critical orders have been identified by critical profiles of the data mining approach. Since this is the result of a single data mining experiment on one input data set, it neither incorporates results from other data mining algorithms (e.g. profiles 11 and 12 in fig. 7-11) nor is it fully representative of an enterprise's expected set of critical profiles. For instance, further data sources (e.g. data from customer complaints) might be available internally, and regular updates of data mining analysis as well as continuous assessment of profiles (see section 4.2.3) increase the number and quality of critical profiles. Moreover, expert knowledge extracted by a qualitative discovery approach (see section 4.2.2.1) is not addressed here. Thus, a much higher degree of identified critical orders is anticipated for real SNEM implementations[22].

Based on the empirical findings, a model for the calculation of communication load and IT resource consumption in a multi-level supply network is proposed to assess the impact of $CCP_j$ on monitoring efficiency. The data gathering strategy for proactive event management in supply networks proposed in section 4.1.2.2 requires that suborder recipients be requested for their suborders' SNEM data. As long as no critical profiles are used

---

[20.]Calculated as *(TP+FP)/allOrders*.

[21.]Calculated as hit-rate=TP/(TP+FP)

[22.]The same principle for discovery of critical profiles can be applied to other types of fulfillment processes, e.g. production or warehousing processes.

in a supply network, every order and all its suborders are monitored and surveillance agents for every order are initialized. IT resource consumption and communication load are at a maximum. In a scenario with critical profiles the situation changes: Every enterprise has its own set of profiles and thus requests data from corresponding suborder recipients. In fig. 7-13 a situation is depicted where an enterprise on supply network level $n+1$ monitors a certain amount of orders and sends data queries for all related suborders to a supplier on level $n$. This supplier already monitors a certain amount of orders itself, because of its own critical profiles. A certain degree of requests from its customer thus refers to orders already monitored (*overlap* indicated in fig. 7-13), but the rest of the customer orders trigger the enterprise on level $n$ to initiate monitoring of further orders: Additional surveillance agents are initialized as defined in the behavior of the coordination agent described in section 5.4.2.2. The same mechanism applies to level $n-1$ as indicated in fig. 7-13.

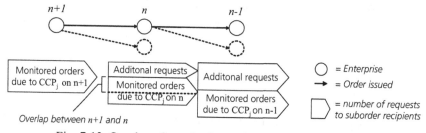

Fig. 7-13. Overlap of monitoring activities in supply networks

A forecast model is proposed that calculates the additional requests for each supply network level and thus the number of additionally initialized surveillance agents. The model builds upon the notion of an overlap ratio *OVR*. *OVR* indicates the ratio between orders monitored both by an enterprise and its customers due to overlapping profiles (for details of the model see appendix F). Additional requests are calculated as *1-OVR* multiplied with the number of orders monitored by a customer.

Different scenarios with varying numbers of monitored orders and different overlap ratios are assessed (see fig. 7-14). Four supply network levels are considered with $n=4$ being an initial customer and three consecutive suborder recipient levels.

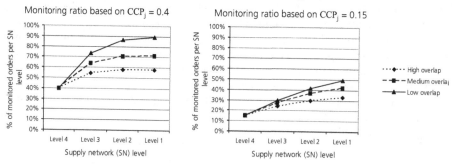

Fig. 7-14. Scenarios for varying monitoring intensities

On the left hand side a very broad approach to definition of critical profiles is chosen by every supply network partner: Each partner monitors 40% of its orders based on its own $CCP_j$. Three variants of overlap ratios are compared which subsequently add additional requests on every network level. For a low overlap ratio $OVR$ (between 0.16 and 0.22 as calculated for the different levels) a maximum of up to 90% monitored orders per enterprise is predicted with a network average of more than 60%. Thus, to effectively decrease monitoring efforts for all supply network partners, each partner has to restrict the number of orders it proactively monitors. The results of the data mining approach showed a 5% monitoring ratio to result in nearly 40% identified critical orders (see above). An increase of the monitoring ratio to 15% will still not yield identification of 100% of all critical orders, but at least a sharp increase is assumed. A scenario where every supply network partner initially monitors 15% of its orders is depicted on the right hand side of fig. 7-14. Depending on the overlap ratio a realistic maximum ratio of around 40% is to be expected, and the overall monitoring ratio for the whole supply network averages at about 30%.

Monitoring ratios are not static within a supply network. A typical scenario when implementing an event management solution is depicted in fig. 7-15. On the left side an initial setup is depicted where customers on higher network levels define more critical profiles than their suppliers. Initially, this is reasonable, because customers realize cumulated negative effects from suborder fulfillment problems and thus identify many potentially critical orders. Over time many smaller problems are handled within one network level due to enhanced reactions enabled by SNEM systems. Thus, customers' profiles will in part become obsolete and be removed from the profile knowledge-base automatically (see section 4.2.3). An improved situation where for instance every partner only monitors 20% of its orders based on critical profiles, reduces the average monitoring ratio within the network from more than 50% to less than 40%.

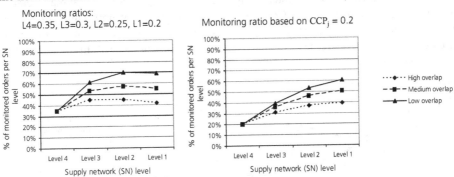

Fig. 7-15. Improvement of monitoring efficiency

Summing up, critical profiles can substantially reduce communication load and IT-resource consumption associated with monitored orders: The number of monitored order and thus the number of active surveillance agents and associated data gathering activities are significantly reduced compared to the situation with complete monitoring. However, this is only achieved, if the definition of profiles is limited and a high quality of profiles regarding their hit-rate is realized. Average monitoring ratios within a network may thus be reduced to about 30%, based on the input of the data mining analysis and the forecast model. This reduction has a substantial effect on monitoring costs, if costs per SNEM cycle are considered (0.05 US-Dollar, see section 7.2.2.2): For instance, if a relatively small number of optimal SNEM cycles (14 as derived from the example in fig. 7-8) is assumed for the 4,122 orders of the LSP analyzed before, monitoring costs would add up to 2,885 US-Dollar and the 70% reduction in monitoring efforts with critical profiles adds up to 2,019 US-Dollar. Reconsidering the business case of the LSP (see section 2.4.1.3), a prediction of similar reductions for all 200,000 orders per year adds up to a decrease of monitoring costs of about 98,000 US-Dollar per year, if critical profiles are employed. Consequently, these reductions have a significant impact on the cost-benefit ratio of event management detailed below.

### 7.2.5.2    Effects in the Cost-Benefit-Model

Up to this point of the analytical evaluation, it is assumed in the cost-benefit-model that 100% of an enterprise's orders are monitored, but only an average of 5% actually encounters disruptive events $DE$. Thus, an average hit-rate of monitoring efforts is also 5%, which in turn means that 95% of all monitoring efforts are wasted. This is depicted by the monitoring efficiency parameter $w=1/hit\ rate = 1/0.05 = 20$ (see section 7.2.3.1). In section 7.2.5.1 it is shown that by using critical profiles $CCP_j$ to focus monitoring efforts, the hit-rate can be increased to about 80%. Thus, the corresponding monitoring efficiency parameter $w$ would be reduced to $w=1.25$. However, within a supply network an average monitoring ratio of about 30% is expected, if critical profiles are well configured. Assuming that with this configuration nearly all 5% critical orders are identified, the hit rate of an average profile is around 16.6%. Thus, a realistic monitoring efficiency parameter is $w=6$. In consequence, a SNEM system configured with $CCP_j$ reduces event management costs $CO_{SNEM}$, and overall costs $CO_{cum}(CYC)$ are similarly lowered. This results in an increase of the optimal number of SNEM cycles. At the same time cumulated costs in the monitoring optimum decrease as depicted in fig. 7-16 for a number of different monitoring efficiencies $w$.

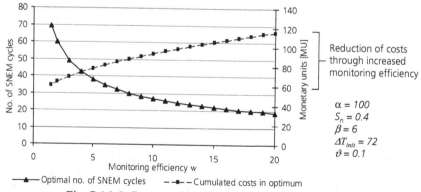

Fig. 7-16. Influence of profiles on monitoring optimum

Again, specific values of optimal SNEM cycles and associated costs vary with parameters in the analytical model. Since changes of cost parameters have been considered before, the influence of monitoring efficiency $w$ and initial time $\Delta T_{init}$, which is derived from average cycle times of monitored orders, is depicted in fig. 7-17.

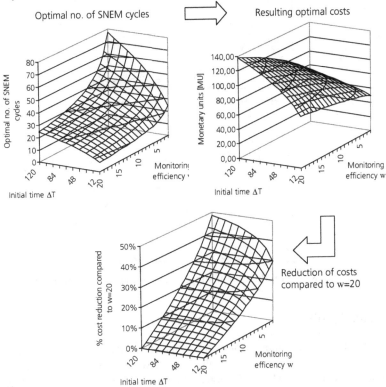

Fig. 7-17. Scenarios for varying profile qualities

With an improved monitoring efficiency (lower $w$) an increase above average of the number of optimal SNEM cycles is achieved for larger $\Delta T_{init}$. Considering these optimality conditions, the resulting cumulated costs decrease and a reduction compared to the initial state of $w=20$ adds up to 20% to 32% for $w=6$. This corresponds to the realistic hit-rate of 16.6% (see above). Further reductions for better hit-rates (see section 7.2.5.1) are possible.

Following the arguments in section 7.2.3.2 the situation for $w=20$ is a benchmark situation that is (potentially) achieved by current SCEM systems. Any additional benefits due to better monitoring efficiencies provided through critical profiles $CCP_j$ are only realized by the agent-based SNEM concept. For the same scenario as in fig. 7-10 the additional benefit of profiles is visualized in fig. 7-18. The optimal number of SNEM cycles is increased from 13.42 to 24.49 with a hit-rate of 16.6% ($w=6$) and costs are reduced compared to the SNEM situation without profiles by 39.7% and compared to the cost level achieved by state-of-the-art SCEM systems by 58.7%. In the example this reduction adds up to about 270 monetary units. Compared to the initial benchmark of a T&T system the SNEM concept even realizes a 78.6% reduction of costs (1,935 MU) in this scenario.

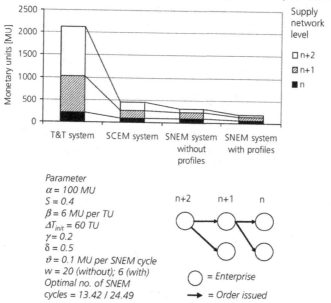

Fig. 7-18. Cost reduction at supply network level with profiles

## 7.2.6   Conclusions

The integrated cost-benefit-model for event management developed in section 7.2 uses the notion of a *SNEM cycle* to determine the time between occurrence and identification of a disruptive event $(\Delta T)$. The model considers costs of disruptive events influenced by the number of SNEM cycles and monitoring costs for each realized SNEM cycle. Typical real-world scenarios (without event management, T&T, SCEM) are characterized by different numbers of SNEM cycles per order, and monetary measurements derived from the cost-benefit-model are applied to these situations. These scenarios are used as benchmarks to investigate differences with respect to the agent-based SNEM concept:

1. Inter-organizational communication between enterprises of multiple supply network levels is not realized with a standardized mechanism by systems other than the agent-based SNEM concept.

2. An increase in monitoring efficiency that reduces costs of monitoring and allows to increase the number of SNEM cycles is provided by no other approach except the agent-based SNEM concept.

For both aspects it is shown individually that costs compared to the highest benchmark depicted by current SCEM systems are effectively reduced by as much as 60%, depending on the parameters chosen in the analytical model. Although specific reductions can vary greatly, they are shown to be significant (more than at least 20%) for parameter configurations which reflect realistic scenarios. Robustness of results is illustrated by a number of scenarios where different parameters are varied in defined steps.

The theoretical cost-benefit-model remains conservative and underestimates benefits of the SNEM concept while slightly overestimating benchmarks for other existing approaches (T&T, SCEM) (see section 7.2.3.2). Costs which remain after implementation of agent-based SNEM are mostly attributed to effects induced by the severity of disruptive events. These costs represent a basic cost level induced by a disruptive event, even if a reaction takes place instantaneously. Such follow-up costs cannot be affected by operational event management. They are determined by structural factors of organizational and process design that are to be improved on a tactical or strategic level (see also section 2.3.1.2). However, operational event management hints to areas of increased risk in fulfillment processes during its automated monitoring activities, but it cannot eliminate sources of disruptive events.

## 7.3 Experimental Evaluation

Experiments with the generic prototype focus on evaluating the impact of SNEM cycles on identification of disruptive events $DE$ (see section 7.3.2.1). Since the analytical model inherently considers $DEs$ which occur early during fulfillment (see section 7.2.1), a generalization of these findings is sought by analyzing effects of $DEs$ at different points in time during a fulfillment process (see section 7.3.2.2). Experimental evaluation concludes with a cost-assessment of benefits measured in experiments (see section 7.3.3).

All experiments are conducted with the simulator presented in section 6.2.2. The simulator agent generates disruptive events and enters corresponding data into simulated ERP systems of enterprises in an experiment. Besides, it logs data in an experiments data base that is used for analysis of experiments' results. The simulator agent controls experiment parameters and allows for instance to vary the date of occurrence of a disruptive event. A second aspect of simulation in the testbed is to simulate reactions to disruptive events. This feature is available to each surveillance agent as defined in section 6.2.2 and detailed in section 7.3.1. The results of all reactions for every enterprise in a simulated supply network are stored in the experiments data base along with the experiments' parameters.

### 7.3.1 Reaction Function

The experiments focus on delays which result from disruptive events $DE$ and propagate from suborders to customers' orders. As described in section 6.2.2 the simulator provides an additional class used by each surveillance agent to realize reactions $R_u$ in case a delay of a suborder is identified. The earlier this identification occurs, the better will be any reaction in reducing the initial delay. Compared to the analytical evaluation approach, not follow-up costs of disruptive events are directly measured but operational effects on fulfillment processes: delays. Thus, time-oriented process metrics are measured in the experiments and associated costs are determined outside the experimental environment in an additional assessment (see section 7.3.3).

The basic mechanism of reactions $R_u$ in the testbed is as follows: A delay is identified by an enterprise, a reaction is realized which reduces the delay and the remaining delay is communicated to the customer affected in the next step. The same mechanism is subsequently applied by the customer (and eventually its customer) until either no delay remains or a final customer in a supply network is reached. The underlying assumption permits reactions $R_u$ only, if event information is available on a suborder and before internal processes of an enterprise have started. Otherwise, it is assumed that internal fulfillment processes cannot be changed anymore. Although in reality such changes might be possible, for the experiment's design a focus on inter-organizational exchange of event information is chosen where internal processes are fixed as soon as these are started. This design assures that a worst-case-scenario is realized, if no event information is provided: A delay propagates completely to the final customer (see also fig. 7-3 in section 7.1.2.3), but the delay is never increased during propagation. Thus, the worst case scenario remains conservative compared to real-world situations where increasing delays over multiple network levels are common (see example in section 2.1.2.3).

The mechanism for reducing a delay assumes that to a certain extent the planned duration of fulfillment processes can be reduced. However, this reduction is limited to a predefined threshold, since in reality fulfillment processes (e.g. a production process) always have some minimum duration (e.g. for working on a product). The maximum potential for reduction is termed the *Maximum Reduction MR*. It is also assumed in the testbed that all suborders are finished, before internal fulfillment processes are conducted. Thus, no overlapping of processes is permitted which might in reality shorten cycle times additionally.

To calculate the reduction achieved by a reaction $R_u$, a *Reaction Factor $RF_n$* is used which indicates how much of the maximum reduction $MR$ is realized by $R_u$ for the $n^{th}$ disruptive event. In case a second or third disruptive event $DE$ is identified ($n > 1$), only the remaining fraction of MR after previous reactions is usable for a further reaction. This remaining fraction is termed the *Remaining Potential for Reduction $RPR_n$*:

$$R_u(n) = RF_n \times RPR_n \text{ with } n \in N, n \geq 1$$

$$DE_1: RPR_1 = MR; \text{ All other } DE_n: RPR_n = RPR_{n-1} - R_u(n-1) \text{ as long as } RPR_n \geq 0;$$

Reactions that are larger than the current $RPR_n$ are truncated to this upper limit and no further reactions $R_u$ are possible for this order afterwards.

The reaction factor $RF_n$ is restricted to the interval between zero and one, where zero indicates that no reaction takes place and one utilizes the complete remaining potential for reduction $RPR_n$ currently available to a specific order. Depending on when event information becomes available, $RF_n$ changes: The earlier information is available the higher is $RF_n$ and vice versa. In fig. 7-19 a possible function to calculate $RF_n$ is depicted. For every order a certain planning period before the order's scheduled start is assumed, during which information on disruptive events in suborder fulfillment is of particular high value. In case a delay of a suborder occurs, the *PlannedStartDate (PSD)* of the superorder cannot be realized, and a new *EstimatedStartDate (ESD)* is provided that incorporates the delay which is propagated by the suborder recipient. If information on a disruptive event is provided after the delayed suborder eventually arrived and internal fulfillment started, this information is no longer of any value and no reaction is realized ($RF_n=0$). This is the case after *ESD* and reflects the specific experiment's design established above.

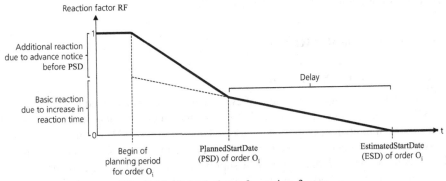

Fig. 7-19. Calculation of reaction factor

A linear function with a break-point is selected for calculating the reaction factor $RF_n$ as depicted in fig. 7-19 (details in appendix G). The intention is to value information higher, if it arrives before the initially *PlannedStartDate* of a monitored order and thus to value advance notices relatively higher than event information after *PSD*. $RF_n$ is determined by the increase in available reaction time. This is indicated by the increasing linear function that is zero at *ESD*. Without inter-organizational communication as part of event management, it is not known before *PSD* whether a suborder is late or not. However, this information is automatically available after *PSD*, because a delay is obvious to the enterprise and event management only has to provide additional information on how long this delay will last. Consequently, the advance notice provides a second informational aspect that is valued additionally in the calculation of $RF_n$, indicated by the break-point at *PSD* and higher increase in $RF_n$ before *PSD*.

In real-world scenarios different reaction functions to calculate a reaction factor $RF_n$ might be realistic (see also section 7.4.2.1). Assuming that such a function is available, it can be incorporated in the reaction mechanism by transforming the $RF_n$ into a $RF_n*$ as indicated in fig. 7-20.

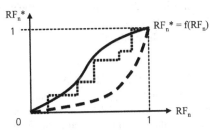

Fig. 7-20. Types of reaction functions

For instance, an increasing function is realistic, if at an early stage of fulfillment (especially during the planning horizon) only informational activities such as scheduling of activities are affected by a disruptive event, while at a later point in time various resources (e.g. personnel, machines) remain idle and induce high costs. However, in the experiments the linear model is used since it tends to underestimate benefits of event management (see also arguments in sections 2.3.4 and 7.2.6).

## 7.3.2    Experimental Results

### 7.3.2.1    Varying SNEM Cycles

The main parameter for effectiveness of event management is assumed to be the number of SNEM cycles as argued in section 7.2.1. This hypothesis is analyzed in experiments conducted on a multi-level supply network as depicted in fig. 7-21. Disruptive events are inserted by the simulator (see section 6.2.2)[23] during fulfillment of a suborder which is placed with *Enterprise 4*. All orders in the supply network have the same planned duration of five days. The initial advance planning horizon for *Enterprise 3* is 15 days and each following enterprise adds the maximum cycle time of its suborder(s) to this initial planning horizon. A maximum reduction *MR* of 10%, which is 12 hours, is defined for every enterprise.

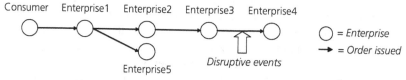

Fig. 7-21. Supply network design for experiments

In fig. 7-22 results of an experiment are depicted where a disruptive event occurs very early during fulfillment at *Enterprise 4* (within the first day of the planning horizon) and results in an initial delay of 100 hours. Measurements are taken at *Enterprise 3* for different numbers of SNEM cycles.

Since a very precautious reaction function with only 10% maximum reduction is chosen, the absolute difference between low and high numbers of SNEM cycles is relatively small. However, the results state that an increase in SNEM cycles results in a sharp decline of the remaining delay similar to that assumed within the analytical evaluation model in sections 7.2.1 and 7.2.3.1. In the experiments the minimum number of SNEM cycles per order is an average of 2.5 which results from fixed intervals between data gathering

---

[23.]The simulator stores the new *DE* in the simulated ERP data base and triggers initial requests for the consumer (= the final customer in the supply network which is also an enterprise) in fig. 7-21. Thus, it is able to control the number of SNEM cycles conducted in the supply network for the complete experiment. In particular, the simulator varies the frequency of requests in different experimental settings and terminates an experiment as soon as the *DE* is identified and a reaction has been realized. All experiment parameters and results are stored in the experiments data base.

rounds and the specific fulfillment duration of an order. According to the benchmark scenarios defined in section 7.2.3.1 the reduction associated with 2.5 SNEM cycles is very
similar to the situation attributed to a common *Tracking and Tracing (T&T)* system. An
increase of SNEM cycles allows to realize nearly the maximum reduction of 12 hours.
Compared to the T&T benchmark (10 hours) this is approximately an additional 20% reduction.

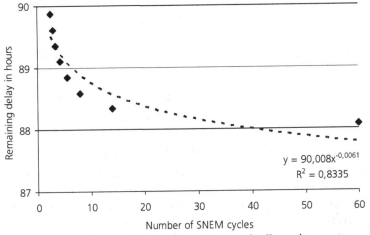

Fig. 7-22. Influence of SNEM cycles on early disruptive event

The theoretical cost-benefit-model of section 7.2 inherently focuses on disruptive events
that occur early within fulfillment processes. This model predicts a sharp decrease of follow-up costs for an increasing number of SNEM cycles. A similar behavior is observed
in the experiments for reductions of delays which supports the mechanisms proposed in
the cost-benefit-model. However, the extent of reductions is not as great which is attributed to the very conservative reaction function used within these experimental settings.
The major influence of the reaction function results in a first conclusion: Agent-based
SNEM is the more effective the higher the potential for reactions is, which is available in
fulfillment processes. Conversely, implementing sophisticated agent-based SNEM systems in an environment with a low impact of potential reactions cannot yield significant
additional benefits compared to simpler monitoring alternatives (e.g. T&T systems).

   To refine these experimental findings, the impact of SNEM cycles on the remaining
delay at *Enterprise 3* for a later disruptive event *DE* (seven days later) is depicted in fig.
7-23. The more erratic pattern of reductions results from fixed intervals for gathering data
and from random occurrence of a disruptive event: In some cases, a disruptive event will
be very close to an update round, even though this update round is one of very few in an
experiment with a low number of SNEM cycles. However, an approximated trend indicates the same pattern as for the early *DE* although the overall reduction is less. This is
due to the later occurrence of the *DE* and thus a reduced reaction time. On a relative basis
the additional reduction realized for more SNEM cycles compared to the T&T-situation
(2.5 cycles) is even larger: 4.5 hours reduction for T&T is compared to 6 hours reduction
for many SNEM cycles. This is an additional reduction of more than 30%.

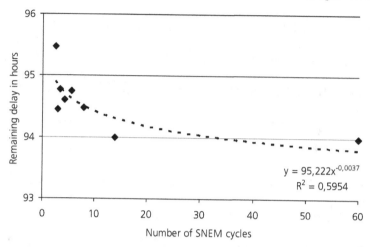

Fig. 7-23. Influence of SNEM cycles on later disruptive events

Propagation of the disruptive event over multiple supply network levels is inevitable: The delay of 100 hours in the experiments cannot be reduced completely, due to the conservative reaction function. However, the influence of earlier information on following supply network levels is illustrated by the results in fig. 7-24. On each following supply network level the reductions are greater for every number of SNEM cycles. This is due to the advance information available through inter-organizational exchange of event management information. For increasing SNEM cycles the difference between reductions on each level diminishes and converges towards the maximum reduction possible for a disruptive event *DE* (in this case 12 hours for the very early type of *DE*).

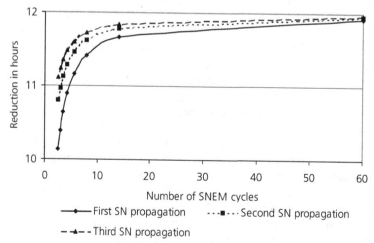

Fig. 7-24. Reductions on multiple supply network levels

### 7.3.2.2    Variation of Occurrence Date

In fig. 7-23 the erratic fluctuation of achieved reductions indicates that the time of occurrence of disruptive events and the number of SNEM cycles result in irregularities regarding achievable reactions $R_u$. Experiments where disruptive events are inserted into the fulfillment processes at different times are depicted in fig. 7-25. A high number of update rounds (every 8.5 hours) realizes a good approximation of the reaction function implemented in the simulator for any disruptive event during fulfillment. In contrast, the less often monitoring updates are realized (= less SNEM cycles) the lower is the achieved reduction (which has already been shown in section 7.3.2.1) and the more step-wise is the truly realized reaction function. For instance, no difference in reduction of the delay is identified for disruptive events that occurred between the third and fifth day when monitored with a 48 hours update-configuration.

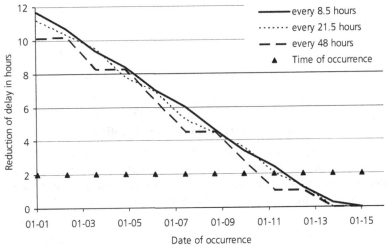

Fig. 7-25. Variation of occurrence date

It turns out that regardless of what form a reaction function might have in theory (see section 7.3.1), in reality a step-wise reaction function will always be realized. Only an approximation of the implemented reaction function is possible. This approximation improves significantly with more SNEM cycles. An example of a realistic reaction function is provided in the showcase evaluation in section 7.4.

## 7.3.3    Cost-Benefit Analysis

In fig. 7-26 the experimental results of fig. 7-22 are rated with costs: Every additional hour of delay is valued with 5 monetary units (MU), and every additional SNEM cycle costs 0.1 MU. The ratio of both cost types corresponds to a realistic minimum of 50:1 defined in section 7.2.3.1. Assuming complete monitoring of all orders and an average hit-rate of 5%, the monitoring efficiency parameter $w$ in this scenario is 20. Cumulated costs indicate a cost optimum for this disruptive event at a little more than 453 MU and 3 to 4 SNEM cycles (see fig. 7-26).

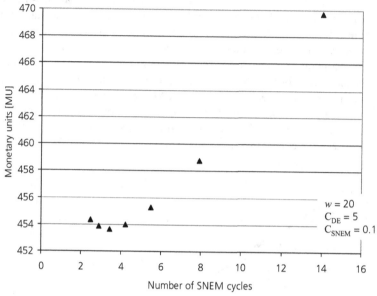

Fig. 7-26. Costs without critical profiles

Assuming that critical profiles $CCP_j$ are used in the scenario, a reduction of the monitoring efficiency parameter $w$ to about 6 is realistic (as is shown in section 7.2.5). The approximated trend in fig. 7-27 indicates that the result is an additional reduction of the cost optimum to about 447 MU and an increase of SNEM cycles to around 8.

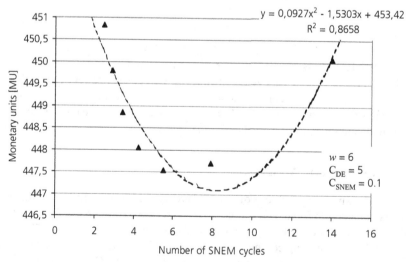

Fig. 7-27. Costs with critical profiles

This result corresponds to the analytical findings of section 7.2, although reductions are much smaller here. There are two reasons for smaller benefits: First, the reaction function is very conservative and permits only small reductions of delays (see section 7.3.1). Thus, cost reductions associated directly to delays are relatively smaller. Second, only the operational effect on fulfillment times is measured and valued in this experiment. Hence, additional indirect effects on follow-up costs, for instance based on reduced stock, higher customer satisfaction, and future sales, are not considered.

Nevertheless, these experimental results indicate that the use of critical profiles improves benefits. An additional effect is improved "robustness" of the optimal SNEM cycle configuration. Comparing fig. 7-26 and fig. 7-27, the interval for nearly optimal costs is much broader with critical profiles than for the case where monitoring efforts are wasted. Thus, agent-based event management with critical profiles provides additional flexibility for configuring event management systems, while at the same time it offers additional benefits regarding follow-up costs of disruptive events.

## 7.3.4  Conclusions

The primary objective of experiments with the generic prototype in a laboratory environment is to validate the hypotheses on potential benefits of agent-based event management which are derived from the analytical evaluation model. As far as the results of experiments are concerned, the same patterns are found regarding reductions of negative effects related to disruptive events:

1. The number of SNEM cycles greatly influences the achievable benefits: A lower number of cycles results in reduced benefits and a worse approximation of reaction functions.
2. An optimal number of SNEM cycles is realizable with agent-based event management, and inter-organizational communication provides benefits on all supply network levels.
3. Implementing critical profiles $CCP_j$ improves the optimal cost situation further and provides additional flexibility in configuring an event management system, because the range of "nearly optimal" configurations is broadened significantly.

However, some constraints are identified that serve as additional criteria when deciding on implementation of an agent-based SNEM system:

1. Effects of event management are significantly reduced, if the ability to react on problems is low (reflected by a very conservative reaction function in the experiments). For instance, in an environment where processes offer little buffers of time or stock and where no flexibility for changing fulfillment plans is given, even early information on disruptive events might not help in reducing negative effects. In these cases a redesign of fulfillment processes with the objective of adding flexibility to the process design is necessary prior to implementing event management systems. Nonetheless, at a supply network level benefits for customers' levels are significant, even if no benefits are achieved within the supplier's enterprise, as long as reaction abilities are available at customers.

2. The quality of approximation of any realistic reaction function and its associated costs depends on the number of SNEM cycles: This poses a specific problem for situations where effects increase non-linear and above average with reduced reaction time: Any delay in identification of disruptive events results in a large increase of associated costs. Thus, for configuration of an event management system the realistic reaction and cost functions need to be assessed. On this basis SNEM cycle configurations need to be defined. For instance, SNEM cycles might be repeated more often at the beginning of fulfillment than close to the end, due to the larger benefits which are thus achieved for non-linear above average reaction and/or cost functions.

## 7.4   Showcase Evaluation

The prototype for the industry showcase presented in section 6.3 is evaluated with respect to its ability for reducing search times and providing advanced services to users at the LSP. The second major aspect is identification of realistic reaction functions based on input data of the LSP to validate the assumptions employed in the experimental evaluation of section 7.3. Finally, a forecast on realistic benefits to be achieved by an agent-based SNEM solution for the LSP is realized.

### 7.4.1   Prototype Assessment

#### 7.4.1.1     Search Times

In section 7.2.2 it is concluded that an agent-based SNEM concept is able to automate SNEM cycles. The showcase prototype PAMAS illustrates this ability. The prototype provides significant improvements compared to the current situation of the LSP where manual monitoring processes are implemented. This manual process and associated process times as determined from interviews with experts of the LSP are depicted in fig. 7-28. A conservative estimation of process times results in a cumulated 125 seconds for finding status information on a certain order and assessing this information. Associated costs are approximately 1.15 Euro per manual SNEM cycle since average costs of personnel are 34 Euro per hour.

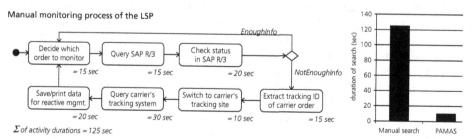

Fig. 7-28. Reduced search times

The showcase prototype provides the same information automatically in a matter of seconds and without manual intervention. Although no direct cost measurements are available for the prototype it is assumed that every update cycle costs at most a few cents (see section 7.2.2.2, 5 US-Cent maximum, thus about 4 Euro-Cent): These costs are due to resource consumption (e.g. computational resources, communication infrastructure) and costs attributed to accessing the SAP data base. However, the latter costs are also incurred in the manual process and not considered in the 1.15 Euro per update round. Hence, the difference between manual and automatic data gathering is at least one Euro per SNEM cycle. This underlines the assumption in section 7.2.3.1 that benchmark costs for a conventional *Tracking-and-Tracing (T&T)* system are underestimated in the theoretical model, because manual monitoring causes additional costs not considered in the cost-benefit-model. Realistic benchmark costs are thus higher, and benefits of automated event management are even greater.

### 7.4.1.2 Scalability

Scalability of an IT-system is important, if a system is to be implemented in a real-world environment. Based on the showcase prototype a measurement of resource consumption in different scenarios is conducted (*Bodendorf et al. 2005*). The main restriction for the showcase prototype is memory consumption: It increases with every additional monitored order, because a new dedicated surveillance agent is initialized for every order. Results for different numbers of surveillance agents are depicted in fig. 7-29. A linear growth of memory consumption is statistically approximated.

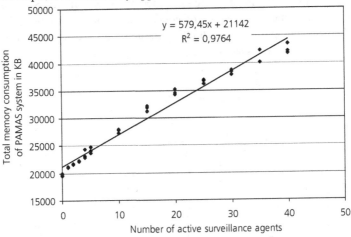

Fig. 7-29. Scalability of prototype

A forecast for the LSP on realistic resource consumption of an agent-based SNEM system adds up to about 104 MB. The forecast is based on the statistical model and the following assumptions: The average cycle time of every international order of the LSP varies between 5 to 15 days. It is assumed that critical orders encounter delays which result in an average of around 20 days cycle time for monitored orders. Based on the data mining results provided in section 7.2.5.1, at least 220 orders would be monitored in a three month period by the LSP. Assuming that additional critical profiles are defined to enhance the quality of monitoring efforts, an additional amount of 200% of the already monitored orders is added as assumed in section 7.2.5.1. This results in a monitoring rate relative to all orders of the LSP of only 16%. Thus, about 220 international transportation orders of the LSP have to be monitored on average per month. Based on the average 20 day cycle time, which complies to the average life-time of a surveillance agent, around 147 surveillance agents are permanently active. The linear statistical model thus predicts about 104 MB memory consumption. Considering that the prototype is not optimized for resource consumption, the scalability of an agent-based SNEM system is not a critical aspect for the LSP and implementation on a regular desktop computing system is viable.

## 7.4.2   Analysis of Follow-up Costs

### 7.4.2.1   Reaction and Cost Function

In section 7.3.4 it is concluded that an assessment of individual reaction and cost functions is necessary prior to implementation of an event management system. For the LSP a process analysis has been conducted which exemplifies a method to determine such functions. The reaction considered in the analysis is conducted in case of severe disruptive events that occur within orders of important European customers: A second delivery has to be triggered since the initial delivery is definitely not arriving at the planned delivery date. Typical reasons for this reaction are - as stated by experts of the LSP - damages during transportation and incorrect routing of goods (e.g. to another country). The reaction process of the LSP and approximated durations of activities are depicted in fig. 7-30.

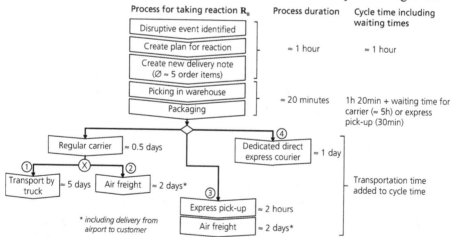

Fig. 7-30. Process analysis: event management reaction of LSP

In every case where a new (second) delivery is initiated due to a disruptive event, internal activities within the administration of the LSP take about one hour and consist of devising a plan for reaction and creating a new delivery note. The internal warehouse processes are well designed with a very short reaction time: About 20 minutes after the delivery note is received in the warehouse, picking and packaging is finished, if goods are available on stock. Packaged goods then wait for pick-up by a carrier.

Four variants depending on the remaining time for reaction exist (see fig. 7-30): Regular transportation by truck to a European destination requires about 5.5 days from order dispatch at the LSP to delivery to the customer (1). By using air freight and a regular service to transport goods to the airport, about 2.5 days are needed (2) which can be reduced to about two days and 2 hours, if an express service courier to the airport is used (3). If only about one day remains a dedicated direct courier with a small and fast transportation vehicle can reach most locations of central Europe within about 24 hours (4). These four alternatives are available to the LSP in case a second delivery is required. The required cycle times associated with processes of the alternatives determine how long each alternative is viable for a specific order's fulfillment.

For each alternative associated costs are gathered in interviews with experts of the LSP and depicted in fig. 7-31. For instance, alternative 2 is cheaper than alternative 3, because a regular carrier is used for sending the goods to the airport while in the latter case an airport express is used.

| | Alternative 1 | Alternative 2 | Alternative 3 | Alternative 4 |
|---|---|---|---|---|
| Internal activities of LSP | 1h20min at 34€/h = 45€ | 45€ | 45€ | 45€ |
| Picking up order from LSP | 74€ per 100kg | 60€ | 160€ for airport express | Direct express courier 660€ |
| Transportation | | 170€ per 100kg air freight | 170€ per 100kg air freight | |
| Cumulated costs | 119€ | 275€ | 375€ | 705€ |

Fig. 7-31. Costs for alternative reactions

Based on the process analysis and associated costs a cost function is devised in fig. 7-32. It illustrates use of the cheapest alternative available for each point in time between the begin of fulfillment of an order and the planned delivery date. In the example, a planned cycle time for orders of 10 days is assumed which is realistic for deliveries to central European countries outside the European Union. For instance, between day zero and four and a half days of fulfillment a second regular transport by truck is viable with lowest costs of 119 Euro. Otherwise, air freight is necessary with a step-wise increase to 275 and 375 Euro. The direct courier results in costs of 705 Euro and if the delivery arrives after the planned delivery date an additional 300 Euro is added as a fine. However, the second delivery still has to arrive as soon as possible after this date which requires a direct express courier[24]. Thus, the final cost level in this example is 1,005 Euro.

---

[24.]At the time of the interviews fines for late delivery were not yet implemented but under discussion. The 300 Euro fine is a realistic assumption used in the cost function.

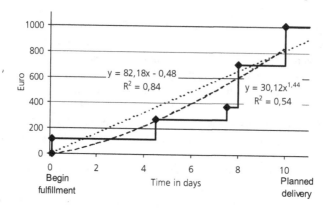

Fig. 7-32. Cost function for European destinations

The step-wise cost function illustrates realistic alternatives for the LSP in relation to the remaining reaction time during an order's fulfillment. Two statistical trends based on a linear and a non-linear trend are depicted to provide comparison to the analytical and experimental results of previous sections. In the example the linear function provides better statistical results and underlines the viability of using linear cost models for assessing the benefits of event management in supply networks. Thus, results obtained from the analytical model and the experimental results are plausible compared to this realistic cost function. The cost function in fig. 7-32 indicates a cost reduction potential for follow-up costs compared to the worst case (after day 10) of more than 80%. Hence, in reality a good ability to realize reactions is identified which is a prerequisite for achieving significant benefits through agent-based SNEM as stated in section 7.3.4.

### 7.4.2.2    Generalized Cost Assessment

The cost function identified in section 7.4.2.1 is only viable for a very specific type of reaction: a second delivery. Other reaction types are appropriate depending on the status and type of an order and the identified disruptive event. Although it is not realistic to determine one generalized cost function which covers all reaction types, it is proposed that, for instance, functions for similar reaction types but different destinations are aggregated. An example in fig. 7-33 illustrates the mechanism: A second cost function (schematic only) is depicted. The fulfillment duration is standardized between zero and one which allows to integrate cost functions for different cycle times. Two statistical trends are depicted which integrate both cost functions. Although this is a schematic example, it illustrates the ability to derive a generalized cost function, if multiple cost functions for specific reaction types are available. While truly realized costs vary greatly for certain points in time of the standardized time scale, an approximation in a continuous cost function provides an average estimation on follow-up costs.

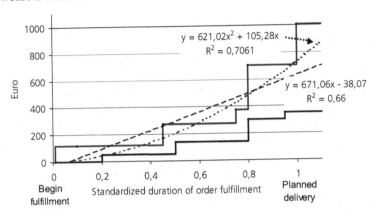

Fig. 7-33. Scenario for generalized cost function

Although the showcase does not provide enough data to approximate such a generalized cost function for the LSP, the mechanism illustrates the ability to assess benefits of event management in realistic environments. Besides assessing direct operational costs associated with typical reactions, further consideration of indirect costs of disruptive events is an option to be considered. Although effects on elements such as stock levels or even future revenue cannot be identified for single orders, a generalized assessment on the enterprise level might be feasible: For instance, if measurements of stock levels over time are associated with average delays of suborders, a cost function for capital costs of stock is identifiable. However, such input data is not available from the showcase and thus, the generalization mechanism only provides an outlook for implementation of SNEM systems.

In addition to identification of generalized cost functions, an assessment of statistical distributions of disruptive events in fulfillment processes hints to configuration options of a SNEM system. For instance, the LSP encounters most disruptive events during transportation processes whereas internal warehouse processes have a much higher process quality. Consequently, monitoring with agent-based SNEM at the LSP focuses on transportation issues. Furthermore, if results from critical profile discovery (see section 7.2.5.1) are available, an overall assessment of potential benefits for an enterprise is possible:

1. Assuming that the cost function of the LSP identified in section 7.4.2.1 is a generalized cost function for the LSP, the majority of disruptive events are encountered during transportation: This would be between day 1 and day 10. As long as no other information is available, the linear approximation is appropriate and an equal probability of encountering disruptive events is assumed. In consequence, a disruptive event occurs on average at day 5.5 (see also arguments in section 7.2.1). About 451 Euro per severe disruptive event are thus forecasted by the linear statistical approximation.

2. Average costs for a single disruptive event are used to forecast effects of agent-based SNEM for all international orders of the LSP. In fig. 7-12 (section 7.2.5.1) data min-

ing results on real-world data indicate that 483 orders had severe problems in a three month period. Assuming that the cost function from above applies to all of these orders, a maximum cost of 485,415 Euro is forecasted, if every disruptive event is identified after day 10. If all orders of the LSP were continuously monitored, the average costs would be decreased by 55% to 218,079 Euro. Implementing the basic critical profiles identified in section 7.2.5.1, only 5.3% of all orders need to be monitored and 37% of all disruptive events would be monitored. Thus, even this first approach to define critical profiles results in a reduction of follow-up costs of about 97,845 Euro.

This sample calculation illustrates the ability to forecast event management benefits. At the same time it provides additional insight into constraints of agent-based SNEM: The use of critical profiles always includes the risk of missing some important disruptive events while focusing monitoring activities and reducing monitoring costs. This issue is further addressed in section 7.5.

### 7.4.3   Conclusions

Evaluation of the showcase prototype and data obtained from the LSP during development of the showcase yield the following results:

1. Manual monitoring compared to automated event management induces significantly higher costs. This is illustrated by the process analysis in section 7.4.1.1.
2. Scalability of agent-based SNEM does not impose severe restrictions on resource consumption, especially in the case of the LSP.
3. Cost functions and possible cost reductions due to early reactions are quantifiable, if a process analysis is conducted within an enterprise and activity-related costs are provided (see section 7.4.2.1).
4. Generalization of cost functions is possible. It provides insight into the overall potential for reduction of follow-up costs in an enterprise (see section 7.4.2.2). Additional information on statistical distributions of disruptive events and quality of critical profiles further improve these forecasts.

Main constraints identified within the showcase are:

1. Realistic cost functions exhibit step-wise developments, while continuous functions (linear or non-linear) are only useful as approximations, especially in cases where multiple cost functions need to be aggregated.
2. Quality of critical profiles determines the amount of those disruptive events which are not identified. Consequently, the risk of neglecting some disruptive events has to be compared to the increased monitoring efficiency achievable with critical profiles (see also section 7.5)

# 7.5  Summary - Benefits and Constraints

Reconsidering the constraints to an evaluation of the SNEM concept, a large field test is not realizable at this stage of development. However, three different perspectives have been selected to provide an answer to the main question of evaluation: *By how much can follow-up costs*[25] *of disruptive events DE be reduced by a SNEM system?*

1. The first perspective is realized by the analytical evaluation approach. It provides a theoretical cost-benefit-model which predicts substantial reductions of follow-up costs in supply networks for agent-based SNEM. Even if compared to state-of-the-art SCEM systems, which resemble the highest benchmark for the agent-based SNEM concept, additional reductions add up to more than 50% in supply networks, depending on cost parameters. Reductions are due to proactive inter-organizational communication between SNEM agent societies and to the use of critical profiles $CCP_j$. Compared to situations which dominate today's business environments, where event management is not implemented or realized manually, follow-up costs of $DE$ are reduced by more than 80%. Essentially, only structural costs of disruptive events remain after implementation of agent-based SNEM. These costs cannot be reduced with operational event management activities but only with strategic process redesigns.

2. The theoretically determined relationship between the number of SNEM cycles and the benefits and costs of event management is similarly found in results of experiments with the generic prototype in a supply network testbed. An optimal number of SNEM cycles is realized through automation of SNEM cycles by the agent societies and effects of disruptive events are reduced within practical limits of the fulfillment processes. In a final cost-assessment it is shown that critical profiles $CCP_j$ allow robust configuration of SNEM systems, because the range of "nearly" optimal costs is widened and a larger set of different SNEM cycle configurations achieves these low costs. Thus, in dynamic environments agent-based SNEM provides economic robustness in the face of changing environmental conditions (e.g. new order types with different cycle times), because "optimal" SNEM cycle configurations apply to a wider range of conditions.

3. The third perspective is provided by the showcase prototype and related data of a logistics service provider (LSP). Evaluation results indicate that substantial reductions of follow-up costs are realistic. A cost function predicts a potential to reduce directly associated follow-up costs of severe disruptive events by as much as 80%, if disruptive events occur early during fulfillment and are identified very soon. A mechanism is proposed to generalize cost functions and in a schematic example an overall potential benefit of nearly 100,000 Euro for a three month period is achieved, if critical profiles are used by the LSP. However, this forecast relies on a number of restrictive assumptions and overestimates realistic benefits, since very severe disruptive

---

[25.]Follow-up costs of disruptive events are considered in a broad sense. They incorporate direct costs such as costs for expediting orders and indirectly related costs such as loss of sales due to dissatisfied customers (see section 2.3.1.2)

events are assumed. Hence, a worst-case scenario for negative effects and a best-case scenario for event management is used which results in an upper-limit of potential benefits. Nonetheless, significant benefits are realistic and assumptions made by the theoretical cost-benefit-model regarding cost functions are substantiated by the showcase results.

Concluding, benefits which are quantified within the analytical evaluation approach for multi-level supply networks are supported by experimental results (regarding the importance of SNEM cycles) and showcase evaluation (regarding cost functions). Although specific benefits depend on the individual (cost) parameters of a supply network, the theoretical cost-benefit-model indicates superior performance of agent-based SNEM compared to all other existing event management approaches.

Besides quantifying the potential monetary benefits of the agent-based SNEM concept, several constraints are identified within the evaluation perspectives that are important for further development and application of SNEM systems:

1. Experiments with very conservative reaction functions indicate that agent-based SNEM is not necessarily the best way to reduce effects of disruptive events. If the ability to react during operational fulfillment is very limited, implementation of a SNEM solution cannot yield significant benefits. Consequently, a redesign of processes has priority. It has the objective to provide additional flexibility to fulfillment processes. Only then is the realization of an agent-based SNEM system beneficial.

2. The number of SNEM cycles determines the quality of approximation of the underlying reaction respectively cost function of a fulfillment process (see section 7.3.2.2). For instance, if the number of economically optimal SNEM cycles is relatively low, an additional improvement of follow-up costs is possible in some situations: It is assumed that a non-linear cost function which either grows fast or exhibits step-wise development is known to an enterprise. Distributing SNEM cycles evenly over the fulfillment process of an order as proposed in section 7.2.1 is not rational in this case. SNEM cycles should better be scheduled either early during order fulfillment for non-linear fast growing functions or before significant step-ups of costs in a step-wise cost function. Thus, before an agent-based SNEM system is implemented, an evaluation of realistic reaction functions and associated costs is required to determine a high-quality SNEM cycle configuration.

3. Implementation of critical profiles $CCP_j$ yields additional cost benefits as indicated by the theoretical cost-benefit-model and additional robustness for SNEM cycle configuration, but it also poses one threat that cannot be neglected: Disruptive events might affect orders which are not proactively monitored based on $CCP_j$ by any supply network partner. Consequently, benefits of agent-based SNEM due to $CCP_j$ identified in the cost-benefit-model are overestimated to the degree that disruptive events are not discovered. A potential solution for a realistic SNEM system is to define $CCP_j$ for potentially critical orders and monitor these with the optimal number of SNEM cycles and to monitor other orders at least once or a few times, depending on their duration. Aspects such as order priority represent additional information to decide on the monitoring intensity of "non-$CCP_j$"orders. As a result a mixed-approach should yield many of the benefits indicated by the analytical model without

adding high risk of severe undiscovered disruptive events.

Concluding, strong evidence for benefits is found that supports implementation of agent-based SNEM systems, if the constraints identified above are considered during development. For supply networks where disruptive events result in significant follow-up costs and reaction ability is given, an assessment of reaction and cost functions is the first step of development before decisions on using critical profiles $CCP_j$ become relevant. Besides this, the theoretical cost-benefit-model provides mechanisms to forecast potential benefits with and without critical profiles. Thus, an instrument is provided to calculate forecasts required for return-on-investment calculations which precede implementation of an agent-based SNEM system.

# Chapter 8

# Conclusions and Outlook

In the remaining sections a final summary of the concept and the prospects of agent-based SNEM in complex supply networks precedes an assessment of related future research opportunities: A focus is on integration of advanced technologies such as *smart labels* or *object chips* which are based on *RFID* technologies. However, further opportunities are identified e.g. in transferring event management techniques to other domains than the supply network domain.

## 8.1  Supply Network Event Management

The notion of event management in supply networks is related to an information deficit in multi-enterprise supply networks regarding timely information on disruptive events and their negative consequences on operational fulfillment processes. This deficit is termed the *Supply Network Event Management (SNEM) Problem* (see section 2.1.1). It is characterized by an "implicit" demand $D_q$ for event-related information which arises at autonomous supply network partners: e.g. customers. This demand cannot be made explicit by these actors, because they do not know when and where disruptive events will occur since events remain uncertain (see section 2.1.3). Information logistics has to satisfy this demand with proactive messages $M_s$ which contain information on disruptive events. This information is needed to realize reactions $R_u$ in order to minimize the negative effects of disruptive events in supply networks.

For an event management system that solves the SNEM problem a set of requirements is defined  (see section 2.2). Above all, proactive behavior regarding data gathering in supply networks and generation of alerts for newly identified disruptive events is required for a SNEM solution. The event-related information needed to satisfy the implicit demand $D_q$ has to provide data that represents the supply network domain. This data is used to aggregate respectively refine measurements of an order's status in order to assess negative consequences of disruptive events. Besides this, disruptive events themselves have to be characterized in detail to promote suitable reactions $R_u$. Several functional requirements are identified to automate the process of gathering, analyzing and distributing event-related information. Important aspects are proactive monitoring of orders and related suborders, thus considering interdependencies in supply networks while adhering to the autonomy of every supply network partner. Furthermore, automated data analysis and flexible distribution of event-related information are required to complete this process.

A large potential for cost-reduction through SNEM is identified in an assessment of potential benefits which is based on a theoretical cost model and substantiated by reported benefits of existing event management solutions (see section 2.3). However, existing approaches cannot satisfy the requirements of a SNEM solution and do not realize the potential benefits (see section 2.4). Hence, a concept for a SNEM solution is developed based on the SNEM requirements.

An integrated data model for event management is developed in section 3.1 and a formal ontology for semantic interoperability is presented in section 3.2. Main data types represent status and control data which characterize an order and the effects any disruptive event has on an order's status. Typical examples are achieved and planned fulfillment dates of processes or quality measurements of products. Specific data types to characterize disruptive events and to provide decision-supporting information are additionally defined. Since a SNEM solution is to be automated, SNEM data is made available in a machine-readable format. To facilitate use of reasoning mechanisms a SNEM ontology is designed. It is formalized and implemented in a standard format accessible to reasoning software. Typical data sources relevant for event management are presented in section 3.3. Besides data bases and Internet sources, new identification technologies based on *Radio Frequency Identification (RFID)* are analyzed. The latter provide the ability to align virtual representations of an order's status with the physical reality of an order.

In chapter 4 several mechanisms are proposed to realize the requirements for the process of gathering, analyzing and distributing event information proactively. These mechanisms are integrated in a process termed the *SNEM process* which is applicable to every enterprise in a supply network. It provides a generic pattern to facilitate inter-organizational proactive event management. Several trigger events are defined that initiate monitoring of orders. An important feature in this decision process is provided through critical profiles which are used to focus monitoring activities on potentially critical orders and which enhance the cost-benefit-relation of event management. Proactive data gathering from internal data sources and from suborder recipients is one of the mechanisms to overcome the "implicity" of the demand $D_q$ in the inter-organizational setting of a supply network. Fuzzy Logic is used to facilitate heuristic human-like assessments of the various data types gathered by a SNEM system. Based on these results Fuzzy Logic is also used to decide on necessary alerts which represent the second mechanism to overcome the "implicity" of the demand $D_q$.

Constraints of supply network partners such as their autonomy of behavior and heterogeneity of specific requirements (e.g. additional data types) are considered in the decision on an IT technology for SNEM solutions (chapter 5): Software agent technology supports autonomous behavior of multiple partners in cooperative networks and advanced communication technologies required to realize the inter-organizational cooperation designed in the SNEM process. An agent society is proposed for every enterprise. Each society consists of four agent types: discourse, coordination, surveillance and wrapper agents. Discourse agents provide the external interface to other supply network partners while coordination agents decide which orders are to be monitored and whether alerts are to be generated. Surveillance agents are dedicated to a single order of an enterprise. They gather SNEM data from internal sources via wrapper agents and from suborder recipients which are related to their monitored order. In addition, they analyze and aggregate SNEM data and cyclically update their knowledge on their order. Wrapper agents provide access to proprietary data sources of an enterprise. Two prototype implementations of the agent-based SNEM concept are presented in chapter 6 as a proof-of-concept: a generic prototype that is used in a laboratory environment for experiments and an industrial showcase that illustrates the ability to realize agent-based SNEM in realistic environments.

The extent to which the agent-based SNEM concept and its implementations are able to realize the potential benefits identified in section 2.3 is evaluated in chapter 7. Three different perspectives are employed to answer the question by how much follow-up costs of disruptive events can be reduced with agent-based SNEM. A theoretical cost-benefit-model is introduced which provides benchmarks for existing event management solutions and hypotheses on optimality conditions for configuration of SNEM systems. Essentially, the model shows that from a conceptual point-of-view agent-based SNEM is superior to existing systems and provides additional benefits not achieved by these systems. At a supply network perspective agent-based SNEM provides substantial reductions of follow-up costs. These are further reduced, if critical profiles are employed for event management. Experimental results and empirical data obtained from a showcase with a logistics service provider substantiate both, the assumptions of the cost-benefit-model and the hypotheses on optimality conditions derived from the model. In addition, some critical constraints are identified (e.g. need for reaction ability in processes) that provide input to an agenda for realization of agent-based SNEM in large-scale pilots.

Summarizing, a concept is developed and evaluated to overcome the "implicity" of the demand for event-related information and to realize benefits not yet achieved by existing event management solutions. However, further potential for development remains regarding the integration of (future) identification technologies (see section 8.2) and open issues for further research are suggested (see section 8.2).

# 8.2 Further Research Opportunities

Three areas for future research are identified and exemplified in the following sections. Besides migrating parts of agents' responsibilities to integrated chips which are attached to physical goods (see section 8.2.1), the use of event management techniques in other domains will provide yet unrealized benefits e.g. in project management (see section 8.2.2). Finally, in order to increase acceptance and dissemination of agent technology in industrial applications, questions of adjustable agent autonomy become increasingly important (see section 8.2.3).

## 8.2.1   Object Chips for Supply Network Event Management

Identification technologies based on *Radio Frequency Identification (RFID)* provide innovative capabilities of transferring information and computational power to physical objects in fulfillment processes. While simple RFID tags only provide an identification number, current state-of-the-art chips store relatively large amounts of data and are rewritable. On a laboratory scale *object chips* are already available that provide additional capabilities: An object chip consists of one or more sensors and effectors (i.e. active transmitters), data management and storage capacities, computing logic and internal energy supply. These three types of electronic tags provide an overview of the spectrum of identification technologies while other technological variants such as sensor chips with reduced computing logic exist. Integration of these types into agent-based SNEM solutions results in three scenarios (see fig. 8-1) which depend on the degree of sophistication of identification technology.

Scenario 1 in fig. 8-1 employs simple RFID tags which only store an identification number. Information on the physical good and its status is stored in a data base which is accessed and updated by a RFID reader management system. This might either be an existing ERP-system or an additional data base as indicated in fig. 8-1. Consequently, access to the reader management system provides an additional data source for timely and verified information on an order's status through monitoring of the order's associated goods during fulfillment processes. Basic agent roles are not changed in this scenario and agent interactions are conducted as defined in the agent-based SNEM concept of chapter 5.

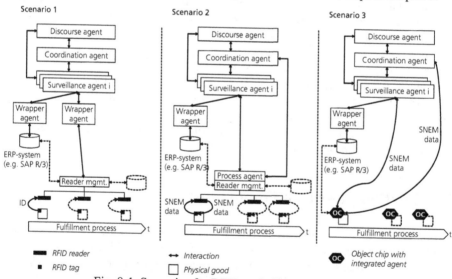

Fig. 8-1. Scenarios for RFID and object chip usage

A new type of agent is introduced in scenario 2 where rewritable RFID tags with extra storage capacity are used. Hence, SNEM data types such as planned fulfillment dates are permanently stored in the tag and updates of estimated fulfillment dates are written to the tag as they become available. This information, which is locally available to actors, is used by a *process agent* that is dedicated to monitoring specific activities or processes. It has access to the reader management system and provides basic analytical capabilities to identify deviations from fulfillment plans of objects that pass a reader. Since at this point during fulfillment data is extracted from the tag anyway, additional costs of analyzing this data are assumed to be very small. Thus, a process agent provides the ability to monitor every passing good as well as its associated order. If it identifies new disruptive events or critical situations, it passes this information on to the coordination agent of its enterprise or to an already existing surveillance agent, if one is known. Besides this, existing surveillance agents send requests for information to a process agent that will return a status response (for instance that a good has not yet achieved a milestone in the process). However, it has to be assumed that in supply networks only parts of all fulfillment processes can be monitored this way while other activities cannot, due to technical or economical restrictions. Thus, existing roles of the agent-based SNEM concept are only enlarged but not replaced.

Integration of agent technology into chips that are tagged to physical objects represents the most advanced situation (scenario 3). The activities conducted by the process agent in scenario 2 are integrated into the object chip which permits permanent assessment of a good's situation and therefore the associated order's situation. Active transmission capabilities permit the object chip to communicate newly identified disruptive events either to a coordination agent or to a surveillance agent. In this scenario a surveillance agent is primarily responsible to gather information on related suborders while internal information is provided whenever possible by the object chip agents in a proactive manner. Thus, the role of the surveillance agent changes significantly. For instance, analytical results derived from suborder-related SNEM data are communicated from a surveillance agent to the respective object chip agent, if the information is relevant for further fulfillment of the associated order. A typical situation might be that a surveillance agent identifies an incomplete delivery of supplied material which will result in a delay of internal processes in the near future. This information is relevant to the object chip agent of the order which is affected by this future delay, because goods tagged with object chips are enabled to coordinate their fulfillment autonomously: Reactions $R_u$ are triggered on the local level by the object chip agent. For instance a negotiation for available resources within a fulfillment process is employed to speed up fulfillment as soon as material will be available. A variety of research results on resource allocation through multi-agent negotiations are available (see section 5.1.3.1) which can be employed in this scenario. Further illustration of a similar scenario is provided in a concept for an integrated information infrastructure in fulfillment processes of the machine and plant construction industry presented in *Müller et al. 2005*. There, it is also shown that object chips are not necessarily built upon RFID technologies, but may also be realized by using existing embedded systems within machines, if these are combined with additional communication infrastructure (e.g. GSM modules).

Summarizing, identification technologies offer additional mechanisms for conducting event management in supply networks which can be integrated into the agent-based SNEM concept. Whether these technologies offer additional benefits that are not achievable with the current version of the SNEM concept is a research topic that might be guided by the ideas presented in the scenarios above.

## 8.2.2　Event Management in other Domains

The agent-based SNEM concept is designed to reduce an information deficit which is characterized by the "implicit" demand for information $D_q$ (see section 2.1.3). Similar information deficits are found in other domains and the agent-based concept can be transferred to these domains. For instance, in the health-care domain patients in hospitals are affected by different disruptive events during their treatment. An emergency caused by a traffic accident will lead to a change in the schedule of an operating room and personnel needed for surgery. This may lead to an additional night stay of a patient, if surgery is conducted later than planned and other treatments have to be postponed. On an abstract level the patient is comparable to a consumer who issues an initial order in a supply network. To fulfill this order several suborders (in the hospital-case different treatments) have to be fulfilled. A disruptive event (e.g illness of a doctor) propagates and affects the patients' treatments negatively. If it is known early enough (= the information logistics task), the effects can be contained within acceptable levels, because managerial reactions are possible (e.g. call in another doctor). A transfer of the formal model of the SNEM problem is possible with only slight changes in definitions. Other potential domains are:

- Project management: Many actors cooperate to conduct a joint project by fulfilling different subtasks. Types of projects span from large industrial projects for building plants to software development or consultancy projects.
- Administrative processes: An example is a budget planning process in a large industrial enterprise (*Vögele 2005*). These processes are conducted according to a defined process model by multiple actors in many different countries. The problem is to coordinate these activities that are often dependent upon each other but are not well synchronized. In many cases, results required as a precondition arrive too late and information on available results is not communicated. Thus an information deficit similar to the "implicit" demand $D_q$ exists that is overcome with an agent-based information logistics solution.

## 8.2.3　Integration and Acceptance Issues

Integration of agent-based SNEM with other multi agent systems (MAS) to form flexible large-scale coordination systems is addressed in the *Agent.Enterprise* approach (*Frey et al. 2003a, Frey et al. 2003b*). In this project several different MAS are connected to develop an agent-based integrated approach for production planning and control in supply networks. Interoperability between the agent societies, which all have different objectives, is achieved with a common ontology for all MAS. One research task is the development of mechanisms to match different ontologies which are used by different MAS in order to facilitate interoperability (*AAAA 2005*).

To reduce reservations of users concerning autonomous behavior of software agents and to increase acceptance of agent technology in the industrial context, an agent has to make its decisions explicit to a user (*AAAA 2005*). Furthermore, a user has to be able to influence the behavior of an agent in certain situations. Concepts to adjust the agent's autonomy (e.g. *Chalupsky et al. 2001*) are required which allow to restrict agent behavior depending on environmental conditions. Critical situations are actively perceived by a software agent and constraints on its competencies are self-inflicted by the agent. In the context of the agent-based SNEM concept adjustable autonomy is especially relevant in situations where reactions are triggered that have severe effects on fulfillment processes (e.g. large-scale replanning). Although these reaction mechanisms are not part of a SNEM solution, knowledge on especially critical constellations might be available from the SNEM solution. In such cases replanning might be triggered automatically but a human actor retains the authority to finally decide on implementation of the new schedule.

# Appendices

## *Appendix A - SNEM Data Model*

| | | Production | Warehousing | Transportation |
|---|---|---|---|---|
| **Basic data** | | Order relations<br>• Superorder-ID<br>• Customer-ID<br>• Suborder-ID<br>• Recipient-ID<br>• Material-/Product-ID<br>• OrderFinished (Y/N)<br>• Order type<br><br>• *Customized data types* | Additional basic data<br>*Order*<br>• Order item(s)<br>• Delivery note<br>• Order value<br>*Customer*<br>• Priority<br>• Adress<br><br>• *Customized data types* | *Product*<br>• Product-/service-Type<br>*Physical*<br>• Volume<br>• Weight<br><br>• Destination<br>• Route<br>• Dispatch type<br>• *Customized data types* |
| **Status data** | Time | • Achieved/estimated date of production start<br>• Achieved/estimated date of production end<br>• Achieved/estimated dates of production milestones | • Achieved/estimated date of dispatch<br>• Achieved/estimated dates of warehousing milestones | • Achieved/estimated date of delivery<br>• Achieved/estimated dates of transportation milestones<br>• Location of order at time x |
| | Quality | • Production quantity<br>• Tolerance in product quality<br>• Number (#) or % of defect parts per order | • Picked / packed quantity<br>• Part quantities<br>• # of picking failures<br>• # of defect goods/pallets/... | • Delivered quantity<br>• Missing quantity<br>• # of defect goods/pallets/... |
| | Costs | • Costs of material / parts<br>• Direct labor costs of order<br>• Activity-based costs | • Costs of packaging material<br>• Activity-based costs | • Transportation costs<br>• Costs of customs procedures<br>• Activity-based costs |
| **Control data** | Time | • Planned date of production start<br>• Planned/promised date of production end<br>• Planned dates of production milestones | • Planned date of dispatch<br>• Planned dates of warehousing milestones | • Planned/promised date of delivery<br>• Planned dates of transportation milestones<br>• Planned location of order at time x |
| | Quality | • Planned production quantity<br>• Tolerance limits | • Ordered quantity | • Ordered quantity |
| | Costs | • Planned costs of material / parts<br>• Planned direct labor costs<br>• Planned activity-based costs | • Planned costs of packaging material<br>• Planned activity-based costs | • Planned transportation costs<br>• Planned customs cost<br>• Planned activity-based costs |
| **Decision data** | | • Disruptive event description<br>• Disruptive event severity | • Date of occurrence<br>• Disruptive event identifier | |
| **Examples of common disruptive events** | | • Machine failure<br>• Material/parts/products defect<br>• Material/parts not available<br>• Capacity shortage<br>• Change of production plan | • Machine failure<br>• Goods damaged<br>• Out-of-stock<br>• Picking failure<br>• Packaging failure<br>• Dispatch deadline missed | Means of transportation<br>• Traffic jam<br>• Truck/Train/Ship/Plane defect<br>• Route blocked<br>• Change of transportation plan<br>Delivery<br>• Address incomplete/wrong<br>• Goods destroyed<br>• Goods lost / not found<br>• Goods damaged<br>• Customs delayed |

## Appendix B - Refined Calculation of Profile Quality Indicator "util"

The *degree of utilization* is presented in section 4.2.3.2. A refined calculation that avoids underestimation of *util*, if a $CCP_j$ fluctuates heavily over time and overestimation of *util* for continuously low usage of a $CCP_j$ compared to more active $CCP_j$ is presented below.

| Formula | Parameters | | Example |
|---|---|---|---|
| $$util = \dfrac{\displaystyle\sum_{i=1}^{12} \dfrac{13-i}{12} \cdot n_i}{\displaystyle\sum_{i=1}^{12} \dfrac{13-i}{12} \cdot u}$$ $$avU = \dfrac{n}{N}$$ $$glU = \dfrac{1}{p}$$ | $i$ | Index of month, $i=1$ latest month, $i=12$ one year ago | $n_1=2; n_2=3; n_3=3; n_4=2;$ $n_5=2; n_6=2; n_7=5; n_8=7;$ $n_9=8; n_{10}=9; n_{11}=8; n_{12}=9$ |
| | $n_i$ | Number of profile usages of a $CCP_j$ in month $i$ | $N=132$  $p=14$ |
| | $u = Max(n_i)$ | Maximum $n_i$ of the last twelve months | $util = \dfrac{\dfrac{12}{12}\cdot 2 + \dfrac{11}{12}\cdot 3 + ...}{\dfrac{12}{12}\cdot 9 + \dfrac{11}{12}\cdot 9 + ...}$ |
| | $N$ | Number of profile usages for all $CCP_j$ | $= 0.405$ |
| | $p$ | Number of active $CCP_j$ in a SNEM system | $avU = \dfrac{62}{429} = 0.145$ $glU = \dfrac{1}{14} = 0.071$ |

Again, the main indicator *util* calculates the average usage of a $CCP_j$ over the past twelve months with emphasis on the last month and continuously decreasing importance of each month before[1]. This average is standardized by relating it to the maximum usage of the last twelve month indicated by $u=Max(n_i)$. In the example of the table above *util* results in a value of 0.405 for a $CCP_j$ with decreasing usage. However, if a $CCP_j$ fluctuates heavily over time, *util* underestimates the $CCP_j$'s utilization while on the other hand continuously low usage results in an overestimation of *util* compared to more active $CCP_j$. For this reason, the indicators *avU* and *glU* are introduced. They are used to correct over- and underestimations of the *degree of utilization (util)*. The value *avU* represents the usage of a specific $CCP_j$ in relation to the overall usage of $CCP_j$. It is compared to *glU* which, in turn, is interpreted as the predicted average usage relation in case that all active

---

[1] The term $\dfrac{13-i}{12}$ assures that the 12th month is included, but weighted lowest with $\dfrac{1}{12}$.

$CCP_j$ are used with the same intensity. If $glU$ is much larger than the $avU$ of a $CCP_j$ and the indicator *util* is very high[2], *util* is reduced, e.g. according to the following rule:

```
IF avU < 0.5*glU AND util > 0.8 THEN util := util - 0.4
```

A similar rule can be applied if a $CCP_j$ is used very often but with varying intensity. This situation results in a low value of *util* and high $avU$ compared to $glU$, e.g.:

```
IF avU > 2*glU AND util < 0.3 THEN util := util + 0.4
```

## *Appendix C - Introduction to Fuzzy Logic*

Fuzzy Logic theory uses the interval between the values *true (1)* and *false (0)* as opposed to a traditional two-valued logic where any proposition is either *true* or *false* (*Bodendorf 2003, pp. 146*)[3]. A fuzzy proposition might be e.g. *partly true* with a value of 0.3. Such a proposition is well suited to reflect human style assessments of situations which are based on logic transformation of *perceptions* (see section 4.3.2). The generic process to define and reason with fuzzy propositions is depicted below. It is subsequently illustrated by a simple example before it is applied to the more complex analytical perspectives of a SNEM solution.

The activity of transforming an exact input value (a *measurement*) into a fuzzy value is referred to as "fuzzification". A fuzzy value is based on fuzzy set theory which enlarges traditional set theory, where any element can either belong completely or not at all to a given set of elements. In the fuzzy set theory a certain element can belong to a *fuzzy set* with a value between *true (1)* and *false (0)* (see above). This value represents a *perception* and it can be interpreted as a probability. As in traditional set theory, one element (= a measurement) can belong to different sets at the same time, but with different values between true and false for each *fuzzy set*. That means different *perceptions* can be associated with one element. In essence, traditional set theory is enlarged to include the notion of a continuous membership to a set (e.g. *partly true*) (e.g. *Grauel 1995, pp. 1*). Applied to the example of the *measurement* "25.6° Celsius", three *perceptions* for the *fuzzy sets cold, warm* and *hot* can be derived for the *linguistic variable Temperature* (see figure below). A *linguistic variable* represents one or more *perceptions* for a certain type of variable (e.g. *Temperature*). It represents values in the form of words or sentences (e.g. *cold*), just like an algebraic variable has numbers as its potential values. Any fuzzy proposition is based on *linguistic variables*. The set of values that a *linguistic variable* can represent is called its *term set*. Each term in the *term set* is a *fuzzy variable* which is represented by a *fuzzy set*.

---

[2.] This case occurrs when a classified critical profile is continuously used with the same low usage rate.

[3.] For a detailed introduction to Fuzzy Logic and the underlying mathematical foundations see e.g. *Zimmermann 1991*.

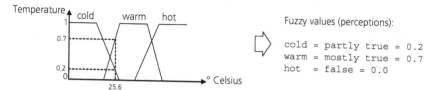

In the figure above three *fuzzy variables* (*cold, warm, hot*) are defined. Each *fuzzy set* is defined by a *membership function* which links the input value (= the *measurement*) which is called "*base variable*" to the *fuzzy variable*. In the example trapezoid *membership functions* are used to tie the *base variable* "°Celsius" to the *fuzzy variables* "cold", "warm", "hot". Other *membership functions* (e.g. triangular or pi-functions) are also possible. The *membership function* realizes the mathematical representation of the *perception* (= *fuzzy variable*) that is associated with a certain *measurement* (= *input value*).

Based on *perceptions* that are defined in the fuzzification activity, reasoning is applied to deduce an interpretation of these *perceptions* (fuzzy inference). This is realized by defining propositions and their consequences as rules. For instance, the consequence of a temperature *perception* might be the adjustment of a temperature control, where *Temp-Control* is also a *linguistic variable* with the *fuzzy sets heat* and *cool*:

```
IF Temperature = cold THEN TempControl = heat
Example:   cold = 0.2 --> heat = 0.2
```

Fuzzy rules can integrate in the *IF*-part a varying number of different *linguistic variables* that are connected with logic operators *AND*, *OR* or *NOT*. Similarly, various consequences can be defined in the *THEN*-part of a rule. Different rules reflect knowledge for interpretation of different types of *perceptions*. These rules represent the heuristic knowledge which a human actor would apply to his *perceptions* (see section 4.3.1.1 and section 4.3.2).

For each fuzzified input value a Fuzzy Logic system checks whether one or more of the fuzzy rules are applicable (*fuzzy inference*). This may result in a variety of matching fuzzy rules, as depicted in the figure below, since one input value may have various possible perceptions as depicted above. However, similar to a human actor, who e.g. deduces an overall assessment of an order's situation, a single output of the *fuzzy inference* is needed as an aggregated interpretation of the input *perceptions*. Mathematically, multiple results which are represented as different *fuzzy sets* are combined to one *fuzzy set,* and methods such as the "center of gravity" are applied to extract a single exact output value. This activity is called "defuzzification" and in the example results in a single control instruction for a temperature regulator (*Regulator = 0.3*, see below).

To sum up, reasoning mechanisms in Fuzzy Logic which are based on definition of rules allow to integrate various data types and to deduce aggregated interpretations of input data which is provided by a SNEM system's data gathering mechanisms. Different strategies of supply network partners, which affect the way in which SNEM data is interpreted (see section 4.3.1.2), are reflected in different rule sets.

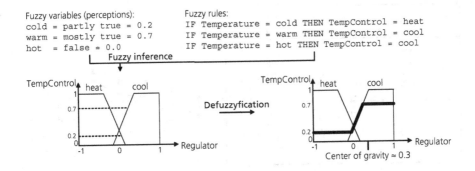

Fuzzy variables (perceptions):
```
cold = partly true = 0.2
warm = mostly true = 0.7
hot  = false = 0.0
```

Fuzzy rules:
```
IF Temperature = cold THEN TempControl = heat
IF Temperature = warm THEN TempControl = cool
IF Temperature = hot THEN TempControl = cool
```

## Appendix D - Results of Fuzzy Logic Tests

Tests have been conducted with the AlertBehavior of the coordination agent.

Varying Fuzzy Logic rule sets

| Endogeneous Disruptive Event Severity | AggregatedOrderStatus | Priority | Overly cautious | Cautious | Optimistic | Very optimistic |
|---|---|---|---|---|---|---|
| 0 | 0.2 | 0.5 | 0.87 | 0.75 | 0.25 | 0.13 |
| 0.2 | 0.2 | 0.5 | 0.87 | 0.75 | 0.43 | 0.25 |
| 0.4 | 0.2 | 0.5 | 0.87 | 0.75 | 0.73 | 0.33 |
| 0.6 | 0.2 | 0.5 | 0.87 | 0.75 | 0.75 | 0.5 |
| 0.8 | 0.2 | 0.5 | 0.87 | 0.87 | 0.87 | 0.75 |
| 1 | 0.2 | 0.5 | 0.87 | 0.87 | 0.87 | 0.87 |
| 0 | 0.5 | 0.5 | 0.87 | 0.5 | 0.24 | 0.13 |
| 0.2 | 0.5 | 0.5 | 0.87 | 0.54 | 0.25 | 0.25 |
| 0.4 | 0.5 | 0.5 | 0.87 | 0.68 | 0.5 | 0.46 |
| 0.6 | 0.5 | 0.5 | 0.87 | 0.75 | 0.75 | 0.54 |
| 0.8 | 0.5 | 0.5 | 0.87 | 0.76 | 0.76 | 0.75 |
| 1 | 0.5 | 0.5 | 0.87 | 0.87 | 0.87 | 0.87 |
| 0 | 0.8 | 0.5 | 0.5 | 0.25 | 0.13 | 0.13 |
| 0.2 | 0.8 | 0.5 | 0.79 | 0.26 | 0.25 | 0.25 |
| 0.4 | 0.8 | 0.5 | 0.79 | 0.33 | 0.25 | 0.25 |
| 0.6 | 0.8 | 0.5 | 0.79 | 0.5 | 0.5 | 0.5 |
| 0.8 | 0.8 | 0.5 | 0.87 | 0.75 | 0.75 | 0.75 |
| 1 | 0.8 | 0.5 | 0.87 | 0.77 | 0.87 | 0.77 |

## Varying priority

| Endogeneous Disruptive Event Severity | Aggregated OrderStatus | Priority | Pessimistic rule set |
|---|---|---|---|
| 0 | 0.5 | 0.5 | 0.5 |
| 0.2 | 0.5 | 0.5 | 0.54 |
| 0.4 | 0.5 | 0.5 | 0.68 |
| 0.6 | 0.5 | 0.5 | 0.75 |
| 0.8 | 0.5 | 0.5 | 0.76 |
| 1 | 0.5 | 0.5 | 0.87 |
| 0 | 0.5 | 0.2 | 0.39 |
| 0.2 | 0.5 | 0.2 | 0.44 |
| 0.4 | 0.5 | 0.2 | 0.55 |
| 0.6 | 0.5 | 0.2 | 0.64 |
| 0.8 | 0.5 | 0.2 | 0.66 |
| 1 | 0.5 | 0.2 | 0.8 |
| 0 | 0.5 | 0.8 | 0.61 |
| 0.2 | 0.5 | 0.8 | 0.63 |
| 0.4 | 0.5 | 0.8 | 0.7 |
| 0.6 | 0.5 | 0.8 | 0.79 |
| 0.8 | 0.5 | 0.8 | 0.79 |
| 1 | 0.5 | 0.8 | 0.9 |

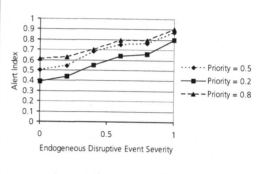

## Varying AOS

| Endogeneous Disruptive Event Severity | Aggregated OrderStatus | Priority | Pessimistic rule set |
|---|---|---|---|
| 0 | 0.2 | 0.5 | 0.75 |
| 0.2 | 0.2 | 0.5 | 0.75 |
| 0.4 | 0.2 | 0.5 | 0.75 |
| 0.6 | 0.2 | 0.5 | 0.75 |
| 0.8 | 0.2 | 0.5 | 0.87 |
| 1 | 0.2 | 0.5 | 0.87 |
| 0 | 0.5 | 0.5 | 0.5 |
| 0.2 | 0.5 | 0.5 | 0.54 |
| 0.4 | 0.5 | 0.5 | 0.68 |
| 0.6 | 0.5 | 0.5 | 0.75 |
| 0.8 | 0.5 | 0.5 | 0.76 |
| 1 | 0.5 | 0.5 | 0.87 |
| 0 | 0.8 | 0.5 | 0.25 |
| 0.2 | 0.8 | 0.5 | 0.26 |
| 0.4 | 0.8 | 0.5 | 0.33 |
| 0.6 | 0.8 | 0.5 | 0.5 |
| 0.8 | 0.8 | 0.5 | 0.75 |
| 1 | 0.8 | 0.5 | 0.77 |

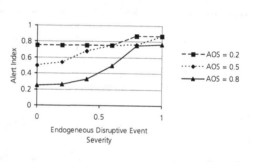

## Extreme input values

| Endogeneous Disruptive Event Severity (EnDS) | Aggregated Order Status (AOS) | Priority | AlertIndex AI (cautious strategy) |
|---|---|---|---|
| 0 | 0 | 0 | 0.75 |
| 0 | 0 | 1 | 1 |
| 0 | 1 | 0 | 0 |
| 1 | 0 | 0 | 0.75 |
| 1 | 1 | 1 | 1 |
| 1 | 1 | 0 | 0.5 |
| 1 | 0 | 1 | 1 |
| 0 | 1 | 1 | 0.25 |

Alert index calculation, if no new disruptive event is identified, but AOS is provided

| Aggregated OrderStatus | Priority | Pessimistic rule set |
|---|---|---|
| 0 | 0.2 | 0.8 |
| 0.2 | 0.2 | 0.67 |
| 0.4 | 0.2 | 0.5 |
| 0.6 | 0.2 | 0.34 |
| 0.8 | 0.2 | 0.21 |
| 1 | 0.2 | 0.12 |
| 0 | 0.5 | 0.87 |
| 0.2 | 0.5 | 0.77 |
| 0.4 | 0.5 | 0.58 |
| 0.6 | 0.5 | 0.42 |
| 0.8 | 0.5 | 0.23 |
| 1 | 0.5 | 0.13 |
| 0 | 0.8 | 0.9 |
| 0.2 | 0.8 | 0.79 |
| 0.4 | 0.8 | 0.66 |
| 0.6 | 0.8 | 0.5 |
| 0.8 | 0.8 | 0.33 |
| 1 | 0.8 | 0.2 |

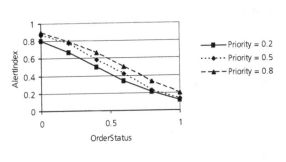

## *Appendix E - Statistical Results - Discovery of Critical Profiles*

Algorithm: J48

=== Run information ===

Scheme:      weka.classifiers.trees.j48.J48 -C 0.25 -M 2
Relation:         QueryResult-weka.filters.unsupervised.attribute.Remove-R3,8-weka.filters.unsupervised.at-tribute.Remove-R2
Instances:   4122
Attributes:  6
        spedition
        auftragsart
        concat('d', weekday(clean.auftragseingangsdatum))
        frankatur
        land
        class
Test mode:    10-fold cross-validation
=== Classifier model (full training set) ===
J48 pruned tree
------------------

land = Deutschland: n (1262.0/88.0)
land = USA: n (54.0/5.0)
land = Schweden
|   concat('d', weekday(clean.auftragseingangsdatum)) = d3: n (26.0/9.0)
|   concat('d', weekday(clean.auftragseingangsdatum)) = d0: n (21.0/1.0)
|   concat('d', weekday(clean.auftragseingangsdatum)) = d1: y (18.0/6.0)
|   concat('d', weekday(clean.auftragseingangsdatum)) = d2: n (31.0/15.0)
|   concat('d', weekday(clean.auftragseingangsdatum)) = d4: n (13.0/1.0)
|   concat('d', weekday(clean.auftragseingangsdatum)) = d5: n (0.0)
|   concat('d', weekday(clean.auftragseingangsdatum)) = d6: n (0.0)
land = Polen
|   concat('d', weekday(clean.auftragseingangsdatum)) = d3: y (4.0/1.0)
|   concat('d', weekday(clean.auftragseingangsdatum)) = d0: n (16.0/4.0)
|   concat('d', weekday(clean.auftragseingangsdatum)) = d1: y (6.0/3.0)
|   concat('d', weekday(clean.auftragseingangsdatum)) = d2: y (4.0/2.0)
|   concat('d', weekday(clean.auftragseingangsdatum)) = d4: y (9.0/3.0)

302

| concat('d', weekday(clean.auftragseingangsdatum)) = d5: n (0.0)
| concat('d', weekday(clean.auftragseingangsdatum)) = d6: n (0.0)
land = Thailand: n (14.0)
land = Gro?britannien: n (385.0/23.0)
land = Luxemburg: n (66.0)
land = Niederlande: n (360.0/43.0)
land = T?rkei
| spedition = B: y (0.0)
| spedition = J: n (5.0/1.0)
| spedition = C: y (33.0/5.0)
| spedition = D: y (0.0)
| spedition = E: y (0.0)
| spedition = F: y (0.0)
| spedition = A: y (0.0)
| spedition = I: y (0.0)
| spedition = K: y (0.0)
| spedition = H: y (0.0)
| spedition = L: y (0.0)
| spedition = M: y (0.0)
| spedition = G: y (0.0)
land = ?sterreich: n (411.0/3.0)
land = Hongkong: n (19.0/2.0)
land = Belgien: n (259.0/4.0)
land = Tschechische Republik: n (70.0/3.0)
land = D?nemark: n (97.0)
land = S?dafrika: y (23.0/7.0)
land = Italien: n (172.0/32.0)
land = Frankreich: n (131.0)
land = Griechenland: y (41.0)
land = Irland: n (45.0/6.0)
land = Finnland: n (75.0)
land = Slowenien: n (37.0)
land = Russland: y (3.0)
land = Norwegen: y (75.0)
land = Portugal: n (61.0)
land = Kanada: n (77.0/35.0)
land = Ungarn: n (49.0/1.0)
land = Brasilien: n (1.0)
land = Lettland: n (1.0)
land = VAE: y (3.0)
land = Slowakei: n (33.0)
land = Ukraine: n (7.0)
land = Bulgarien
| concat('d', weekday(clean.auftragseingangsdatum)) = d3: y (0.0)
| concat('d', weekday(clean.auftragseingangsdatum)) = d0: y (0.0)
| concat('d', weekday(clean.auftragseingangsdatum)) = d1: n (3.0/1.0)
| concat('d', weekday(clean.auftragseingangsdatum)) = d2: y (3.0/1.0)
| concat('d', weekday(clean.auftragseingangsdatum)) = d4: y (0.0)
| concat('d', weekday(clean.auftragseingangsdatum)) = d5: y (0.0)
| concat('d', weekday(clean.auftragseingangsdatum)) = d6: y (0.0)
land = Spanien: n (9.0/2.0)
land = Singapur: n (63.0/3.0)
land = Kroatien: n (13.0/3.0)
land = Australien: y (4.0/2.0)
land = Litauen: n (6.0)
land = Estland: y (2.0)
land = Schweiz: n (2.0)

Number of Leaves  : 69
Size of the tree : 74
Time taken to build model: 0.13 seconds
=== Stratified cross-validation ===
=== Summary ===
Correctly Classified Instances        3775          91.5818 %
Incorrectly Classified Instances       347           8.4182 %
Kappa statistic                     0.4661
Mean absolute error                 0.1288
Root mean squared error              0.2586
Relative absolute error             62.2221 %
Root relative squared error         80.3976 %
Total Number of Instances            4122
=== Detailed Accuracy By Class ===
TP Rate  FP Rate  Precision  Recall  F-Measure  Class
0.366    0.011    0.812      0.366   0.505      y
0.989    0.634    0.922      0.989   0.954      n
=== Confusion Matrix ===
  a    b   <-- classified as
177  306 |   a = y
 41 3598 |   b = n

## Algorithm: JRip

=== Run information ===
Scheme:      weka.classifiers.rules.JRip -F 3 -N 2.0 -O 2 -S 1
Relation:        QueryResult-weka.filters.unsupervised.attribute.Remove-R3,8-weka.filters.unsupervised.at-
tribute.Remove-R2
Instances:   4122
Attributes:  6
          spedition
          auftragsart
          concat('d', weekday(clean.auftragseingangsdatum))
          frankatur
          land
          class
Test mode:    10-fold cross-validation
=== Classifier model (full training set) ===
JRIP rules:
===========

(land = Norwegen) => class=y (75.0/0.0)
(land = Griechenland) => class=y (41.0/0.0)
(land = T?rkei) => class=y (38.0/9.0)
(frankatur = FCA) and (spedition = K) => class=y (23.0/7.0)
 => class=n (3945.0/322.0)
Number of Rules : 5
Time taken to build model: 0.98 seconds
=== Stratified cross-validation ===
=== Summary ===
Correctly Classified Instances        3764          91.3149 %
Incorrectly Classified Instances       358           8.6851 %
Kappa statistic                     0.4139
Mean absolute error                 0.153
Root mean squared error              0.2792
Relative absolute error             73.898  %
Root relative squared error         86.8082 %
Total Number of Instances            4122
=== Detailed Accuracy By Class ===

| TP Rate | FP Rate | Precision | Recall | F-Measure | Class |
|---------|---------|-----------|--------|-----------|-------|
| 0.302 | 0.006 | 0.874 | 0.302 | 0.449 | y |
| 0.994 | 0.698 | 0.915 | 0.994 | 0.953 | n |

=== Confusion Matrix ===

```
  a    b   <-- classified as
146  337 |  a = y
 21 3618 |  b = n
```

## Algorithm: PART

=== Run information ===

Scheme:     weka.classifiers.rules.part.PART -M 2 -C 0.25 -N 3

Relation:     QueryResult-weka.filters.unsupervised.attribute.Remove-R3,8-weka.filters.unsupervised.attribute.Remove-R2

Instances:  4122

Attributes:  6

    spedition
    auftragsart
    concat('d', weekday(clean.auftragseingangsdatum))
    frankatur
    land
    class

Test mode:  10-fold cross-validation

=== Classifier model (full training set) ===

PART decision list

------------------

land = Deutschland: n (1262.0/88.0)
land = ?sterreich: n (411.0/3.0)
land = Gro?britannien: n (385.0/23.0)
land = Belgien: n (259.0/4.0)
land = Frankreich: n (131.0)
land = D?nemark: n (97.0)
land = Finnland: n (75.0)
land = Norwegen: y (75.0)
land = Tschechische Republik: n (70.0/3.0)
land = Luxemburg: n (66.0)
land = Singapur: n (63.0/3.0)
land = Portugal: n (61.0)
land = Ungarn: n (49.0/1.0)
land = USA AND
frankatur = FCA: n (45.0/1.0)
land = Niederlande: n (360.0/43.0)
land = Italien: n (172.0/32.0)
land = Irland: n (45.0/6.0)
land = Griechenland: y (41.0)
land = Slowenien: n (37.0)
land = T?rkei AND
spedition = C: y (33.0/5.0)
land = Slowakei: n (33.0)
land = Schweden AND
concat('d', weekday(clean.auftragseingangsdatum)) = d2: n (31.0/15.0)
land = Schweden AND
concat('d', weekday(clean.auftragseingangsdatum)) = d3: n (26.0/9.0)
land = Schweden AND
concat('d', weekday(clean.auftragseingangsdatum)) = d0: n (21.0/1.0)
land = S?dafrika: y (23.0/7.0)
land = Hongkong: n (19.0/2.0)
land = Schweden AND

concat('d', weekday(clean.auftragseingangsdatum)) = d1: y (18.0/6.0)
land = Kanada: n (77.0/35.0)
land = Polen AND
concat('d', weekday(clean.auftragseingangsdatum)) = d0: n (16.0/4.0)
land = Polen: y (23.0/9.0)
land = Thailand: n (14.0)
land = Schweden: n (13.0/1.0)
land = Kroatien: n (13.0/3.0)
land = USA: n (9.0/4.0)
land = Spanien: n (9.0/2.0)
land = Ukraine: n (7.0)
land = Litauen: n (6.0)
land = T?rkei: n (5.0/1.0)
land = Russland: y (3.0)
land = VAE: y (3.0)
land = Bulgarien AND
concat('d', weekday(clean.auftragseingangsdatum)) = d1: n (3.0/1.0)
: n (13.0/6.0)
Number of Rules : 42
Time taken to build model: 0.45 seconds
=== Stratified cross-validation ===
=== Summary ===
Correctly Classified Instances        3765          91.3392 %
Incorrectly Classified Instances       357           8.6608 %
Kappa statistic                     0.4494
Mean absolute error                 0.1299
Root mean squared error             0.2588
Relative absolute error            62.7389 %
Root relative squared error        80.4697 %
Total Number of Instances           4122
=== Detailed Accuracy By Class ===
TP Rate  FP Rate  Precision  Recall  F-Measure  Class
0.354    0.012    0.792      0.354   0.489      y
0.988    0.646    0.92       0.988   0.953      n
=== Confusion Matrix ===
  a    b   <-- classified as
171  312 |   a = y
 45 3594 |   b = n

## Appendix F - Forecast Model - Monitoring Efficiency

The model to forecast effects of critical profiles on communication load and resource consumption in multi-level supply networks is based on the notion of an *Overlap Ratio OVR* that determines additional requests generated on every supply network level (see schematic in fig. 7-13 (section 7.2.5.1)). The model builds upon the following definitions:

- A *Profile Monitoring Ratio MR$_P$* is defined by the critical profiles $CCP_j$ an enterprise employs. For instance, as a result of the data mining analysis in section 7.2.5.1 about 5.3% of all orders are monitored due to $CCP_j$ with $MR_P = 0.053$.
- A *Real Monitoring Ratio MR$_{real}$* is calculated for every enterprise. $MR_{real}$ integrates all monitored orders of an enterprise: internally monitored orders due to $CCP_j$ and *Additional Status Requests (AddReq)* from customers that force an enterprise to initiate monitoring of an order it does not yet monitor at all (see schematic in fig. 7-13 (section 7.2.5.1)).

- An *Overlap Ratio OVR* indicates how much overlap between external status requests and already monitored internal orders exists. The *OVR* determines how many additional requests *AddReq* are encountered.
- An *Average Monitoring Ratio* $\emptyset MR$ depicts the average between the real monitoring rate $MR_{real}$ of a customer and the profile monitoring ratio $MR_P$ of one of its suppliers. It is used as an indicator to determine the overlap ratio *OVR* between two supply network partners (see below).

Communication load and resource consumption with critical profile usage in a multi-level supply network is calculated for an enterprise on level $n$ and its supplier on level $n$-$1$ as depicted below.

Supply network levels

Level n+1 (A) $Add\,Req_{n+1}$

= Enterprise
= Order issued

Level n

(B) $MR_{real_n} = \dfrac{x_n \cdot MR_{P_n} + Add\,Req_{n+1}}{x_n}$

(C) $\emptyset MR_n = \dfrac{MR_{real_n} + MR_{P_{n-1}}}{2}$

(D) $OVR_n = f(\emptyset MR_n) = (\emptyset MR_n)^q$

(E) $Add\,Req_n = x_n \cdot MR_{real_n} \cdot (1 - OVR_n)$

High overlap
$0 < q < 1$

OVR

ØMR

Low overlap
$q > 1$

Level n-1

(F) $MR_{real_{n-1}} = \dfrac{x_{n-1} \cdot MR_{P_{n-1}} + Add\,Req_n}{x_{n-1}}$

$x_n$ identical for all n,
since suborders 1:N or 1:1

1. Depending on the number and quality of critical profiles defined by the enterprise on level $n$ a certain percentage of orders is monitored proactively. This is defined by the monitoring ratio *MR* due to internal critical profiles (*P*) on level $n$ written as $MR_{P_n}$. The actual number of monitored orders is calculated by multiplying the number of orders fulfilled by an enterprise $x$ on level $n$ defined as $x_n$ with $MR_{P_n}$.
2. An enterprise on supply network level $n$ will receive additional status requests from level $n$+$1$ (its customer) which it does not yet proactively monitor due to its own critical profiles. These additional requests are written as $AddReq_{n+1}$. Thus, a real monitoring ratio $MR_{Real_n}$ for level $n$ is calculated in formula (B). $MR_{Real_n}$ is the effective monitoring ratio which the enterprise on level $n$ has to realize. For all suborders an equivalent number of status requests (determined by $MR_{Real_n}$) is communicated to the enterprise(s) on level $n$-$1$.
3. To calculate the real monitoring rate of an enterprise on the next supply network level $n$-$1$ ($MR_{Real_{n-1}}$) all additional requests from level $n$ ($AddReq_n$) have to be sorted

out that are not already monitored by the enterprise on level $n-1$ due to its own critical profiles as defined by its monitoring ratio $MR_{P_{n-1}}$.

- In a first step a simple average of the real monitoring ratio on level $n$ ($MR_{Real_n}$) and the profile monitoring ratio on level $n-1$ ($MR_{P_{n-1}}$) is calculated as $\emptyset MR_n$ (see formula (C)). In a simple model $\emptyset MR_n$ represents the overlap ratio $OVR_n$ for order monitoring between network levels $n$ and $n-1$. It indicates the ratio of orders to be monitored by both enterprises according to the following heuristic: If the ratio of monitored orders is larger on level $n$ than on $n-1$ the overlap ratio will be larger than the profile monitoring ratio on level $n-1$ and vice versa. Note that the overlap ratio calculates a percentage of the profile monitoring ratio on level $n-1$. For instance, if $MR_{P_{n-1}} = 0.6$ and $OVR_n$ is 0.5 only 30% of all orders ($MR_{P_{n-1}} \times OVR_n$) on level $n-1$ are already monitored on level $n$.

- In reality the overlap ratio $OVR_n$ depends on factors such as the ratio of disruptive events that propagate to customers and thus induce these to create critical profiles for the same orders. Thus, the very basic heuristic for calculating the $OVR_n$ is refined by allowing different overlap scenarios. This is realized by a function $f$ based on $\emptyset MR_n$ that links to the $OVR_n$ as depicted in the figure above on the right side. In the model a function is proposed with $OVR_n = f(\emptyset MR_n) = (\emptyset MR)^q$ which assures that for $\emptyset MR_n = 0$ and $\emptyset MR_n = 1$ (minimum and maximum) a corresponding $OVR_n$ of zero or one is calculated: If all orders are monitored by the customer, all suborders are queried and for situations where no orders are monitored by a customer no overlap exists. A high overlap ratio is indicated for $0<q<1$ and a low overlap for $q>1$.

- Additional requests $AddReq_n$ on level $n$ for the suborder level $n-1$ are then calculated according to formula (E). The term $1-OVR$ is multiplied with the actually monitored number of orders on level $n$ as $x_n \times MR_{Real_n}$, because all monitored orders on level $n$ that are not monitored on level $n-1$ are to be identified which is determined by $1-OVR$. As a result, the additional requests $AddReq_n$ from level $n$ to $n-1$ are forecasted based on the different types of monitoring ratios on level $n$ and $n-1$.

4. For level $n-1$ the real monitoring ratio $MR_{Real_{n-1}}$ is calculated in formula (F) which is the same as (B) but for level $n-1$ instead of $n$. With this recursive forecast model multiple levels of supply networks are calculated and different scenarios depending on monitoring ratios and profile qualities are assessed.

## *Appendix G - Reaction Function of Simulator*

Definitions

Reaction Factor RF for $n^{th}$ disruptive event DE: $RF_n$
Time of identification of $n^{th}$ disruptive event DE: $T_n$
PlannedStartDate of monitored order: PSD
EstimatedStartDate of monitored (delayed by disruptive event DE): ESD
Begin of planning horizon: BOP
Planning horizon: PH
% remaining planning horizon: $PH_{rel}$
% remaining delay: $RD_{rel}$
Weight of advance notice: $W_{AN}$
Maximum reduction: MR
Remaining Potential for Reduction: $RPR_n$
Reaction for $n^{th}$ disruptive event DE (= reduction of delay): $R_u(n)$

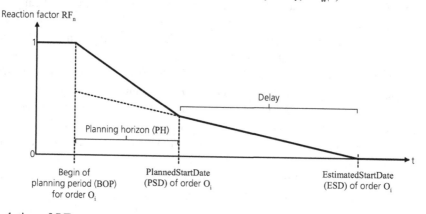

Calculation of $RF_n$

$$RF_n = \begin{cases} 0 \text{ for } T_n > ESD \\ 1 \text{ for } T_n < BOP \\ (1 - W_{AN}) \cdot PH_{rel} + W_{AN} \cdot RD_{rel} \text{ for } BOP \leq T_n \leq ESD \end{cases}$$

$$PH_{rel} = \begin{cases} 0 \text{ for } PH = 0 \\ 0 \text{ for } T_n \geq PSD \\ 1 - \left(\dfrac{T_n - BOP}{PH}\right) \text{ for all else} \end{cases} \text{ and } RD_{rel} = \begin{cases} 1 \text{ for } (PH > 0 \wedge T_n < PSD) \\ \dfrac{ESD - T_n}{ESD - PSD} \text{ for all else} \end{cases}$$

Calculation of reduction

First DE: $MR = RPR_0$; $R_u(1) = RF_1 \times MR$; $RPR_1 = RPR_0 - R_u(1)$

All other DE: $R_u(n) = RF_n \times RPR_{n-1}$; $RPR_n = RPR_{n-1} - R_u(n)$ as long as $RPR_n \geq 0$

# References

AAAA 2005     AAAA: Adaptive Agent-Applications and -Autonomy (A4). http://www.wi2.uni-erlangen.de/index.php?id=en_253, accessed on 2005-04-29.

Aart 2005     van Aart, Chris: Beangenerator for Protege. http://hcs.science.uva.nl/usr/aart/beangenerator/index25.html, accessed on 2005-03-31.

Alvarenga et al. 2003     Alvarenga, Carlos; Schoenthaler, Robert: A new Take on Supply Chain Event Management. In: Supply Chain Management Review, 7 (2003) 2, pp. 28-35.

Ambient Networks 2004     Ambient Networks: Integrated project (IP) within the Information Society Technology (IST) area of the 6th FP of the EU Commision, http://www.ambient-networks.org, accessed on 2004-09-29.

Atkinson 2001     Atkinson, William: Gaining Supply Chain Visibility. In: Supply Chain Management Review Web Exclusives, http://www.manufacturing.net/scm/article/CA182735.html?text=atkinson, 2001-11-15, accessed on 2005-04-15.

Augustin 1998     Augustin, Siegfried: Informationslogistik. In: Klaus, Peter; Krieger, Winfried (eds.): Gabler Lexikon Logistik. 1st edition, Gabler, Wiesbaden 1998, pp. 183-186.

Austin 1962     Austin, John L.: How to do things with words. Oxford University Press, London 1962.

Baader et al. 2003     Baader, Franz; Horrocks, Ian; Sattler, Ulrike: Description Logics as Ontology Languages for the Semantic Web. In: Hutter, Dieter; Stephan, Werner (eds.): Festschrift in honor of Jorg Siekmann. Springer (LNAI), Berlin 2003, pp 21-42.

Barrows 2003     Barrows, Trevor: Using the SCOR Model to Map Collaborative Multi-Agent Systems (MAS) Business Environments. Presentation at Supply-Chain World-Australia/New Zealand 2003, Exe Technologies, http://www.supplychainworld.org/ANZ2003/presentations/Barrows_EXE_SCWANZ03.zip, accessed on 2004-04-15.

Basra et al. 2005     Basra, Rajveer; Lü, Kevin; Rzevski, George; Skobelev, Petr: Resolving Scheduling Issues of the London Underground Using a Multi-agent System. In: Marík, Vladimír; Brennan, Robert W.; Pechoucek, Michal (eds.): Holonic and Multi-Agent Systems for Manufacturing, Second International Conference on Industrial Applications, of Holonic and Multi-Agent Systems (HoloMAS 2005). Copenhagen, Springer (LNCS 3593), Berlin 2005, pp.188-196.

310

| | |
|---|---|
| Bauer 2001 | Bauer, Bernhard: UML Class Diagrams Revisited in the Context of Agent-based Systems. In: Wooldridge, M.; Ciancarini, P.; Weiss, G. (eds.): Proceedings of Agent-oriented Software Engineering (AOSE 01), Montreal. Springer (LNCS 2222), Berlin 2001, pp. 1-8. |
| Bauer 2002 | Bauer, Jürgen: Produktionscontrolling mit SAP-Systemen - effizientes Controlling, Logistik- und Kostenmanagement moderner Produktionssysteme. Vieweg, Braunschweig 2002. |
| Bauer et al. 2004 | Bauer, Bernhard; Müller, Jörg: Methodologies and Modeling Languages. In: Luck, M.; Ashri, R.; D'Inverno, M. (eds.): Agent-Based Software Development. Artech House, Boston 2004, pp. 77-131. |
| Bellifemine et al. 2003 | Bellifemine, Fabio; Caire, Giovanni; Poggi, Agostino; Rimassa, Giovanni: JADE - A White Paper. In: exp 3 (2003) 3, pp. 6-19, http://exp.telecomitalialab.com/articolo.asp?id=2&idart=1, accessed on 2005-04-15. |
| Bittner 2000 | Bittner, Michael: E-Business Requires Supply Chain Event Management - The Report on Supply Chain Management. AMR Research, Boston 2000. |
| Bodendorf 1999 | Bodendorf, Freimut: Wirtschaftsinformatik im Dienstleistungsbereich. Springer, Berlin 1999. |
| Bodendorf 2003 | Bodendorf, Freimut: Daten- und Wissensmanagement. Springer, Berlin 2003. |
| Bodendorf et al. 2005 | Bodendorf, Freimut; Zimmermann, Roland: Proactive Supply Chain Event Management with Agent Technology. Accepted for: International Journal of Electronic Commerce, Inderscience Enterprises Ltd., 2005. |
| Bonabeau et al. 2001 | Bonabeau, Eric; Meyer, Christopher: Swarm Intelligence - a Whole New Way to Think about Business. In: Harvard Business Review 79 (2001) 5, pp. 106-114. |
| Borgo et al. 1996 | Borgo, Stefano, Guarino, Nicola, Masolo, Claudio: Stratified Ontologies: The Case of Physical Objects. In: Proceedings of the Workshop on Ontology Engineering, ECAI96. http://old.ulstu.ru/people/SOSNIN/umk/Basis_of_Artificial_Intelligence/mirrors/www.ladseb.pd.cnr.it/infor/ontology/Papers/StratOntologies.pdf, accessed on 2005-04-15. |
| Bretzke et al. 2002 | Bretzke, Wolf-Rüdiger; Stoelzle, Wolfgang; Karrer, Michael; Ploenes, Patrick: Vom Tracking & Tracing zum Supply Chain Event Management - aktueller Stand und Trends. KPMG Consulting AG, Duesseldorf 2002. |
| Brock et al. 2001 | Brock, David L.; Milne, Timothy P.; Kang, Yun Y.; Lewis, Brendon : The Physical Markup Language- Core Components: Time and Place, White paper. Auto-ID initiative, Cambridge (MA) 2001. |
| Brooks 1986 | Brooks, Rodney A.: A robust layered control system for a mobile robot. In: IEEE Journal of Robotics and Automation 2 (1986)1, pp. 14-23. |
| Brueckner 2000 | Brueckner, Sven A.: Return from the Ant - Synthetic Ecosystems for Manufacturing Control. PhD Thesis, Berlin 2000. |

| | |
|---|---|
| Bryce 2000 | Bryce, Ciaran: A Security Framework for a Mobile Agent System. In: Cuppens, Frédéric; Deswarte, Yves; Gollmann, Dieter; Waidner, Michael (eds.): Proceedings of Computer Security - ESORICS 2000, 6th European Symposium on Research in Computer Security, Springer (LNCS 1895), Heidelberg 2000, pp.273-290. |
| Buechner et al. 2000 | Buechner, Heino; Zschau, Oliver; Traub, Dennis; Zahradka, Rik: Web Content Management - Websites professionell betreiben. Galileo Press, Bonn 2000. |
| Bunch et al. 2005 | Bunch, Larry; Breedy, Maggie R.; Bradshaw, Jeffrey M.; Carvalho, Marco M.; Suri, Niranjan: KARMEN: Multi-agent Monitoring and Notification for Complex Processes. In: Marík, Vladimír; Brennan, Robert W.; Pechoucek, Michal (eds.): Holonic and Multi-Agent Systems for Manufacturing, Second International Conference on Industrial Applications, of Holonic and Multi-Agent Systems (HoloMAS 2005). Copenhagen, Springer (LNCS 3593), Berlin 2005, pp.197-206. |
| Burmeister 1996 | Burmeister, Birgit: Models and Methodology for Agent-Oriented Analysis and Design. In: Fischer, Klaus (ed.): Working Notes of the KI'96 Workshop on Agent-Oriented Programming and Distributed Systems, DFKI, Saarbrücken 1996, ftp://ftp.dfki.uni-kl.de/pub/Publications/Documents/1996/D-96-06.tar.gz, accessed on 2005-04-15. |
| Busch et al. 2002 | Busch, Axel; Lange, Heiko; Langemann, Timo: Marktstudie: Standardsoftware zum Collaborative Supply Chain Management. Dangelmaier, Wilhelm (ed.), ALB/HNI, Paderborn 2002. |
| Bussmann et al. 2000 | Bussmann, Stefan; Schild, Klaus: Self-organizing Manufacturing Control: an Industrial Application of Agent Technology. In: Proceedings 4th Int. Conf. on Multi-agent Systems (ICMAS'2000), Boston, IEEE Computer Society 2000, pp. 87-94. |
| Bussmann et al. 2004 | Bussmann, Stefan; Jennings, Nicholas R.; Wooldridge, Michael: Multiagent Systems for Manufacturing Control - A Design Methodology, Springer, Berlin 2004. |
| Caire et al. 2004 | Caire, Giovanni; Cabanillas, David: JADE TUTORIAL - Application-defined Content Languages and Ontologies, TILab S.p.A., 2004, http://jade.tilab.com/doc/CLOntoSupport.pdf, accessed on 2005-03-31. |
| Calisti et al. 2004 | Calisti, Monique; Lozza, Thomas; Greenwood, Dominic: An Agent-Based Middleware for Adaptive Roaming in Wireless Networks. In Proceedings of AAMAS 2004, Workshop on Agents for Ubiquitous Computing, ACM, New York 2004. |
| Calisti et al. 2005 | Calisti, Monique; Dorer, Klaus; Dannegger, Christian: Living Systems Adaptive Transportation Networks. In AgentLink News 17, http://www.agentlink.org/newsletter/17/AL-17.pdf, accessed on 2005-10-21. |

312

| | |
|---|---|
| Callot et al. 2000 | Callot, Martine; Delprat, Sylvie; Hugues, Emmanuel; Brimble, Richard; Oldham, Keith; Stokes, Melody; Klein, Rüdiger; Danino, David; Redon, Romaric; Sellini, Florence: Methodology and Tools Oriented to Knowledge-based Engineering Applications - Final Synthesis, DELIVERABLE D4.3. 2000-06, http://web1.eng.coventry.ac.uk/moka/Documents/consortium/d4-3.pdf, accessed 2004-08-18. |
| Chalupsky et al. 2001 | Chalupsky, Hans; Gil, Yolanda; Knoblock, Craig A.; Lerman, Kristina; Oh, Jean; Pynadath, David V.; Russ, Thomas A.; Tambe, Milind: Electric Elves: Applying Agent Technology to Support Human Organizations. In: Hirsh, Haym; Chien, Steve (eds.): Proceedings of the Thirteenth Innovative Applications of Artificial Intelligence Conference. AAAI, Seattle 2001, pp. 51-58. |
| Chun et al. 2000 | Chun, In-geol; Lee, Jin-goo; Lee, Eun-seok. I-SEE: An Intelligent Search Agent for Electronic Commerce. In: International Journal of Electronic Commerce, 4 (2000) 2, pp. 83-98. |
| Conen et al. 2004 | Conen, Wolfram; Sandholm, Tuomas: Anonymous Pricing of Efficient Allocations in Combinatorial Economies. In Proceedings of Third International Joint Conference on Autonomous Agents and Multiagent Systems - Volume 1 (AAMAS'04), ACM, New York 2004, pp. 254-260. |
| Cornelsen 2000 | Cornelsen, Jens: Kundenwertanalysen im Beziehungsmarketing - theoretische Grundlegung und Ergebnisse einer empirischen Studie im Automobilbereich. PhD thesis, GIM, Nuremberg 2000. |
| Cossentino et al. 2002 | Cossentino, Massimo; Potts, Colin: A CASE Tool supported Methodology for the Design of Multi-agent Systems. In: Proc. of the 2002 International Conference on Software Engineering Research and Practice (SERP'02). Las Vegas, 2002, http://www.pa.icar.cnr.it/~cossentino/paper/SERP02.pdf, accessed on 2005-04-15. |
| DeLoach et al. 2001 | DeLoach, Scott A.; Wood, Mark F.; Sparkman, Clint H.: Multiagent Systems Engineering. In: International Journal of Software Engineering and Knowledge Enineering 11 (2001) 3, pp. 231-258. |
| DHL 2004 | DHL Express: Alles über Track und Trace - Schwarz auf Weiß - Anwenderhandbuch. DHL Deutschland, 2004. |
| Dörr et al. 2001 | Dörr, Martin; Guarino, Nicola; López, Mariano Fernández; Schulten, Ellen; Stefanova, Milena; Tate, Austin: State of the Art in Content Standards. In: Nicola Guarino, Milena Stefanova (eds.): Deliverable 3.1 of IST Project IST-2000-29243 OntoWeb: Ontology-based Information Exchange for Knowledge Management and Electronic Commerce. Amsterdam 2001, http://ontoweb.ontoware.org/About/Deliverables/D3.1.pdf, accessed on 2005-04-15. |
| Dordowsky et al. 1997 | Dordowsky, Frank; Kampmann, Peter: EURO-LOG - ein vernetztes Informationsverarbeitungssystem zur Unterstützung der unternehmensübergreifenden Transportlogistik. In: Wirtschaftsinformatik 39 (1997) 2, pp. 113-121. |

| | |
|---|---|
| Dorer et al. 2005 | Dorer, Klaus; Calisti, Monique: An Adaptive Solution to Dynamic Transport Optimization. In: Klügl, Franziska; Bazzan, Ana L.C.; Ossowski, Sascha (eds.): Applications of Agent Technology in Traffic and Transportation. Whitestein Series in Software Agent Technologies, Birkhäuser, Basel 2005 . |
| EAN 2003 | EAN International: EANCOM, http://www.ean-int.org/eancom.html, accessed on 2003-09-10. |
| ebXML 2001 | ebXML Business Process Specification Schema Version 1.01, http://www.ebxml.org/specs/ebBPSS.pdf, accessed on 2005-01-18. |
| ebXML 2003 | ebXML Initiative, http://www.ebxml.org, accessed on 2003-11-18. |
| Eisenbiegler et al. 2003 | Eisenbiegler, Joern; Erdmann, Michael; Jekutsch, Sebastian; Kazakos, Wassilios; Weber, Herbert; Rothfuss, Gunther; Ried, Christian (eds): Content Management mit XML - Grundlagen und Anwendungen. 2nd edition, Springer, Berlin 2003. |
| Eller et al. 2005 | Eller, Michael; Makedonska, Kristina; Schiemann, Bernhard: Distributed visualization of Multi Agent Systems. Submitted to: ATOP Workshop at AAMAS 2005. |
| EPCglobal 2004a | EPCglobal: EPC Tag Data Standards Version 1.1 Rev.1.24, Standard Specification 2004. http://www.epcglobalinc.org/, accessed on 2005-01-19. |
| EPCglobal 2004b | EPCglobal: Object Name Service (ONS) 1.04, Working Draft Version 2004. http://www.epcglobalinc.org/, accessed on 2005-01-19. |
| Epistemics 2004 | Epistemics: PcPACK4. http://www.epistemics.co.uk/Notes/55-0-0.htm, accessed on 2005-04-15. |
| ERIKA 2003 | Research project ERIKA: Final report. Participants: Department of Information Systems II (Prof. Bodendorf), Institute for Computer Sciences III (Prof. Dal Cin), MID GmbH, BIK GmbH, Nuremberg 2003. |
| Esteva et al. 2001 | Esteva, Marc; Rodriguez, Juan Antonio; Sierra, Carles; Garcia, Pere; Arcos, Josep Lluis: On the Formal Specifications of Electronic Institutions. In: Dignum, Frank R.; Sierra, Carles (eds.): Agent Mediated Electronic Commerce - The European AgentLink Perspective. Springer (LNAI), Heidelberg 2001, pp.126-147. |
| Esteva et al. 2002 | Esteva, Marc; de la Cruz, David; Sierra, Carles: ISLANDER: an Electronic Institutions Editor. In: Proceedings of First International Joint Conference on Autonomous Agents and Multiagent Systems (AAMAS 2002). Bologna 2002, pp. 1045-1052. |
| Eymann 2003 | Eymann, Torsten: Digitale Geschäftsagenten. Springer, Berlin 2003. |
| Eymann et al. 2005 | Eymann, Thorsten; Ardaiz, O.; Catalano, M.; Chacin, P.; Chao, I.; Freitag, F.; Gallegati, M.; Giulioni, G.; Joita, L.; Navarro, L.; Neumann, D.; Rana, O.; Reinicke, M.; Schiaffino, S. B., Ruben Carvajal; Streitberger, W.; Veit, D.; Zini, F.: Catallaxybased Grid Markets. In: Proceedings of the First International Workshop on Smart Grid Technologies (SGT05), Utrecht 2005. |

314

| Fadel et al. 1994 | Fadel, Fadi G.; Fox, Mark S.; Grüninger, Michael: A Resource Ontology for Enterprise Modelling. In: Third Workshop on Enabling Technologies-Infrastructures for Collaborative Enterprises, West Virginia University, 1994, pp. 117-128. |

FedEx 2002 — FedEx Express: Service Guide, Vol. 1. http://www.fedex.com/downloads/services/pdf/no_ServiceGuide.pdf?link=4, accessed on 2003-11-27.

FedEx 2005 — FedEx Express: FedEx Ship Manager API XML Transaction Guide, Version 3.1. http://www.fedex.com/us/solutions/wis/pdf/xml_transguide.pdf?link=4, 2005.

Fensel 2001 — Fensel, Dieter: Ontologies: A Silver Bullet for Knowledge Management and Electronic Commerce. Springer, Berlin 2001.

Ferber 1994 — Ferber, Jacques: Simulating with Reactive Agents. In: Hillebrand, E.; Stender, J. (eds.): Many-Agent Simulation and Artificial Life. IOS-Press, Amsterdam 1994, pp. 8-30.

Ferber 1999 — Ferber, Jacques: Multi-Agent Systems - An Introduction to Distributed Artificial Intelligence. Addison-Wesley, London 1999.

Fewster 2001 — Fewster, Paul: SAP Java Connector & Java Proxy Generation. Presentation Slides, SAP AG Australia 2001.

Fillion et al. 1995 — Fillion, Florence; Menzel, Chris; Blinn, Thomas; Mayer, Richard: An Ontology-Based Environment for Enterprise Model Integration. In: Proceedings of the IJCAI Workshop on Basic Ontological Issues in Knowledge Sharing. AAAI Press 1995.

Finkenzeller 2002 — Finkenzeller, Klaus: RFID-Handbuch - Grundlagen und praktische Anwendungen induktiver Funkanlagen, Transponder und kontaktloser Chipkarten. 3rd edition, Carl Hanser, Munich 2002.

FIPA 2001 — Foundation for Intelligent Physical Agents: FIPA Interaction Protocol Library Specification. 2001, http://www.fipa.org/specs/fipa00025/XC00025E.pdf, accessed on 2005-04-15.

FIPA 2002a — Foundation for Intelligent Physical Agents: FIPA ACL Message Structure Specification. 2002, http://www.fipa.org/specs/fipa00061/SC00061G.pdf, accessed on 2005-02-15.

FIPA 2002b — Foundation for Intelligent Physical Agents: FIPA Request Interaction Protocol Specification. 2002, http://www.fipa.org/specs/fipa00026/SC00026H.pdf, accessed on 2004-09-24.

FIPA 2002c — Foundation for Intelligent Physical Agents: FIPA Query Interaction Protocol Specification. 2002, http://www.fipa.org/specs/fipa00027/SC00027H.html, accessed on 2004-09-24.

FIPA 2002d — Foundation for Intelligent Physical Agents: FIPA SL Content Language Specification. 2002, http://www.fipa.org/specs/fipa00008/SC00008I.pdf, accessed on 2004-09-24.

FIPA 2004 — Foundation for Intelligent Physical Agents: FIPA Agent Management Specification. 2004, http://www.fipa.org/specs/fipa00023/SC00023K.pdf, accessed on 2005-02-15.

FIPA OS 2005  Emorphia: FIPA-OS agent platform. http://fipa-os.sourceforge.net, accessed on 2005-04-15.

Fleischmann et al. 2002  Fleischmann, Bernhard; Meyr, Herbert; Wagner, Michael: Advanced Planning. In Stadtler, Hartmut; Kilger Christoph (eds.): Supply Chain Management and Advanced Planning. Springer, Berlin 2002, pp. 71-96.

Floerkemeier et al. 2003  Floerkemeier, Christian; Anarkat, Dipan; Osinski, Ted; Harrison, Mark. PML Core Specification 1.0. Auto-ID Center Recommendation, 2003, http://www.epcglobalinc.org/standards_technology/Secure/v1.0/PML_Core_Specification_v1.0.pdf, accessed on 2005-04-15.

Föcker et al. 2000  Föcker, Egbert; Lienemann, Carsten: Informationslogistische Dienste für Unternehmensportale. In: Wissensmanagement 3 (2000) 2, pp. 18-22.

Forgy 1982  Forgy, Charles: Rete: A Fast Algorithm for the Many Pattern/Many Object Pattern Match Problem. In: Artificial Intelligence 19 (1982) 1, pp.17-37.

Fortras 2002  FORTRAS - Forschungs- und Entwicklungsgesellschaft Transportwesen mbH: Datensatz für Statusberichte. Release 2, Osnabrück 2002.

Fox et al. 1995  Fox, Mark S.; Barbuceanu, Mihai; Grüninger, Michael: An Organisation Ontology for Enterprise Modelling: Preliminary Concepts for Linking Structure and Behaviour. In: Computers in Industry 29 (1995) 1/2, pp. 123-134.

Fox et al. 1997  Fox, Mark S.; Grüninger, Michael: On Ontologies and Enterprise Modelling. In: Kosanke, Kurt; Nell, James G. (eds.): Enterprise Engineering and Integration: Building International Consensus - Proceedings of the International Conference on Enterprise Integration Modelling Technology 97, Torino. Springer, Berlin 1997, http://www.eil.utoronto.ca/enterprise-modelling/papers/fox-eimt97.pdf, accessed on 2005-04-15.

Fox et al. 2000  Fox, Mark S.; Barbuceanu, Mihai; Teigen, Rune: Agent-oriented Supply Chain Management. In: International Journal of Flexible Manufacturing Systems, 12 (2000) 2/3, pp. 165-188.

Freitas 2002  Freitas, Alex A.: Data Mining and Knowledge Discovery with Evolutionary Algorithms. Springer, Berlin 2002.

Frey et al. 2003a  Frey, Daniel; Stockheim, Tim; Woelk, Peer-Oliver; Zimmermann, Roland: Integrated Multi-agent-based Supply Chain Management. In: Proceedings of the 12th IEEE International Workshops on Enabling Technologies: Infrastructure for Collaborative Enterprises (WETICE-2003). IEEE, 2003, pp. 24.29.

Frey et al. 2003b  Frey, Daniel; Mönch, Lars; Stockheim, Tim; Woelk, Peer-Oliver; Zimmermann, Roland: Agent.Enterprise - Integriertes Supply-Chain-Management mit hierarchisch vernetzten Multiagenten-Systemen. In: Proceedings der GI Jahrestagung 2003, pp. 47-63.

Friedmann-Hill 2003  Friedmann-Hill, Ernest: JESS in Action - Rule Based Systems in Java. Manning Publications, Greenwich, 2003.

Friedrich 1997  Friedrich, Alfred: Logik und Fuzzy-Logik. 1st edition, expert-verlag, Renningen-Malmsheim 1997.

316

Furness 2004 — Furness, Anthony: Present and Future Smart Active Label (SAL) Enabling Technologies - An Introductory Overview. The Smart Active Labels Consortium. http://www.sal-c.org/pdfs/Overview%20on%20Current%20and%20Future%20SAL%20Technologies.pdf, accessed on 2004-09-29.

Geerts et al. 2000 — Geerts, Guido; McCarthy, William: The Ontological Foundation of REA Enterprise Information Systems. Working paper, Michigan State University 2000, http://www.msu.edu/user/mccarth4/Alabama.doc, accessed on 2005-04-15.

Gerhardt 2003 — Gerhardt, Stefan: Europamarkt für Supply Chain Event Management (SCEM). Frost&Sullivan Report B141 (12/02), http://www.marketing-marktplatz.de/VerVkf/EuSupplyCem.htm, accessed on 2003-03-19.

Genesereth et al. 1987 — Genesereth, Michael R.; Nilsson, Nils J.: Logical Foundations of Artificial Intelligence. Morgan Kaufman, Los Altos 1987.

Giorgini et al. 2003 — Giorgini, Paolo; Müller, Jörg P.; Odell, James (eds.): Agent-Oriented Software Engineering IV, 4th International Workshop, AOSE 2003, Melbourne, Australia. Springer (LNCS 2935), Berlin 2003.

Gollwitzer et al. 1998 — Gollwitzer, Michael; Karl, Rudi: Logistik-Controlling. Langen/Müller, Munich 1998.

Grauel 1995 — Grauel, Adolf: Fuzzy-Logik: Einführung in die Grundlagen. Wissenschaftsverlag, Mannheim 1995.

Gray 2003 — Gray, Jim: Distributed Computing Economics. Technical Report, Microsoft Research, Redmond 2003, http://arxiv.org/ftp/cs/papers/0403/0403019.pdf, accessed on 2005-04-27.

Grebasch et al. 2003 — Grebasch, Dennis; Samberger, Martin; Stepan, Dirk: Erstellung von Auftragsprofilen mithilfe der Data Mining Workbench WEKA. Student research project, Nuremberg, 2003.

Gruber 1993 — Gruber, Thomas R.: A translation approach to portable ontologies. In: Knowledge Acquisition 5 (1993) 2, pp. 199-220.

Grüninger et al. 1994 — Grüninger, Mihai; Fox, Mark S.: The Role of Competency Questions in Enterprise Engineering. In: Proceedings of the IFIP WG5.7 Workshop on Benchmarking - Theory and Practice, Trondheim (Norway), 1994, http://www.eil.utoronto.ca/enterprise-modelling/papers/benchIFIP94.pdf, accessed on 2005-04-15.

Grüninger et al. 1995 — Grüninger, Mihai; Pinto, Javier A.: A Theory of Complex Actions for Enterprise Modelling. In: Working Notes AAAI Spring Symposium Series 1995: Extending Theories of Action: Formal Theory and Practical applications, Stanford, 1995, http://www.eil.utoronto.ca/enterprise-modelling/papers/gruninger-aisymp95.pdf, accessed on 2005-04-15.

Guarino 1998 — Guarino, Nicola: Formal Ontology and Information Systems. In: Guarion, Nicola (ed.): Formal Ontology in Information Systems, Proceedings of the 1st International Conference of Formal Ontology in Information Systems, IOS Press, Amsterdam 1998, pp. 3-15.

| Hannotin et al. 2002 | Hannotin, Xavier; Maggi, Paolo; Sisto, Riccardo: Formal Specification and Verification of Mobile Agent Data Integrity Properties: A Case Study. In: Picco, Gian Pietro (ed.): Proceedings of Mobile Agents, 5th International Conference 2001, Springer (LNCS 2240), Heidelberg 2002, pp. 42-53. |
| --- | --- |
| Haugen et al. 2000 | Haugen, Robert; McCarthy, William: REA: A Semantic Model for Internet Supply Chain Collaboration. In Online-Proceedings of Business Object Component Design and Implementation Workshop VI: Enterprise Application Integration - The ACM Conference on Object-Oriented Programming, Systems, Languages, and Applications 2000, Minneapolis, http://www.jeff-sutherland.org/oopsla2000/mccarthy/mccarthy.htm, accessed on 2005-04-18. |
| Haque et al. 2005 | Haque, Nadim; Jennings, Nicholas R.; Moreau, Luc: Resource allocation in communication networks using market-based agents. In Bramer, Max; Coenen, Frans; Allen, Tony (eds.): Proceedings of Twenty-fourth SGAI International Conference on Innovative Techniques and Applications of Artificial Intelligence. Springer, London 2005, pp. 187-200 |
| Helin et al. 2005 | Helin, Heikki; Klusch, Matthias; Lopez, Antonio; Fernandez, Alberto; Schumacher, Michael; Schuldt, Heiko; Bergenti, Federico; Kinnunen, Ari: Context-aware Business Application Service Coordination in Mobile Computing Environments. In Proceedings of the International Workshop on Ambient Intelligence - Agents for Ubiquitous Environments, 4th International Joint Conference on Autonomous Agents and Multi Agent Systems, Utrecht 2005, . |
| Hofmann 2000 | Hofmann, Oliver: Konfigurierbare Softwareagenten zur Unterstützung von Koordinationsvorgängen in Electronic Business Networks, PhD thesis, dissertation.de 2000. |
| Holsapple et al. 2002 | Holsapple, Clyde W.; Joshi, Kshiti D.: A Collaborative Approach to Ontology Design. In: Communications of the ACM 45 (2002) 2, pp. 42-47. |
| Horrocks et al. 2002 | Horrocks, I., Fensel, D., Broekstra, J., Decker, S., Erdmann, M., Goble C., van Harmelen, F., Klein, M., Staab, S., Studer, R., Motta, E.: The Ontology Inference Layer OIL. Http://www.ontoknowledge.org/oil/papers.shtml, accessed on 2002-03-25. |
| Huget 2002 | Huget, Marc-Philippe: Agent UML Class Diagrams Revisited. In: Kowalczyk, Ryszard; Müller, Jörg P.; Tianfield, Huaglory; Unland, Rainer (eds.): Agent Technologies, Infrastructures, Tools, and Applications for E-Services, NODe 2002 Agent-Related Workshops, LNCS 2592, Springer, Berlin 2003, pp. 9-60. |
| Hunsel et al. 2000 | Hunsel, Lothar; Zimmer, Michael: Kundenwert und Kundenloyalität. In: Hofmann, Markus; Mertiens, Markus (eds.): Customer-Lifetime-Value Management - Kundenwert schaffen und erhöhen - Konzepte, Strategien, Praxisbeispiele. Gabler, Wiesbaden 2000, pp. 115-128. |
| IBM 2005 | IBM: WebSphere software, http://www-306.ibm.com/software/websphere/, accessed on 2005-01-18. |
| Icosystems 2005 | Icosystems: Technology, http://www.icosystem.com/technology.htm, accessed on 2005-10-21. |

318

| | |
|---|---|
| Ihde 2001 | Ihde, Gösta B.: Transport, Verkehr, Logistik - gesamtwirtschaftliche Aspekte und einzelwirtschaftliche Handhabung, 3rd edition, Vahlen, München 2001. |
| ILOG 2003 | ILOG: ILOG Business Rule Components - Product Datasheet, 2003, http://www.ilog.com/products/rules/ds_rules.pdf, accessed on 2005-04-18. |
| JACK 2005 | Agent Oriented Software: JACK - Agent Platform. http://www.agent-software.com, accessed on 2005-04-18. |
| JADE 2005 | JADE Steering Board: JADE - Agent Platform. http://jade.cselt.it, accessed on 2005-04-18. |
| Jennings et al. 1998 | Jennings, Nicholas R.; Sycara, Katia; Wooldridge, Michael: A Roadmap of Agent Research and Development. In: Autonomous Agents and Multi-Agent Systems 1 (1998) 1, pp. 275–306. |
| Jennings et al. 2000a | Jennings, Nicholas R.; Faratin, Peyman; Norman, Timothy J.; O'Brien, P.; Odgers, Brian; Alty, James L.: Implementing a Business Process Management System using ADEPT: A Real-World Case Study. In: Int. Journal of Applied Artificial Intelligence 14 (2000) 5, pp. 421-463. |
| Jennings et al. 2000b | Jennings, Nicholas R.; Faratin, Peyman; Norman, Timothy J.; O'Brien, P.; Odgers, Brian: Autonomous Agents for Business Process Management. In: Int. Journal of Applied Artificial Intelligence 14 (2000) 2, pp. 145-189. |
| Jennings 2001 | Jennings, Nicholas R.: An Agent-Based Approach for Building Complex Software Systems. In: Communications of the ACM 44 (2001) 4, pp. 35-41. |
| Jennings 2004 | Jennings, Nicholas R.: On the Application and Future of Agents and Multi-agent Systems. In: Künstliche Intelligenz (KI) 16 (2004) 2, pp. 38-40. |
| JESS 2005 | Java Expert System Shell (JESS), http://herzberg.ca.sandia.gov/jess/index.shtml, accessed on 2005-04-18. |
| Kantardzic 2003 | Kantardzic, Mehmed: Data Mining – Concepts, Models, Methods, and Algorithms. IEEE Press, Indianapolis 2003. |
| Karrer 2003 | Karrer Michael: From Tracking&Tracing to Supply Chain Event Management - theoretical point of view and first empirical results. Working paper, Chair for Management (Logistics and Transport Management), University of Duisburg-Essen 2003. |
| Khan 2005 | Khan, Andy: Java Excel API, http://www.andykhan.com/jexcelapi/, accessed on 2005-03-31. |
| Kilgore et al. 2002 | Kilgore, Stacie; Orlov, Laurie; Nakashima, Taichi: Grading Apps for Inventory And Order Visibility. The TechStrategy Report, Forrester Research 2002, http://www.viewlocity.co.kr/materialGrading%20Apps%20for%20Inventory%20and%20Order%20Visibility%20Final%207-02.pdf, accessed on 2005-04-18. |
| Kim et al. 1995 | Kim, Henry M.; Fox, Mark S: An Ontology of Quality for Enterprise Modelling. In: Fourth Workshop on Enabling Technologies-Infrastructures for Collaborative Enterprises WETICE 1995, IEEE Computer Society 1995, pp. 105-116. |

Kind et al. 2003    Kind, Thomas; Gurzki, Thorsten; Lebender, Markus: Web-Service-basierte Kollaborationsplattform für vertikale Logistikverbünde. Presentation at Workshop 2003 SpiW - Mobile Speditionen im Web - Leipzig, Fraunhofer IAO, Stuttgart 2003.

Klaus 1998    Klaus, Peter: Supply Chain Management. In: Klaus, Peter; Krieger, Winfried: Gabler Lexikon Logistik. 1st edition, Gabler Verlag, Wiesbaden 1998, pp. 434-441.

Klaus et al. 2000    Klaus, Peter; Distel, Stefan; Prockl, Guenter; Stein, Andreas; Zimmermann, Roland; Baresel, Andreas: Integrated Suppliers - ECR is also for Suppliers of Ingredients, Raw Materials and Packaging. ECR Europe, Nuremberg 2000.

Kloth 1999    Kloth, Ralph: Waren- und Informationslogistik im Handel. Gabler, Wiesbaden 1999.

Klügel 2000    Klügel, Franziska: Multiagentensimulation, Addison Wesley, München 2000.

Klügel 2004    Klügel, Franziska: Applications of software agents. In: Künstliche Intelligenz (KI) 16 (2004) 2, pp. 5-10.

Klusch et al. 2004    Klusch, Mathias; Ossowski, Sascha; Kashyap, Vipul (eds.): Proceedings of Cooperative Information Agents VIII: 8th International Workshop, CIA 2004, Erfurt. LNCS 3191, Springer, Berlin 2004.

Klusch 2005    Klusch, Mathias: International Workshop Series CIA on Cooperative Information Agents, http://www.dfki.de/~klusch/IWS-CIA-home.html, accessed on 2005-02-15.

Krieger et al. 2001    Krieger, Winfried; Bonsen, Gesine: Tracking und Tracing in kleinen und mittelständischen Unternehmen des Straßengüterverkehrs - Potentiale und Risiken der Integration von Sendungsverfolgungssystemen in internetbasierte Seehafenportale. Report on the VIKING project supported by the European Union Directorate General for Transport, Flensburg 2001.

Lang 2005    Lang, Florian: Developing Dynamic Strategies for Multi-Issue Automated Contracting in the Agent Based Commercial Grid. In: Proceedings of the IEEE International Symposium on Cluster Computing and the Grid (CCGrid05), Workshop on Agent Based Grid Economics (AGE05), Cardiff, 2005.

Larman 1997    Larman, Craig: Applying UML and Patterns - An Introduction to Object-Oriented Analysis and Design. 1st edition, Prentice Hall PTR, Indianapolis 1997.

Lee et al. 1997    Lee, Hau; Padmanabhan, Paddy; Whang, Seungjin: The Bullwhip Effect in Supply Chains. In: Sloan Management Review 38 (1997) 3, pp. 93-102.

Lee 1998    Lee, Ronald M.: Bureaucracies as deontic systems. In: ACM Transactions on Office Information Systems 6 (1988) 2, pp. 87-108.

320

| | |
|---|---|
| Liebig et al. 1996 | Liebig, Thorsten; Rösner, Dietmar: Modelling of Reusable Product Knowledge in Terminological Logics - a Case Study. In: Proceedings of the Workshop on Product Knowledge Sharing for Integrated Enterprises - First International Conference on Practical Aspects of Knowledge Management. Basel 1996, http://www.informatik.uni-ulm.de/ki/Liebig/papers/pakm96-liebig.ps.gz. |
| Lienemann 2001 | Lienemann, Carsten: Informationslogistik - Qualität im Fokus. In: Deiters, Wolfgang; Lienemann, Carsten (eds.): Report Informationslogistik - Informationen just-in-time. Symposion Publishing, Düsseldorf 2001, pp.13-34. |
| Lin et al. 1996 | Lin, Jinxin; Fox, Mark S; Bilgic, Taner: A Requirements Ontology for Concurrent Engineering. In: Concurrent Engineering: Research and Applications, 4 (1996) 4, pp. 279-291. |
| Lind 2001 | Lind, Jürgen: Iterative software engineering for multiagent systems: The MASSIVE method. LNCS 1994, Springer, Berlin 2001. |
| Lockamy et al. 2002 | Lockamy, Archie; McCormack, Kevin: Supply Chain Event Management Best Practice Models, Presentation held at Supply Chain World - Conference and Exhibition 2002, http://www.logis-net.co.kr/wwwboard/data/1/sc-mpractice.pdf, accessed on 2005-04-18. |
| Lonvick 2001 | Lonvick, Chris: The BSD syslog Protocol - RFC 3164, The Internet Society, 2001, http://www.ietf.org/rfc/rfc3164.txt, accessed on 2004-07-16. |
| LostWax 2005 | LostWax E-commerce Platform, http://www.lostwax.com/solutions/products/ecommerce/, accessed on 2005-10-21. |
| Luger 2001 | Luger, George F.: Künstliche Intelligenz - Strategien zur Lösung komplexer Probleme. Pearson Studium, Munich, 2001. |
| Luck et al. 2005 | Luck, Michael; McBurney, Peter; Shehory, Onn; Willmott, Steve: Agent Technology Roadmap - A Roadmap for Agent-based Computing. AgentLink II, 2005, http://www.agentlink.org/roadmap, accessed on 2005-10-21. |
| Mädche et al. 2001 | Mädche, Alexander; Staab, Steffen; Studer, Rudi: Ontologien. In: Wirtschaftsinformatik 43 (2001) 4, pp. 393-395. |
| Marbacher 2001 | Marbacher, Albert: Demand & Supply Chain Management - Zentrale Aspekte der Gestaltung und Überwachung unternehmensübergreifender Leistungserstellungsprozesse betrachtet aus der Perspektive eines Markenartikelherstellers aus der Konsumgüterindustrie.Verlag Paul Haupt, Bern 2001. |
| Mascada 1998 | MASCADA EU-Projekt, ESPRIT LTR 22728, WP1 Dissemination Report: Analysis and evaluation of change and disturbances in industrial plants, 1998, http://www.mech.kuleuven.ac.be/pma/project/mascada/welcome.html, accessed on 2005-04-18. |
| Masing 2003 | Masing, Natascha: Supply Chain Event Management as Strategic Perspective – Market Study: SCEM Software Performance in the European Market, diploma thesis, 2003, http://www.cata.ca/files/PDF/Resource_Centres/hightech/reports/studies/SupplyChainEventMgt.pdf, accessed on 2005-04-18. |

| Maturana et al. 2005 | Maturana, Francisco P.; Staron, Raymond J.; Tichý, Pavel; Slechta, Petr; Vrba, Pavel: A Strategy to Implement and Validate Industrial Applications of Holonic Systems. In: Marík, Vladimír; Brennan, Robert W.; Pechoucek, Michal (eds.): Holonic and Multi-Agent Systems for Manufacturing, Second International Conference on Industrial Applications, of Holonic and Multi-Agent Systems (HoloMAS 2005). Copenhagen, Springer (LNCS 3593), Berlin 2005, pp.111-120 |
|---|---|
| McCarthy 1982 | McCarthy, William E.: The REA Accounting Model: A Generalized Framework for Accounting Systems in a Shared Data Environment. In: The Accounting Review 57 (1982) 3, pp. 554-578. |
| Menzel et al. 1996 | Menzel, Christopher; Mayer, Richard J.: Situations and Processes. In: Concurrent Engineering: Research and Applications 4 (1996) 3, pp. 229-246. |
| Meyr et al. 2002 | Meyr, Herbert; Rohde, Jens; Schneeweiss, Lorenz; Wagner, Michael: Architecture of selected APS. In: Stadtler, Hartmut; Kilger, Christoph (eds.): Supply Chain Management and Advanced Planning, Springer, Berlin 2002, pp. 293-304. |
| Milton 2003 | Milton, Nick: Information on Knowledge Acquisition, http://www.epistemics.co.uk/Notes/63-0-0.htm, accessed on 2004-08-18. |
| Montgomery et al. 2001 | Montgomery, Nigel; Waheed, Rekha: Supply Chain Event Management Enables Companies To Take Control of Extended Supply Chains. AMR Research 2001. |
| Montgomery 2003 | Montgomery, Nigel: EXE Technologies-Europe Outperforms U.S. Division and Expects Further Growth Through EXceed/SNx Rollout, AMR Research Alert, January 14, 2003, http://www.amrresearch.co.uk/Content/View.asp?pmillid=15548, accessed on 2005-04-20. |
| Moukas et al. 2000 | Moukas, Alexandros; Zacharia, Giorgios; Guttmann, Robert; Maes, Pattie Agent-Mediated Electronic Commerce: An MIT Media Laboratory Perspective. In: International Journal of Electronic Commerce 4 (2000) 3, pp. 5-22. |
| Müller 1996 | Müller, Jörg P.: The Design of Intelligent Agents - A Layered Approach, LNAI 1177, Springer, Berlin 1996. |
| Müller et al. 2005 | Müller, Jörg P.; Zimmermann, Roland: An Ambient Intelligence Information Infrastructure for Production-to-Maintenance Processes. Accepted paper for IFAC 2005, Prague. |
| Nado et al. 1996 | Nado, Robert; Chams, Melanie; Delisio, Jeff; Hamscher, Walter: Comet: An Application of Model-Based Reasoning to Accounting Systems. In: Proceedings of the Eighth Innovative Applications of Artificial Intelligence Conference, AAAI Press / The MIT Press 1996, pp. 1482-1490. |
| Nimis et al. 2004 | Nimis, Jens; Lockemann, Peter: Robust Multi-Agent-Systems: The Transactional Conversation Approach. In Proceedings of SASEMAS 2004, New York. |
| Nonaka 1992 | Nonaka, Ikujiro: Wie japanische Konzerne Wissen erzeugen. In: Harvard Manager, 14 (1992) 2, pp. 95-103. |
| NRC 2004 | NRC - National Research Council Canada: NRC FuzzyJ Toolkit for the Java Platform, http://www.iit.nrc.ca/IR_public/fuzzy/fuzzyJDocs/, accessed on 2005-04-20. |

| Odell et al. 2001 | Odell, James J.; Parunak, H. Van Dyke; Bauer, Bernhard: Representing Agent Interaction Protocols in UML. In: Ciancarini, P.; Wooldridge, M. (eds.): Agent-Oriented Software Engineering. Springer, Berlin 2001, pp. 121–140. |
|---|---|
| Odell et al. 2004 | Odell, James; Giorgini, Paolo; Müller, Jörg P. (eds.): Agent-Oriented Software Engineering V - 5th International Workshop AOSE 2004, New York. LNCS 3382, Springer, Berlin 2004. |
| Odette 2003 | Odette: Supply Chain Monitoring, Version 1.0, Recommendation Mai 2003, http://www.odette.org/html/scmopr.htm, accessed on 2005-04-19. |
| OMG 2005a | Object Management Group: Agent Platform Special Interest Group, http://agent.omg.org/, accessed on 2005-02-15. |
| OMG 2005b | Object Management Group: UML. http://www.uml.org/, accessed on 2005-02-15. |
| Oracle 2001 | Oracle Corporation: Web Services Technical White Paper - Oracle 9i Application Server. Redwood Shores 2001. |
| Oracle 2005 | Oracle Corporation: Oracle 10g Application Server, http://www.oracle.com/appserver/index.html, accessed on 2005-01-18. |
| Parunak et al. 1999 | Parunak, H.van Dyke; Savitt, Robert; Riolo, Rick; Clark, Steven: DASCh: Dynamic Analysis of Supply Chains, http://www.erim.org/~vparunak/dasch99.pdf, download 2002-05-28. |
| Parunak 2000 | Parunak, H.van Dyke: A Practitioners' Review of Industrial Agent Applications. In: Autonomous Agents and Multi-Agent Systems 3 (2000) 4, pp. 389-407. |
| Parunak et al. 2005 | Sauter, John A.; Matthews, Robert; Parunak, H. Van Dyke; Brueckner, Sven A.: Performance of Digital Pheromones for Swarming Vehicle Control. Accepted for Fourth International Joint Conference on Autonomous Agents and Multi-Agent Systems (AAMAS'05), Utrecht, Netherlands. |
| Paschke et al. 2003 | Zimmermann, Roland; Paschke, Adrian: PAMAS - an Agent-based Supply Chain Event Management System. In: Proceedings of AMCIS 2003, Minitrack on Intelligent Agents and Multi-Agent Systems, AIS, Tampa 2003, pp. 1892-1900. |
| Pfeiffer et al. 1994 | Pfeiffer, Werner; Weiss, Enno: Lean Management - Grundlagen der Führung und Organisation lernender Unternehmen. 2nd revised edition, Erich Schmidt, Berlin 1992. |
| Pflaum 2001 | Pflaum, Alexander: Transpondertechnologie und Supply Chain Management – Elektronische Etiketten als bessere Identifikationstechnologie in logistischen Systemen?. PhD thesis, Dt. Verkehrs-Verlag, Hamburg 2001. |
| PSI 2005 | PSI Logistics: ABX LOGISTICS (Deutschland) GmbH, http://www.psilogistics.com/download/file/Referenzblatt_ABX_0507_en.pdf, accessed on 2005-10-21. |
| Radjou et al. 2002 | Radjou, Navi; Orlov, Laurie M.; Nakashima, Taichi: Adapting to Supply Network Change. Forrester Research Inc., Cambridge (MA) 2002. |

| | |
|---|---|
| Rao et al. 1992 | Rao, Anand S.; Georgeff, Michael P.: An abstract Architecture for Rational Agents. In: Proceedings of the Third International Conference on Principles of Knowledge Representation and Reasoning (KR'92), ACM Press, New York 1992, pp. 439-449. |
| Rao et al. 1995 | Rao, Anand S.; Georgeff, Michael P.: BDI agents: From Theory to Practice.In: Proceedings of ICMAS 95 - First International Conference on Multi-Agent Systems, AAAI Press, Cambridge MA, pp. 312-319. |
| Rätzmann 2003 | Rätzmann, Manfred: Software-Testing. 1st edition, Galileo Press, Bonn 2003. |
| Reichwein 2004 | Reichwein, Georg: Order Monitoring mit mobilen Internetgeräten. Quantum.Logistics GmbH, http://www.quantum-logistics.com, accessed on 2004-09-23, 2004. |
| Reinicke et al. 2005 | Reinicke, M.; Streitberger, W.; Eymann, T.: "Evaluation of Service Selection Procedures in Service Oriented Computing Networks". In: Proceedings of the First International Workshop on Smart Grid Technologies (SGT05), Utrecht, Niederlande, 2005. |
| Reiter 2002 | Reiter, Harald: Supply Chain Event Management: Business Benefits and ROI. 2002, http://www.edifice.org/82plenary/TI-SCEM-Reiter-TI-final.pdf, accessed on 2005-04-20. |
| RFID Journal 2005 | RFID Journal: RFID System Components and Costs. http://www.rfidjournal.com/article/articleprint/1336/-1/129/, accessed on 2005-04-20. |
| Roberti 2005 | Roberti, Mark: Retailers Say RFID Will Take Time. In: RFID Journal, Jan 17, 2005, http://www.rfidjournal.com/article/articleprint/1344/-1/1/, accessed on 2005-04-20. |
| Rogers 2005 | Rogers, A.; David, E.; Schiff, J.; Kraus, S.; Jennings, Nicholas R.: Learning Environmental Parameters For The Design Of Optimal English Auctions With Discrete Bid Levels. In: Proceedings of 7th International Workshop on Agent-Mediated E-Commerce, Utrecht 2005, pp. 81-94. |
| Roth 2003 | Roth, Anselm: Transparenz in der Wertschöpfungskette durch Supply Chain Event Management. Presentation at 5. Paderborner Frühjahrstagung 2003, http://fb5-cim.uni-paderborn.de/alb/pdf/5pbft/Roth.pdf, accessed on 2005-04-20. |
| Sandholm et al. 2003 | Sandholm, Tuomas; Suri, Subhash: BOB: Improved winner determination in combinatorial auctions and generalizations. In: Artificial Intelligence 145 (2003) 1-2, pp. 33-58. |
| Sandholm et al. 2005 | Sandholm, Tuomas; Gilpin, Andrew; Conitzer, Vincent: Mixed-Integer Programming Methods for Finding Nash Equilibria. In: Veloso, Manuela M.; Kambhampati, Subbarao (eds.): Proceedings of the Twentieth National Conference on Artificial Intelligence and the Seventeenth Innovative Applications of Artificial Intelligence Conference 2005, AAAI Press / The MIT Press, Pittsburgh 2005, pp. 495-501. |
| SAL-C 2005 | SAL: Smart Active Labels (SAL) Consortium. http://www.sal-c.org, accessed on 2005-01-19. |

| | |
|---|---|
| Saltare 2001 | Saltare Leap 2.0: Intelligent Supply Chain Event Management. In: Supply-ChainBrain.com, August 2001, http://www.glscs.com/archives/8.01.Saltare.htm?adcode=10, accessed on 2005-04-20. |
| SAP 2001 | SAP AG: Allgemeine Einführung in die BAPIs (CA-BFA), Release 4.6C, 2001, http://help.sap.com/printdocu/core/Print46c/de/data/pdf/CABFABA-PIREF/CABFABAPIEINF.pdf, accessed on 2005-04-21. |
| SAP 2002 | SAP AG: SAP Advanced Planner and Optimizer (SAP APO), Release 3.1. Release Notes, http://www.sap.com/solutions/business-suite/scm/pdf/RN_APO_31_EN.pdf, accessed on 2005-02-04. |
| SAP 2004a | SAP AG: SAP Advanced Planning and Optimization 4.0 (SAP APO 4.0 ). 2003, http://www.sap.com/solutions/scm/brochures/solutions/scm/pdf/BWP_APO40.pdf, accessed on 2004-04-22. |
| SAP 2004b | SAP AG: Software-Agenten - die fleißigen Helfer im Verborgenen. 2004, http://www.sapinfo.net/public/en/index.php4/article/Article-319013cc3e1f67b1b6/de. accessed on 2004-09-29. |
| SAP 2005a | SAP AG: Interface Repository. http://ifr.sap.com/index.html, accessed on 2005-01-18. |
| SAP 2005b | SAP AG: Netweaver Solutions. http://www.sap.com/solutions/netweaver/index.aspx, accessed on 2005-01-18. |
| Sashima et al. 2005 | Sashima, Akio; Izumi, Noriaki; Kurumatani, Koichi: Social Role Awareness for Ambient Intelligence. In Proceedings of the International Workshop on Ambient Intelligence - Agents for Ubiquitous Environments, 4th International Joint Conference on Autonomous Agents and Multi Agent Systems, Utrecht 2005, pp. 64-67. |
| SCC 1997 | Supply-Chain Council: SCOR-Modell Version 2.0, August 1997. |
| SCC 2005 | Supply-Chain Council: Supply-Chain Operations Reference-model - Overview, Version 7.0. http://www.supply-chain.org/galleries/default-file/SCOR%207.0%20Overview.pdf, accessed on 2005-04-21. |
| Schissler et al. 2001 | Schissler, Martin; Mantel, Stephan; Ferstl, Otto K.; Sinz, Elmar J.: Unterstützung von Kopplungsarchitekturen durch SAP R/3. FORWIN working paper FWN-2001-008, Bamberg 2001, http://www.forwin.de/download/berichte/Internet_FWN_2001-008.pdf, accessed on 2005-04-21. |
| Schlenoff et al. 1996 | Schlenoff, Craig; Knutilla, Amy; Ray, Steven: Unified Process Specification Language: Requirements for Modeling Process. NISTIR 5910, National Institute of Standards and Technology, Gaithersburg 1996, http://www.mel.nist.gov/msidlibrary/doc/schlen96/req-paper.pdf, accessed on 2005-04-21. |
| Schlenoff et al. 2000 | Schlenoff, Craig; Gruninger, Michael; Tissot, Florence; Valois, John; Lubell, Joshua; Lee, Jintae: The Process Specification Language (PSL) Overview and Version 1.0 Specification. NISTIR 6459, National Institute of Standards and Technology, Gaithersburg 2000, http://www.mel.nist.gov/msidlibrary/doc/nistir6459.pdf, accessed on 2005-04-21. |

| | |
|---|---|
| Schreiber et al. 2000 | Schreiber, Guus; Akkermans, Hans; Anjewierden, Anjo; De Hoog, Robert; Shadbolt, Nigel; Van de Velde, Walter; Wielinga, Bob: Knowledge Engineering and Management: The CommonKADS Methodology. Cambridge (MA), MIT Press, 2000. |
| Searle 1969 | Searle, John R. Speech Acts - An Essay in the Philosophy of Language. Cambridge University Press, Cambridge 1969. |
| Seifert 2001 | Seifert, Dirk: Efficient Consumer Response: strategische Erfolgsfaktoren für die Wertschöpfungspartnerschaft von Industrie und Handel. Hampp, München 2001. |
| ServiceObjects 2005 | Service Objects: Packtrack web services, http://www.serviceobjects.com/products/dots_packtrack.asp, accessed on 2005-01-18. |
| Shim et al. 2003 | Shim, Richard; Gilbert, Alorie. Wal-Mart to throw its weight behind RFID. In: CNET News.com June 5, 2003, http://news.zdnet.com/2100-9584_22-1013767.html?tag<br>=nl, accessed on 2005-01-19. |
| Shingo 1993 | Shingo, Shigeo: Das Erfolgsgeheimnis der Toyota-Produktion, 2nd edition, verlag moderne industrie, Landsberg/Lech 1993. |
| Siek et al. 2003 | Siek, Katja; Erkens, Elmar; Kopfer, Herbert: Anforderungen an Systeme zur Fahrzeugkommunikation im Straßengüterverkehr. Working paper, Chair of Logistics, Bremen 2003, http://www.logistik.uni-bremen.de/download/pubs/siek_erkens_kopfer<br>_lm_03.pdf, accessed on 2005-04-21. |
| Singhal 2003 | Singhal, Vinod R.: Quantifying the Impact of Supply Chain Glitches on Shareholder Value. SAP White Paper, SAP AG, Walldorf 2003, http://www.sap.com/solutions/business-suite/scm/pdf/BWP_Quantify.pdf, accessed on 2005-04-22. |
| Songini 2001 | Songini, Marc L.: Policing the Supply Chain. In: Computerworld 2001-04-30, http://www.itworld.com/App/808/CWD010430STO60017/pfindex, accessed on 2002-05-06. |
| Soundararajan et al. 2005 | Soundararajan, K.; Brennan, Robert W.: A Proxy Design Pattern to Support Real-Time Distributed Control System Benchmarking. In: Marík, Vladimír; Brennan, Robert W.; Pechoucek, Michal (eds.): Holonic and Multi-Agent Systems for Manufacturing, Second International Conference on Industrial Applications, of Holonic and Multi-Agent Systems (HoloMAS 2005). Copenhagen, Springer (LNCS 3593), Berlin 2005, pp.133-143. |
| SPSS 2004 | SPSS Inc.: Clementine 9.0 – Specifications, 2004, http://www.spss.com/pdfs/CLM9SPClr.pdf, accessed on 2005-02-11. |
| Stadtler et al. 2002 | Stadtler, Hartmut; Kilger, Christoph (eds.): Supply Chain Management and Advanced Planning, Springer, Berlin 2002. |
| Stadtler 2002 | Stadtler, Hartmut: Production Planning and Scheduling. In: Stadtler, Hartmut; Kilger, Christoph (eds.): Supply Chain Management and Advanced Planning, Springer, Berlin 2002, pp. 177-193. |
| Stein et al. 1998 | Stein, Andreas; Krieger, Winfried; Pflaum, Alexander; Dräger, Heinrich: Sendungsverfolgung zwischen Marketinginstrument und Produktionsunterstützungstool. GVB Schriftenreihe No. 40, GVB, Nürnberg 1998. |

326

| | |
|---|---|
| Sun 2005 | Sun Microsystems: Sun Grid, http://www.sun.com/service/sungrid/overview.jsp, accessed on 2005-04-27. |
| Swaminathan et al. 1998 | Swaminathan, Jayashankar M.; Smith, Stephen F.; Sadeh, Norman M.: Modeling Supply Chain Dynamics: A Multiagent Approach. In: Decision Sciences 29 (1998) 3, pp. 607-632. |
| Tham et al. 1994 | Tham, Donald, Fox, Mark S., and Gruninger, Michael: A Cost Ontology for Enterprise Modelling. In: Proceedings of the Third Workshop on Enabling Technologies: Infrastructure for Collaborative Enterprises. IEEE Computer Society Press, Morgantown 1994, pp. 197-210. |
| Thelen et al. 2000 | Thelen, Klaus; Wilkens, Christian: CLV-M-basiertes Kundenmonitoring als innovatives Controlling-Instrument in Marketing und Vertrieb. In: Hofmann, Markus; Mertiens, Markus (eds.): Customer-Lifetime-Value Management - Kundenwert schaffen und erhöhen - Konzepte, Strategien, Praxisbeispiele. Gabler, Wiesbaden 2000, pp. 143-153. |
| Timmermann 2002 | Timmermann, Dirk: Sicherheit, Kommunikation und Energie: Offene Fragen wirklich mobiler Systeme. Invited speach at Collaborative Symposium of DFG priority programs "Softwareagents" and "IT Security", Schloss Dagstuhl, Wadern 2002, . |
| Többen et al. 2005 | Peters, Richard; Többen, Hermann: A Reference-Model for Holonic Supply Chain Management. In: Marík, Vladimír; Brennan, Robert W.; Pechoucek, Michal (eds.): Holonic and Multi-Agent Systems for Manufacturing, Second International Conference on Industrial Applications, of Holonic and Multi-Agent Systems (HoloMAS 2005). Copenhagen, Springer (LNCS 3593), Berlin 2005, pp. 221-232. |
| Tohamy et al. 2003 | Tohamy, Noha; Radjou, Navi; Hudson, Ryan: Grading Order Fulfillment Solutions. TechStrategy Report, Forrester Research, 2003. |
| Tomczak et al. 2001 | Tomczak, Torsten; Rudolf-Sipötz, Elisabeth: Bestimmungsfaktoren des Kundenwertes: Ergebnisse einer branchenübergreifenden Studie. In: Günter, Bernd; Helm, Sabrina (eds.): Kundenwert - Grundlagen, innovative Konzepte, praktische Umsetzungen. Gabler, Wiesbaden 2001, pp. 127-154. |
| Unece 2003 | United Nations Economic Commission for Europe: United Nations Directories for Electronic Data Interchange for Administration, Commerce and Transport. http://www.unece.org/trade/untdid/welcome.htm, accessed on 2002-05-02. |
| Uschold et al. 1995 | Uschold, Mike; King, Martin: Towards a Methodology for Building Ontologies. In: Proceedings of Workshop on Basic Ontological Issues in Knowledge Sharing, held in conjunction with IJCAI-95, 1995, http://citeseer.ist.psu.edu/uschold95toward.html, accessed on 2005-04-22. |
| Uschold et al. 1998a | Uschold, Mike; King, Martin; Moralee, Stuart; Zorgios, Yanniy: The Enterprise Ontology. In: The Knowledge Engineering Review 13 (1998) 1, pp. 31-89. |

| | |
|---|---|
| Uschold et al. 1998b | Uschold, Mike; Healy, Mike; Williamson, Keith; Clark, Peter; Woods, Steven: Ontology reuse and application. In: Guarino, Nichola (ed.): Proceedings of the Int. Conf. on Formal Ontology in Information Systems - FOIS'98 (Frontiers in AI and Applications v46). IOS Press, Amsterdam 1998, pp. 179-192. |
| van Brussel et al. 1998 | van Brussel, Hendrik; Wyns, Jo; Valckenaers, Paul; Bongaerts, Luc; Peeters, Patrick: Reference architecture for holonic manufacturing systems. In: Computers in Industry 37 (1998) 3, pp. 255-274. |
| Vernadat 1996 | Vernadat, Francois B.: Enterprise Integration: On Business Process and Enterprise Activity Modelling. In: Concurrent Engineering: Research and Applications 4 (1996) 3, pp. 219-228. |
| Viewlocity 2002 | Viewlocity: Bridge the Chasm Between Planning and Execution with Supply Chain Event Management. Viewlocity Whitepaper Series, 2002. http://www.viewlocity.com/news/pdf/bridgechasm.pdf, accessed on 2005-04-22. |
| Viewlocity 2003 | Viewlocity: Product Modules, http://www.viewlocity.com/solutions/prodmap.html, accessed on 2003-09-09. |
| Viewlocity 2005 | Viewlocity: Architecture Overview on SWA, http://www.unitopia.com/e/solutions/ViewlocitySWA_4.html, accessed on 2005-01-11. |
| Vögele 2005 | Vögele, Bernd: Konzeption und prototypische Realisierung eines agentenbasierten Systems zur Unterstützung eines mehrdimensionalen Vertriebsplanungsprozesses in der Industrie. Diploma thesis, Nuremberg 2005. |
| W3C 2005 | World-Wide-Web Consortium (W3C): Ontology Web Language - OWL, http://www.w3c.org/2004/OWL/, accessed on 2005-01-18. |
| Wacker 2001 | Wacker, Jeff: Beyond Thinking Sand and Tamed Lightning - The new frontier for embedded chips. EDS, Plano 2001. |
| Wagner et al. 2001 | Wagner, Thomas; Phelps, John; Qian, Yuhui; Albert, Erik; Beane, Glen: A modified architecture for constructing real-time information gathering agents. In: Wagner, Gerd; Karlapalem, Kamalakar; Lesperance, Yves; Yu, Eric (eds.): Proceedings of the 3rd International Workshop on Agent Oriented Information Systems (AOIS), iCue Publishing, Berlin 2001, pp. 121-135. |
| Wagner et al. 2002a | Wagner, Michael; Meyr, Herbert: Food and Beverages. In: Stadtler, Hartmut; Kilger, Christoph (eds.): Supply Chain Management and Advanced Planning, Springer, Berlin 2002, pp.353-370. |
| Wagner et al. 2002b | Wagner, Thomas; Guralnik, Valerie; Phelps, John: Software agents: enabling dynamic supply chain management for a build to order product line. In: Arabnia, Hamid R.; Mun, Youngsong (eds.): Proceedings of the International Conference on Internet Computing, IC'2002, CSREA Press, Las Vegas 2002, pp. 689-696. |
| Ward 2004 | Ward, Diane M.: 5-Cent Tag Unlikely in 4 Years. In: RFID Journal 2004-08-26, http://www.rfidjournal.com/article/articleprint/1098/-1/1/, accessed on 2005-01-18. |
| Weiß et al. 2005 | Weiß, Gerhard; Jakob, Ralf: Agentenorientierte Softwareentwicklung. Springer, Berlin 2005. |

328

Weka 2005          Weka 3: Data Mining Software in Java. University of Waikato, New
                   Zealand, http://www.cs.waikato.ac.nz/~ml/weka/, accessed on 2005-02-11.

Whitestein         Whitestein Technologies: Agent Modeling Language, Language Specifica-
2004               tion, Version 0.9, http://www.whitestein.com/resources/aml/
                   wt_AMLSpecification_v0.9.pdf, accessed on 2005-10-21.

Wieser et al.      Wieser, Oswald; Lauterbach, Bernd: Supply Chain Event Management mit
2001               mySAP SCM (Supply Chain Management). In: HMD Praxis der
                   Wirtschaftsinformatik, 41 (2001) 3, pp. 65-71.

Willmott et al.    Willmott, Steven; Cortés, Ulises; Cabanillas, David: Standards for Agent
2004               Development. In: Luck, Michael; Ashri, Ronald; D'Inverno, Mark (eds.):
                   Agent-Based Software Development. Artech House, Boston 2004, pp. 133-
                   166.

Wilson 2001        Wilson, Tim: Event Tools Alert Partners. In: InternetWeek.com, 2001-02-
                   21, http://www.internetweek.com/newslead01/lead022101.htm, accessed
                   on 2002-06-09.

Winston 1992       Winston, Patrick H.: Artificial Intelligence. Addison Wesley Longman,
                   Cambridge 1992.

Witten et al.      Witten, Ian H.; Frank, Eibe: Data Mining - Praktische Werkzeuge und Tech-
2001               niken für das maschnielle Lernen. Hanser, München 2001.

Wooldridge         Wooldridge, Michal J.: The Logical Modelling of Computational Multi-
1992               Agent Systems. Ph.D. Thesis, Manchester 1992, http://www.csc.liv.ac.uk/
                   ~mjw/pubs/thesis.pdf, accessed on 2005-02-15.

Wooldridge et      Wooldridge, Michael J.; Jennings, Nicholas R.: Intelligent Agents: Theory
al. 1995           and Practice. In: Knowledge Engineering Review 10 (1995) 2, pp. 115-152.

Wooldridge         Wooldridge, Michael J.: Intelligent agents. In: Weiß, Gerhard (ed.): Multi-
1999               Agent Systems. MIT Press, Cambridge (MA) 1999, pp. 27-77.

Wooldridge et      Wooldridge, Michael J.; Jennings, Nicholas R.; Kinny, David: The GAIA
al. 2000           Methodology for Agent-Oriented Analysis and Design. In: Autonomous
                   Agents and Multi-Agent Systems 3 (2000) 3, pp. 285-312.

Yu et al. 1996     Yu, Eric; Mylopoulos, John; Lesperance, Yves: AI Models for Business Pro-
                   cess Reengineering. In: IEEE Expert 11 (1996) 4, pp. 16-23.

Zadeh 1999         Zadeh, Lotfi A.: Some Reflections on the Relationship Between AI and
                   Fuzzy Logic (FL) - A Heretical View. In: Ralescu, Anca L.; Shanahan,
                   James G. (eds.): Fuzzy Logic in Artificial Intelligence. Springer, Berlin
                   1999, pp. 1-8.

Zambonelli et      Zambonelli, Franco; Jennings, Nicholas R.; Wooldridge, Michael: Develop-
al. 2003           ing Multiagent Systems: The Gaia Methodology. In: ACM Transactions on
                   Software Engineering Methodology 12 (2003) 3, pp. 317-370.

Zebraxx 2004       ZEBRAXX AG Europe, http://www.zebraxx.com/, accessed on 2004-09-
                   23.

Zimmermann         Zimmermann, Hans-Jürgen: Fuzzy set theory and its applications, 2nd edi-
1991               tion, Kluwer, Norwell (MA) 1991.

| Zimmermann et al. 2002 | Zimmermann, Roland; Butscher, Robert; Bodendorf, Freimut: An ontology for agent-based supply chain monitoring. In: Timm, Ingo J.; Schleiffer, Ralf; Davidsson, Paul; Kirn, Stefan (eds.): Workshop-Proceedings "Agent Technologies in Logistics" ECAI 2002, Lyon, 2002, pp. 65-78, http://www.ide.bth.se/~pdv/Papers/proceedingsECAI-02-WS-Logistics.pdf, accessed on 2005-04-22. |
| Zimmermann et al. 2003a | Zimmermann, Roland; Paschke, Adrian: PAMAS - an Agent-based Supply Chain Event Management System. In: Proceedings of Americas Conference on Information Systems AMCIS 2003, Mini-track on Intelligent Agents and Multi-Agent Systems. AIS, Tampa 2003, pp.1892-1900. |
| Zimmermann et al. 2003b | Zimmermann, Roland; Butscher, Robert; Bodendorf, Freimut; Huber, Alexander; Görz, Günther: Generic Agent Architecture for Supply Chain Tracking, In: Moeness, Amin; Kokou, Yétongnon: The 2nd IEEE International Symposium on Signal Processing and Information Technology. IEEE-Press, Marrakesh 2002, pp. 203-207. |
| Zimmermann et al. 2005 | Zimmermann, Roland; Käs, Simone; Butscher, Robert; Bodendorf, Freimut: An Ontology for Agent-Based Monitoring of Fulfillment Processes. In: Tamma, Valentina; Cranefield, Stephen; Finin, Tim W.; Willmott, Steven (eds.): Ontologies for Agents: Theory and Experiences. Whitestein Series in Software Agent Technologies, Birkhäuser, Basel 2005, pp. 323-345. |